Preparing for the Project Management Professional (PMP®) Certification Exam

Third Edition

Preparing for the Project Management Professional (PMP®) Certification Exam

Third Edition

Michael W. Newell, PMP, ENP

AMACOM

American Management Association

New York • Atlanta • Brussels • Chicago • Mexico City • San Francisco
Shanghai • Tokyo • Toronto • Washington, D.C.

Special discounts on bulk quantities of AMACOM books are available to corporations, professional associations, and other organizations. For details, contact Special Sales Department, AMACOM, a division of American Management Association, 1601 Broadway, New York, NY 10019.
Tel.: 212–903–8316. Fax: 212–903–8083.
Web site: www.amacombooks.org

This publication is designed to provide accurate and authoritative information in regard to the subject matter covered. It is sold with the understanding that the publisher is not engaged in rendering legal, accounting, or other professional service. If legal advice or other expert assistance is required, the services of a competent professional person should be sought.

"PMI" and the PMI logo are service and trademarks registered in the United States and other nations; "PMP" and the PMP logo are certification marks registered in the United States and other nations; "PMBOK", "PM Network", and "PMI Today" are trademarks registered in the United States and other nations; and "Project Management Journal" and "Building professionalism in project management" are trademarks of the Project Management Institute, Inc.

Library of Congress Cataloging-in-Publication Data

Newell, Michael W., 1945–
        Preparing for the project management professional (PMP) certification exam / Michael W. Newell.—3rd ed.
            p.   cm.
        Includes bibliographical references and index.
        ISBN 0-8144-0859-1 (pbk.)
        1. Project management—Examinations, questions, etc.   I. Title.

    HD69.P75N49   2005
    658.4' 04' 076—dc22

                                                        2004030682

Printing Number

10   9   8   7   6   5   4   3   2   1

This book is dedicated to my wife, Saralee, who still corrects my spelling and puts up with all my foolishness.

CONTENTS

Preface xv

Introduction to Project Management 1

 What Is Project Management Anyway? 2
  Standards and Regulations *2*
 A True Story 5
 Advantages of Project Management 6
 Organizing for Project Management 7
  The Projectized Organization *7*
  The Functional or Traditional Organization *9*
  The Matrix Organization *11*
 The Project Office and the Project Management Office 12
 How the Project Manager Makes Projects Successful 13
 The Project Life Cycle 14
 Project Management Processes 15
 Summary 17

1. Scope Management 18

 Initiation of the Project 19
  Project Charter *19*
   Statement of Work 20
   Business Need 20
   Scope Description 20
   Environmental and Organizational Factors 21
   Organizational Process Assets 21
   Change Management Procedure 21
   Risk Control Procedures 21
  Organizational Knowledge Bases *21*
  Constraints and Assumptions *22*
  Project Selection Methods *22*
 Who Are Those Stakeholders? 22
  Cost and Its Relationship to Price *23*
  Overbid or Underbid: Which Is Better for Your Company? *24*
 Getting to the Scope Baseline 26
 Work Breakdown Structure 28
  Systems Approach to Work Breakdown Structure *31*

    Work Breakdown Structure Dictionary — *32*
    Additional Project Breakdown Structures — *32*
  Scope Verification — 33
  Change Management — 33
  Project Justifications — 34
    The Breakeven Chart — *35*
      Problems with Breakeven Charts — 36
    Average Rate of Return on Investment — *36*
    Present Value of Money — *37*
    Internal Rate of Return on Investment — *40*
  Summary — 46

2. Time Management — **47**

  Activity Definition — 47
  Activity Sequencing — 48
    Activity on Arrow Diagramming — *49*
    Gantt Charts and Milestone Charts — *50*
    Precedence Diagramming Method (PDM) — *51*
  Logical Relationships — 52
    Finish-Start Relationship (FS) — *52*
    Start-Start Relationship (SS) — *52*
    Finish-Finish Relationship (FF) — *54*
    Start-Finish Relationship (SF) — *55*
    Leads and Lags — *56*
  Diagramming Relationships — 56
    Project Start and Project Finish Events — *57*
    Logical Precedence Diagram — *57*
      Activity Durations — 57
      Building the Network Diagram — 58
      Buffering the Schedule — 63
    Reverse Resource Allocation Scheduling — *67*
  Critical Path Method (CPM) — 68
  Program Evaluation and Review Technique (PERT) — 68
  Monte Carlo Simulation — 73
    The Simulation — *73*
    Output from the Monte Carlo Simulation — *74*
  Critical Chain Theory — 74
  Summary — 76

3. Cost Management — **77**

  Why We Need Cost Management — 77
  Project Life Cycle and Project Cost — 78

Using the Work Breakdown Structure   78
Project   *78*
Cost Estimating   79
Types of Estimates   *79*
    Top-Down Estimates   79
    Bottom-Up Estimates   79
    Analogous Estimates   80
    Parametric Estimates   80
    Control Estimates   81
Cost Budgeting   82
Cost Control   84
Earned Value Reporting   *84*
    Cumulative Reporting   85
    Earned Value Parameters   86
    Difficulties in Data Collection   87
    Reporting Work Complete   88
    Examples   88
    Calculated Values for Earned Value Reports   90
Financial Measures   *93*
    Return on Sales   96
    Return on Assets   96
    Economic Value Added   97
Depreciation   *98*
    Straight Line Depreciation   99
    Accelerated Depreciation   99
      Sum of the Years' Digits   *100*
      Double Declining Balances   *101*
Summary   101

4. Quality Management   **103**

Quality Planning   104
Quality Assurance   105
Cost of Quality   105
Deming's Fourteen Points   *107*
Quality Control   107
Inspection   *108*
Sampling Inspection   108
Acceptable Quality Level (AQL)   *109*
Buyer's Risk and Seller's Risk   *109*
Other Quality Control Techniques   110
Flowcharts and Diagrams   *110*

Cause and Effect Diagrams   110
Pareto Charts   110
Control Charts   113
Run Charts   116
Checklists   116
Kaizen   116
Benchmarking   117
Summary   117

5. Human Resources Management   118

Project Manager Roles and Responsibilities   119
Responsibility-Accountability Matrix   119
Project Schedule   120
Staffing Plan   120
Training Plan   120
Organization Chart   121
Strong Matrix, Weak Matrix, and Balanced Matrix Organizations   121
Strong Matrix   121
Weak Matrix   122
Balanced Matrix   122
Making Matrix Management Work   123
Personnel and Personal Evaluations   124
Motivation   125
Importance of Motivation   125
Industrial Revolution   125
Scientific Management   125
Learning Curve Theory   125
Depression Era   126
World War II   126
Post–World War II   127
Motivational Ideas   127
Procedures vs. Motivation   127
Expectancy Theory   129
Maslow's Hierarchy of Needs Theory   129
Hertzberg's Motivation/Hygiene Theory   131
Supervisory Style and Delegation   132
Job and Work Design   132
Job Enlargement   133
Job Enrichment   134
Quality Circles   134
Power   135
Forms of Power   135
Coercive Power and Reward Power   135

Legitimate Power 136
Referent Power 136
Expert Power 136
Representative Power 137
Leadership 137
Theory X and Theory Y Managers 137
Conflict Resolution 137
Forcing 138
Smoothing 139
Compromise 139
Problem Solving 140
Withdrawal 140
Managing Meetings 140
Managing Meetings Effectively 142
Before the Meeting 142
Beginning the Meeting 142
Summary 143

6. Communications Management 144

Lessons Learned 144
General Model of Communications 146
Thinking 146
Encoding 146
Symbols 146
Transmitting 147
Perceiving 147
Decoding 147
Understanding 147
Barriers to Communications 147
Distorted Perceptions 147
Distrusted Sources 147
Transmission Errors 148
Improving Communications 148
Make the Message Relevant for the Receiver 148
Reduce the Message to Its Simplest Terms 148
Organize the Message into a Series of Stages 148
Repeat the Key Points 149
Verbal and Written Communications 149
Formal and Informal Communications 150
Formal Communications 150
Informal Communications 150

Improving Listening   151
   Don't Interrupt   *151*
   Put the Speaker at Ease   *152*
   Appear Interested   *153*
   Cut Out Distractions   *153*
   Periodically Sum Up What Was Said   *153*
Networking   153
   Circular Networks   *154*
   Chain Networks   *154*
   The Wheel   *155*
   Free and Open Communications   *155*
Management by Walking Around   157
Performance Reviews   157
Summary   158

7. Risk Management   **160**

When to Do Risk Management   161
The Risk Process   162
Risk Management Planning   162
   Risk Breakdown Structure   *162*
Risk Identification   163
   Documentation Reviews   *163*
   Brainstorming   *163*
   Delphi Technique   *164*
   Nominal Group Technique   *165*
   Crawford Slip   *165*
   Expert Interviews   *165*
   Root Cause Identification   *166*
   Strengths, Weaknesses, Opportunities, and Threats (SWOT) Analysis   *166*
   Checklists   *166*
   Analogy   *167*
   Diagramming Techniques   *167*
   Recording of Risks Identified   *169*
Risk Assessment   169
   Qualitative Risk Analysis   *170*
   Risk Tolerance   *170*
   Risk Probability   *172*
     The Addition Rule   174
     The Multiplication Rule   176
   Risk Impact   *178*
   Expected Value   *178*
   Decision Trees   *180*

Risk Quantification 183
   Comparative Ranking 184
   Sensitivity Analysis 184
   Grouping the Risks 185
   Affinity Diagramming 186
Risk Response Planning 186
   Risk Response Strategies 186
   Avoidance 187
   Transfer 187
   Contracting 188
   Acceptance 188
   Mitigation 189
   Budgeting for Risk 189
Risk Monitoring and Control 190
Summary 191

8. Contract and Procurement Management   192

Contract Management 193
   Make or Buy 194
   Contract Life Cycle 194
      Requirement Process 195
      Requisition Process 195
      Solicitation Process 196
      Award Process 197
      Trade-Off Studies 197
      Contract Process 198
   Contract Administration 198
   Contract Types 199
      Fixed-Price or Lump-Sum Contract 199
         Firm Fixed-Price Contract 200
         Fixed-Price Plus Economic-Adjustment Contract 200
         Fixed-Price Plus Incentive Contract 201
      Cost-Plus Contract 201
         Cost Plus Fixed-Fee Contract 202
         Cost Plus Award-Fee Contract 202
         Cost Plus Incentive-Fee Contract 203
      Time-and-Material Contract 203
Procurement Management 203
   Commodities 203
   Unique Products and Services 204
   Forward Buying 204

    Blanket Orders   *205*
    Split Orders   *205*
  Summary   206

9. Professional Responsibility   207

  Task 1   208
  Task 2   209
  Task 3   209
  Task 4   210
  Task 5   211
  Code of Professional Conduct   211

10. What Is the PMP Exam Like?   213

  Domain 1: Initiating the Project   214
  Domain 2: Planning the Project   215
  Domain 3: Executing the Project   216
  Domain 4: Controlling the Project   216
  Domain 5: Closing the Project   217
  Domain 6: Professional Responsibility   217
  Types of Questions on the Exam   218
  Taking the Exam   219
  Use of Practice Questions   220
  The Application for PMP Certification   221
  The Education Qualification   223
  Joining PMI   223
  Recertification   224

Practice Questions   *225*

Practice Questions Answer Key   *303*

Appendix: Probability Distributions   *357*

Bibliography   *365*

Index   *367*

About the Author   *379*

PREFACE

This book has been written to help those preparing for the Project Management Professional Examination. It is aimed at those who want to learn project management methodology. It is not intended to be a drill in exam questions; there are more than enough of those around. It is intended to cover all of the material that the Project Management Institute (PMI®) considers important enough to be included in the exam. This book has been revised to reflect the changes in the Project Management Professional Examination put into effect as of the third quarter of 2005 and reflects the *Guide to the Project Management Body of Knowledge*®, Third (2004) Edition.

I have been working in the field of project management for the past thirty years and was managing projects long before that and long before there was a methodology called project management. Once I began to consider project management as a profession and a disciplined methodology, it became clear to me what had gone wrong with some of my projects in the past.

From that point on I began applying the tools and techniques of project management, and slowly the unification and completeness of the methodology became clear. Project management works as a unified body of knowledge, but all of the tools and techniques depend on one another to succeed. You cannot do a good job of cost estimating if you have not developed a good set of deliverables for the project any more than you can produce a good schedule without taking the time necessary to develop good estimates of the task durations.

If you practice project management using the methodology outlined in this book and the Project Management Institute's *Guide to the Project Management Body of Knowledge*, you will become a good project manager. Learning project management is more than studying a book or even a group of books. Project management must also be learned in the field with experience and exposure to real responsibility on real projects. The Project Management Professional (PMP®) certification is designed to certify project managers who meet the criteria for both knowledge and experience. To qualify for certification you must have both. PMI requires that you have at least 4,500 hours of experience if you have a bachelor's degree. Some of this experience must extend past more than the last three years, but not more than past the last six years. There is also a criterion for people not holding a bachelor's degree. This requires more experience—7,500 hours—but allows the hours to be over a five-year period and not exceeding eight years.

In addition, there is a requirement of thirty-five hours of project management education. This requirement is really not very difficult to fulfill, since there is no time limit and the training can be provided by practically anyone.

The forms for applying for the certification are not included in this book, because they change fairly often and can be easily downloaded from the Project Management Institute's Internet site at www.pmi.org/certification/.

This book is intended to cover the subject matter of the PMP exam. Since the PMP exam is a comprehensive examination of your knowledge of project management tools and techniques, the book is also comprehensive. However, every answer to every question on the PMP examination is not in this book. Nor is it in any other book. PMI is continually introducing new questions and replacing questions that have been around for some time. I do the best job I can to keep aware of the nature of the examination and pass this information on to you.

My philosophy is that no one should be able to pass the PMP exam without having an extremely good working knowledge of the practice of project management. In this book I have tried to explain the nature of project management, how all of the tools and techniques relate to one another, and how it all goes together to make a unified methodology that can be used to successfully manage projects.

There are a few comments to be made about how this book relates to the PMBOK®. There is not a direct chapter to chapter relationship between this book and the PMBOK. If you are preparing for the PMP examination, read the entire PMBOK several times. I do not want to sell you another copy of the PMBOK. Instead I have made an effort to explain the methodology of project management and supplement the PMBOK. This book is largely based on the knowledge areas of the PMBOK. I believe that organizing the project management methodology by knowledge areas is much clearer, and this is the way the PMBOK is organized with a few exceptions. For example, in my book there is no chapter on the integration knowledge area. The topics in the integration chapter of the PMBOK are covered better by discussing them in the knowledge areas that relate to them. For instance, developing the project charter and scope statement fit much better into a discussion of the scope knowledge area. Developing the project management plan must be done in all of the knowledge areas and so on. I did not fill the pages with endless lists of the ITTOs, PMI's inputs, outputs, tools, and techniques. You will see plenty of these in the PMBOK.

I hope that this book will help you prepare for the Project Management Professional certification and that you will embark on a long and prosperous career in project management.

I would appreciate your comments. My e-mail address is:
Mnewell@PSMconsult.com.

Preparing for the Project Management Professional (PMP®) Certification Exam

Third Edition

INTRODUCTION TO PROJECT MANAGEMENT

Project management is quickly becoming the method of management for more and more industries. Projects are being done for everything from building the largest skyscrapers to planning the smallest wedding. Many large companies now have a stated policy to manage their entire company using project management methods. We hope to encourage the use of project management in all businesses, and we hope to encourage and help project managers learn more about the profession of project management and pass the Project Management Professional (PMP®) examination.

If the professional organization for project managers, the Project Management Institute (PMI®), has been instrumental in promoting project management, we should be able to get some idea of the growth of project management by looking at the growth of the membership in this organization. Founded in 1969, PMI has now been in existence more than thirty-five years. When I joined PMI in 1989 they boasted of having about 5,000 members and a thousand Project Management Professionals (PMPs). Since 1989 the organization has experienced fantastic growth. In 2004, PMI's membership was well over 100,000, and the number of PMPs was over 75,000. These numbers represent a growth greater than even PMI had anticipated.

Of course, all project managers and those working in the project management profession are not members of PMI, just as all people practicing any profession do not join a professional organization. If the growth of PMI is any indication of the growth in the project management profession itself, then it can easily be said that the profession is growing by great leaps.

PMI has done much for the growth of project management as a profession. It has set the standards for the body of knowledge that makes up the project management profession. In 2001 PMI received ISO 9001 recognition for its PMP certification program from the International Organization for Standardization (ISO). This indicates that PMI's program for certifying individuals as PMPs meets the highest international quality standards. According to the ISO, a standard is a "document approved by a recognized body, that provides, for common and repeated use, rules, guidelines, or characteristics for products, processes, or services with which compliance is not mandatory."

In addition PMI was able to obtain American National Standards Institute (ANSI)

---

recognition for the *Guide to the Project Management Body of Knowledge* (PMBOK®). This certification makes this guide the standard document for project management knowledge.

Other factors have contributed to the growth of the profession as well. The body of knowledge that comprises project management contains very few tools and techniques that were not around before we started calling the work of doing projects "project management." Gantt charts have been around for nearly a hundred years, PERT analysis was a tool invented in the 1950s, and concepts of teamwork and participative management have been around for that long as well. What project management as a profession does is draw these tools together into a homogeneous whole and forge them into a new tool that produces reliable results in the management of projects.

What Is Project Management Anyway?

The *Guide to the PMBOK* defines project management as follows:

> Project Management is the application of knowledge, skills, and techniques to project activities in order to meet stakeholder needs and expectations from a project.

So project management is using a set of tools and techniques to manage projects. But it isn't fair to use the words you are defining as the definition. We had better first talk about what a project is and then see if we can come up with something better.

There are certain areas of expertise that are required for a project team to manage projects in the most effective way. These are: the *Guide to the PMBOK*, applicable standards and codes for the project, technical ability, general management ability, human resource skills, and the project surroundings.

Standards and Regulations

A *standard* is an agreed upon set of rules that are designed to achieve the optimum degree of order in the desired results. These are usually published by some authority on the subject. An example of a standard would be the octane ratings of gasoline used in their manufacture.

A *regulation* is a set of rules issued by some government agency. Regulations lay down a set of rules that are mandatory for compliance to this agency. Examples of regulations are occupational health and safety regulations.

A *project* is a temporary endeavor undertaken to provide a unique product or service. That is the definition from the *Guide to the PMBOK*. The word temporary means that any project done must have a beginning and an end. A project generally begins when some sort of official document proclaims the project to have an official life. This document, the project charter, usually creates some means of collecting the cost and expenses of the project. Often the end of the project is when all of the project goals have been met and all of the work of the project has been accomplished. Some projects will end when for various reasons it has been decided to abandon the project or stop work on it. This is generally because the goals of the project cannot be achieved practically.

Some distinction is made between the terms *project* and *program*. Most project managers feel that the project management profession can manage projects of any size and that the methodology that is used to manage them all is nearly the same, with modifications made to accommodate different sized projects. The methods used in the project management process are the same. While discussing the difference between projects and programs it would be well to note that there is a hierarchy of endeavors of this type starting at the largest, the strategic plan, followed by the portfolio, the program, the project, and even the subproject.

Most projects will have the characteristic of being developed through what is called "progressive elaboration" in the *Guide to the PMBOK*. This simply means that projects are progressively developed. For example, the project scope is only broadly defined in the beginning of the project. As the project progresses the scope becomes more clearly defined and more detailed. Ultimately a baseline is developed to define the scope of the project in a detailed way.

According to the *Guide to the PMBOK*, a program is a group of projects managed in a coordinated way to obtain benefits not able to be obtained by managing them separately. Programs are generally ongoing. This definition is familiar when we speak of very large programs, but all projects are really subprojects of larger projects or are composed of subprojects. From the perspective of a subproject manager, he or she is in charge of his or her own project. From the perspective of the manager of these managers, he or she is responsible for his or her own project. The difficulty of this definition is that there is no clear distinction between the size of a project and that of a program. It is also true that in some organizations, programs may even be considered to be subprojects of other projects. All of this goes to show that project management is not a strict science but has some artistic aspects to it as well. We will see that there are many differences in terminology throughout the project management profession. PMI has made a remarkable effort to try to separate and standardize terminology.

When we speak of portfolio management, we are talking about a number of projects that are grouped together to help meet strategic business goals. In this way projects that advance the strategic goals of the company are included together, and an effort is made to ensure that each project not only is justified on its own merits but that it also supports the strategic goals of the organization.

It is important to realize that the end of the project is not the same as the end of the goods or services that the project produces. A project to build a nuclear power plant usually ends when the goal of building the plant and making it operate at some expected level of production has been achieved. The plant continues to operate, far into the future, even though the project has ended. Although the project itself may come to an end from the standpoint of the project manager and the project team, it is important to understand that the effects of the project may continue for much longer. Life cycle costs can frequently be incurred over the useful life of the project. These costs include warranty repair work and project liability and many others. Since the project is usually closed when these costs occur, they must be recognized by the project team and allowed for as future costs by management.

The project team, the project manager, and upper management of the company must also consider the project environment. The social environment must be understood. This is how the project affects people and how their wishes and desires will affect the project. In some projects the political environment is important. This will determine the effect of local customs, regulations, and laws that will affect the project. Lastly, the physical environment is important. The project must be done within the bounds of the physical environment in which it takes place and under the conditions present.

The word *unique* in our definition means that the good or service that the project provides is to some extent different from anything that has been produced before. However, unique does not mean that the project is completely unique but that it is to have certain parts that are unique and that those parts are unique enough to require a planning process to organize the effort to be done.

Many projects build on the results of other projects and have many things in common with projects the organization has done in the past. A project is unique because there is something that sets each project apart from others. If it were not for this it could not be a project. Instead, it would be a routine repetition of something done before and would not require many of the project management tools and techniques.

Projects are "progressively elaborated," which means that the products of a project are progressively developed throughout the project. The goals and objectives are stated at the beginning of the project. These goals and objectives are elaborated on and made clearer and become more detailed as the project progresses. Initially the project will be broadly defined. As time passes and more about the project becomes known the definition of the project becomes clearer and more specific.

From this, the idea that project management can be used to do almost anything comes easily to mind. Of course, those of us in project management sometimes like to think that members of our profession can manage projects better than anyone else.

Projects are always going to be temporary endeavors, because they are intentionally put together for the purpose of accomplishing something. Once this "something" has been accomplished, the resources that were put together for this purpose can be assigned to other projects. This means that the people and resources that can be brought together for a project can be the right ones, and the project team can be formed specifically for the purpose of that project.

In modern project management, project teams bring together resources as they are required. One of the great advantages of project management is its ability to form multi-disciplined project teams of the right people at the right time. The obvious advantage of this is that scarce skills can be brought to a project when needed.

Projects always have limited resources, but sometimes there are projects where the cost and amount of resources seem to be unlimited. Projects like the Apollo Project in the 1960s and the Manhattan Project in the 1940s come to mind, but even these projects had some resource constraints on them. To the project manager who is trying to get a project completed with scarce or unavailable resources this might seem like a wonderful way to manage a project, but these types of projects usually come with severe schedule requirements.

The person or organization that has something at stake in the results of a project we call the "stakeholder." Projects will always have more than one stakeholder, and each of the stakeholders will have different needs and expectations.

The "client" or "sponsor" is the main stakeholder in the project. Without this stakeholder the project probably would not go forward. This person or organization usually puts up the money for the project and has the most interest in its success.

So, we can now understand the PMBOK definition, "project management is the application of the tools and techniques that are necessary to satisfy the expectations of the stakeholder or stakeholders of the project."

A True Story

"Of course I don't look busy—I did it right the first time." This one-liner brings to mind the problem that so many of us face in implementing project management strategies and methods in our businesses. It seems that people are resistant to change even when it is good for them, and they don't appreciate people getting things done if they don't look busy enough. As a newly certified project management professional, you will undoubtedly run into some resistance when you try to implement new ideas, and project management techniques seem to be full of new ideas.

There is a story (probably true) about a project manager who went to work for a company that produced computer software. This project manager was hired to complete a project that was to produce a significant amount of the company's income for the year, and it had a strict deadline of twelve months.

As time went by, the project manager settled in, and after a couple of weeks the project manager's boss asked her how many lines of code had been written for the project (a not too unusual measure for computer programming types).

She replied, "Well, none at the moment. We are describing the user's requirements and doing some planning for the project, but no, we have no lines of code written."

This seemed to satisfy her manager for the time being, and the project manager continued her work. After about a month the project manager's boss showed up again and asked the same question, "How many lines of code have you and your project team written?"

The project manager, recognizing the concern of her manager, said, "Well, none, but we are getting organized. We have defined our deliverables for the project, and we have made a work breakdown structure for the project, and we have started our risk analysis, but no, we have no lines of code written." Somewhat shaken, the manager left.

This went on for some time. The project manager did planning and organizing for the project execution to take place, and her manager grew more and more frantic with each passing day.

To make a long (twelve months) story shorter, after about eleven months, the project was completed. The customer and all the stakeholders were happy. The project was fully tested and it met all the requirements as specified. The customer accepted the system and paid the bill.

The project manager's boss decided to throw a party for the entire project team. So, one Friday afternoon, the office was closed and everyone took a break for pizza and beer. The project manager's boss took her aside during the party and said, "I want to congratulate you on getting this project done within the time required, but it seems to me that if you had not been messing around doing that planning stuff and gotten busy writing code from the start, we would have been done about two months sooner."

This is the kind of reward you can expect when you follow good project management practices and you are working in an environment where all of this is new to the management of your organization. Sometimes a little training in the ways and methods of project management is in order. Often we find companies that are spending many thousands of dollars training people who will manage projects are not training any of the managers above those project managers. When the project managers try to implement something new that they have learned, they are frequently frustrated by upper management's resistance to change.

Sometimes it seems that getting these executive managers into some sort of project management course is a lost cause. But it is imperative that we do so, if only so that they will appreciate and understand some of the things that our new project managers are trying to do.

Advantages of Project Management

Project management brings together many of the things that are needed to make endeavors like projects successful. But what do we mean by a successful project? A successful project is one that meets the expectations of the stakeholders of the project.

By organizing the project in a way that concentrates the efforts of the project team in the direction of accomplishing the project, a great deal of motivation is achieved. This allows for the project teams to concentrate on the project and not be distracted by all of the other projects and business activities that are going on in the area around them.

The stakeholders have consistent points of contact with the project team, and the project manager is a reliable source of information about the project and all that is going on within it.

The tools and techniques of project management are tried and tested and can be used on any project with success. Nearly all of them have been available for many years but have been somewhat difficult to use without the aid of personal computers. Project management brings many of these tools together in one methodology that can be successfully applied.

In project management we frequently speak of the triple constraints of project scope, project budget, and project time. This means that projects must meet the stakeholders' expectations and must be able to be done within the budget that was allocated to them and in the time that was allocated to them.

Organizing for Project Management

Most projects are smaller than the organizations to which they belong. The management of a project is strongly influenced by the organizational environment to which they belong. The organization's maturity with respect to project management will have a great influence on how the project manager is able to perform the work of managing the project. For example, project managers who have a management style of participative management may have trouble managing projects in a strongly hierarchical environment.

Referring to Figure I-1, there are really only three ways that organizations can be structured. All organizations are derivations or combinations of these structures. At one end of the spectrum of organizations is the "projectized" or pure project organization. At the other end is the functional or traditional organization. In the middle is the matrix organization.

The Projectized Organization

In project management, the pure project organization is not the organization that we are most interested in. It is a developmental stepping-stone to the matrix organization that is so important to the proper use of project management. Let us look at these organizations one at a time.

The first type of organization used was probably the pure project organization. In this type of organization the project manager is the supreme authority, and all questions regarding the project are directed to him or her as the ultimate authority. The project manager makes all of the decisions. When the Egyptian pyramids were built, this type of

Figure I-1. Project management versions.

	Functional	Weak Matrix	Balanced Matrix	Strong Matrix	Pure Project
Person's Authority in Projects	No Authority	Some Authority	Moderate to Low Authority	High to Moderate Authority	High Authority
Project Manager's Time in Role	Part Time	Part Time	Full Time	Full Time	Full Time
Common Titles for Manager	Project Coordinator, Project Leader	Project Coordinator, Project Leader	Project Manager	Project Manager, Program Manager	Project Manager, Program Manager
Percent of Project Team Assigned Full-Time	0%	15%	50%	75%	100%

organization was used. The project manager answered directly to the pharaoh, and there were thousands of people dedicated to the completion of the project. The project took place far from the formal organization, and most resources were completely dedicated to the project.

People who work in this kind of organization are generally dedicated to the project until it is over. In some early projects, such as building the Egyptian pyramids, people worked on these projects until they—the people or the projects—were finished. This type of project organization is necessary when there is a very large project of great importance or when the project is taking place a great distance from the main organization. The relationship between having a good focus on the goals of the project and good motivation is clear, and people respond well to a clear focus.

In this type of organization, the focus of the project team and the project goals are clear. Communications between the customer and the project team are usually quite good.

There are some disadvantages to this kind of organization, however. The first is one of efficiency. If persons with a special skill are needed, they must generally be brought to the project for the duration of time that their skills are needed, even if the skills are needed only part of the time. A stone carver who specializes in carving birds might be needed for only one week a month, but because of the distance and difficulty transporting him to and from the project site, he would have to be employed full time. For the other three weeks of the month this person would have to be utilized in some other capacity.

The second problem with this type of organization is what to do when it is over. There are thousands of people working on a pyramid out there in the desert. They all had the goal of constructing a pyramid. They all had a deadline of getting it done before the pharaoh dies. When the pyramid is finished, so is the project—and so is the team. There is usually a big celebration with everyone patting each other on the back while the project manager comes around and hands out everyone's termination notice.

In modern times the same thing happens in this type of organization. An example is the Apollo Program. President John F. Kennedy gave his famous speech and said, "I believe this nation should commit itself to the goal of sending a man to the moon before the end of the decade and returning him safely to Earth." As we all know, this goal was met in July of 1969 when Neil Armstrong first stepped on the surface of the moon and returned home safely. At that same time, NASA managers were figuring out what to do now that the program was over. For a time they were able to keep life in the program, but eventually the funding dried up, and many of the highly skilled aerospace engineers and managers were terminated. When NASA, a few years later, tried to start up the space shuttle program, many of these former employees had changed careers and were happy in their new occupations.

We can say that this organization can be used for special projects that are large in size or remote from their home organization. For most of the projects that we will be involved in, this type of organization has too many serious disadvantages to be used successfully. This brings us to the next organization we will consider.

The Functional or Traditional Organization

The functional organization has been with us for quite some time—it has been the dominant form of organization for over a hundred years. The development of "scientific management" by such persons as Fredrick Taylor and Henry Ford led to the extensive use of the concepts of this type of organization, which are still used today. In this type of organization the intention is to place people into jobs that they do best, train them to do their jobs even better, and organize the work so that it takes advantage of their skills in the most effective way.

This kind of organization is set up primarily on the basis of organizing people with similar skills into the same groups, working under a manager who is similarly skilled. In this way the skills are concentrated into pools of workers in such a way that the manager can distribute the work to those who are best qualified for a specific job. The manager of this group, being experienced in this type of work, is also an appropriate person to recommend training and career-enhancing assignments to each of the members of the group.

In the past, traditional organization people became specialists in their jobs and became very good at what they did. This allowed them to become somewhat complacent about what they did. As long as they were continually asked to do things that were familiar and within their area of expertise they were successful. With people working this way companies became this way as well. They were very good at what they did as long as they could keep on doing it over and over again with little change. Companies like these were not easily changed when market demands and new technology entered their business areas.

Suppose Sally worked for a large automotive company in the 1970s. Her job was to design disk brake assemblies for all of the cars that this company made. She was very good at it. In fact, you could say that she was as good at it as anyone in the business. She was so good at designing disk brakes that she was employee of the month and received many awards for her designs in terms of quality and cost. She had been with the company since leaving college and progressed through the ranks and received regular raises. She received training to help enhance her skills and was allowed to go to a limited number of conferences held for people in her profession. She knew that in a few years she would be the head of a design group and perhaps some day be manager of a department.

Things changed and the company decided to diversify. One new line of business was producing a super-lightweight vehicle. This vehicle required the design of a disk brake assembly of the lightest weight possible. For Sally this meant that she would have to design the brake assembly using materials that she had never used before. This bothered her, and she delayed starting the task. She had no contact with the customer and knew nothing about the strategic objectives of this project.

Meanwhile, her boss was also less than enthusiastic about the project. Fortunately for him, the new ultra-lightweight vehicle was only a minor part of the work that was going on in his department. As a result he did not monitor Sally too much on the design of the disk brake assembly. To him it seemed that there was the more important work of the company's normal business to take care of. This new, here-today-and-gone-tomorrow, super-lightweight vehicle was just another dream of the marketing department and nothing to be concerned about when there were thousands of customers continuing to buy the standard products of the company.

In another department of the company, where the bulk of the vehicle design work was taking place, the manager was under a lot of pressure to get this design completed. It represented a large amount of the work that had to be done in that department. His job was all the more difficult since his fellow department heads were not concerned with this project. In addition, this manager probably had very little direct contact with the customer, and the communications problem of going through the marketing and sales people to find out what the customer really wanted was formidable.

As long as companies are doing the same sorts of things that they always did, this type of organization works well. Each person has a boss who knows what that person's job is and how well the person does it. The boss knows how to administer salaries, training, and all the other administrative things that employees need. By being familiar with the work and the people doing the work, the boss is able to best use the skills that are available.

However, the problem with this kind of organization is that it is difficult to make a change in what people do. Sally avoided working on the ultra-lightweight brake because it was more difficult to learn new things to get the job done. She was measured by the amount of designs she completed and to a lesser extent by the difficulty of the designs. She naturally avoided the difficult and new in favor of the tried and true. Since the whole company worked this way, it was very resistant to change and the development of new products.

The Matrix Organization

The matrix organization came into being in the 1970s. It was an attempt to put the best of the projectized and the traditional organizations together.

In the matrix organization, all of the employees report to functional managers much like the managers in the traditional organization. The employees are organized strictly by skills. In the traditional organization, there are many exceptions to organizing by skills. An electrical engineer might be in a department of mechanical engineers, for example. In matrix organizations this does not take place. All people of the same skill report to the same functional manager. The functional managers are responsible for project managers' staffing and direct the administrative work that is needed for the employees. The project managers direct the bulk of the work done by the employees.

There is an organization of project managers as well. The project managers are responsible for the work that is done, but not for the administrative work that must be done for the employees actually doing the work. This allows the project managers to form teams that can concentrate on the project at hand without getting bogged down by administrative work. It allows the project team to focus on the customer, the stakeholders, and the project much as in the projectized organization.

In operation, the project manager puts together the project plans and develops a list of people needed to work on the team. He or she then meets with the functional manager and negotiates for the people who are available and who have the proper skills to work on the project. Together, they develop the staff that will work on the project. The functional managers do this with all of the project managers who require skills that are in their organizations. Here is one way of thinking about this: If a project manager has a Gantt chart that lists all of the activities in a project, the functional manager has a similar chart listing all of the employees in the organization and the projects that they are assigned to work on, shown as bars against a timeline.

There are several difficulties with this kind of organization. There needs to be a balance of power between the project managers and the functional managers. If there is not, one group will dominate the other. If the project managers become too powerful, they can force the functional managers to allocate the best people to their projects, or even allocate more people than their projects require. The result of this is that all of the people end up reporting to project managers, who then can trade people between projects without consulting with the functional managers. The functional managers end up being underutilized. This type of organization where the project managers are very powerful is called a strong matrix organization.

If the balance of power is toward the functional managers, we end up with the traditional organization, only now we have a group of project managers as well. Sooner or later someone will realize that the functional managers are assigning and monitoring all the work and the project managers are merely expediting projects. This type of organization, where the project manager has less power than the functional manager, is called a weak matrix organization.

Balance can be achieved by deciding when work should be done by the project team and when work should be assigned to the functional department organizations themselves. For example, organizations can make a rule that any work done that requires a person to work full time for more than one month will be done in the project under the direction of the project manager, and any work that takes less time than this will be assigned to the functional organization. This allows work to be done in the functional areas as well as in the projects. This type of organization, where there is a balance of power between the functional managers and the project managers, is called a balanced matrix organization.

The Project Office and the Project Management Office

"Project management office" is a term that has come into use in the past few years. It should be noted that, in common usage, the term "project office" is different from "project management office." The project office is the place where the project team is managed and where the project manager and the project team reside. As companies become more project oriented, quite a lot of inefficiency can result. This is because project managers want to have direct control of all the work that goes on inside their project. But it is not practical for all project teams to have complete independence.

For example, although they might find it desirable, each project team cannot have their own high-speed copy machine, accounting group, payroll department, purchasing department, and so on. Common services that are required for several projects can be organized into a project management office (PMO). One PMO can support the needs of several project teams. It can be much more efficient to have one large copy machine serving the needs of several project teams. Other resources are appropriately shared through the PMO. The PMO can also be very helpful in helping to coordinate project policies, procedures, reports, and documentation. In addition the PMO can be useful in coordinating quality efforts, communications, and mentoring.

The danger of having the responsibilities of the project team handled by the PMO is that the authority of the project team may be eroded. For example, it might be economically practical to have one copy machine shared by several project teams and to locate the copy machine in the PMO. What happens if we decide that it makes sense to have the PMO produce the project schedule or some of the other reports that are generated regularly by all projects? What if those using the project schedule will now come to the scheduler in the PMO to make project schedule changes? Before we know it the PMO may end up giving advice and literally running aspects of the project that should be done by the project team. This is leading us away from the idea of project management and back to the functional organization.

What project management brings to the table is the ability to coordinate all of these activities and at the same time help to motivate people to work on them. By bringing people together into a project team, the work of the project is coordinated through a project manager who is in close contact with the client and stakeholders. This allows the project manager to focus the project team on the completion of the project.

The project manager and his or her team are able to focus on the goals of the project with relatively little distraction. To the project team, this project is the main thing in their working life for the time being. People with the proper skills can be brought into close proximity to each other, and by having this close proximity they develop a synergy of mutual assistance and complete the work with remarkable results.

How the Project Manager Makes Projects Successful

When we think of project managers we should think of them as small business managers. Many of the characteristics that are required to be successful in the managing of a small business are the same as those needed for the proper management of projects. In fact, since many project managers today are rooted in technical disciplines, it is surprising that the skills they are called upon to have were previously considered unusual skills for technical managers.

Today the project manager is expected to be familiar with and have considerable knowledge in the areas of finance, accounting, sales, marketing, manufacturing, research and development, strategic and operational planning, the characteristics of organizations, personnel, administration, managing work relationships, motivation, and other people skills. This is necessary because project managers are managing projects much like people manage small businesses. The multidisciplined project team becomes an entity in itself, focused on the needs of the project and trying to satisfy those needs in the best way possible.

The Project Life Cycle

Projects of any size, large or small, can be managed using the project management methodology. Because all projects are unique in some way, it might be helpful to look at the life cycle or phases of projects and note the many similarities between projects and that all projects go through similar phases. The project life cycle defines the beginning and the end of a project and various phases within it. At various points in the project life cycle the project is reevaluated and a decision is made whether to go forward with the project or to stop work on it. The points between the beginning and the end of the project vary considerably depending on the type of business and the specific project being done. The definition of specific phases will differ greatly from organization to organization with most organizations defining their own phases. Most often a phase's completion is marked by some sort of management review and a decision to move into the next phase. This is not always the case since phases will overlap especially when "fast tracking" a project.

During the life cycle of a project there will be accomplishments made at each phase. The completion of these accomplishments results in the creation of a "deliverable," a tangible verifiable product of the work being done on the project. These may be products that are delivered external to the project or something needed for other project work to take place, which are considered to be "internal deliverables."

If we consider the project life cycle as having at least three phases—an initial phase, a final phase, and one or more intermediate phases—we see that projects share many characteristics.

PMI describes the project management processes as the initiating processes, planning processes, executing processes, controlling processes, and closing processes. These processes are repeated over and over in each phase of the project life cycle.

As can be seen in Figure I-2, in a project's initial phase, cost and staffing levels are low. There are only a few key people who spend their time on the project at this point. Few if any materials have been purchased, and the company's financial commitment is not great. At this phase there is the greatest chance that the project will never be completed. Many projects reach this phase only to be discontinued when it is determined that the cost of doing the project meets or exceeds the benefits received from doing the project. At this phase of the project there is little known about the project.

As the project moves into the second phase the rate of spending increases for the project. This is a result of having more people working a greater amount of time on the project. At this time the cost of changes and the impact of the risks increases as well, since it will take more effort and time to make corrections.

At some point the project's rate of spending begins to decrease. This is because some of the people on the project team have completed their work and are moving on to other projects. Much of the material and equipment has been purchased. From this point on the project will spend less and less.

Figure I-2. Typical daily cost of projects during project phases.

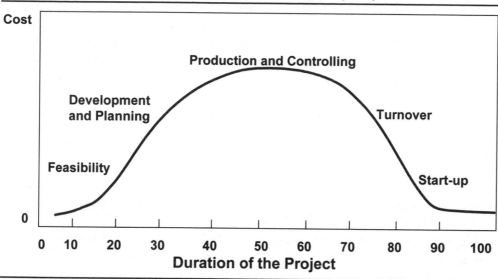

At the final phase of the project it is important that the project manager make a transition of the stakeholders, changing from the project team to an ongoing maintenance and support group. If this is not done the good relationship that the project team has with the stakeholders will come back to haunt the team members. Stakeholders have enjoyed working with the project team and are familiar with the members of the team and what they do. The team members have not moved to other projects and will spend much of their time working with previous project stakeholders. This can be difficult if the stakeholders are major customers or our own upper management.

Project Management Processes

In the *Guide to the Project Management Body of Knowledge*, the basic project management processes are discussed. This approach to finding a way to look at the project management process uses the systems management approach to project management. By this we mean that project management is a process that takes inputs, processes them, and produces outputs. Within the project management process are other process groups: the initiating process group, the planning process group, the executing process group, the monitoring and control process group, and the closeout process group.

The *initiating process group* includes the processes that authorize the start of a new project or the next phase of a project. The rough estimates of the project success are estimated and a preliminary scope definition is made. These estimates are used to perform, at least, a preliminary project justification. The project is authorized by the project charter. Prior to the issuing of the project charter, the project does not officially exist.

The *planning process group* includes the processes that make it possible to plan the project. At this time the project is "progressively elaborated" (sometimes called "rolling wave planning"), and the project scope is matured and more clearly defined. These processes are used to gather much additional information about the project from many sources both inside and outside of the project.

The *executing process group* includes the processes that are required to actually do and complete the work defined in the project plan. This work will result in the accomplishment of the project's objectives and the delivering of the deliverables to the stakeholders. During the execution process there will be more resources used than at any other time in the project. A great deal of effort must be spent coordinating these resources. It is therefore necessary to have a quality effort that will ensure that the project will meet the stakeholder expectations.

The *monitoring and control process group* includes the processes that are required to monitor and control the execution phase. The project is monitored for results and performance according to the project plan. Recommendations for corrective action are made and the results of the corrective actions are monitored. The change management system is part of this group and is essential to controlling "scope creep" and "creeping elegance."

The *closing process group* includes the processes that are required to formally terminate the project. With this group we put an end to the project. The deliverables are delivered and accepted by the stakeholders, accounts that were opened for the project are closed, and purchasing activities are reconciled.

Of course, each of the knowledge areas mentioned in the *Guide to the PMBOK* operates in each of these major processes. For example, the knowledge area of cost management is concerned with the initiation process, because we must have preliminary estimates for a project to be able to move forward into the planning phase or process. We must have cost information for the planning process, because we must know how much our project is going to cost when it is actually done. In the execution process we must collect actual cost data to allow us to control the project. In the closeout phase of the project we must have cost information to close out the accounts and make sure that all of the bills associated with the project are paid.

The process groups all take place over the life of the project. That is, if we look at a project from beginning to end each of the process groups will have taken place. It is important to note that all of the process groups will take place during each phase or subproject of the project. In other words, if a particular phase of a project produces deliverables, either internal or external, we must go through the initiation processes, the planning processes, the execution processes, the monitoring and control processes, and the closeout processes. It is also important to note that the process groups do not necessarily occur in sequence. There can be considerable overlap from one process or process group to the next.

In each of the knowledge areas—integration management, scope management, time management, cost management, quality management, human resources management, communications management, risk management, and contracts and procurement management—it can be seen that they all may apply to each and every one of the processes. One could say that some knowledge from each of the knowledge areas is required in every one of the process groups.

Summary

Project management is quickly becoming the management method of choice not only in the United States but around the globe as well. The reasons for this are that project management works, and people are finding out that it is the most comprehensive method of management available today.

CHAPTER 1

Scope Management

Without a doubt, the most common reason that projects fail is because of poor scope definition. By that I mean that the expectations of the stakeholders, and especially the client or sponsor, are different from the expectations of the project team. This is a most difficult problem, but it is critical to the success of the project that it is overcome. There are many reasons why a project fails, and understanding them will give us insights as to how to avoid them.

The relationship between the project team and the customer has to reverse itself at the time of scope definition. Up to this point the customer's main contact has been someone from a sales organization. During this part of the project the salesperson has been trying to convince the customer that the project is a good project to do. Sometimes the salesperson becomes overly enthusiastic about the project and intentionally or unintentionally leads the customer to believe that everything imaginable is actually going to be produced by the project. This is rarely the case.

When the project team is formed and begins to hold meetings with the customer to develop the scope of the project, the customer already has the notion that the project is already defined. As a result the customer views the whole process of scope definition as a waste of time. In fact the customer may actually resist the scope definition process because of reluctance to commit to defining the project.

It becomes very difficult for the project team to convince the customer that both the project team and the customer have the same goal for the project, that is, that the goal of the project is to give the customer something that is useful and something that does what is wanted in the first place. There is no point in having an adversarial relationship between the customer and the project team. Both want the project to succeed, and both want the project to be useful and serve the purpose for which it was intended.

The project team needs to understand the customer as well. The team should not be frustrated if the customer seems to know less about the project than the project team. After all, the reason that the project team is doing the project is that they are expert at accomplishing the project. The customer is not expert in doing the project. That is why the project team was formed in the first place.

Sometimes extraordinary means must be used to develop the scope of the project. It may be necessary for one or more project team members to work in the customer's area for a period of time and become trained in the work that the project is supposed to enhance. This is a good technique when the customer is not willing or able to cooperate in devoting the necessary time and manpower to working with the project team. The project team member simply becomes a surrogate customer and learns enough about the customer's operation to speak for the customer.

Of course it is much more desirable to have the customers themselves play this role. The customer should be represented in the project team, as should all of the project stakeholders. The greater the involvement and the greater the level of communications that you have with all of the stakeholders, the sounder the project will be. This will start with the definition of the scope of the project.

Initiation of the Project

A project comes into existence with the creation of a formal document called the project charter. The project charter is a small document but one that is extremely important to getting a project started in the right direction. Projects are done for a number of reasons. Generally, for commercial companies, the reason for doing a project is to make money. There are many other reasons for doing projects, such as establishing goodwill, conforming to government regulations and laws, and attempting to stay current with developing technology.

Project Charter

In the third edition of the *PMBOK®*, PMI® has chosen to expand the content of the project charter. It also recommends that the contract with the customer be completed before the approval of the project charter. Some considerations must be made for this approach. The more information that is put into the project charter, the greater the possibility for people to disagree. If there is much disagreement about the project charter and its specific contents, there will have to be discussion and clarification in order to get managers to approve it. Since the project charter officially begins the project, work that is done prior to project charter approval may not be accounted for properly. This means that the effort taken prior to the approval of the project charter may not be properly accounted for. This in turn understates the true cost of the project and leads to underbudgeting of future projects when this project is used as a reference. I feel that project charters should be kept to a minimum in order to speed approval. The host of documents PMI considers could easily be done after the completion and approval of the project charter. For these reasons, in the real world of project management, some caution must be used when following the *PMBOK* recommendations for the project charter.

The project charter should contain a statement of the purpose of the project and the project name. It should also contain the business case for doing the project, the needs and expectations of the stakeholders, a rough schedule and budget for the project, and a list of the assumptions and constraints that we recognize at this point in the project.

The project charter formally authorizes the project to begin and names the project manager. This is usually done by creating some sort of financial account that will allow costs to be accumulated for this project.

The project charter is written by the project manager, but it must be distributed under the signature of the person who is authorized to initiate or sponsor the project and create funding for the project. It would make no sense to have project managers creating and authorizing their own projects. However, it is important that the project manager actually write the project charter, because this is the first opportunity for the project manager to define the project as he or she sees it. Several documents should be done prior to the creation of the project charter.

Statement of Work

The statement of work is a narrative that describes what work will be done in the course of completing this project. The statement of work for the project can come in many forms. It can be part of the bid process or the request for proposals process. When coming in the form of a bid, the statement of work is defined by the organization requesting the bid. In the case of a request for proposals from outside the company, the statement of work is only functionally defined by the requestor and the detailed statement of work is proposed by the proposing organization. It can also be a statement of work required by part of our own organization.

Business Need

The business need is a statement of the need to do the project. This can be in the form of a request for a needed product or service that will result from doing the project.

Scope Description

The project scope description is a statement of the requirements of the project as they are seen today. The scope of the project at this point is not terribly detailed and will be progressively elaborated as the project plan unfolds. The project scope should be sufficiently detailed so that it can be used for planning purposes. The scope description should also show how the items described in the scope description relate to the business needs that were to be addressed by the project.

Environmental and Organizational Factors

This document should address all of the organizational factors surrounding the project and the marketplace. It should identify strengths and weaknesses in the environment in which the project will have to be done and the ability of the company to carry on the project. Since projects are so dependent on information, a statement of the company's management information systems is appropriate. Stakeholder and industry risk tolerance should be estimated and addressed. Personnel administration should also be addressed as the company's hiring and firing practices will have an effect on the ability of the project manager to add and remove people from the project team.

Organizational Process Assets

These items, included in the project charter or subsequent documentation, are the principal company documentation of standards and procedures already completed and available for the project to use. They include any standards that have been created for managing projects as well as lessons learned from previous projects, both successes and failures.

Also included are all procedural standards and communication policies, such as distribution of reports, the frequency of distribution, reporting of actual cost during the project, and the method used for reporting progress and performance of the project team. It should be noted that when we refer to the project team we include people normally considered outside the project, such as vendors and functional departments that do work for the project.

Change Management Procedure

The project charter should include the change management procedure. This procedure will need to be followed as soon as the baselines of the project are established. The procedure itself needs to be in place early so that stakeholders and project team members are aware of how changes to project scope, cost, and schedule should be processed.

Risk Control Procedures

As companies become more mature in the management of projects, the need for good risk management becomes more important. The project charter should contain the risk management procedures, the methods of identifying risk, and the methods for calculating impact, probability, and severity.

Organizational Knowledge Bases

The project charter should contain the lessons-learned documents, including progress and performance, identified risks and the results of risk management, financial data, issue and defect management, and history from previous related projects.

Constraints and Assumptions

In addition to the project charter, any constraints that will limit the project team's choices in any of the project activities must be noted. Predetermined or edicted project schedules, project completion dates, and project budgets need to be reckoned with early in the project.

Assumptions must be made for the purpose of planning the project. These will be considerations for the availability of resources, other needs and expectations, vendors, start dates, contract signing, and others. Assumptions are not a bad thing—we make assumptions every day. From the moment we get out of bed each morning we assume that the electricity will work and the water will come out of the faucets. To successfully plan a project many assumptions will be made or the project will never get started.

Project Selection Methods

This section of the project charter should outline the standard methods that should be used in justifying projects. It should include the methods that can be employed during different times of the project life. In the early stages of the project when only small commitments are being made, fairly easy but less accurate justification methods, such as "breakeven" analysis or the calculation of "payback points," can be employed. As the project develops, more complete and accurate justification methods can be used. As the amount of money committed to the project increases it is necessary to have more detailed and accurate project justifications, such as the "internal rate of return on investment" calculation. These will be discussed in detail later in this chapter.

Who Are Those Stakeholders?

First of all we should say that the *stakeholders* are all of the people who have something to gain or lose in the project. By this definition we must include, among others, the project team. If we consider all of the far-reaching effects of doing almost any project, we can see that there are a lot of stakeholders indeed. We must be careful that we consider all of the stakeholders in a project, some to a lesser extent than others.

Our main concern is going to be the "key" stakeholders. The first problem is to identify them. How can we best accomplish this task? For some reason there is reluctance on the part of project managers to contact all of the key stakeholders in the project, let alone the ones that are not so critical. This results in a poor definition of what the project is all about. With a poor definition of what the project is all about, there is no hope of ever being able to construct a project plan and determine the cost, schedule, and scope objectives that project managers hold so dear to their hearts.

One of the techniques that can be used is to have seven to ten members of your project team get together and use one of the group dynamics techniques to come up with the names of all the stakeholders for the project. One technique that is gaining in popularity these days is called the *Crawford slip*.

Using this technique, each person in the group is given ten pieces of paper. The facilitator asks the question, "Who is the most important stakeholder in this project?" Each of the participants must answer the question with the best answer he or she can think of. This is all done in silence, and the answers are not discussed at this time. The facilitator waits one minute, exactly, and asks the same question again. Each time the question is asked, the participants must answer the question. An answer cannot be used more than one time by each participant.

After the question has been asked ten times, the group should have generated 70 to 100 responses. If the group has been picked carefully so that there is diversity among the participants, there is a good chance that a high percentage of the stakeholders have been identified.

At this point the list of stakeholders can be compiled and distributed to the participants for additions and corrections. With this technique we have gone a long way toward identifying the stakeholders for the project.

Cost and Its Relationship to Price

One of the things that seems to be confusing is the relationship between cost and price. So, the first thing we should do is to make certain that we are all using the same meanings for these two words.

Price is the amount of money (or something else) that a customer or stakeholder is willing to give you in order to receive something from you. Generally, in terms of project management, the thing that is being done for the stakeholder is the project, and the things that the customer and stakeholders receive are the deliverables of the project. These things can be either goods or services. Money is usually the thing that is given in exchange for doing the project. *Cost,* on the other hand, is the amount of resources (money, people, materials, equipment, and so on) that are consumed in order to produce the delivered goods or services, the results of the project.

What is the relationship between cost and price? Are we satisfied if we are able to make a reasonable profit on what we do for our stakeholders? Are we satisfied if the cost of doing a project is less than the selling price by some accepted percentage?

Let's explore this a bit. Suppose we say we would be satisfied if our total project cost was 85 percent of the selling price. We must first ask where the selling price came from. Did our sales and marketing people try to get the highest price they could, or were they satisfied by being able to get the acceptable 15 percent markup from the customer?

Eliyahu Goldratt said in his book *It's Not Luck* that the price of something should be determined by "the perceived value to the buyer." What this means is that the selling price of anything we do should be determined by what the customer and the stakeholders are willing to pay. Having determined what the stakeholders are willing to pay, we then need to determine whether it is profitable enough for us to do the work. To determine this we must determine cost.

In order for us to stay competitive in a world of global competition it is important that we recognize this. In the beginning of a product life cycle or when a new service is being offered for the first time, it is important that the stakeholders pay the price equivalent to the value of the goods or services they receive. It is also important that the project team produce the deliverables of the project for the minimum cost.

This will leave what may seem like an excessive profit. It is important for the future of the company that these excessive profits be used to invest in improving the company's ability to produce future projects for less cost. The competition will be eager to come into a highly profitable and growing new business area. When they do, they will be willing to reduce the price to your customers to entice them away from your organization. And when this happens the company that started it all had better have been making cost improvements all the while or risk the loss of a major market share.

So, a couple of things are important here. One is that we ask the customer to pay a price that is relevant to the perceived value of what they receive. The second is that the company providing the goods or services takes the extra profit and invests it in its ability to reduce costs as the product matures and competition enters the market.

Overbid or Underbid: Which Is Better for Your Company?

We said that it was important to price things according to the perceived value to the customer. In other words, if a project has a high value to stakeholders and customers, they should pay a price that is high as well.

Now, suppose we are in a bidding situation. Our organization is in the kind of business where the stakeholders publish requirements and companies like ours submit a firm fixed price to do the work specified. Many construction projects work this way, but other types of projects are done this way, too. A number of companies are bidding for the same project.

The question is then: Is it better for companies to underbid or overbid projects like this? Most people would say, "It is better to overbid the project because if I underbid I may win the project but lose money trying to complete it." Let us explore this issue.

A company that underbids a project and wins the bid finds that the cost estimate for doing the work was too low and as a result they did not charge enough to the stakeholder to make a profit. In fact the company may actually lose money on this project. This gives the company immediate feedback: They know soon after starting the work that there will not be enough money coming from the customer to pay all the costs and expenses associated with the project. At this point lots of unhappy things take place.

The company may go to the customer or stakeholders and ask for additional funds. The company may have to grin and bear it and lose money or at least not make as much money as they would like. The company may try to reduce the requirements to save cost, with or without the customer's approval. Panic may follow, leading to a very unhappy situation all around.

But, every cloud has a silver lining. The company in this situation at least knows where it stands, and one way or another, the next time the company bids on a job it will increase the price. Companies in this situation either learn from this experience or they soon find another line of work.

In the other situation we talked about—where the company overbids the work—only two things can happen: The company bids too high and does not get the work, or the company bids high and gets the work anyway.

In the first case, the company loses the bid and does not get to work on the project. This may or may not have a positive effect on future business. If the company was convinced that the bid it submitted was just too high, it might look into the cost estimating process or some of the costs associated with the way it is doing things. Many companies don't do this. They become convinced that for some unknown reason the competition got the job and they did not. You will hear about how so-and-so's brother-in-law was a friend of the purchasing agent or so-and-so's wife is in a bridge club with the company's owner, and so on. Companies are reluctant to admit that they may be doing something wrong, and they wait for the next opportunity to come along.

Now let's consider the case where the company overbids the project and is awarded the contract anyway. This could actually be the worst thing for the company. Where the company overbid and lost the project, there at least was some feedback to the company that something was wrong, providing the impetus for doing business differently in the future.

When a company overbids a project and is awarded the contract, what budget will the company assign to the project manager of this project? It will probably take the bid price, reduce it by some acceptable level of profit, and ask the project manager to complete the project with those funds.

This sounds right except that, in this situation, the company overbid the project. As a result, the company is going to over-budget the project. The reason is that it doesn't really know that it had overbid the project in the first place.

The project manager will measure the progress and the performance of the project according to the allocated budget. As long as the project is completed on time and under budget, and the requirements are all satisfied, no one is likely to complain about the project performance. As time goes by, more jobs like this are bid and won, and the company continues on with an acceptable profit. The projects are completed, and everyone is happy. Ignorance is bliss.

However, sooner or later a competitor is going to figure out that there is extra profit to be made in this type of business. The competitor discovers this by doing a better cost analysis than our company and starts to bid the same jobs but at a lower price.

At first, there is no reaction. Lost work is considered just part of the normal business cycle. As time goes by and there is less and less business, the company may eventually come to its senses, realize that its costs are too high, and take some corrective action.

This is very hard for companies to do. They are in the situation where for years they have been doing things the way they always have and been successful. Now they are losing business, and they have a lot of trouble figuring out why. If they had had good cost estimates they still might have been able to overbid the projects, but the budget for the projects would have been based on more accurate cost estimates, and the profits would have been larger. What must happen next is that the company must take those excess profits and invest them in the company and modernize before being forced to do so by their competition.

We can see that the worst thing that could happen to companies is that they overestimate costs. From that, they overbid work, over-budget projects, and learn inefficient ways to do things. From all of that, they may go out of business.

Getting to the Scope Baseline

We are concerned about two major things in defining the scope of the project, the project scope and the product scope. The *product scope* is all of the features and functions that the completion of the project will provide to the stakeholders, whereas the *project scope* is the work that must be done to deliver the product scope to the stakeholders.

The first thing that happens in a project is usually characterized by the feeling of wild and unbridled enthusiasm. This results in a great many things being included as the needs of the project. In many respects this is a good thing. If the project has many good things that can result, it is probably a good project to do. The problem is that many of these things are not necessary or may be impractical. Many of the items may just not be the things that the stakeholder needs or really wants.

The solution is to have the project team and the stakeholders come together one or more times and separate out the needs that everyone agrees are not going to be practical or necessary for the project to be useful. When we reduce the needs of the project by deleting the ones that everyone agrees are not part of the project, the result is a list of the "requirements."

We are not nearly finished at this point. We have only reduced the project by the items that everyone agrees to eliminate. We will need to further reduce these items by the items that may not be good for the project. These items are not so obvious and will not have the agreement of all the stakeholders. There will have to be some investigation and some justification applied to make these items acceptable or not acceptable to the project. When this analysis is completed the result is the project's *scope baseline*. This is the first baseline that we will develop. We need to have the scope baseline before the remaining two baselines, cost and schedule, can be completed.

When moving from requirements to scope baseline, the items that are eliminated from the project must be documented as exclusions to the project. It is important to do this since, at one time, these items were thought to be good for the project by at least some of the stakeholders. If their exclusion is not properly documented, they will return again and again as new requirements to be considered.

In all of these items that will or will not be included in the project there are a number of factors that must be considered, such as cost, expense, time to develop, service, and maintenance. These items are called the *deliverables* of the project or the product scope definition.

It is critically important that all of the stakeholders be involved with the parts of the project in which they have a stake. To accomplish this there must be a good cooperative relationship between the stakeholders and the project team. Detailed descriptions of the intentions of the project must be obtained.

All items making it to the scope baseline must be fully documented and clearly defined. There must be measurable tangible results that will be achieved. These should be documented along with the acceptance criteria as part of the scope definition. When this is not done, scope cannot be controlled, and project scope tends to creep ever upward with requests from the stakeholders that start out by saying, "There is one little change that we need to make to the project" or "This item should have been included in the original scope of the project."

When all of this is completed, we will have developed a set of deliverables that the stakeholders and the project team can agree upon. These deliverables must be formally agreed to by all stakeholders, and there should be a formal sign-off. Everything should be done to impress all of the participants in the project that the deliverables list is a conclusive, exhaustive list of the things that the project is going to produce. There should be no doubt in anyone's mind that the deliverables list that has been agreed to is final unless a formal change is approved and paid for by someone. They must also know that approved changes to the project after this point are going to result in increases in cost. Oftentimes these changes are paid for by the customer or sponsor, but frequently the changes will be absorbed by the company organization doing the project. In any case, if the scope changes the project budget should be adjusted as well.

To make all this possible, each of the project deliverables must be clear and concise. Each deliverable must have tangible, measurable criteria that determine that the deliverable has been completed and accepted by the stakeholder. Every effort must be made to avoid describing deliverables in a way that can be misunderstood. The situation where the project team thinks they have completed a deliverable and the customer disagrees must be avoided. It is also important when defining the scope that the *acceptance criteria* for each of the deliverables be defined as well. The stakeholders are likely to accept the acceptance criteria early in the project but will be more reluctant to accept the *test criteria* later in the project. This is because as the project progresses and the stakeholders find additional requirements they will attempt to include them in the test criteria for acceptance.

For example, a project team determines that a user manual for the system they are proposing will be required. The deliverable that they put into the scope of the project is entered as "User Manual," with no additional description. The customer sees this and agrees to the item.

When the user manual is delivered to the customer, it is a five-page document that basically says to hit the green button to start and hit the red button to stop. The project team does not want to give too much information to the customer, because they want their own maintenance and support people to take care of problems that might arise in the life of the product they are delivering.

On the other hand, the customer's expectations were for a fully detailed user manual that would allow them to understand the inner workings of the product delivered—200 or 300 pages of detailed information about the product and its use. Stakeholders want this information because they do not want to be committed to the supplying company forever. They are concerned that they may have to maintain the product after they have terminated their relationship with the supplying company. They are also concerned that the supplying company may go out of business.

When this dilemma becomes known, usually late in the project when there are many things to be done, the project team says that they have met the agreed-upon requirement with their five-page user manual, and the stakeholders disagree. Generally, at this point, the stakeholders appeal to higher levels of management in the project team's company, and eventually the project team will write that 300-page manual.

At this point in the development of the project scope we have determined what all of the project deliverables are, and we have gotten full agreement from all of the stakeholders. All of the deliverables are tangible and measurable items that cannot be easily misunderstood. There has been a formal sign-off on the deliverables that are due to each stakeholder. In addition to the deliverables being developed from a preliminary definition to a detailed baseline for scope, there should be a development of risk in parallel to the scope development. An order of magnitude estimate should be done to determine if the project is feasible.

Work Breakdown Structure

At this point in our project development we have determined the deliverables that are due to all the stakeholders. But we cannot plan the project from this list of deliverables. To plan the project we must convert these into individual pieces of work that must be done to complete the project. For this we need the "work breakdown structure," or WBS.

The work breakdown structure is the most central item in the project plan. Without it we do not have a definition of the work that has to be done to complete the project. Without knowing the work that has to be done we cannot possibly determine the cost of the project or determine the schedule of the project.

Without knowing the cost or schedule of the project how will it be possible to control the project or determine how much should be spent to complete it? The amount of resources that must be used on the project and when they must be made available cannot be determined without knowing the schedule. Funding to do the project cannot be scheduled to be in place when the project needs it without a time-phased budget for the project. Without knowing the work to be performed on the project, risk management cannot be done in a satisfactory way. These things cannot be done without the work breakdown structure.

According to the *Guide to the PMBOK,* the definition of a *work breakdown structure* is:

> A deliverable oriented grouping of project components that organizes and defines the total scope of the project. Each descending level represents an increasing detailed definition of the project work. The WBS is decomposed into work packages. The deliverable orientation of the hierarchy includes both internal and external deliverables.

Work outside the WBS is outside the scope of the project. In this definition of the WBS, we are striving for a method to identify the work that is required to produce all of the deliverables of the project. As we will see, with many projects it will be possible to identify close to 95 percent of the work that must be done in the project.

To create a WBS is a simple task: The project is first broken down into a group of subprojects. Each of these subprojects can be broken down to sub-subprojects. The sub-subprojects can be broken down again and again until the desired level of detail is reached. The level of detail is termed the *work package* level. The work package is the lowest level of management that the project manager needs to manage. Below the work package other project team members may break down their parts of the project into additional levels.

The reason this technique is so effective is that it follows the principle of "divide and conquer." If we were to hold a meeting and write down a list of all the things that had to be done to complete the project, the meeting would not produce a very good list. In a meeting of this type where there is little focus, attention will drift into one area and do a pretty good job of listing the work needed in that area and ignore other areas of the project.

A better way to do this is to break the project into smaller projects or products of the project. When we do this we can think of each one of these subprojects as producing one or more of the deliverables of the whole project. In this way we can also think of the WBS as a product-oriented breakdown as well. This allows project management to become a methodology that will work well on the largest of projects or programs as well as the smallest. At the top levels of the project, particularly large projects, think of these early levels of breakdown as product breakdowns. This is because on larger projects there can be a grouping of deliverables into large deliverables that might be called products.

So, initially the project is broken up into a group of subprojects. These subprojects are further broken down into sub-subprojects, and so on. In this way the largest project we can imagine could be broken down into subprojects. Since each of these subprojects could be considered to be a project in its own right, any large project can be thought of as a family of smaller projects that are interrelated.

A project can also be thought of as a microcosm or a macrocosm. At any level in the breakdown structure, from the standpoint of the manager in charge of a particular part of the project, there is a separate project for which he or she is responsible. All projects are part of some larger project, and all projects have subprojects within them. It is just a matter of perspective.

For example, in the 1960s the United States took on the challenge of getting a man to the moon and safely back to Earth. The resulting project was very large, employing many thousands of people. The project manager lived in Washington, D.C., and spent most of his time dealing with Congress and other parts of the government.

When the Apollo Program was in full swing in the 1960s, it was a very large project indeed. There were perhaps 40,000 people working on it at any given time. There was a project to develop the engines for the Saturn V booster, the first stage of the launch vehicle. This project had a project manager and many people involved. The engine development project had several locations and several hundred people working on it. Within this project there were other projects, such as engine testing, fuel systems, fuel delivery, cooling, and so on.

Although the engine development project for the Apollo program was a large effort, it was only a small part of the program. Depending on where you were in the hierarchy of the program, you might consider yourself as a program manager, a project manager, or even a subproject manager.

As a matter of practicality, it does not make sense for the top-level program manager or project manager to manage all of the details of the project. In fact it is not necessary for him or her to even know about them. So, we can see that extremely large projects result in smaller projects or subprojects. The subprojects are themselves projects in their own right and have their own work breakdown structures. Each project may be part of some bigger project or macrocosm, and each project may have smaller projects, or microcosms, within it.

The important thing about project management is that it is a powerful methodology that adapts to any size project or program. The tools and methodology that are used are similar in all projects. The WBS is the tool that allows all projects to be broken down into smaller, more manageable projects.

The end result of the WBS is a group of individual pieces of work defined. Each of these small individual pieces of work must be assigned to one person on the project team. The primary purpose of the WBS is to divide the project into subprojects until a point is reached where this assignment of the individual pieces of work can be made.

For a large project the WBS might stop at a rather high level. This may be the level of control for the project manager. As mentioned above, this level of the WBS is generally called the work package. It must be understood that at this high level other project managers will take the lowest level of the initial breakdown and further break it down until the individual piece of work is reached.

The bottom level of any project, then, must be the place where an individual piece of work that can be done by one person or a group is described. This person or group of persons is actually going to accomplish the work rather than manage the work. This level is considered to be the task or activity level.

There is a change in terminology in this area, and the *Guide to the PMBOK* is not entirely clear as to the terms used. The WBS breaks down the project into manageable pieces but stops at the work package level. The work package is the lowest level that the project manager would have under his or her direct control. It is then possible to break the work packages down further before the actual work assignments at the detail level are made. Work packages can be broken down into "activities," and activities can be further broken down into "tasks."

The *Guide to the PMBOK* refers to the lowest level of the WBS as the work package level. Work package managers will further divide the work of the project into what they consider to be subprojects and work packages. Common usage has the task or activity at the lowest level of the ultimate WBS.

I recommend that the WBS be developed just for one purpose—to discover all of the work that must be done to complete the project. If an attempt is made to use the WBS to simultaneously produce an organization chart, a chart of accounts for the project, or any of the other organizational requirements of the project, it is likely that the attempt to discover all of the work to be done will fail. These items, the "organizational breakdown structure" (OBS) and the "chart of accounts" should be separate items from the WBS that are related through the lower level elements of the WBS.

Systems Approach to Work Breakdown Structure
At this point we have broken the project down into subprojects and continued this breakdown to the work package level. In smaller projects, the work package level may be the task or activity level where the work actually takes place. In larger projects it may be that the work package has a work package manager who continues to divide the work into lower levels until the task or activity level is reached.

It is extremely important that each of the lowest levels have only one person responsible for the work that is to be done to satisfy that work component, regardless of whether it is called work package, task, or activity.

What's next? We have identified all the work in the project. Our ability to do this, however, defines only about 90 percent of the work that is necessary. We would like to be able to more accurately identify more of the work that is required.

According to the systems management concept, *all work is considered to be a system where the work is a process that converts inputs to outputs.* Taking this concept to the project level, we can describe a project as a process that converts inputs, resources, money, and people's effort into outputs, the deliverables of the project.

If we apply this concept to our work breakdown structure, we could say that each task at the bottom level of our WBS is a process that converts inputs to outputs. The inputs are something that the task owner needs from some other part of the project or from somewhere external to the project. The outputs are items that are needed in some other part of the project or are items that represent all or part of a deliverable.

We can apply these ideas to our definition of project work. Each person responsible for a task looks to other tasks to find the items needed for a specific task. Each will also look for other parts of the project to deliver the outputs. In this way each person on the project team must look at each input and output at least two times. All inputs to a task must come from somewhere inside the project or from some external source. All outputs from a task must go to another task in the project or directly contribute to the delivery of a deliverable.

Input items that cannot be found externally or from outputs of other project tasks must be added to other project tasks. Output items that cannot be delivered to other parts of the project or to a deliverable can be considered extra work. In this way almost all of the additional work not already in the plan can be discovered. In addition, all of the work that has been developed in the project that can be considered "creeping elegance" can be dropped from the project plan.

Last of all, there is a good chance that duplicated work can be eliminated as well. When a task owner who is seeking input for the task work finds more than one task supplying the same or nearly the same input, one or the other may be eliminated.

Work Breakdown Structure Dictionary

The work breakdown structure dictionary is used to expand on the information for each of the elements in the WBS. For each element it should contain an elemental statement of work, schedule and duration, budget, all of the associated elements and activities related to it, the organization responsible, and the risks associated with it.

Additional Project Breakdown Structures

It is important to recognize that there are many other types of breakdowns used in projects. The WBS that we have been discussing must be used only to generate the individual pieces of work that must be done in the project. To try to use the WBS to develop anything else would confuse the effort and make the identification of work less effective.

Other breakdown structures that are used that should not be confused with the WBS are:

- *Contractual WBS (CWBS)*. This breakdown is used to define the reporting information and the timeliness of information that a supplier will supply to the buyer. It is usually not as detailed as the WBS that is used to plan the work that is going to be done.
- *Organizational Breakdown Structure (OBS)*. The main purpose of this structure is to show the organization of resources and of the people who will work on the project. In the OBS, the work components of the WBS are shown related to the groups of individuals and resources that will accomplish the work.
- *Resource Breakdown Structure (RBS)*. This is a refinement of the OBS in that the detail of the RBS generally goes to the individual level.
- *Bill of Material (BOM)*. The various product components are included in the BOM in a hierarchical way. Products produced, subassemblies, and lower level of assembly are shown as a "goes into" hierarchy.
- *Risk Breakdown Structure (RBS)*. This is a hierarchical listing of the project risks according to the risk categories that were developed for this project.

Scope Verification

Scope verification takes place at the end of the project. Once the scope of the project has been defined and delivered, the scope of the project delivered must be verified. This means getting approval of the delivered scope of the project from all of the stakeholders. Generally it is a good practice to get the stakeholders to agree to the acceptance criteria at the beginning of the project rather than the end of it. A set of acceptance criteria is drawn up and the acceptance criteria are agreed to when the project scope is accepted by the stakeholders.

Change Management

A change control process must be put in place to control the project once the scope baseline has been set. The change control process is a formal process that controls the project scope baseline. The change management must be in place early in the project, certainly no later than the completion of the scope baseline.

The point of the change management process is to establish recognition for changes in the project funding whenever there is a change in the project scope. Changes in scope and funding do not necessarily mean increases in project scope and funding. Many times there can be agreed-upon changes that reduce the project scope or increase it.

In the change management process there are certain essentials that must be included regardless of whether the project changes are funded internally or externally to the project. The proposed change must first be evaluated as to how much time and effort it will take to evaluate the implementation of the change. Stakeholders who ask for new things to be incorporated into the project can bog down a project team. The investigation of these changes can cost much in time and effort. So, the first thing that needs to take place in the change management process is that the stakeholder must authorize funding to investigate the change itself.

Once this funding is approved, the project team can bring in additional resources to complete the investigation. The investigation must include the effect that the change has on all other things that are being done in the project. Once the effect on cost, schedule, and scope of the project is determined, a justification for the change can take place. If the justification is adequate and the stakeholder wishes to authorize the funds for the change, the change can move into the project plan.

The change management process is actually a small project plan. All of the things that must be done in planning a project must be done for project changes as well. When all of this has been done, the project baselines of cost, schedule, and scope are changed, and the new project plan is implemented.

Project Justifications

There are many reasons for doing projects. Some of them are more tangible than others. Projects may be a response to a government order, such as a redesign of an unsafe automobile or changing a process that is found to be polluting air or water. Other projects may be justified by the opportunity to create a new business or enter a new field. The potential benefits of a project can be the result of a market demand for a product, a customer request, a government requirement, or meeting or creating new competition or social needs.

Of course, one of the strongest and most compelling project justifications is the concept of a benefit occurring to the organization after making some effort. The most efficient way to measure this is to compare the monetary benefits to the monetary cost of the project. To this end, many justification methods have been developed over the years. It is important to use the appropriate method for project justification. The selection of a justification technique has its own costs and benefits. Some methods produce results that consider many aspects of the project costs and benefits, while others consider only some of these factors. Of course, the more aspects of the project that are considered, the higher will be the cost of the justification itself.

These analysis techniques are forms of cash flow analysis. *Cash flow analysis* is measuring the cash flowing into and out of an organization over time. Projects that have more cash flowing into the organization than cash flowing out of the organization are good projects. In most projects it is necessary to make an investment in the project (cash outflow) before the benefits can begin (cash inflow).

The Breakeven Chart

The breakeven chart is useful when comparing two or more alternatives. In the question of justifying a project, doing the project can be compared to not doing the project. Where there is more than one choice, several alternatives can be considered at the same time.

Refer to Figure 1-1. The vertical axis shows dollars, and the horizontal axis shows time. The variable cost of each of the alternatives is plotted over time and is plotted from time zero. In the case of an alternative requiring that money be spent before the benefits of the project can be realized, the variable cost is plotted from a point on the vertical axis representing the total fixed, one-time cost of the project. In the case of an ongoing alternative, the choice of doing nothing, there is no fixed cost. At some point in time, if the project has an overall benefit, the lines will cross. This is the "breakeven point," the point where the benefits of doing the project outweigh the cost of doing the project when compared to not doing the project at all. The point on the horizontal time axis is the point in time when this occurs. This point in time is also called the "payback period."

For example, suppose a manufacturing plant has a machine that is used to make left-handed widgets. The machine is getting old. The machine can manufacture widgets

Figure 1-1. Breakeven chart.

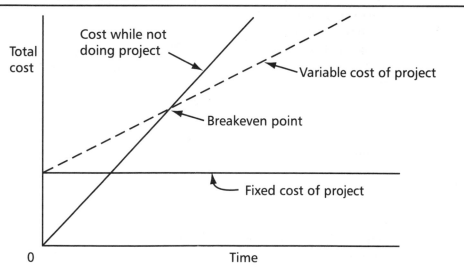

for $2 per widget. A new machine can be purchased and installed that will manufacture widgets for $1.50 each. If the company makes 25,000 widgets per month, and the new machine costs $200,000, what is the breakeven point of the project? (See Figure 1-2.)

Problems with Breakeven Charts

I said earlier that the simpler methods of justification are less expensive to use but produce results that do not consider as many factors as other techniques. The breakeven-point method has some shortcomings.

The time that exists after the breakeven point is reached is not considered. This means that projects that have a high early return will be favored over projects that may have higher returns in the long run. For example, buying a cheap machine that wears out quickly and has high maintenance costs is favored over a machine that is built to last longer but costs more to buy.

Because breakeven-point charts are used as a very rough justification method, it is usually assumed that the production rates are constant, allowing the use of linear variable cost lines.

Average Rate of Return on Investment

One way to add a little more accuracy to our justification technique is to eliminate the problem of shortsightedness that exists in the breakeven-point and payback-period analy-

Figure 1-2. Example of a breakeven chart.

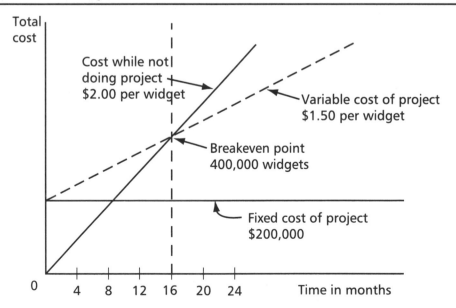

ses. In these techniques the analysis stops when the payback point or the breakeven point is reached.

The "average-rate-of-return-on-investment" method solves this problem by using the same time period to compare alternative projects. Regardless of when the project has its payback point or breakeven point, the time period in this justification method covers the approximate life of the project. It then measures all of the cash flows from the beginning of the investment to the end of the useful life of the project. In this way we consider all of the money that is being spent.

For example, to expand on our example from above, let's say that the sales forecast for widgets changes over time, and that the maintenance cost of the new machine is now recognized. Table 1–1 summarizes the data. We can see from the table that the total cash flow for this project was a positive $935,000. This represents a return on our investment of $200,000, or 468 percent, an average rate over ten years of 46.8 percent.

This method of project justification is not often used these days because the more sophisticated methods of justification have become easier to calculate since the appearance of the personal computer. However, using these methods requires more time and effort to collect data and make forecasts.

Present Value of Money

Before we talk about the more sophisticated methods of justification, we should look at the present value of money and the net present value of money.

Suppose I borrow $100 from you today and pay you back $100 tomorrow. This is a reasonable transaction among friends. But suppose I borrow $100 from you and don't pay it back to you for two years. Is this still a fair arrangement? You should say "No!" because I have had the use of your money for two years and have paid you nothing for the use of your money. If I had not borrowed the money from you, you could have invested the money in something, and you would have had something more than the $100 you started with.

This is the idea behind using the present value of money. Money that I receive in the future is worth less than money I receive now. This is not to say that money I receive in the future is worthless—it's just worth less than money I get today. The further into the future I receive the money, the less valuable it is to me today. In the example, I should have given you back $115 for borrowing $100 from you for two years.

The calculation that I use to figure out what my $100 will be worth two years from now is the compound interest formula:

If you invest $100 at 7 percent interest for one year, you would receive $107.

$$FV = PV + (PV \times I)$$

where *PV* is the present value of the money, *FV* is the future value of the same money, and *I* is the interest rate paid by the investment.

Table 1-1. Cash flow.

Year	Annual Sales Volume	Annual Revenue	Maintenance	Cost	Cash Flows	Cumulative
0	0	0	0	$200,000	−$200,000	−$200,000
1	$300,000	$150,000	0		150,000	−50,000
2	300,000	150,000	$5,000		145,000	95,000
3	300,000	150,000	5,000		145,000	240,000
4	250,000	125,000	5,000		120,000	360,000
5	250,000	125,000	10,000		115,000	475,000
6	250,000	125,000	10,000		115,000	590,000
7	200,000	100,000	10,000		90,000	680,000
8	200,000	100,000	15,000		85,000	765,000
9	200,000	100,000	15,000		85,000	850,000
10	200,000	100,000	15,000		85,000	935,000

$$107 = 100 + (100 \times .07)$$

If you leave the money in the bank at the same interest rate, you would get more the next year.

$$FV = 107 + (107 \times .07)$$
$$FV = 107 + 7.49$$
$$FV = 114.49$$

With a little manipulation, the series of calculations can be generalized into the compound interest formula:

$$FV = PV (1 + I)^n$$

The new term in this formula is n, the number of time periods that the interest is applied.

Your \$100 invested at 7 percent for two years looks like this:

$$FV = 100 (1 + .07)^2$$
$$FV = 100 (1.07)^2$$
$$FV = 100 (1.1449)$$
$$FV = 114.49$$

Now that we have reviewed compound interest calculations, it is time to look at calculating the present value of money that we will get in the future. This is really just the compound interest calculation solved for the present value instead of the future value.

Start with the compound interest formula:

$$FV = PV (1 + I)^n$$

Solve for the present value:

$$PV = FV / (1 + I)^n$$

Now let's say that we can do something that will result in a return of \$100 two years from now. We would like to know what the equivalent present value of that money is. Remember that money we receive in the future is worth less than money we receive now. Here we are trying to determine the present value of the \$100 we will receive two years from now.

$$PV = FV / (1 + I)^n$$
$$PV = 100 / (1.07)^2$$
$$PV = 100 / 1.1449$$
$$PV = 87.34$$

You can check this number by calculating the future value of \$87.34 invested at 7 percent for two years. The result should be \$100.

To bring all this into the context of a project, projects usually start out by investing an amount of money at the beginning of the project and receiving benefits from the project in the future. By using the present value calculations we can now more accurately determine the true value of the project. Projects that have very high returns early in the project's useful life will be considered better projects than projects that have the same returns but later in the project.

"Net present value" is the sum of all the cash flows of a project adjusted to present values. For example, suppose we have two projects that have the same initial cost of $100,000. The two projects have the same net cash flows as well, but the time that the money comes to us is different. The interest rate for borrowing money is 7 percent. Table 1–2 illustrates the present value cash flow.

Notice that here the two projects have the same total return over the ten-year life of the projects, but project A gets more of the returns sooner, making the net present value of the money higher. Remember, the present value of the money is the value today of money that will be received in the future.

In this justification analysis, we considered much more than in previous methods. Here we recognized all of the costs and revenues that occur over the useful life of the project. If this were a project to buy a machine, for example, we would look at the cash flows over the expected life of the machine. This would allow us to consider the effect of changing sales forecasts and changing maintenance costs. Then we can adjust for the time value of the money that is involved in the project. This method gives us a pretty good idea of which projects should be selected over other projects.

There is one difficulty with this method. There is a problem distinguishing small projects that have small investments and relatively small returns when compared to large projects. The method of justification we have just seen tells us only the net present value of the project. It does not tell us whether we would be better off selecting a number of small projects or a few large ones. What we need is a method of justification that gives us a single value that will be highest for the most favorable project, regardless of size. If we had a method like that, we would be able to rank all of our potential projects by this value and use the ranking order to pick the projects that are the most favorable for financial reasons.

Internal Rate of Return on Investment

The internal rate of return on investment (IRR) method meets all of the criteria for a justification method that gives a single value. It is, however, the most complicated of them all. For practical reasons, a computer is required to make the calculations.

In the last example we looked at the cash flows of two different projects. Both of the projects had the same total cash flow at the end of their useful life, but one of them was favored because of the adjustment of the value of future monies received. The factor in our calculations that brought about this result was the interest rate that was used. It

Table 1-2. Present value cash flow.

	Project A		7% Interest		Project B		7% Interest	
Year	Outflow	Inflow	PV	NPV	Outflow	Inflow	PV	NPV
0	−100,000	0		−100,000	−100,000	0		−100.000
1		60,000	56,075	−43,925		30,000	28.037	−71.963
2		50,000	43,672	−253		30,000	26.203	−45.759
3		40,000	32,652	32,399		30,000	24.489	−21.271
4		30,000	22,887	55,285		30,000	22.887	1.616
5		20,000	14,260	69,545		30,000	21.390	23.006
6		20,000	13,327	82,872		30,000	19.990	42.996
7		20,000	12,455	95,327		30,000	18.682	61.679
8		20,000	11,640	106,967		30,000	17.460	79.139
9		20,000	10,879	117,846		30,000	16.318	95.457
10		20,000	10,167	128,013		30,000	15.250	110.707
Total		300,000	228,013			300,000	210,707	

should be clear that if the interest rate were zero, both projects would be the same in terms of desirability.

What we are really talking about here is what we can do with our money. We usually want to use money to finance projects that will return money to us in the future. But all of these projects have risk attached to them. There is the possibility that we will spend all the money on the project, and it will not work. The marketplace might change, and the expected revenues are not what we had predicted. Many other things can go wrong in any business venture.

Since all of the projects we run into in business have some risk associated with them, we might want to consider what a risk-free investment might be. There is such a thing. For example, investing in U.S. Treasury bills is considered a risk-free investment. Generally speaking, however, investing in the projects of a company and taking advantage of business opportunities are going to generate a higher return on our investment than putting the same money into U.S. Treasury bills.

Suppose interest rates were higher. If they were high enough, we could consider putting money into the risk-free investment of U.S. Treasury bills. If they were not high enough, we would invest in projects. At any given interest rate, it would be wise to invest in some projects and not in others. With this in mind, we can come up with another justification system.

In the internal rate of return on investment justification method, we are calculating the interest rate on Treasury bills that would make the proposed project and investing in the Treasury bills "equal opportunities."

To make the calculation we compare the net present value of the project at the end of its useful life to the net present value of the risk-free investment. At low interest rates the project with the risk and relatively higher cash flows into the organization will be favored. As interest rates increase, the difference between the two investments will change and become smaller until the interest rate is high enough to make investing in the risk-free investment as favorable as investing in the risky investment.

Notice that when we look at projects this way, the size of the project does not matter. Only the value of the project matters.

These calculations need to be done by a computer, because the calculations cannot be handled algebraically but must be solved in an iterative manner. An example will show this best.

Suppose we take the project from the previous example and look at what the cash flows would be at various interest rates (Table 1–3). If we calculate the present value of each of the cash flows, we will find that at the end of the time period of the project, the net cash flows are either positive or negative. We have the cash flows already calculated at 7 percent interest. Now we will calculate the net present value cash flows for various interest rates.

Table 1-3. Cash flow at various interest rates.

| | Project A | | 7% Interest | |
Year	Outflow	Inflow	PV	1.07
0	$100,000.00	$0.00	− $100,000.00	
1		$60,000.00	$56,074.77	
2		$50,000.00	$43,671.94	
3		$40,000.00	$32,651.92	
4		$30,000.00	$22,886.86	
5		$20,000.00	$14,259.72	
6		$20,000.00	$13,326.84	
7		$20,000.00	$12,454.99	
8		$20,000.00	$11,640.18	
9		$20,000.00	$10,878.67	
10		$20,000.00	$10,166.99	
Total			$128,012.88	

| | Project A | | 60% Interest | |
Year	Outflow	Inflow	PV	1.6
0	$100,000.00	$0.00	− $100,000.00	
1		$60,000.00	$37,500.00	
2		$50,000.00	$19,531.25	
3		$40,000.00	$9,765.63	
4		$30,000.00	$4,577.64	
5		$20,000.00	$1,907.35	
6		$20,000.00	$1,192.09	
7		$20,000.00	$745.06	
8		$20,000.00	$465.66	
9		$20,000.00	$291.04	
10		$20,000.00	$181.90	
Total			− $23,842.39	

(continues)

Table 1-3. (Continued).

Year	Project A Outflow	Project A Inflow	40% Interest PV	1.4
0	$100,000.00	$0.00	− $100,000.00	
1		$60,000.00	$42,857.14	
2		$50,000.00	$25,510.20	
3		$40,000.00	$14,577.26	
4		$30,000.00	$7,809.25	
5		$20,000.00	$3,718.69	
6		$20,000.00	$2,656.21	
7		$20,000.00	$1,897.29	
8		$20,000.00	$1,355.21	
9		$20,000.00	$968.01	
10		$20,000.00	$691.43	
Total			$2,040.68	

Year	Project A Outflow	Project A Inflow	50% Interest PV	1.5
0	$100,000.00	$0.00	− $100,000.00	
1		$60,000.00	$40,000.00	
2		$50,000.00	$22,222.22	
3		$40,000.00	$11,851.85	
4		$30,000.00	$5,925.93	
5		$20,000.00	$2,633.74	
6		$20,000.00	$1,755.83	
7		$20,000.00	$1,170.55	
8		$20,000.00	$780.37	
9		$20,000.00	$520.25	
10		$20,000.00	$346.83	
Total			− $12,792.43	

Table 1-3. (Continued).

Year	Project A Outflow	Project A Inflow	45% Interest PV	1.45
0	$100,000.00	$0.00	− $100,000.00	
1		$60,000.00	$41,379.31	
2		$50,000.00	$23,781.21	
3		$40,000.00	$13,120.67	
4		$30,000.00	$6,786.55	
5		$20,000.00	$3,120.25	
6		$20,000.00	$2,151.90	
7		$20,000.00	$1,484.07	
8		$20,000.00	$1,023.50	
9		$20,000.00	$705.86	
10		$20,000.00	$486.80	
Total			− $5,959.88	

Year	Project A Outflow	Project A Inflow	42.5% Interest PV	1.425
0	$100,000.00	$0.00	− $100,000.00	
1		$60,000.00	$42,105.26	
2		$50,000.00	$24,622.96	
3		$40,000.00	$13,823.42	
4		$30,000.00	$7,275.48	
5		$20,000.00	$3,403.73	
6		$20,000.00	$2,388.59	
7		$20,000.00	$1,676.20	
8		$20,000.00	$1,176.28	
9		$20,000.00	$825.46	
10		$20,000.00	$579.27	
Total			− $2,123.34	

We use the equation:

$$FV = 1 / (1 + int)^n$$

where *FV* is the future value of the cash flow, *int* is the proposed equivalent interest rate in decimal form, and *n* is the number of the time periods from present to future value.

When we have reached the point when the net cash flows are no longer positive, then, for the time period in question, we have found the equivalent interest rate that would make investing in a risk-free investment equal to investing in the project. Referring to Table 1–3, we can see that this interest rate is between 40 percent and 42.5 percent.

Summary

The most common reason for project failure is not clearly identifying what exactly is to be delivered by the project. The project charter is a device that helps get the project off the ground and headed in the right direction. It allows project managers to express their understanding of the project and what its accomplishments are intended to be.

All of the stakeholders in the project must be identified. A stakeholder is any person who has something to gain or lose in the carrying out of the project. The project team, the customer, the management of the supplying company, and many others are all stakeholders.

The project manager must have input into the pricing of the project. The price should not be determined by the cost of the project, but the cost of the project is a very real consideration in making sure that the project benefits are high enough to justify the cost.

The scope baseline is the first of the three baselines that measure the success of the project. Without the scope baseline it is not possible for the cost and schedule baselines to be meaningful.

The work breakdown structure is the heart of the project. From the work breakdown structure it is possible to determine the detailed definitions of the work that has to be done in the project. It is the basis for making a bottom-up estimate and for producing the project schedule.

Change management is initiated as soon as it is practical in the definition of the scope of work for the project. It must be implemented by the time the scope baseline is defined. From that point on all changes to the project scope should be traceable to an authorized change.

All projects must be justified. There are many justification methods for projects. With the exception of mandated projects, projects are justified on the basis of cost versus benefits. Today, because of the availability of sophisticated, fast computers, the internal rate of return on investment (IRR) has become the most popular method of financial justification of projects.

CHAPTER 2

Time Management

The *Guide to the Project Management Body of Knowledge*® describes project time management as "the process used to ensure the timely completion of the project." The guide goes on to say that there are five major processes that are required to do proper project time management:

1. *Activity Definition.* Defining the specific activities that are necessary to complete the project and produce all of the project deliverables.

2. *Activity Sequencing.* Identifying the sequence in which the activities must be done. This is the same as identifying the interdependencies that the activities have between each other and inputs external to the project.

3. *Activity Duration Estimating.* In addition to the cost estimate for each activity in the project plan, the duration of time that is necessary for each activity must be estimated.

4. *Schedule Development.* Analyzing all of the data available to determine the project schedule that will work for the project.

5. *Schedule Control.* Controlling changes that occur in the project that affect the project schedule.

Activity Definition

The main tool that is required for the definition of the activity as well as the determination of the duration and sequence of activities is the work breakdown structure (WBS). If you recall, in our discussion of the WBS, we found that it was used to methodically break down the project into manageable subprojects.

The end result of this breakdown process is the creation of the lowest level of breakdown. This lowest level of breakdown comprises the individual pieces of work that must be done to complete the project. Because the WBS is a representation of the entire project in various levels of detail, it represents all the work that must be done to complete the project. The WBS defines the lowest level of control that the project manager is required to manage. This is the *work package level*. From the viewpoint of the subproject manager, this level of control may reach down to the work package; it may be broken down further to the activity level or still further to the individual activity level.

The result of this decomposition is that the work packages are decomposed into activities. The activities represent the necessary work that must be done to complete all of the deliverables of the project. If there is similarity to projects that have been planned successfully in the past then it is possible to start with a template from the previous project as a starting point for the activity descriptions.

The WBS represents all of the work that the project team must do to complete the project. Before the scheduling work can begin, the scope statement, the constraints and assumptions, and any other historical information must be reviewed to be certain that the work definition is correct and complete.

The schedule, like the project plan, can be progressively elaborated. This is called *rolling wave planning*. This approach is helpful in large or long-term projects where there is some uncertainty about continuing with the project beyond a certain point in time. In this technique the work packages that are further in the future are planned at only a high level. Work packages that are closer in time are planned in detail. The result of this technique is that we can save a lot of planning time by not planning things that have a relatively high chance of never reaching execution. An example of this type of project would be the development of a pharmaceutical product. Many new drugs reach the experimental stage but few of them are actually brought to market.

Planning components may be included in the WBS. These components can be used for planning later parts of the project. These components may also contain accounting information and separate account numbers to collect the cost of the planning work when it is done.

Activity Sequencing

The activity's identity comes from the work breakdown structure. When the WBS is completed, the bottom of the work breakdown structure defines the individual pieces of work that are necessary to complete the project. These individual pieces of work are the same items that become the activities in the project schedule. One of the things that is done in the development of the WBS is to check that each of the activities has inputs for the work required. Each output from an activity is used by another activity or is required as a part of a project deliverable. Since an activity requires something from another activity, which is that activity's output, both activities must be done in sequence or at least partly so. An activity that is not complete but delivers enough of its outputs to the dependent activity to allow it to start can overlap the dependent activity. Taking advantage of this and scheduling activities to be done in parallel when they would have otherwise been done in sequence is called *fast tracking*.

Dependencies can be categorized as mandatory, discretionary, or external, and they can be restricted by constraints and assumptions. Mandatory dependencies are those that are required as part of the nature of the work. These dependencies are sometimes called "hard" dependencies. For example, the walls of a house cannot be built until the foundation is completed. Discretionary dependencies are those that are defined by management. These are preferred ways of doing things and may be determined by past experiences. External dependencies are those that are external to the project. These are all of the inputs that are supplied by anyone or anything outside the project.

Activity on Arrow Diagramming

Activity on arrow diagramming (AOA) is a network diagramming method that is seldom used today. Still, there are a number of places where these can still be seen (mainly in the *PMBOK*). Nearly all, if not all, software programs that are available for project management scheduling have stopped using this diagramming method. However, because they are still present in the latest release of the *Guide to the PMBOK*, we will discuss them here very briefly.

In activity on arrow diagrams the network diagram will always be shown with the activity information on the arrows instead of in the nodes of the diagram. The nodes of an activity on arrow diagram will always be shown as circles. This diagramming nomenclature is always followed.

Each activity in the diagram has two events associated with it. These events are of zero duration and are located at the beginning of the arrow and at the end of the arrow. This means that there are three things associated with each activity in the diagram: the activity description itself, the starting event of the activity, and the ending event of the activity.

The one advantage of this diagramming method is that, since the arrow is a line, the length of the line can be varied in proportion to the duration of the activity. This can be helpful in recognizing the magnitude of the duration of the activity. However, most project management professionals feel that the complexity and difficulty in using this diagramming method is not compensated for by this feature.

Since the arrows in the diagram in Figure 2-1 represent the activities, it is necessary to create dummy activities to show multiple dependencies in the project being represented.

Calculations of schedules using this diagramming method are a bit more compli-

Figure 2-1. Activity on arrow diagram.

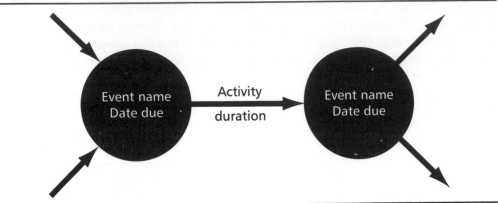

cated than the activity on node network diagram (Figure 2-2), but the results will be the same.

Gantt Charts and Milestone Charts

Once the schedule has been determined it is necessary to communicate it to those who will use it for information about the project schedule. Both of these techniques are good communication techniques and have their place alongside of the network diagram.

The *Gantt chart* is the familiar bar chart that we have all seen many times. It has horizontal bars, one for each activity. There is a timescale that is usually linear. The bars are drawn proportional to their duration with the start and finish of the activity corresponding to the dates on the timescale. Using project management software it is possible to annotate the bars with color and text information from the database for the project. Care must be taken to limit the amount of data displayed so that clutter does not occur.

Figure 2-2. Activity on node diagram.

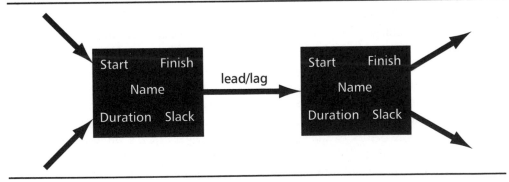

The *milestone chart* is a simplification of the Gantt chart. In the days before computers, Gantt charts were done on large pieces of paper, usually several large pieces of paper. If each of the projects were to submit the full schedule to the project manager's manager the volume of paper would be overwhelming. To solve this problem, the project managers instead reported milestones. A milestone represents a group of work activities, usually an element in the work breakdown structure. Milestones have a duration of zero. The milestones could all be plotted on one chart for the manager, called the milestone chart.

Milestones can be created in project management software by creating an activity that has a duration of zero. Project management software actually gives us a better choice, and it is done automatically. If the WBS is entered into the software it will automatically create summary activities that show the start and finish dates for the earliest start and the latest scheduled finish date for the activities subordinate to them. If all of the WBS is entered there will be a summarizing hierarchy of all of the elements in the WBS including a project summary bar, which shows the start and finish schedule for the project.

Precedence Diagramming Method (PDM)

Precedence diagramming is the method currently being used in nearly all of the project management scheduling software available today. This diagram is used to explain the mechanics of scheduling.

Precedence diagrams can be easily recognized. The network diagram will always be shown with the activity information on the nodes instead of on the arrows of the diagram. The nodes of an activity on precedence diagrams will always be shown as rectangles. This diagramming form is always followed.

In its simplest form the diagram contains boxes to indicate the activities in the schedule and arrows connecting them. The boxes can contain any activity information that is desired, and all of the project management scheduling software today has a great deal of flexibility in this regard. Today, all of this is done through the use of computer software for project management scheduling. The software allows you to annotate the boxes in the diagram with nearly any information you desire. Color and symbols can be used effectively to describe the diagram more fully.

The basic information normally included in the precedence diagram boxes is the activity number, description, early start, early finish, late start, late finish, and duration. The arrows connect the activities according to the logic that is required by the project. The arrows indicate the logical order that the activities may be worked on. The logic of the schedule can be considered as two activity pairs at a time. A pair of activities is any two (and only two) activities that are joined by an arrow. The tail (the part without the head) of the arrow indicates the independent activity of the pair, and the head of the arrow indicates the dependent activity. Reading the logic of the diagram is easy if you keep this in mind and always consider the logical relationships of the network two activities at a time.

By saying that a relationship exists between two and only two activities, I do not mean to say that any activity cannot have more than one relationship. An activity might have two or more predecessors, and it might have two or more successors (Figure 2-3). The relationship has only two activities associated with it, however.

Logical Relationships

Four logical relationships are possible. These relationships can be remembered if you use the same statement to describe the relationship and simply substitute the letters designating the relationship. The statement is: The independent activity must (first letter of the relationship) before the dependent activity can (second letter of the relationship), as shown in Figure 2-4.

Finish-Start Relationship (FS)
Most projects that you are likely to encounter will use the logical relationship of finish-start more often than any other relationship. This relationship is stated like this: The independent activity in the relationship must *finish* before the dependent activity can *start*.

This simply says that where there are two activities connected by an arrow, the one that is connected to the tail of the arrow must be finished before the dependent activity connected to the head of the arrow is allowed to start. It does not say that the dependent activity *must* start at that point; it could start later, but it is not allowed to start any sooner than the finish of the independent activity.

For example, I have two activities to complete in my project, which is to construct a wedding cake. The activities are to make the cake and put on the frosting. The finish-start relationship says that I cannot start putting the frosting on the cake until I have baked the cake layers. Notice that I could, logically, put the frosting on any time after that. The relationship constricts the *start* of the activity of frosting the cake to be no sooner than the *finish* of baking the cake.

Start-Start Relationship (SS)
The start-start relationship is stated in the same way as the finish-start relationship except that the word *start* is substituted for *finish*. The relationship is stated like this: The independent activity in the relationship must *start* before the dependent activity can *start*.

This simply says that where there are two activities connected by an arrow, the one that is connected to the tail of the arrow must start before the activity connected to the head of the arrow is allowed to start. It does not say that the dependent activity must start then. The activity could start later than that time, but it is not allowed to start any sooner than the start of the independent activity.

Figure 2-3. Precedence diagram.

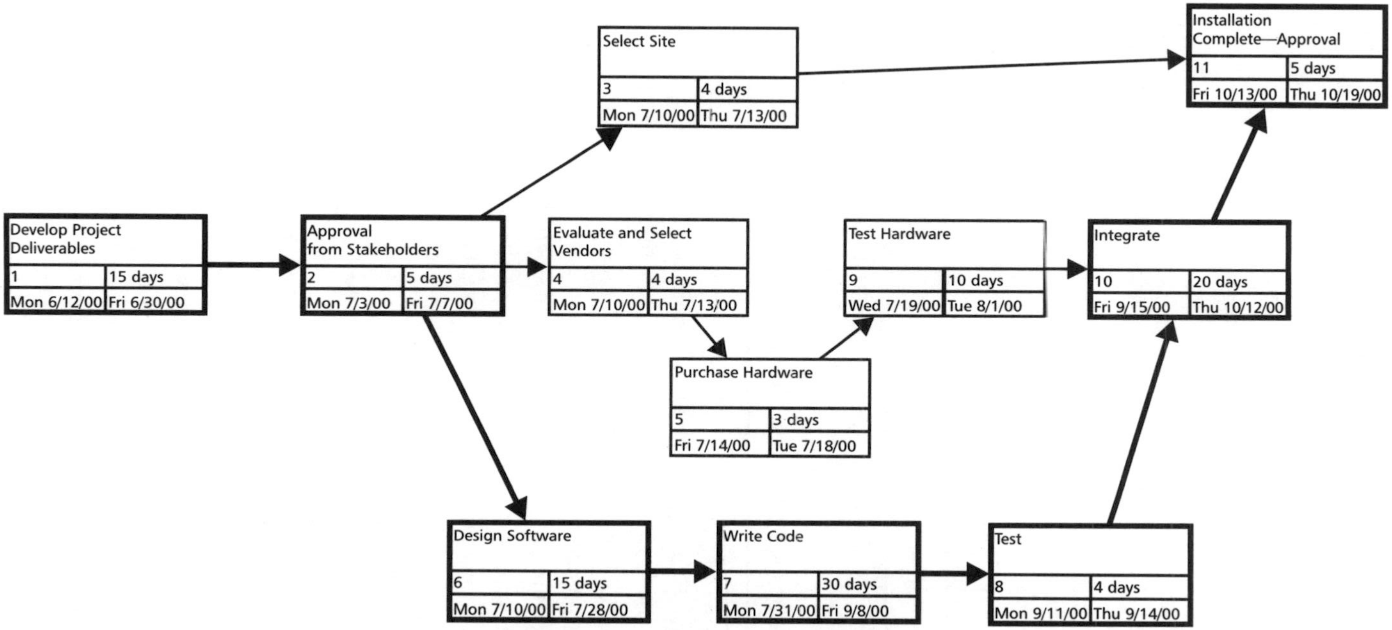

Develop Project Deliverables		
1	15 days	
Mon 6/12/00	Fri 6/30/00	

Approval from Stakeholders		
2	5 days	Fri 7/7/00
Mon 7/3/00		

Select Site		
3	4 days	
Mon 7/10/00	Thu 7/13/00	

Evaluate and Select Vendors		
4	4 days	Thu 7/13/00
Mon 7/10/00		

Purchase Hardware		
5	3 days	Tue 7/18/00
Fri 7/14/00		

Test Hardware		
9	10 days	Tue 8/1/00
Wed 7/19/00		

Design Software		
6	15 days	Fri 7/28/00
Mon 7/10/00		

Write Code		
7	30 days	Fri 9/8/00
Mon 7/31/00		

Test		
8	4 days	Thu 9/14/00
Mon 9/11/00		

Integrate		
10	20 days	Thu 10/12/00
Fri 9/15/00		

Installation Complete—Approval		
11	5 days	Thu 10/19/00
Fri 10/13/00		

Figure 2-4. Precedence relationships.

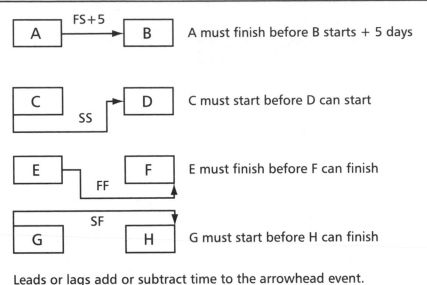

Leads or lags add or subtract time to the arrowhead event.

For example, using the above example of constructing a wedding cake, I do not want to apply the frosting to the cake until the master chef is on scene. The two activities then are: (1) apply frosting to cake, and (2) master chef supervises cake construction. The start-start relationship says that I cannot start putting the frosting on the cake until I have the master chef present. Notice that I could, logically, put the frosting on any time after that. The relationship constricts the start of the activity of frosting the cake to be no sooner than the beginning of the master chef supervising the cake construction.

Finish-Finish Relationship (FF)
The finish-finish relationship is expressed in the same way as the finish-start relationship except that the word *finish* is substituted for *start*. The relationship is stated like this: The independent activity in the relationship must *finish* before the dependent activity can *finish*.

This says that where there are two activities connected by an arrow, the one that is connected to the tail of the arrow must finish before the activity connected to the head of the arrow is allowed to finish. It does not say that the dependent activity must finish then. The activity could finish later than that time, but it is not allowed to finish any sooner than the finish of the independent activity.

For example, using the example of applying the frosting to the wedding cake, I must have the master chef there until the frosting is complete so that he or she can approve it.

The master chef is then restricted from finishing the supervising activity until the frosting activity is finished. The two activities are: (1) apply frosting to cake, and (2) master chef supervises cake construction. The finish-finish relationship says that the master chef cannot finish supervising the cake construction until the frosting is completed. Notice that I could, logically, have the master chef continue supervising after that. The relationship constricts the finish of the master chef supervising activity to be no sooner than the finish of the frosting activity.

Start-Finish Relationship (SF)

The start-finish relationship is very seldom used and has even been dropped from some of the project management scheduling software packages. This relationship is stated in the same sentence as the finish-start relationship except that the words *start* and *finish* are substituted for *finish* and *start*. The relationship is stated like this: The independent activity in the relationship must *start* before the dependent activity can *finish*.

This says that where there are two activities connected by an arrow, the one that is connected to the tail of the arrow must start before the activity connected to the head of the arrow is allowed to finish. It does not say that the dependent activity must finish then. The dependent activity could finish later than that time, but it is not allowed to finish any sooner than the start of the independent activity.

For an example, using the wedding cake example again, the project is still to construct a wedding cake, and the activity is to apply the frosting to the cake. We do not want to finish applying the frosting to the cake until the master chef is on the scene. The two activities then are: (1) apply frosting to cake and (2) master chef supervises cake construction. Remember that the start-start relationship says that I cannot start putting the frosting on the cake until I have the master chef present. The start-finish relationship says that I can start putting on the frosting of the cake before the master chef is present, but I am not allowed to finish putting on the frosting until the master chef has started supervising. Notice that I could, logically, start putting the frosting on any time before the master chef begins to supervise. The relationship constricts the finish of the activity of frosting the cake to be no sooner than the beginning of the master chef supervising the cake construction.

These relationships must be available to project managers and schedulers in order to be able to schedule all of the real relationships that are necessary to properly schedule a project. They are seldom used until attempts are made to reduce total schedule time.

In the examples involving frosting the cake, I related the frosting of the cake to the presence of the master chef to supervise the operations. At first the relationship was a start-start relationship, in which the frosting operation had to wait until the master chef began supervising. If we were trying to shorten the schedule, one of the things that might help would be to change the relationship between these two activities to a start-finish relationship. This would allow the frosting of the cake to begin much sooner but still require that the master chef supervise the completion of the activity.

Leads and Lags

To complete our discussion of relationships between schedule activities we must discuss leads and lags. Leads and lags are delays that are imposed in the relationship between the independent and dependent activity. They can help to shorten schedules as well as allow for delays between activities. Leads and lags are designated by adding a plus for lags, and a minus for leads, as well as the number of time periods that the lead or lag adds to the schedule.

A *lag* causes the dependent activity of the pair of activities in the relationship to have a designated number of time periods added to the start or finish of the dependent activity. A *lead* causes the dependent activity of the pair of activities in the relationship to have a designated number of time periods subtracted from the start or finish of the dependent activity.

For example, in the two activities previously discussed, baking the cake and putting the frosting on the cake, we established a finish-start relationship between the two activities. This said that we could not apply the frosting until the cake was baked. This is all right if the baking the cake activity included the time for the cake to cool. If it did not, and the cake activity ended when it was removed from the oven, then it would be necessary to insert a lag between the two activities. It is not possible to put the frosting on a hot cake, since it would melt and make a mess. This may be necessary because the cake baker would like to have closure on the baking activity and go about doing other things, and we may not want him to be responsible for waiting until the cake cools.

We would change the relationship from an FS to an FS + 1. This would force the schedule to allow one time period between completion of the baking activity and the start of the frosting activity.

A lead, on the other hand, allows the dependent activity to start sooner than the logical relationship would normally allow. In the example showing the start-finish relationship, we wanted to show that the frosting activity could start sooner in this relationship than if it used a start-start relationship. The problem with the start-finish relationship is that the frosting activity could start very much earlier than the supervising activity. The result of this might mean that the person responsible for the frosting cannot get closure on the activity until the master chef arrives. Another way to show this relationship is to make it an SS − 1 relationship. This means that the frosting operation could start as early as one time period before the master chef arrives.

Diagramming Relationships

The convention used in network diagramming of relationships and leads and lags is that the relationship is shown on the logical arrow only if it is *not* a finish-start relationship. If there are no leads or lags, no designation is given.

Project Start and Project Finish Events

Each activity in the diagram will always have a predecessor and a successor if the following convention is used. The convention is to create two events, the start of the project and the finish of the project. An event is a project activity that has zero duration and marks a place of significance in the project. Creating a start and finish event for the project allows all other activities to have at least one predecessor and at least one successor. This convention keeps the diagram tidy and avoids having multiple places in the diagram where the project can start and finish. These are called "danglers."

Since nodes (the boxes) represent the activities in the diagram, it is not necessary to create dummy activities to show multiple dependencies in the project being represented. Notice that it is easy to show multiple relationships between activities. Activity 4 in the diagram in Figure 2-3 is dependent on activity 1 and activity 2, as well as the start of the project.

Logical Precedence Diagram

At this point it is possible to lay out the logical relationships of the project activities. The activities themselves came from the work breakdown structure. There should be a one-to-one correspondence between the activities that resulted at the bottom of the work breakdown structure and the activities that are in the schedule. The logical relationship between the activities is also determined in the development of the work breakdown structure. We accomplished this when we developed the inputs and outputs for each activity in the work breakdown structure. Since inputs required for one activity are the outputs for another activity, this gives us much of the information we need for sequencing the order of the activities.

Activity Durations

The durations of the activities were developed when we estimated the cost of the project. Again, this was done with the help of the work breakdown structure. When we broke the project down to the individual activities that had to be done in the project, we were able to do a bottom-up estimate on cost for the project. While estimating the cost of each of the activities in the project we must also estimate the duration for each activity as well. The duration of an activity will not necessarily be the same as the effort to do the activity. Please refer to Chapter 3, Cost Management, for a complete discussion of the estimating process.

Effort is the number of people-hours needed to do the activity and will help us estimate cost. We speak of effort as being one hundred people-hours. This means that I might have one person working on the activity for one hundred hours, or I might have one hundred people working on the activity for one hour.

Duration is the length of time that it takes to do an activity. This would be the number of days that one person or more actually work on the activity. If project activity is scheduled to be done on Monday and Tuesday by Mary and Joe, Wednesday and

Thursday by Madelyn and Joe, and Friday by Nancy and Fran, the duration of the activity is five days. If a project activity is scheduled to be done on Monday and Tuesday by Mary and Joe, no work is scheduled on Wednesday and Thursday, and work is scheduled on Friday for Nancy and Fran, and on Monday and Tuesday for Madelyn and Joe, the duration of the activity is still five days. Wednesday and Thursday are considered to be nonworking days and contribute nothing to the activity's duration. This is a split activity. It is easy to think of this type of activity as being two activities, or parts A and B of the same activity. The important thing is to realize that the duration of the activity does not include the time when the activity is not being worked.

The *span* of an activity is different from duration as well. Span is the time that elapses between the start and finish of the activity. Span is simply the number of days that go by between the start and finish of the activity, regardless of whether the activity is being worked on.

Continuing the above example with Mary, Madelyn, Joe, Nancy, and Fran, note that the activity started on Monday of the first week and finished on Tuesday of the second week. The span of the activity is seven days, the duration of the activity is five days, and the effort of the activity is ten people-days.

Fortunately for the sake of our sanity, project schedules are put together without very much use of interrupted activities. This is usually an inefficient way to schedule work. The interrupted activity is, however, often used in adjusting schedules for problems that appear during project execution.

Building the Network Diagram

Now that we have the durations and logic of the project, we can actually build the schedule. A sequence of steps should be followed in developing the schedule:

1. Create a list of the activities that are to be scheduled.
2. Assign a duration to each of the activities.
3. Determine the predecessor for each activity.
4. Calculate the forward pass, the early schedule for each activity.
5. Calculate the backward pass, the late schedule for each activity.
6. Calculate the float for each activity.
7. Determine the critical path.
8. Determine if the predicted project completion is earlier than the promise date.
9. Adjust schedule or promise date.
10. Apply resources and determine resource constraints.
11. Adjust the schedule to allow for resource constraints.
12. Determine if the predicted project completion is earlier than the promise date.
13. Adjust schedule or promise date.
14. Get approval on schedule.

Calendars must be entered if project management software is used. They must be considered when scheduling even when software is not being used. A calendar is the data that tells precisely when a resource is available for work. It defines the holidays, days off each week, and the time of day that the resource is available. A separate calendar is necessary for each resource that has a different work schedule, but resources having the same work schedule can use the same calendar. For example, Arnie and Zara are working on the same project. Arnie works from 8:00 A.M. to 5:00 P.M. with an hour off for lunch from 12:00 noon to 1:00 P.M. He works Monday through Saturday and takes off all of the company standard holidays. Zara works from 8:00 A.M. to 5:00 P.M. with an hour off for lunch from 12:00 noon to 1:00 P.M. She works Monday through Friday and takes off all of the company standard holidays. Zara and Arnie would require separate calendars.

The first thing we do is to create a list of activities (1) that will be in our schedule. This list is identical to the bottom level of the work breakdown structure. The duration of each activity (2) was determined during the estimating process. The predecessor of each activity (3) was determined during the final stages of the construction of the work breakdown structure.

Calculating the early schedule for each activity (4) requires the adoption of a few scheduling conventions. These conventions are accepted by the scheduling community. The first activity is always scheduled to start on the project start date. This date is input as part of the project plan. The first start date is the project start. The early finish date is the early start date plus the duration of the activity. Here another convention comes into play. Each activity is considered to have started at the beginning of the period that it starts on and to finish at the end of the period it finishes on. This means that if an activity has a duration of one day and it starts on January first, it ends on January first, too. Due to this convention the early finish of any activity equals the early start plus the duration minus one. So, activity 1 starts on day 1 and finishes on day 15 (Table 2-1).

The next activity must start at the beginning of the time period it starts in. This means that the next activity starts in the next available time period. Since activity 1 finishes on day 15, activity 2 must start on day 16, and it finishes on day 20.

Activities 3 and 4 present a new problem. Both of these activities depend on activity 2 to be completed before they can start. Both have an early start date of day 21. The schedule development continues.

In order to complete the backward pass (5) we must start at the last activity that was completed in the early schedule. The rationale for this is that if the early schedule was the soonest that the project could be completed, then what we seek in the backward pass is the latest that each of the activities can be done so that the final completion of the project can be made.

We begin by taking the latest of the early finish times from the last activity to be completed. This is the late finish time. The duration is then subtracted from the late

Table 2-1. Precedence.

Activity	Description	Duration	Predecessor	ES	EF	LS	LF	Float
1	Develop project deliverables	15	—	1	15	1	15	0
2	Approval from stakeholders	5	1	16	20	16	20	0
3	Select site	4	2	21	24	86	89	65
4	Evaluate and select vendor	4	2	21	24	53	56	32
5	Purchase hardware	3	4	25	27	57	59	32
6	Design software	15	2	21	35	21	35	0
7	Write code	30	6	36	65	36	65	0
8	Test software	4	7	66	69	66	69	0
9	Test hardware	10	5	28	37	60	69	32
10	Integrate hardware and software	20	9, 8	70	89	70	89	0
11	Install and final acceptance	5	3, 10	90	94	90	94	0

finish time to get the early finish time. The late schedule times, late start and late finish, for activity 11 are thus days 90 and 94. Since activity 11 has a late start date of day 90, activities 10 and 3 must be finished no later than day 89. This will be the late finish date for both of them. It is the latest that they can be finished in order to support the project completion on day 94 and the latest start of activity 11.

Remember the convention that says that the activity work always starts at the beginning of the work period and ends at the end of the work period. A late finish of day 94 and a duration of 5 days means that the activity must have started on day 90. Days 90, 91, 92, 93, and 94 are the five days worked. The durations are subtracted to get the late start dates for each activity. When we come to activity 2 we must be careful to choose a late finish date that supports the late start dates of activities 3, 4, and 6. Since the late start dates for activities 3, 4, and 6 are days 86, 53, and 21, respectively, the latest that activity 2 can be finished is day 20.

Now, referring to Table 2-1, we see that we have completed the calculation of the early start, early finish, late start, and late finish dates for our schedule.

When we calculated the early and late schedule dates for our project we found that sometimes the early and late schedule dates were the same, and in other activities the dates were different. In these activities there was a difference between the earliest day that we could start an activity and the latest day we could start the activity. The difference between these two dates is called "float," or sometimes "slack." These terms mean exactly the same thing and can be used interchangeably. The *float* of an activity is the amount of time that the activity can be delayed without causing a delay in the project.

To calculate the float (6) for each activity, subtract the early start day from the late start day of the activity. Incidentally, the subtraction could be performed using the late finish and the early finish days as well, since the difference between start and finish dates is simply the duration, and that is the same for the early and late schedules.

The critical path (7) is really not a path at all. In the days when activity on arrow diagramming was used, the activities formed a path through the project schedule. Today, with the use of computerized project management scheduling software, the critical path can be more versatile. The *critical path* is defined as the group of activities that cannot be delayed without delaying the completion date for the entire project. In other words, it is the series of activities that have "zero float."

Using computerized project management scheduling software, we can modify the list of activities on the critical path to include activities that are nearly on the critical path. This is important, since the critical path method is a management method for managing project schedules. The activities that have zero float are the activities that cannot be delayed without delaying the completion of the project. These are the activities that must be monitored closely if we want our project to finish on time. Conversely, the activities that are not on the critical path, those activities that have something other than zero float, need not be managed quite as closely. In addition, it is important to know which activities in the project may be delayed without delaying the project completion. Resources from activities having float could be made available to do a "workaround" if the need should arise.

Now that we have determined our schedule for the earliest completion of the project it is time for a reality check (8). The schedule should be showing a completion date that is earlier than the promise date that may have already been given to the stakeholders. If this is not the case, then warning flags should be up and waving.

The schedule that we have produced so far does not yet include delays that will occur if resources are not available when they are needed. Schedule reserves have not yet been added to allow for the effect of known and unknown risks. We also have not taken into consideration the normal variations that will occur between the predicted and actual project activity durations.

Next, we must adjust the schedule or the promise date (9). We have two situations, a schedule that has a promise date that is earlier than the predicted date, and a schedule that has a promise date that is later than the predicted date. If the predicted date of the schedule is later than the promise date we must compress the schedule. Crashing or fast tracking must be used. *Crashing* a schedule is doing anything at all to reduce the scheduled completion of the project. Examples of crashing would include reducing the scope of the project, adding additional resources for selected activities, eliminating activities, and changing the process to eliminate steps.

Fast tracking is a special case of crashing. In fast tracking activities that would have been scheduled in sequence are scheduled to be done with some overlap instead. The use of leads in the logical relationships between activities can be used to facilitate this, or the relationships can be changed completely.

For example, suppose the project is to paint a house (Figure 2-5). The original schedule called for one crew of people to scrape off the loose paint, apply the primer, and then apply the finish coat. The schedule calls for the three activities to be done in sequence.

To improve on the scheduled completion of the project, some of the activities could

Figure 2-5. Painting a house.

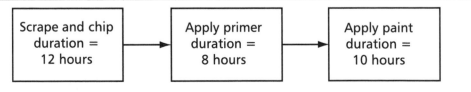

Project duration is 30 hours.

be fast tracked. Instead of one crew, two crews could be utilized. The first crew starts chipping and scraping. Eight hours later the second crew starts applying the primer to the scraped areas. When the first crew finishes scraping and chipping the house they can begin painting the finish coat over the primer that the second crew has been applying and which is now half done.

The overall effect on the project is to reduce the time for doing the project from 30 hours to 22 hours. The work content, the effort, remains the same at 30 person-hours. If the crew size were 2 people, then the project effort would be 60 person-hours. The disadvantage of fast tracking the schedule as we have done here, and the disadvantage of crashing any schedule, is that cost or risk, or both, will increase.

In this example, the overall cost of the project did not go up according to what we have measured. However, the real cost of the project, if all things were considered, would have gone up. Transportation of the additional crew to the job site would have increased. The cost of the additional equipment needed for two crews would have gone up.

The risk of the project goes up as well. If a mistake is made by one crew or the other, there will be little time to recover before the project schedule is affected. For example, if the wrong primer was used by the second crew, the finish coat may have already been applied before the mistake is found (Figure 2-6).

Buffering the Schedule

The other problem that we addressed was what to do if the schedule is earlier than the promise date (12) of the project to the stakeholders. This is a much more pleasant problem than trying to shorten the schedule. It is a very important problem to solve, however. This must be done after allowing for reserve schedule time, normal fluctuations in the activity durations, and resource limitations on the schedule (Figure 2-7). If after all of this the schedule time is less than the promise date, buffering may be applied.

Figure 2-6. Painting a house.

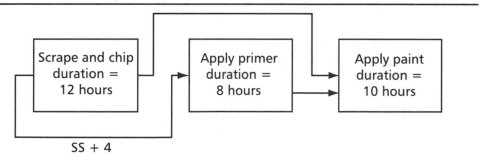

Project duration is 22 hours.

Figure 2-7. Schedule without contingency.

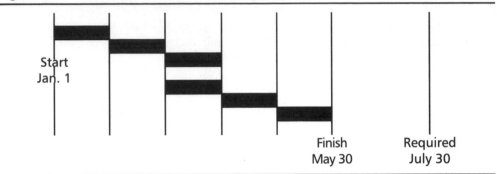

A project schedule should not be adjusted by lengthening the duration of the activities (see Figure 2-8). If this is done, each of the people responsible for a scheduled activity will essentially be given the extra allowance and will probably work to this schedule. The schedule should also not be left as it is, since this is an optimistic schedule with no allowances for the items we discussed earlier.

A better way to schedule the project is with a buffer (Figure 2-9). *Buffering* a schedule is simply adding float to selected activities. In some project management scheduling software this feature is available. If it is not a part of your software, it can still be done. There are two methods: using lags in the relationships and creating buffer activities.

Using relationship lags is easily done but is tedious to accomplish. Each pair of activities must be considered and a lag added wherever it is desired to add buffer. To increase the project's scheduled completion time, a lag may be added between any two activities on the critical path. Changing the relationship from a normal finish-start to an FS + 10 would add 10 days of float to the activity and also shift the project completion day to ten days later.

Figure 2-8. Schedule with contingency.

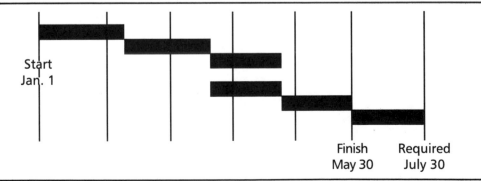

Figure 2-9. Schedule with buffer.

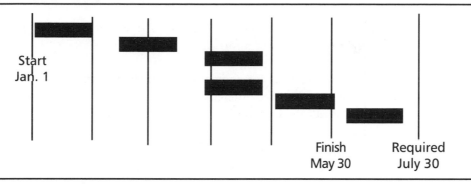

Start
Jan. 1

Finish
May 30

Required
July 30

Another technique is to create a duplicate activity for each activity that is to be buffered (Figure 2-10). The activity created is inserted between the independent activity to be buffered and the dependent activity in the relationship. If there was originally an FS relationship between activities A and B, the new relationship would add activity A'. This gives us an FS relationship between A and A' and another between A' and B. When this technique is used, the buffering dummy activities can be selected out of the schedule so that they will not appear. The remaining activities in the schedule will show with their correct dates.

Which activities should be buffered? This can be answered in a number of ways. The amount of buffer time that is applied to activities can be proportioned according to the risk of the activity, the dependencies that follow it, or any other reason that seems appropriate to the project manager.

In all project management scheduling software available today there is the ability to constrain the project with the use of resources (10). The unavailability of the resources may cause schedule delays. This problem occurs when an activity is scheduled that uses a

Figure 2-10. Buffering.

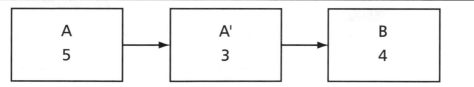

Without buffer: 9 days.
With buffer: 12 days.

particular person or equipment and that piece of equipment is being used in some other part of the project or on some other project altogether.

To enter the resource information into any project management scheduling software package, a number of different pieces of information must be entered:

• *Work Calendar*. This describes the work schedule of the resources. Many of these may be necessary to take care of all the different work patterns of the various resources. The days of the week worked, the time of day that is worked, and holidays that are not worked must be entered.

• *Resource Availability*. The availability of the resource in terms of when the resource is available as well as the quantity of the resource that is available.

• *Resource Requirement*. The amount of the resource required and when it is required.

Next, we adjust the schedule to allow for resource constraints (11). The resource-leveling function in all scheduling software packages is useful for a first look at this problem but is not intelligent enough to solve any but the simplest resource problem. To solve this problem the software contains a feature called the "resource histogram" (Figure 2-11).

The *resource histogram* is done in a split screen format. Generally, the upper portion of the screen shows the Gantt chart with the activities that are using the resource in question. In the bottom portion of the screen, vertical bars indicate the amount of re-

Figure 2-11. Overallocation of resource (resource histogram).

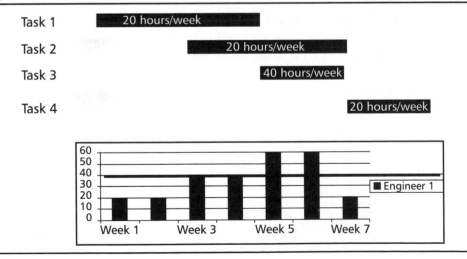

source that is necessary for the time period in question. The time scales that are used are the same for both views.

By looking at the two parts of the screen in Figure 2-11, it can be seen that during weeks 1 and 2 the resource is underutilized, and that in weeks 5 and 6 the resource is overutilized. While the underutilized resource may be employed somewhere else in the project, it will be very difficult to make the overutilized resource work 20 hours of overtime for those two weeks.

To resolve the problem, activity 2 was scheduled to be interrupted for two weeks (Figure 2-12). By doing this the workload of this resource was leveled out, and no overtime was required.

Now, with the resource constraints and the schedule adjusted to meet promise dates, another check is made to be sure that the schedule can be met (12). If the promise date and the planned date are still not consistent, then it is time to readjust the schedule one more time (13). Before the plan can be finalized it is important that the plan be approved (14) and that there is a formal sign-off for this schedule baseline.

Reverse Resource Allocation Scheduling

Some projects are required to be completed on a specific date regardless of the resources needed. This makes it necessary to schedule the resource in reverse. The end date of the project minus the time needed for the resource determines the start date for using that resource.

Figure 2-12. Overallocation of resource resolved (resource histogram).

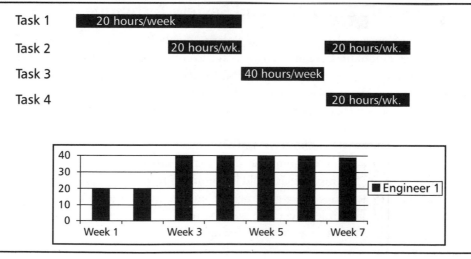

Critical Path Method (CPM)

The critical path is a method of managing a project effectively. We have seen how the critical path is determined and how the float or slack is determined. Using the notion of float, the project manager can direct his or her efforts where they will do the most good.

Activities that are found to have float, particularly those that have large amounts of float, can be managed less intensely than other activities in the project plan. This is because activities with float can be delayed without affecting the project completion date. Of course, activities that have large amounts of float can be delayed a considerable amount before they affect the project completion (Figure 2-13).

Conversely, the activities that have zero float cannot be delayed without affecting the project completion date. These activities should be managed carefully by the project manager and the project team.

In the critical path method of managing projects, another term for float is "free float." This is somewhat different than the float we have discussed up until now. One of the problems with managing by float is that if an activity is delayed within its float, it may be necessary to reschedule many other activities as a result. *Free float* is the amount of time an activity can be delayed without affecting the project completion date *or* requiring any other activity to be rescheduled. This is important because rescheduling the remaining activities in the project can cause great confusion for the project team, and the project manager can quickly lose credibility. The use of free float prevents much of this problem.

Program Evaluation and Review Technique (PERT)

The PERT system was developed for the Polaris Missile Program in the 1950s. At that time there was a lot of pressure on the U.S. Navy to complete the Polaris Missile Program. The Cold War was raging, and the United States needed a deterrent that would discourage the threat of nuclear weapons by Russia. A mobile missile that could be carried aboard a submarine and launched from beneath the surface of the sea would be a formidable weapon.

The problem for the U.S. Navy was that there were two separate projects to be done. One was to develop a submarine that could launch these missiles. The second project was to develop a missile that could be launched from a submarine. The durations of the project plan activities had a great deal of uncertainty in them. The navy needed a method to predict the project schedule with better reliability than was possible in the past. PERT was developed to assist in analyzing projects where there was uncertainty in the duration of the activities.

The normal probability distribution relates the event of something happening to the

Figure 2-13. Critical path method.

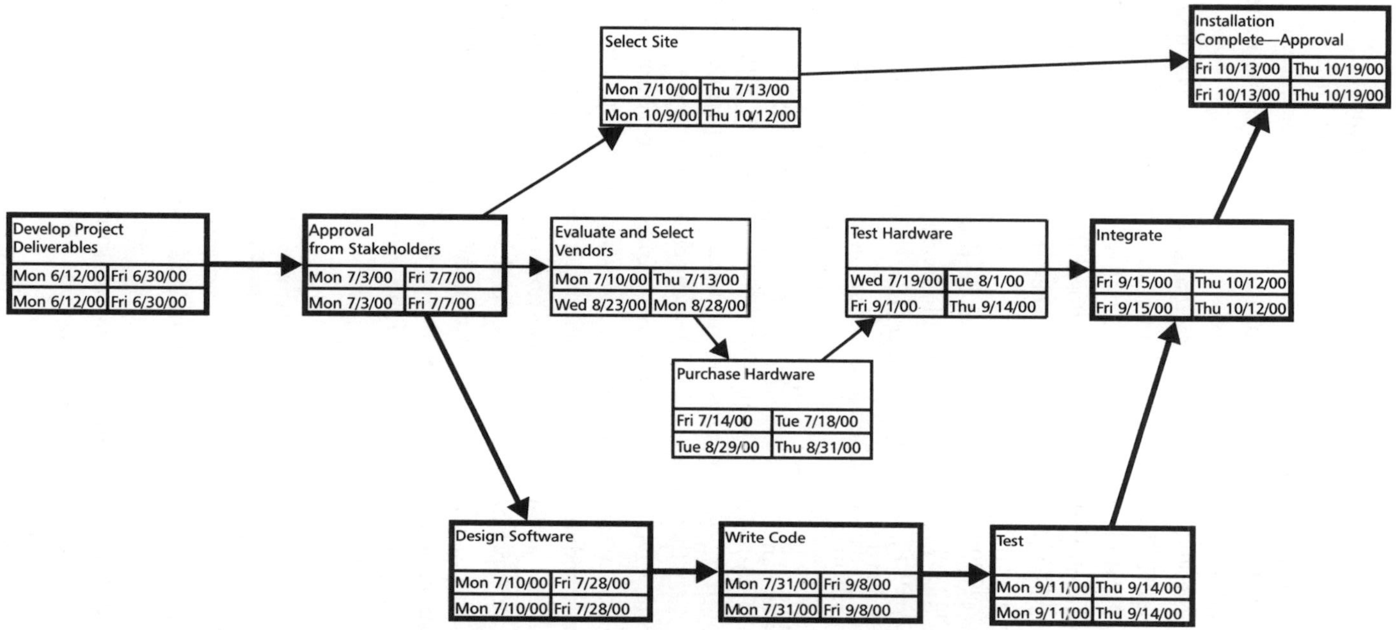

Develop Project Deliverables		
Mon 6/12/00	Fri 6/30/00
Mon 6/12/00	Fri 6/30/00

Approval from Stakeholders		
Mon 7/3/00	Fri 7/7/00
Mon 7/3/00	Fri 7/7/00

Select Site		
Mon 7/10/00	Thu 7/13/00
Mon 10/9/00	Thu 10/12/00

Evaluate and Select Vendors		
Mon 7/10/00	Thu 7/13/00
Wed 8/23/00	Mon 8/28/00

Purchase Hardware		
Fri 7/14/00	Tue 7/18/00
Tue 8/29/00	Thu 8/31/00

Test Hardware		
Wed 7/19/00	Tue 8/1/00
Fri 9/1/00	Thu 9/14/00

Design Software		
Mon 7/10/00	Fri 7/28/00
Mon 7/10/00	Fri 7/28/00

Write Code		
Mon 7/31/00	Fri 9/8/00
Mon 7/31/00	Fri 9/8/00

Test		
Mon 9/11/00	Thu 9/14/00
Mon 9/11/00	Thu 9/14/00

Integrate		
Fri 9/15/00	Thu 10/12/00
Fri 9/15/00	Thu 10/12/00

Installation Complete—Approval		
Fri 10/13/00	Thu 10/19/00
Fri 10/13/00	Thu 10/19/00

probability that it will occur. It turns out that by experiment, the normal distribution describes many phenomena that actually occur. The duration as well as the estimated cost of project activities comes close to matching a normal distribution. In reality, another distribution, called the beta distribution, fits these phenomena better, but the normal curve is close enough for practical purposes.

Suppose we have a scheduled activity that has an expected completion time of thirty-five days. In Figure 2-14, the curve shows the probability of any other day occurring. Since thirty-five days is the expected value of the activity, it follows that it would have the highest probability of all of the other possibilities. Another way of saying this is that, if all of the possibilities are shown, then they represent 100 percent of the possibilities and 100 percent of the probability.

If it were possible for this project to be done thousands and thousands of times, sometimes the time to do the activity would be 35 days, other times it would be 33 days, and still other times it would be 37 days. If we were to plot all of these experiments we would find that 35 days occurred most often, 34 days occurred a little less often, 30 days even less, and so on. Experimentally, we could develop a special probability distribution for this particular activity. The curve would then describe the probability that any particular duration would occur when we really decided to do the project and that activity. In the experiment, if 35 days occurred 134 times and the experiment was performed 1,000 times, we could say that there is a 13.4 percent chance that the actual doing of the project would take 35 days. All 1,000 of the activity times were between 20 and 50 days.

It is impractical to do this activity a thousand times just to find out how long it will take when we schedule it. If we are willing to agree that many phenomena, such as schedule durations and cost, will fit the normal probability distribution, then we can avoid doing the experiment and instead do the mathematics. To do this we need only have a simple way to approximate the mean and standard deviation of the phenomena.

The mean value is the middle of the curve along the x-axis. This is the average or expected value. A good approximation of this value can be obtained by asking the activity estimator to estimate three values instead of the usual one. Ask the estimator to estimate the optimistic, the pessimistic, and the most likely. (The estimator is probably doing this anyway.) The way people perform the estimating function is to think about what will happen if things go well, what will happen if things do not go well, and then what is likely to really happen. This being the case, the three values we need are free for the asking. These are the optimistic, the pessimistic, and the most likely values for the activity duration.

If we have these three values, it becomes simple to calculate the expected value and the standard deviation. For the expected value we will take the weighted average:

Expected value = [Optimistic + Pessimistic + (4 × Most likely)] / 6

Figure 2-14. Schedule probability.

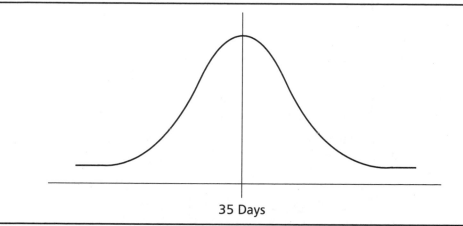

35 Days

Standard deviations can be calculated using the formula:

Standard deviation = (Pessimistic − Optimistic) / 6

As can be seen in Table 2-2, with these two simple calculations we can calculate the probability and a range of values that the dates for the completion of the project will have when we actually do the project. For the purpose of ease of calculation, if we were to decide that 95.5 percent probability would be sufficient for our purposes, then it turns out that this happens to be the range of values that is plus or minus 2 standard deviations from the mean value.

If the expected value of the schedule is 93 days and the standard deviation is 3 days, we could make this statement: This project has a probability of 95 percent that it will be finished in 87 to 99 days.

For example, suppose we use the same example we used earlier. This time we have probabilistic dates instead of the specific ones that we had before. We have collected estimates on the duration of each of the activities and show the optimistic, pessimistic, and most likely values in the table. The expected value is from the formula:

EV = [Optimistic + Pessimistic + (4 × Most likely)] / 6

The standard deviations can be calculated using the formula:

Standard deviation = (Pessimistic − Optimistic) / 6

One thing must be pointed out here. Unlike cost estimating, where the cost of every activity in the project must be added up to get the total cost, the sum of the time it will take to do the project is the sum of the expected value of the items that are on the critical

Table 2-2. PERT exercise.

Activity	Description	Optimistic	Pessimistic	Most Likely	EV	SD	Variance	CP EV	CP Variance
1	Develop project deliverables	13	16	15	14.83	0.50	0.2500	14.83	0.2500
2	Approval from stakeholders	4	6	5	5.00	0.33	0.1111	5.00	0.1111
3	Site selection	4	4	4	4.00	0.00	0.0000		
4	Evaluate and select vendor	4	5	4	4.17	0.17	0.0278		
5	Purchase hardware	3	3	3	3.00	0.00	0.0000		
6	Design software	14	17	15	15.17	0.50	0.2500	15.17	0.2500
7	Write code	24	33	30	29.50	1.50	2.2500	29.50	2.2500
8	Test software	4	4	4	4.00	0.00	0.0000	4.00	0.0000
9	Test hardware	9	11	10	10.00	0.33	0.1111		
10	Integrate hardware and software	20	23	20	20.50	0.50	0.2500	20.50	0.2500
11	Install and final acceptance	5	5	5	5.00	0.00	0.0000	5.00	0.0000
					Sum =			94.00	3.1111
					sq. rt. var. = SD				1.763834

path only. Other activities in the project do not contribute to the length of the project, because they are done in parallel with the critical path.

The sum of the durations for the critical path items is 18.3 days. The standard deviation is 2.3 days. We can say that there is a 95 percent probability that the project will be finished in 13.7 days to 22.9 days.

Monte Carlo Simulation

When a schedule with activities that have uncertainty associated with their durations is encountered, the PERT method can be used to help predict the probability and range of values that will encompass the actual duration of the project. While the PERT technique uses the normal and beta distributions to determine this probability and range of values, there is a serious flaw in the results. The assumption made in the PERT analysis is that the critical path of the project remains the same under any of the possible conditions. This is, of course, a dangerous assumption. In any given set of possibilities, it is quite possible that the critical path may shift from one set of activities to another, thus changing the predicted completion date of the project.

In order to predict the project completion date when there is a possibility that the critical path will be different for a given set of project conditions, the *Monte Carlo* simulation must be used. The Monte Carlo simulation is not a deterministic method like many of the tools that we normally use. By that I mean that there is no exact solution that will come from the Monte Carlo analysis. What we will get instead is a probability distribution of the possible days for the completion of the project.

Monte Carlo simulations have been around for some time. It is only recently that personal computers and third party software for project management have become inexpensive enough for many project managers to afford.

The Simulation

In our project schedule, the predecessors and successors form a critical path. As I explained earlier, the critical path is the list of activities in the project schedule that cannot be delayed without affecting the completion date of the project. These are the activities that have zero float. Float is the number of days an activity can be delayed without affecting the completion date of the project.

When we have uncertainty in the duration times for the activities in the schedule, it means that there is at least a possibility that the activity will take more time or less time than our most likely estimate. If we used PERT to make these calculations, we already have calculated the mean value and the standard deviation for the project and all of the activities that have uncertainty.

The Monte Carlo simulator randomly selects values that are the possible durations for each of the activities having possible different durations. The selection of a duration for each activity is made, and the calculation of the project completion date is made for that specific set of data. The critical path is calculated, as well as the overall duration and completion date for the project.

The simulator usually allows for the selection of several probability distributions. This can be done for one activity, a group of activities, or the entire project. Depending on the software package being used, a selection of probability distributions is offered, such as: uniform, binomial, triangular, Poisson, beta, normal, and others.

The Monte Carlo simulation works in a step-by-step way:

1. A range of values is determined for the duration of each activity in the schedule that has uncertainty in its duration.
2. A probability distribution is selected for each activity or group of activities.
3. If necessary, the mean and standard deviation are calculated for each activity.
4. The network relationships between the activities are entered.
5. The computer simulation is begun.
6. A duration time is selected for each activity in the schedule, whether it is on the critical path or not.
7. The critical path, duration of the project, float, and other schedule data are calculated.
8. This process is repeated many times until the repetitions reach a certain predefined number of cycles or until the results reach a certain accuracy.
9. Output reports are generated.

Output from the Monte Carlo Simulation

The most common output from a Monte Carlo simulation is a chart showing the probability of each possible completion date. This is usually shown as a frequency histogram. Generally, a cumulative plot is made as well. In this way you may see graphically the probability of each of the possible dates. This clearly shows the most likely dates for project completion. Because of the shifting of the critical path, it is quite possible for early dates and late dates to be the most likely, with unlikely dates in between them.

A cumulative curve is also generated showing the cumulative probability of completing the activity before a given date. The criticality index can also be calculated. This is the percentage of the time that a particular activity is on the critical path. In other words, if a simulation were run 1,000 times and a particular activity was on the critical path 212 times, its *criticality index* would be 21.2 percent.

Critical Chain Theory

Eliyahu Goldratt wrote several books that explain his ideas. Since he is now mentioned in the *Guide to the PMBOK*, it might be worthwhile to read about his work. He has written a series of novels—*The Goal, It's Not Luck,* and *Critical Chain*—that explain many of his ideas. Since they are written as novels, it is rather pleasant reading and a painless way to learn some new ideas about managing and project management.

His critical chain theory is relevant to scheduling. The first idea is that a real project's resource constrained schedule will usually have a large number of activities that have reasonably large amounts of float. Unlike the types of schedules that we see in the classroom, real project schedules will have several hundred activities. Real projects will also have many activities on the critical path that are buffered or resource constrained causing a lengthening of the project completion date. This in turn creates float and free float in the activities not on the critical path.

Referring to Figure 2-15, you can think of the series of activities that make up the critical path (those that have zero float or close to zero float) as the critical chain activities. The activities not on the critical chain generally fall into groups of activities that are dependent on each other but as a whole are done independent of the critical path activities until one of them joins the critical path. That is, until an activity has a critical path activity dependent on it. These groups of activities are called feeder chains.

Normally most projects are scheduled according to the early schedule dates or the early schedule. When this is done the float for the feeder chains collects at the end of the feeder chain. When this is done the last activity in the feeder chain will be completed long before it joins the critical chain of activities. Goldratt says that this is a mistake because any knowledge gained as a result of experience and risk events in activities on the

Figure 2-15. Feeder chains and critical chains.

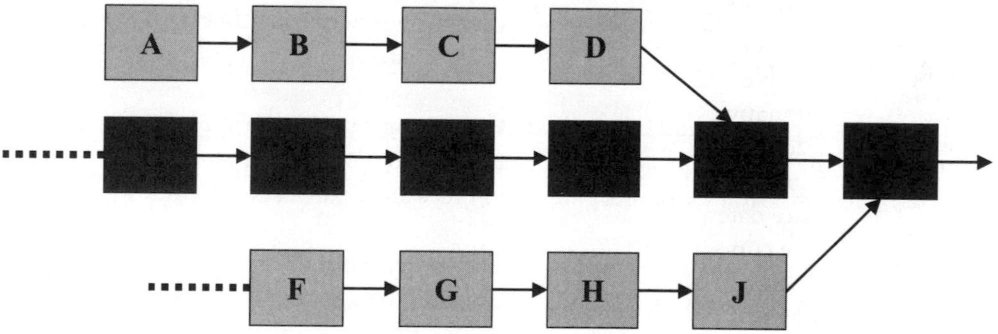

		A	B	C	D	Tot.
Expected value		30	20	25	10	85
Standard deviation		3	3	4	2	6.2

critical path will not benefit the activities on the feeder chains. By delaying the start schedule for these activities we can take advantage of the knowledge that is gained working on the critical activities.

Of course if we delay the start of the feeder chain activities too much, they will become part of the critical chain and this is not good. The feeder chains must be buffered to be completed two standard deviations before their late finish dates. Of course, if we expect to make the promise date for our customer, the critical chain activities must be buffered two standard deviations as well, and this must be done before buffering the feeder chains (see the section on buffering schedules earlier in this chapter).

Summary

Time management of a project produces the schedule baseline. The activities of the project must be defined before they can be scheduled. The work breakdown structure provides the individual activities to be scheduled. There is a one-to-one relationship between the activities described at the bottom of the work breakdown structure and the activities that are scheduled in the project schedule. Activity durations for the schedule are determined in the estimating process.

The activities are sequenced in the logical order in which they are done. This logical ordering is represented in a network diagram. The network diagramming method in use today is the precedence diagram. With the use of the correct logical relationship and the leads and lags, every logical relationship in the schedule can be diagrammed.

Fast tracking and crashing are two techniques for reducing schedules that must meet a promise date sooner than what is predicted by the schedule. Buffering is a technique for increasing schedules that have a promise date later than the date predicted by the schedule.

The critical path method is a method of managing a project by applying the management effort of the project manager and the efforts of the project team in the most effective way. Activities with little or no float are given more attention than activities with float or great amounts of float.

PERT is a technique that is used to predict project completions when there is a great deal of uncertainty in the estimated durations. PERT makes a statistical approximation of the project completion by using the estimate for the optimistic, pessimistic, and most likely duration for each activity.

The Monte Carlo simulation is used to eliminate a problem associated with PERT, which is that the critical path may move from activity to activity under different conditions. Monte Carlo is a simulation technique that runs many schedules with selected durations, statistically calculates the effect of variable durations, and reports (statistically) the results.

CHAPTER 3

Cost Management

Cost management is the completion of the project management triple constraint of cost, schedule, and scope. Each of these must be completed in order to complete the project on time and on budget and to meet all of the customer's expectations. In order to meet the cost goals of the project, the project must be completed within the approved budget.

Why We Need Cost Management

The project manager is primarily concerned with the direct cost of the project, but the trend in project management is that the role of the project manager in cost control will increase to include more of the nontraditional areas of cost control. In the future it will be expected that more project managers will have a great deal of input into the indirect costs and expenses of the project.

Regardless of what the project manager is or is not responsible for, it is critical that the project be measured against what the project manager is responsible for and nothing else. If the project manager does not have responsibility for the material cost of the project, then it makes no sense for the project manager to be measured against this metric.

Timing of the collection of cost information is also important to the cost measurement system. The project budgets must be synchronized with the collection of the project's actual cost. For example, if a project team is responsible for material cost, should the budget show the expenditure when the commitment by the project team to buy the product is made, when the item is delivered, when it is accepted, or when it is paid for? Timing issues like these can make project cost control a nightmare.

If the project team does not properly control cost, the project will invariably go out of control, and more money will be spent than anticipated. It is the purpose of cost management to prevent this.

Project Life Cycle and Project Cost

Lately, it has become important to consider the cost of the project for the full useful life of the product or service that is created. This means that the cost of the project does not end when final acceptance of the project has been completed. Guarantees, warranties, and ongoing services that have to be performed during the life of the project must be considered.

With regard to project life cycle, cost decisions are made with a clearer picture of the future commitments that the project will require. If life cycle cost is considered, better decisions will be made. An example of this would be the project of creating a software program for a customer. The project team can create a working software program without organization or documentation. This is usually called "spaghetti code." Considering the cost of the project as delivered, the spaghetti-coded project will be less costly. When you consider the life cycle cost of the project, however, this approach will be more costly. This is because the cost of debugging and modifying the software after delivery of the project will be more difficult.

Using the Work Breakdown Structure

The work breakdown structure (WBS) is the key to successful projects. The WBS produced a list of the individual pieces of work that must be done to complete a project. These are the building blocks of the project. Each of these represents a portion of the work of the project. Each must be the responsibility of one and only one person on the project team. The person responsible for an individual piece of work is similar to the project manager and is responsible for all that happens in the project regarding that piece of work. That person is responsible for scheduling, cost estimating, time estimating, and of course seeing that the work gets done. Like the project manager, the person responsible may not be required to do all the work. He or she is, however, responsible for seeing that it gets done.

Project

In order to determine the project cost accurately enough to be considered the project cost baseline, a bottom-up estimate must be made. This estimate must have an accuracy of −5 percent to +10 percent. This type of estimate will be produced by estimating the cost of each item at the bottom level of the WBS and then summarizing or rolling up the data to the project level.

Bottom-up estimates are inherently more accurate because they are a sum of individual elements. Each of the individual elements has a possibility of being over or under the actual cost that will occur. When they are added together, some of the overestimates will cancel out some of the underestimates.

Cost Estimating

A cost estimate is a prediction of the likely cost of the resources that will be required to complete all of the work of the project.

Cost estimating is done throughout the project. In the beginning of the project proof of concept estimates must be done to allow the project to go on. An "order of magnitude" estimate is performed at this stage of the project. Order of magnitude estimates can have an accuracy of −50 percent to +100 percent. As the project progresses, more accurate estimates are required. From company to company the specified range of values for a given estimate may vary as well as the name that is used to describe it. For example, *conceptual estimates* are those that have an accuracy of −30 percent to +50 percent. *Preliminary estimates* are those that have an accuracy of −20 percent to +30 percent. *Definitive estimates* are those that have an accuracy of −15 percent to +20 percent. Finally, the *control estimate* of −10 percent to +15 percent is done. Early in the project there is much uncertainty about what work is actually to be done in the project. There is no point in expending the effort to make a more accurate estimate than the accuracy needed at the particular stage that the project is in.

Types of Estimates

Several types of estimates are in common use. Depending on the accuracy required for the estimate and the cost and effort that can be expended, there are several choices.

Top-Down Estimates

Top-down estimates are used to estimate cost early in the project when information about the project is very limited. The term *top down* comes from the idea that the estimate is made at the top level of the project. That is, the project itself is estimated with one single estimate. The advantage of this type of estimate is that it requires little effort and time to produce. The disadvantage is that the accuracy of the estimate is not as good as it would be with a more detailed effort.

Bottom-Up Estimates

Bottom-up estimates are used when the project baselines are required or a control type of estimate is needed. These types of estimates are called "bottom up" because they begin by estimating the details of the project and then summarizing the details into summary levels. The WBS can be used for this "roll up." The advantage of this kind of estimate is that it will produce accurate results. The accuracy of the bottom-up estimate depends on the level of detail that is considered. Statistically, convergence takes place as more and more detail is added. The disadvantage of this type of estimate is that the cost of doing detailed estimating is higher, and the time to produce the estimate is considerably longer.

Analogous Estimates

Analogous estimates are a form of top-down estimate. This process uses the actual cost of previously completed projects to predict the cost of the project that is being estimated. Thus, there is an analogy between one project and another. If the project being used in the analogy and the project being estimated are very similar, the estimates could be quite accurate. If the projects are not very similar, then the estimates might not be very accurate at all.

For example, a new software development project is to be done. The modules to be designed are very similar to modules that were used on another project, but they require more lines of code. The difficulty of the project is quite similar to the previous project. If the new project is 30 percent larger than the previous project, the analogy might predict a project cost of 30 percent greater than that of the previous project.

Parametric Estimates

Parametric estimates are similar to analogous estimates in that they are also top-down estimates. Their inherent accuracy is no better or worse than analogous estimates.

The process of parametric estimating is accomplished by finding a parameter of the project being estimated that changes proportionately with project cost. Mathematically, a model is built based on one or more parameters. When the values of the parameters are entered into the model, the cost of the project results.

Resource cost rates must be known for most types of estimates. This is the amount that things cost per unit. For example, gasoline has a unit cost of $1.95 per gallon; labor of a certain type has a cost of $150.00 per hour, and concrete has a cost of $25.00 per cubic yard. With these figures known, adjustments in the parameter will allow revising of the estimate.

If there is a close relationship between the parameters and cost, and if the parameters are easy to quantify, the accuracy can be improved. If there are historical projects that are both more costly and less costly than the project being estimated, and the parametric relationship is true for both of those historical projects, the estimating accuracy and the reliability of the parameter for this project will be better.

Multiple parameter estimates can be produced as well. In multiple parameter estimates various weights are given to each parameter to allow for the calculation of cost by several parameters simultaneously.

For example, houses cost $115 per square foot, software development cost is $2 per line of code produced, an office building costs $254 per square foot plus $54 per cubic foot plus $2,000 per acre of land, and so on.

Control Estimates

Control estimates are of the bottom-up variety. This is the type of estimate that is used to establish a project baseline or any other important estimate. In a project, the WBS can be used as the level of detail for the estimate. The accuracy of this estimate can be made to be quite high, but the cost of developing the estimate can be quite high and the time to produce it can be lengthy as well.

Control estimates are based on the statistical central limit theorem, which explains statistical convergence. If we have a group of details that can be summarized, the variance of the sum of the details will be less significant than the significance of the variance of the details themselves. All that this means is that the more details we have in an estimate, the more accurate the sum of the details will be. This is because some of the estimates of the details will be overestimated, and some will be underestimated. The overestimates and underestimates will cancel each other out. If we have enough detail, the average overestimates and underestimates will approach a zero difference.

If we flip a coin one time, we can say it comes up 100 percent heads or 100 percent tails. If we continue flipping the coin a large number of times, and the coin is a fair coin, then 50 percent of the flips will be heads and 50 percent of the flips will be tails. It may be that there are more heads than tails at one time or another, but if we flip the coin long enough, there will be 50 percent heads and 50 percent tails at the end of the coin flipping.

If we know the mean or expected values and the standard deviations for a group of detailed estimates, we can calculate the expected value and the standard deviation of the sum. If we are also willing to accept that the probability of the estimate being correct follows a normal probability distribution, then we can predict the range of values and the probability of the actual cost.

Using the same estimates for the expected value and the standard deviation that we used in the PERT method for schedules, we can make these calculations. These are only approximations of these values, but they are close enough to be used in our estimating work.

$$\text{Expected Value} = [\text{Optimistic} + \text{Pessimistic} + (4 \times \text{Most Likely})] / 6$$
$$\text{Standard Deviation} = (\text{Pessimistic} - \text{Optimistic}) / 6$$

Where do these values come from? Most estimators report a single value when they complete a cost estimate. However, they think about what the cost will be if things go badly, and they think about what the cost will be if things go well. These thoughts are really the optimistic and pessimistic values that we need for our calculations. They do not cost us a thing to get. All we have to do is to get the estimator to report them to us.

For control estimates we are usually happy to get a 5 percent probability of being correct. As luck would have it, this happens to be the range of values that is plus or minus 2 standard deviations from the mean or expected value.

For example, suppose we want to estimate the cost of a printed circuit board for an electrical device of some sort. In Table 3-1, the optimistic, pessimistic, and most likely values that were estimated are entered in columns 3, 4, and 5. From these estimated values the expected value of the individual components can be calculated. This is shown in column 6. The expected value of the assembly can be reached by adding the expected values.

The standard deviation for each component is calculated and shown in column 7. In order to add the standard deviations they must first be squared. These values are shown in column 8. Next, the square of each of the standard deviations for each component is added, and the square root is taken of the total. This is the standard deviation of the assembly.

The expected value of the assembly is $5.54, and the standard deviation is 7.4 cents. We are interested in the range of values that have a probability of containing the actual cost of the assembly when it is produced. The range of values that would have a 95 percent probability of occurring is plus or minus 2 standard deviations from the expected value. In our example we can say that the assembly has a 95 percent probability of costing between $5.39 and $5.67.

Cost Budgeting

Cost budgeting is the process of allocating cost to the individual work items in the project. Project performance will be determined based on the budget allocated to the various parts of the project. The result of the cost budgeting process will be to produce the cost baseline of the project.

The cost baseline for the project is the expected actual cost of the project. The budget for a project should contain the estimated cost of doing all of the work that is planned to be done for the project to be completed. In addition, cost must be budgeted for work that will be done to avoid, transfer, and mitigate risks. Contingency must be budgeted for risks that are identified and may or may not come to pass. A reserve must be budgeted for risks that are not identified as well.

On most projects, the expected value for risks is budgeted. This is reasonable since it reflects the average risk exposure for the project. Using the worst case or the best case situation for the project would be overly pessimistic or optimistic and make the project overfunded or underfunded, neither of which is a good thing.

Table 3-1. Estimate of the cost of a printed circuit board.

Item	Description	Optimistic	Pessimistic	Most Likely	Expected Value	Standard Deviation	SD Squared
1	100 ohm resistor	0.04	0.06	0.05	0.050	0.0033	0.00001111
2	200 ohm resistor	0.06	0.09	0.07	0.072	0.0050	0.00002500
3	10 ohm resistor	0.03	0.04	0.03	0.032	0.0017	0.00000278
4	10 mf capacitor	0.22	0.25	0.22	0.225	0.0050	0.00002500
5	20 mf capacitor	0.28	0.36	0.33	0.327	0.0133	0.00017778
6	5 mf capacitor	0.11	0.13	0.12	0.120	0.0033	0.00001111
7	Integrated circuit	1.66	1.88	1.79	1.783	0.0367	0.00134444
8	Wire	0.33	0.33	0.33	0.330	0.0000	0.00000000
9	Circuit board	1.7	2.05	1.98	1.945	0.0583	0.00340278
10	Connector	0.57	0.7	0.67	0.658	0.0217	0.00046944
				Total Cost	5.542	Sum of Squares	0.00546944
						Standard Deviation	0.07395569

Accounting for this money can be confusing and misleading. We do not want to give each of the people who are responsible for an activity the operating budget for the planned work *plus* the contingency budget for the work that may or may not have to be done. People being what they are, this money would all be spent to complete the activity whether or not the risk occurs.

One way to avoid this is to separate the contingency reserve and place it into a contingency activity with zero duration. When a problem occurs in an activity the money needed to correct the problem is taken from the associated contingency activity and placed into the operating budget for that activity.

There is a distinction between the contingency budget and the management reserve. The *contingency budget* is set up for the risks that can be identified but may or may not take place. The *management reserve* is money that is budgeted for the project for risks that are not even identified but where through experience or even intuitive insight we feel that the money will be needed. Contingency budgets should be approved by a manager one level higher than the normal approving manager or person doing the work. The money from the management reserve requires an approval by a person two levels higher.

Cost Control

Cost control is the process of controlling the project cost and taking corrective action when the control indicates that corrective action is necessary. It is important that our cost control system be thoroughly understood by those who are measuring with it as well as by those who are being measured. Inappropriate responses to cost and schedule variances can result in serious quality problems and higher than acceptable risk levels.

Earned Value Reporting

The earned value reporting system is now the most commonly used method of performance measurement and project control. The reason for the popularity of this reporting system in project management is that it reports performance to cost and performance to schedule in one report. Schedule and cost are both measured in dollars. Where earned value reporting is not used, reports favor measuring performance to schedule or performance to budget.

In any reporting system, the principle is to set some standard, measure the actual performance to that standard, and then report on the observed differences. In the earned value reporting system we use the planned budget and schedule and then measure the actual progress in the budget and schedule.

Frequently, a Gantt chart is used to show progress and performance to schedule, but this does not state the case clearly. If a scheduled activity is shown to be three days behind schedule, it is important to know whether there is one person involved in this activity or whether there are twenty.

In reporting cost, actual cost is frequently compared to budget cost to date. This does not show the full picture either. If a project is behind schedule, the actual cost could be tracking nicely to the expected budgeted expenditures, and the project could still be in a great deal of trouble.

Using the earned value reporting system the progress of the project in terms of cost is measured in dollars. The progress of the project in terms of schedule is also measured in dollars. This may sound confusing to people who are used to thinking of schedules in terms of days ahead or days behind. In fact, it is a more informational description of the condition of the project schedule. If a project activity is reported as being five days behind schedule, and there is one person working on the activity part time, it is very different from an activity that is behind five days and has twenty people working on it.

Obviously, what is needed is a reporting system that combines performance, schedule, and budget. This is the purpose of the earned value reporting system.

Cumulative Reporting

Earned value reports are cumulative reports. The values collected for the current reporting period are added to the values from the last reporting period, and the total is plotted.

Cumulative values will never go down unless a value is reversed. As can be seen in Figure 3-1, cumulative cost curves have a characteristic "S" shape. This is because projects typically start out spending money slowly and gradually increase their spending rate until a peak is reached, and then they gradually decrease their rate of spending until the project is finally completed.

Figure 3-1. Cumulative work hours.

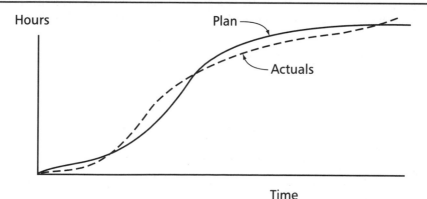

One difficulty in showing the cumulative cost curve for a large project is that the scale required in order to show the entire cost of the project may be so compact that relatively large variations are not visible. A $400 million project plotted on an 8.5-by-11-inch page would show a million-dollar variation in only one-fiftieth of an inch of space.

Where large numbers are used, a plot of the variance can be used. The scale of this type of chart can be much less compact and still show the needed information. It is made by simply drawing a line as a zero base and then plotting the difference between actual and expected values (Figure 3-2).

Earned Value Parameters

The earned value reporting system depends on the tracking of three measurements of the project. In this book I am showing the old and new designations for the earned value reports. In the 2000 edition of the *Guide to the PMBOK*, PMI chose to change the names of these parameters. In reviewing the 2004 edition of the *Guide to the PMBOK*, I found that PMI is still listing both designations in their index. In this book I will at least show the relationship between the two designations for each of the earned value parameters.

1. Budgeted cost of work scheduled (BCWS), or planned value (PV). When we established the three project baselines, we definitively set the cost and schedule baselines. Each of the activities in the project had its own estimated cost and schedule. The PV is the cumulative budget plotted on a time axis showing when the expenditure is supposed to be made according to the project plan.

2. Actual cost of work performed (ACWP), or actual cost (AC). As the project progresses, actual cost is accumulated. This cumulative actual cost is plotted along the same time axis. The actual cost is plotted for every reporting time period.

3. Budgeted cost of work performed (BCWP), or earned value (EV). This is the cumulative plot of the value of the work actually completed. The value of the work is equal to the budget that was estimated for the work. The cumulative earned value is

Figure 3-2. Cumulative variance report.

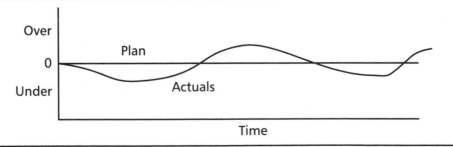

plotted on the same time axis. The earned value is plotted every time period based on the actual work that was accomplished.

If the project follows the project plan, each of these three parameters will be exactly the same. Significant deviations between the values of the three parameters—PV, AC, and EV—are cause for concern (Figure 3-3) (see the section "Calculated Values for Earned Value" below for definitions of EAC and BAC).

Difficulties in Data Collection

Plotting the PV is rather straightforward. Care must be taken that the timing and amounts that are plotted as PV are the same and that the timing is the same as when they are reported as actual expenditures.

In the area of material cost, the timing of the budget and the reporting of the actual expenditures are important. An expenditure may be recognized when the commitment is made to purchase the material, when the material is delivered, when the material is accepted, when it is invoiced, or when it is paid for. All of these dates may be quite different points in time. Care must be taken so that the timing of the PV matches the timing of the AC.

In the area of labor cost, difficulties frequently arise in the development of these estimates as well. Companies often do not like to have their estimators know the salary cost of individual employees. People are generally grouped together by similar skills. Within the group there can be a wide range of salaries. Since it is usually not possible to

Figure 3-3. Earned value reports.

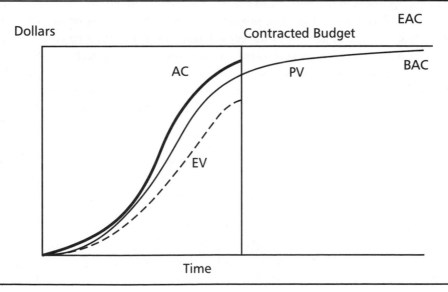

determine exactly who will be working on a project when the work is actually done, the average cost of a person in the group is used for estimating purposes. When the project is actually done, the average cost of a person in the group is still used.

It may seem that this is the right thing to do, but look at the effect on the project manager. The project manager is going to be charged the same amount per hour regardless of which person in the group is used to do the work. The project manager will naturally try to get the best person of the highest skill and experience regardless of the real needs of the project. This situation creates demand for the more senior people, while the junior people are underutilized.

A better situation would be to budget to the average cost for a person in the skill group and then collect the actual cost according to the person's actual salary. This would allow the project manager to select the less skilled person if possible and trade time and rework for lower salary cost.

Reporting Work Complete

There is frequently difficulty in reporting work complete on the project. Many people tend to report that the percent that is complete on an activity is the same as the percent of the time that has elapsed. Thus, if 50 percent of the time to do an activity in the project has passed but only 25 percent of the work is actually done, misleading reports could result.

There are several approaches to solving this problem. The *50-50 rule* is one such approach. In this approach to earned value data collection, 50 percent of the earned value is credited as earned value when the activity begins. The remaining 50 percent of the earned value is not credited until all of the work is completed.

The 50-50 rule encourages the project team to begin working on activities in the project, since they get 50 percent of the earned value for just starting an activity. As time goes by, the actual cost of work performed accumulates, and the project team is motivated to complete the work on the activity so that the additional 50 percent of the earned value can be credited. This creates an incentive to start work and another incentive to finish work that has been started. This solves the problem of reporting percent complete, and there should be few arguments about whether work has actually begun or has been completed on a project activity.

There are many variations of the 50-50 rule. Popular variations include the 20-80 rule and the 0-100 rule. These allow differing percentages of the earned value of the work to be claimed at the start and completion of the work.

Examples

In Figure 3-4, the EV is higher than the PV. This means that the project is ahead of schedule. More activities have been completed than were planned to be completed at this time. This can be good. The AC is higher than the PV as well. It is also higher than

Figure 3-4. Earned value example A.

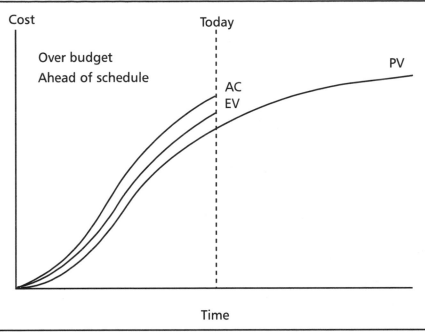

the EV. This means that we are spending more money to accomplish the work than we had planned, and we are spending more money to accomplish work than the EV for that work.

This could mean that the manager of this part of the project is working people overtime in anticipation of a problem that may come to pass in the near future. There could be many explanations for these irregularities. The report tells us that we should investigate to find out the cause for this.

In Figure 3-5, the EV is above the PV. Again, this means that the project is ahead of schedule. More activities are being completed, and their earned value is being credited faster than planned. The AC is lower than the EV. This means that we are spending less money than the earned value of the work that is being completed.

While this looks like a good situation—ahead of schedule and under budget—it is still not following the project plan. It is possible that things are just going well. It is also possible that some of the work is not being done as planned and that the quality of the work performed is suffering.

In Figure 3-6, the EV is less than the PV. This means that the project is behind schedule. The AC is less than the EV. This means that work is being accomplished with less cost than planned. A possible explanation for this situation is that the project is

Figure 3-5. Earned value example B.

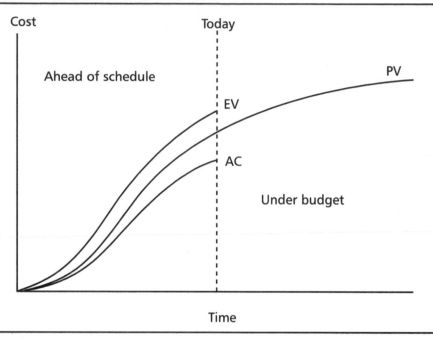

understaffed, but the people working on the tasks that are being done are doing a better-than-average job.

Calculated Values for Earned Value Reports

• *Budget at Completion (BAC)*. The BAC is a point representing the total budget of the project. On a cumulative plot it will be the last point on the PV curve. The PV cannot be greater than the BAC.

• *Cost Variance (CV)*

$$CV = EV - AC$$

This is the difference between the work that is actually completed and the cost expended to accomplish the work. A positive variance is good, and a negative variance is bad.

• *Schedule Variance (SV)*

$$SV = EV - PV$$

Figure 3-6. Earned value example C.

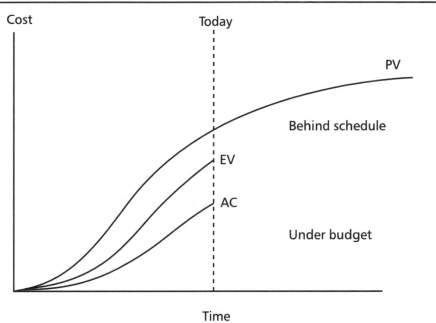

This is the difference between the work that was actually completed and the work that was expected to be completed at this time. A positive variance is good, and a negative variance is bad.

- *Cost Performance Index (CPI)*

$$CPI = EV / AC$$

- *Schedule Performance Index (SPI)*

$$SPI = EV / PV$$

Indexes are used when consistent numbers are required. Cost and schedule variance is measured in dollars. In a large project, say $100 million, a $100,000 cost or schedule variance might not be too significant, but in a small project, say $300,000, a $100,000 cost or schedule variance might be significant.

Cost and schedule variances also vary depending on what phase the project is in. Early in the project small variances may be significant, and later in the project these same size variances may not be terribly significant.

For this reason we use indexes. The values of indexes are the same for the same significance. The cost performance index is the EV divided by the AC. This is the amount of work accomplished per dollar of actual cost spent. The schedule performance index is the EV divided by the PV. This is the amount of work accomplished per dollar of budgeted cost expected to be spent.

• *Estimate at Completion (EAC)*

$$EAC = BAC / CPI$$

The EAC is an estimate of the project cost at the completion of the project. This is the BAC adjusted for current performance to date, cost wise. It says that if the project continues along at its present level of performance to cost, the EAC will be the final project cost. This is a pessimistic value since it says that the mistakes that have been made in the project are expected to continue for the remainder of the project.

This is often used for calculating the EAC. There are several other forms of the EAC that can be used that yield different results. One form is identical to the one above:

$$EAC = AC + Remaining\ PV / CPI$$

Since the remaining PV in the project is simply the difference between the total work that must be done to complete the project (the BAC) and the work that has been completed to date (the EV):

$$Remaining\ PV = BAC - EV$$

And the AC could be stated as:

$$AC = EV / CPI$$

The CPI is just EV / AC

Substituting, we get:

$$EAC = EV / CPI + (BAC - EV) / CPI$$
$$EAC = ((EV \times AC) / EV) + (BAC - EV) \times AC / EV$$
$$EAC = AC + ((BAC \times AC) / EV) - (EV \times AC) / EV$$
$$EAC = AC + BAC / CPI - AC$$
$$EAC = BAC / CPI$$

The above method for calculating the EAC is the one that is required for any questions on the PMP® examination. This method has been shown to represent the true EAC for most projects. Much research has been done to support the use of this calculation for EAC. The trouble with this calculation, while statistically supportable, is that your boss may not like it very much.

A more optimistic approach would be to assume that the mistakes on the project that have occurred so far are not going to continue and that the project from now on will go according to plan. It is the sum of the AC, which is what has been spent to date and cannot be improved on now, plus the amount of work remaining to be done.

$$EAC = AC + \text{Remaining PV}$$
$$EAC = AC + BAC - EV$$

Of course, the most optimistic view is that not only will the project improve its performance from now until the end of the project but also the expenditures over the budget to date will be recovered by the end of the project. This is a mistake often made by project managers. Generally speaking, if a project is over budget when 25 percent of the project is complete, the project will be completed with an over-budget condition greater than 25 percent, not less than 25 percent.

- *Estimate to Complete (ETC)*

$$ETC = EAC - AC$$

The ETC is the remaining budget required to complete the project if work continues at the present performance rate.

There are many other calculations used in the earned value reporting system, but these are the calculations that are accepted by most people (Table 3-2).

Financial Measures

The business risks of a project can be best understood by looking at some of the financial measurements that are commonly applied to business decisions. It is important to recognize that many of the costs associated with a project do not stop once the project has been delivered and each of the stakeholders has accepted the project.

The simplest way to think of project desirability is to consider the *benefit cost ratio:* all of the benefits of doing something divided by all of the costs to accomplish it. Any sort of business consideration can be evaluated with this simple measure. If the benefit cost ratio is 1.0 or greater, the project is desirable. If it is less than 1.0, the project is not desirable.

Life cycle costing is the cost and benefits of a project that begin when the first effort is made on behalf of the project and continue through the conceptual phase, the planning phase, the execution phase, the closeout phase, the warranty period, and on until the project is disposed of. When projects are delivered to the customer, there are many costs that will continue through the life of the project. Maintenance, service, additions, and modifications are items that will continue after delivery. Some of these will result in additional cost, such as warranty repairs, and others will result in additional benefits, such as additions and modifications.

"Sunk cost" is a term used to indicate the amount of money that has already been spent on a project. This is money that we no longer have any control over. Although it seems that if a project is currently very much over budget it would make sense to complete the project and collect the benefits, most financial managers hold that sunk costs should not be considered in making decisions as to whether to continue a project.

Table 3-2. Earned value example.

Week	PV	AC	EV	CV	SV	CPI	SPI	EAC	ETC
1	1,000	1,000	1,000	0	0	1.00	1.00	16,000.00	15,000.00
2	2,000	2,000	2,000	0	0	1.00	1.00	16,000.00	14,000.00
3	4,000	5,000	4,000	−1,000	0	0.80	1.00	20,000.00	15,000.00
4	7,000	8,000	6,000	−2,000	−1,000	0.75	0.86	21,333.33	13,333.33
5	10,000	12,000	9,000	−3,000	−1,000	0.75	0.90	21,333.33	9,333.33
6	12,000	13,000	11,000	−2,000	−1,000	0.85	0.92	18,909.09	5,909.09
7	13,000	14,000	11,500	−2,500	−1,500	0.82	0.88	19,478.26	5,478.26
8	14,000	14,500	13,000	−1,500	−1,000	0.90	0.93	17,846.15	3,346.15
9	15,000	15,000	14,500	−500	−500	0.97	0.97	16,551.72	1,551.72
10	16,000	16,000	15,500	−500	−500	0.97	0.97	16,516.13	516.13
11	16,000	17,000	16,000	−1,000	0	0.94	1.00	17,000.00	0.00
BAC	16,000								

For example, a $300,000 project is 50 percent complete but is over budget by 30 percent. Revenue from the project is estimated to be $350,000. Based on this information it is estimated that the project, when complete, will cost $400,000. Should the project be continued? If the project stops today, $200,000 is sunk cost, and no revenue is made. If the project is completed, a loss of $50,000 will occur. From the point of view of many managers, all other things being equal, it would be better to stop the project and invest the remaining $250,000 that it would have taken to complete the project in another project that is more profitable. Of course, customer commitments and future revenue based on the completion of this project may influence this decision.

Financial measures are rooted in the accounting and financial worlds. The first thing that must be understood is that the fundamental reports in accounting—the income statement and the balance sheet—are of particular interest to the project manager, since the project manager's decisions directly influence these reports. The current trend in project management is to make project managers responsible for the revenue cost and expenses of the project. These are the basic reports of accounting for any business. In these statements, the words *profit* and *income* are frequently interchanged. The reason that project managers must be aware of these financial measures is that if the financial measures applied to the project are favorable and the company can keep all of its projects favorable, then the company's financial measures will also be favorable. The fundamental accounting equation is:

Assets = Liabilities + Owner's Equity

Assets are the things that a company owns, like cash, buildings, materials, and so on. Liabilities are what a company owes, such as unpaid bills, long- and short-term debt, and so on. The owner's equity is the value of the assets after the liabilities have been subtracted. In the successful operation of a company, the company takes on liabilities in order to produce goods and services that are then sold. When the goods and services are sold there is, hopefully, a positive difference in revenue generated versus costs and expenses incurred to allow the goods and services to be sold. At the end of a project the assets that are increased should be greater than the liabilities incurred. To balance the accounting equation, this difference increases the owner's equity.

The income statement (Figure 3-7) shows where the cash flowing into and out of the company came from, and the net profit after taxes is the sum of all the money flowing into the company and all of the money flowing out of the company.

The balance sheet (Figure 3-8) is the statement that shows a breakdown of the items in the fundamental accounting equation. The assets must balance the liabilities and owner's equity.

Project managers have an influence on the numbers on the company's financial reports. But the company's reports are just the summation of the different projects and other activities of the company. It is therefore sensible to consider these financial measures

Figure 3-7. Income statement.

Gross sales
 Less cost of goods sold
= Gross profit
 Less operating expenses
  Salaries and commissions
  Rent expenses
  Depreciation
  Selling expenses
  Other operating expenses
= Net operating income
 Plus other income
  Interest revenue
 Less other expenses
  Interest expense
= Net income before taxes
 Less income tax
= Net income after taxes

as they apply to the individual projects as well. If all projects being done by the company are individually profitable, then the company itself must be profitable. These measures are frequently called financial ratios.

Return on Sales

Return on sales, or ROS, equals the net profit after taxes divided by the gross sales. This is another way of saying how much profit is generated for each dollar of sales. The higher the value of ROS the better. Typically, for American business this ratio is usually nearly 5 percent. Note that the net profit after taxes is what is left of the revenue after all costs, expenses, and taxes have been deducted. Net profit is sometimes called the net operating profit after taxes, or NOPAT.

For example, a project generates revenue of $400,000. After deducting the project's share of all the costs, expenses, and taxes, the net profit after taxes is $23,000.

$$ROS = NOPAT / Gross Revenue$$
$$ROS = \$23,000 / \$400,000$$
$$ROS = 5.75\%$$

Return on Assets

Return on assets, or ROA, equals the net profit after taxes divided by total assets. This is another way of saying how much profit was generated for each dollar of invest-

Figure 3-8. Balance sheet.

Assets:
    Current assets
        Cash
        Accounts receivable
        Inventory
        Prepaid expenses
    Fixed assets
        Plants and equipment
        Furniture and fixtures
        Less accumulated depreciation
        Total assets
Liabilities:
    Current liabilities
        Accounts payable
        Unpaid salaries
    Long-term liabilities
        Long-term debt
Owner's equity:
    Common stock
    Preferred stock
    Retained earnings

ment in the company. The higher the value of ROA the better. Typically, for American business, this value is nearly 9 percent. Since the assets of a company represent the money that is invested in the company, it is important to know how much profit is being made per dollar of investment.

For example, a project uses a share of the company's assets equal to $240,000. After deducting the project's share of all of the costs, expenses, and taxes, the net profit after taxes is $23,000.

$$ROA = NOPAT / Total\ Assets$$
$$ROA = \$23,000 / \$240,000$$
$$ROA = 9.6\%$$

Economic Value Added

The economic value added is also called the EVA. In this financial measurement we are interested in finding whether a project's NOPAT is sufficient to cover the cost of maintaining the assets that it uses. In other words, if a project uses a share of the company's assets, those assets have certain expenses associated with them. These expenses are the cost of interest on borrowed funds and the compensation paid to shareholders in the company. The rationale here is that the only way a company can acquire assets is by borrowing the money to purchase them, having investors purchase stock in the company, or generating profits. Organizations that lend money to companies are compensated in the form of interest payments. Stockholders are compensated in the form of dividends on their share of the company. The revenue generated by the project must be enough to meet all of the project's costs and expenses as well as offset the interest expense and dividends to the stockholders.

The first thing we will have to calculate is the cost of capital. This is the weighted average cost of the money paid to the stockholders in the form of dividends and the money paid to the lenders in the form of interest payments.

Suppose a company's assets are financed by 70 percent in stock sold to investors and 30 percent in funds borrowed from banks and other financial institutions in the form of loans. The average interest that is paid on the loans is 7 percent, and the company dividends are 17 percent. What is the cost of capital for this company?

Seventy dollars out of every $100 of the company's assets are financed by stockholders at 17 percent, or $11.90 per year. Thirty dollars of every $100 of the company's assets are financed by lenders at 7 percent, or $2.10 per year. The total cost of capital per $100 is $14, or 14 percent of the company's assets.

If we take the capital or the assets that are used for this project and multiply by the cost of capital, we will get the *weighted average cost of capital* (WACC).

Let's say that the capital that the project uses is $500,000 and the cost of capital is 14 percent:

$$\text{WACC} = \$500,000 \times 14\% = \$70,000$$

If the net operating profit after taxes is $116,000:

$$\text{EVA} = \text{NOPAT} - \text{WACC}$$
$$\text{EVA} = \$116,000 - \$70,000$$

Project economic value added, or EVA, would be $46,000.

Depreciation

Depreciation is a necessary function in financial management, because without depreciation the irregularities in the fundamental financial reports of a company would vary considerably and make it difficult to compare one year or one quarter to the next. This is because large investments in assets do not occur on a regular basis. If the total cost of an investment were reflected in the financial time period in which it occurred, the effect on net profits would be considerable in this period, and then the net profit would rise significantly in the next period.

What is done with depreciation? The cost of the new asset is spread out over the life of the asset. This allows the company to claim some of the cost each year rather than the total cost of the asset all at one time.

Straight Line Depreciation

Straight line depreciation is the depreciation method that allows an equal amount of depreciation to be taken each year. The amount of depreciation is determined by subtracting the salvage value of the asset at the end of its useful life from the purchase price of the asset. The remaining value is called the book value. The book value is divided by the number of years, and this amount is expensed from the asset each year.

For example, a company buys a large machine for $1 million. The purchase is made with cash. In the accounts for this transaction, the cash account is reduced by $1 million, and the machine account is increased by the amount of $1 million. There is no effect on the liabilities or the owner's equity side of the accounting equation, and it remains balanced. The cost of this machine must eventually be recognized.

The machine has a useful life of ten years and is worth $100,000 at the end of its useful life in terms of scrap value or the ability to sell the machine to someone else. This means that the value of the machine that must be depreciated is $900,000. Since the life of the machine is ten years, the value depreciated each year is $90,000. This is known as straight line depreciation (Table 3-3).

Accelerated Depreciation

Accelerated depreciation methods are used to allow the expenses that are depreciated from the assets to be applied earlier in the useful life of the asset. The reason for this is to

Table 3-3. Straight line depreciation.

Year	Purchase Price	Salvage Value	Depreciation	Current Book Value
0	1,000,000	100,000	0	900,000
1			90,000	810,000
2			90,000	720,000
3			90,000	630,000
4			90,000	540,000
5			90,000	450,000
6			90,000	360,000
7			90,000	270,000
8			90,000	180,000
9			90,000	90,000
10			90,000	0
		Total	900,000	

reduce the net profit after taxes (NOPAT). If NOPAT is reduced in a given year, the amount of tax that a company pays is less by this amount.

In accelerated depreciation methods the total amount of depreciation is the same as in straight line depreciation, but the time that it is taken is much earlier in the useful life of the asset. This means that more equipment expense is recognized and lower taxes are paid in the early part of the useful life of the asset purchased. In later years the taxes will be higher than in straight line depreciation. Because of the present value of the money, taxes that are deferred to later years allow us to use that money in the present years.

Two types of accelerated depreciation are commonly used: sum of the years' digits and double declining balances.

Sum of the Years' Digits. There is no scientific basis for the sum of the years' digits method. There is no financial reason for using this calculation except that it has become a standard accounting practice.

The calculation is made by totaling the digits representing the years of the useful life of the equipment. Thus, as can be seen in Table 3-4, for a ten-year useful life, the total is 55 (10 + 9 + 8 + 7 + 6 + 5 + 4 + 3 + 2 + 1 = 55).

The amount of depreciation in the first year is determined by taking the highest digit year and dividing this by the sum of the years' digits. In the first year, the last year's digit is used, making the calculation 10 divided by 55. This number is then multiplied by the book value.

In the remaining years, the next lower year's digit is used. In the second year, the depreciation is calculated by dividing 9 by 55. Each year the numerator declines by one year.

Table 3-4.   Sum of the years' digits.

Year	Purchase Price	Salvage Value	Sum of Year Digits	Depreciation	Current Book Value
0	1,000,000	100,000		0	900,000
1			10/55	163,636	736,364
2			9/55	147,273	589,091
3			8/55	130,909	458,182
4			7/55	114,545	343,636
5			6/55	98,182	245,455
6			5/55	81,818	163,636
7			4/55	65,455	98,182
8			3/55	49,091	49,091
9			2/55	32,727	16,364
10			1/55	16,364	0
				Total 900,000	

Double Declining Balances. Like the sum of the years' digits depreciation, there is no scientific basis for the double declining balance calculation either. It is, however, a consistent method for accelerating the depreciation of equipment and has become a standard accounting practice.

The percent of depreciation is taken on the depreciable value of the item. The next year's depreciation is taken on the remaining depreciable value of the item, and so on until the salvage value is reached. With this method the amount taken as depreciation in the early years is much higher than in the later years (Table 3-5).

Summary

Cost management is a necessary part of project management, for it makes it possible to manage the cost baseline of the project. Without cost management, projects would use more or less money than allocated, and it would be impossible to fund future projects. The project manager, as in all things, is the person responsible for project cost management.

The work breakdown structure is the basis for the cost estimate. Since the WBS identifies all of the project work in a detailed workable way, it becomes the best place to determine the cost of the project. A cost estimate done this way produces a detailed estimate that can be rolled "bottom up" to any level of detail desired.

Cost estimating is done over the life of the project. In the beginning of the project only a small amount of information is known about the project and inaccurate estimates

Table 3-5. Double declining balances.

Year	Purchase Price	Salvage Value	50% Depreciation	Current Book Value
0	1,000,000	100,000	0	900,000
1			450,000	450,000
2			225,000	225,000
3			112,500	112,500
4			56,250	56,250
5			28,125	28,125
6			14,063	14,063
7			7,031	7,031
8			3,516	3,516
9			1,758	1,758
10			879	879
			Total 899,121	

are appropriate. In the creation of baselines for cost and schedule it is important that definitive, 5 percent to 10 percent estimates be reached.

Cost control in project management is best achieved through the use of the earned value reporting system. This reporting system makes it possible to measure performance to schedule and performance to budget in the same system. Project performance over or under budget is measured in dollars. Project performance ahead or behind schedule is measured in dollars.

In addition to the earned value reporting system, the project manager must face many of the financial decisions that a small-business manager must face and be aware of the financial world of reporting.

CHAPTER 4

Quality Management

One of the goals of project management is to meet the expectations of the stakeholders of the project. Managing the quality of the project is the function that will allow this to happen. Quality management will include all the work that is necessary to ensure that each of the objectives of the project is met. In the latest edition of the *Guide to the Project Management Body of Knowledge*, PMI emphasizes that the purpose of the project is to meet the requirements of the stakeholders. In the past, the project goal was to meet or exceed the customer's expectations.

Quality should be concerned with prevention rather than detection. The cost of preventing a defect in our project is much less than the cost of finding a defect and correcting it. Worse, the cost of not finding a defect and having to correct it in the field is even higher.

We have discussed methods of controlling the project costs and schedule in Chapter 2, Time Management, and Chapter 3, Cost Management. These controls cover only two of the sides of the triple constraint triangle. Quality management controls the third side of the triangle, scope, as well as provides guidance for and assurance of meeting the other two constraints of cost and schedule.

It is important in modern project management to meet the stakeholders' expectations. It is also important that the expectations of the stakeholders are not exceeded. The customer contracts for certain deliverables; delivering something that was not asked for can be a waste of time and money. In some cases delivering more than is asked for can make matters worse.

Quality should not be confused with grade. Quality that is low is always going to be a problem, while a low grade is not necessarily a bad condition. A product may be developed and marketed to appeal to those who want an inexpensive product that will have a limited useful life and functionality. This product may also have a lower cost.

Stakeholders should get what they pay for. The quality of the item means that it is indeed what it was intended to be.

Project quality management addresses both the quality of the project and the quality of the product that is produced. The quality management of projects is generally the same for all projects, but the quality management of the product produced by the project will vary with the application. What we mean by this is that the measurements and techniques that are used to ensure the quality of the construction of a tool shed will be different from the measurements and techniques for ensuring the quality of the construction of a nuclear power plant.

The *Guide to the PMBOK* defines three processes for quality management: quality planning, quality assurance, and quality control. It is important that a distinction be made among them.

The *quality planning function* is the process that determines which quality standards should be used to accomplish the goal of ensuring that the scope of the project fulfills the stakeholders' expectations.

The *quality assurance function* is a process that monitors the overall ability of the project to meet the expectations of the stakeholders. The purpose of the quality assurance function is to provide the confidence that the project will have the proper controls to be able to meet the standards that are expected by the stakeholders. The quality assurance function ensures that the quality of the project will be sufficient.

The *quality control function* is the process used to measure the specific items that must be monitored to determine that the project will meet the stakeholders' expectations.

The philosophy of modern quality management is that mistakes should be prevented rather than detected. It is much better to create an environment that prevents mistakes from happening rather than to spend much time and effort trying to detect problems that may have already occurred. "You can't inspect quality into a product" is the phrase used to state this idea.

Quality Planning

The quality planning process must accomplish several things if the project is to be successful. It involves identifying all of the standards that are relevant to the project. For environmental issues, all government regulations, rules, standards, and guidelines specific to the specific project must be considered. There must be an overall quality policy, or company guidelines, regarding projects of this type. Generally, this is the common policy that will be used by all projects that the company will accomplish. Each project and each interrelated project must modify the guidelines and gain approval on changes that will be required for a particular project.

The result of the quality planning process is the *quality plan*. This plan describes how the quality of the project will be assured and the functions that will be carried out by the project team to accomplish this. The plan also serves to provide the additional activities that will be added to the project scope, budget, and schedule that will allow these things to happen.

The quality plan should reflect the information that is gathered throughout the project. All of the other areas of the management of the project should complement the quality plan. Risk is of major importance in the quality plan. Areas of the project that are high in risk should have a significant influence on the quality plan. The quality planning function will produce the quality metrics that will be used to measure the quality of the project in very specific terms.

It is important that a continuous process improvement plan be developed. This plan details how the project processes will be measured and how the processes can be analyzed so that continuous improvements can be made and measured. This could include the process boundaries, configurations, and metrics as well as targets for improved performance.

Quality Assurance

The *Guide to the PMBOK* defines quality assurance as:

> The application of planned and systematic quality activities to ensure that the project will employ all processes needed to meet all stakeholder expectations and provide the confidence that the product of the project will fulfill the requirements of quality.

Quality audits are performed to review certain important areas of the project. Audits make it possible to determine what is happening in the project and whether the project quality is meeting the standards that were determined in the quality plan.

The quality assurance function includes the means to continuously improve the quality of future projects as well. Lessons learned from one project are applied to the quality plans of future projects so that there can be an ever-improving level of quality in projects completed by the organization.

Each member of the project team, including each of the stakeholders of the project, is essential to the quality assurance of the project. In modern thinking on quality it is the individual person performing work who is really responsible for assuring the quality of the product.

Cost of Quality

As in all things in project management, there should be a favorable ratio of benefits and cost to quality (Figure 4-1). This is usually referred to as prevention rather than cure.

Figure 4-1. Economics of quality.

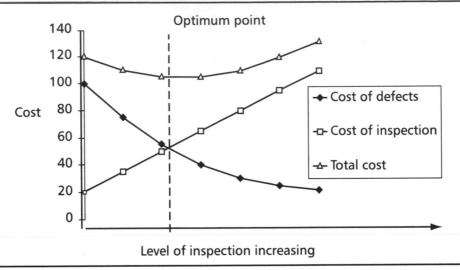

The total cost of curing a problem once it has occurred is generally higher than the cost of preventing the problem in the first place. It is apparent that the potential savings between the cost of defects and the cost of prevention are great. Generally, many of the costs of defects are not recognized in an organized way to reflect their true cost. This is because when some of the costs of these defects are recognized, the project has been turned over to a maintenance and support function. The project team may have been dissolved, and the members may be working on other projects.

As in other projects, a cost-benefit analysis of the proposed methods of implementing quality should be done on each of the proposed methods. According to Edward Deming, "Eighty-five percent of the costs of quality is the direct responsibility of management."

The following is a listing of the considerations for these costs:

Costs of Prevention

- Additional planning
- Education and training of project team and stakeholders
- Inspection and testing of the internal and external deliverables of the project
- Improved designs for quality purposes
- Quality staff
- Quality audits
- Quality plan and execution

Costs of Defects

- Scrap
- Rework
- Repair
- Replacement of defective parts and inventory
- Repairs after the delivery of the product
- Loss of future business with the stakeholder
- Legal issues for nonconformance
- Liability for defect
- Risk to life and property

Deming's Fourteen Points

Edward Deming is probably best known for his fourteen points on quality (Figure 4-2). These guidelines were developed during Deming's work with Japanese industries and serve as a guideline for the practice of practical quality management.

Quality Control

The function of quality control is to monitor specific project results to ensure that the results match the standards that were set for the project. The quality control function utilizes a number of techniques to accomplish this. Many of these tools and techniques are rooted in the concepts of probability and statistics.

Figure 4-2. Deming's fourteen points.

• Constancy of purpose	• Drive out fear
• Adopt a new philosophy	• Break down barriers
• Eliminate need for inspection	• Eliminate slogans, targets, and the like
• Only consider total cost, not price	• Eliminate management by standards and quotas
• Improve constantly	• Remove barriers to pride of workmanship
• Initiate OJT	• Institute education and self-improvement
• Initiate leadership	• Get everyone involved

Many times statistical methods are used in project quality control. These techniques can improve the performance of those involved in quality control by allowing less than 100 percent inspection of all of the products produced.

As a result of a good quality control program recommended corrective and preventive actions will be generated as well as recommendations for the repair of defects and inspection methods for the later repaired defect.

Inspection

Inspection is carried out by the observation of attributes or measurements. An item that is supposed to be a certain size can be measured directly, and the data regarding its dimensional size can be collected. All items accepted will be within the acceptable allowed tolerance on the item.

Items may also be inspected by *attribute*. In this technique the item to be inspected is made to fit or not fit into a specially designed gauge or special measuring device. If the part fits into the "Go" gauge and does not fit into the "No Go" gauge, then the part is acceptable. If the part does not fit into the "Go" gauge or fits into the "No Go" gauge, the part is considered to be bad. All attribute inspections have a *yes* or *no* outcome.

Attribute sampling has several advantages over measurement methods. In attribute sampling the inspection is fast and cheap, and there is little room for mistakes on the part of the inspector. Measurements take a certain amount of skill and concentration. As such, measurements are prone to human errors stemming from fatigue and boredom.

For example, suppose a motor shaft has a design tolerance of 1.5 inches and an allowable tolerance of plus or minus .015 inches for its diameter. This means that an acceptable part will have to be between 1.515 and 1.485 inches.

To test this attribute, a gauge is constructed with a hole that has a diameter of exactly 1.515 inches. This is a "Go" gauge. Parts that have a diameter of less than 1.515 inches will fit into this gauge, and those that are larger than 1.515 inches will not fit.

Another gauge is constructed with a hole of 1.485 inches in diameter. Parts that fit into this gauge will be unacceptable, since their diameter is less than 1.485 inches. This is the "No Go" gauge.

The inspection of shafts is quick, easy, and nearly foolproof. A part is taken and first applied to the "Go" gauge. If it passes this gauge, it is immediately put into the "No Go" gauge. If it fails to fit this gauge, it is an acceptable part.

Sampling Inspection

Unless there are unusual requirements for extreme quality, as when death can result from a defective part, most customers will accept a certain amount of defects. The reason for this is stated in the law of diminishing returns. As the desire to locate each and every defect is satisfied, it becomes more and more costly to find them. One hundred percent inspections are expensive and require much time and effort. In 100 percent inspections there is also the problem of the inspection itself causing damage to some of the parts. This entire concept is based on the fact that the customer is willing to accept a small number of defective parts rather than pay the high cost of trying to locate each and every defect.

This policy of allowing a few unacceptable parts must be considered carefully. The ultimate use of the parts must be considered. In particular, it is important that the part that is defective not create danger to life. There can be no value placed on a human life, and many court cases have awarded large settlements against companies that attempted to do so.

For this reason, *statistical sampling* was developed. Without going into the statistical details that support sampling inspection, it can be described. Sampling inspection plans have been worked out and are available to quality managers to determine the parameters desired and to set up an inspection plan that will fit the type of work that they are doing.

In a sampling inspection, the sample size to be taken and inspected from a given lot size is determined. A sample size of fifteen parts may be taken from a lot of parts. Again, according to precalculated procedures, the fifteen-piece sample can contain no more than three unacceptable parts. If fewer than three parts in the sample are unacceptable, the lot passes, and if more than three parts are unacceptable, then the lot is rejected.

Acceptable Quality Level (AQL)

The rationale behind this technique is that if the acceptable quality level (AQL) was 3 percent and a sample of fifteen parts was taken from a lot of a thousand parts, there would be a very small chance that some of the bad parts would show up in the sample. If more than three parts were to show up in the sample, it could be said that the whole lot had more bad parts than the 3 percent allowed by the AQL.

Because discovering all of the defective parts can be a very costly process, most customers and suppliers agree that a certain level of defects is to be allowed in the normal process. As long as this acceptable quality level is maintained, the lot of parts is acceptable to the customer. The AQL says that a lot that has fewer than 3 percent bad parts in it is acceptable.

Buyer's Risk and Seller's Risk

When we perform sampling inspections, there is a risk that the sample will give misleading information. There are four possible outcomes to this inspection process. The possibilities are:

1. The lot is good, and the sample inspection says that it is good. This is what we want.

2. The lot is good, and the sample inspection says that it is not good. This is not what we want.
3. The lot is bad, and the sample inspection says that it is good. This is not what we want.
4. The lot is bad, and the sample inspection says that it is bad. This is what we want.

If the sampling inspection accepts a lot that is good or rejects a lot that is bad, then the inspection process is working. If the sampling process accepts a lot that is really bad, this means that a lot that is really unacceptable is shipped as a good lot to the customer. This is called "buyer's risk" (see Figure 4-3). If the sampling process rejects a lot that is really good, this means that a lot that is really acceptable is rejected. This is called "seller's risk."

Other Quality Control Techniques

Flowcharts and Diagrams
Flowcharts can be helpful in understanding the cause and effect relationships between the process of performing work and the results that are inspected through measurement or attribute inspection. A flowchart is simply an organized way to look at the steps that have to be carried out to perform some goal. There are many techniques and styles of flowcharting.

Cause and Effect Diagrams
The cause and effect diagram, also known as the *fishbone diagram* because of its appearance, was developed by Kaoru Ishikawa. This is a way of diagramming the flow of work that is useful in determining the cause and effect of problems that are encountered.

As can be seen in Figure 4-4, the process is separated logically into branches. Each of the branches can be dealt with separately. If the work on one branch is excessive, a separate meeting may be used to investigate it or any other branches requiring input from more people or more time to consider the branch.

Like the work breakdown structure, the cause and effect diagram allows for an orderly consideration of each of the possible causes of a problem and then allows for the consideration of each effect and the solution that will reduce the problem.

Pareto Charts
Vilfredo Pareto is given credit for developing the concept of 80–20 rule. He was an economist who found that typically 80 percent of the wealth of a region was concentrated in 20 percent of the population. This concept describes a number of phenomena that

Figure 4-3. Seller's risk versus buyer's risk.

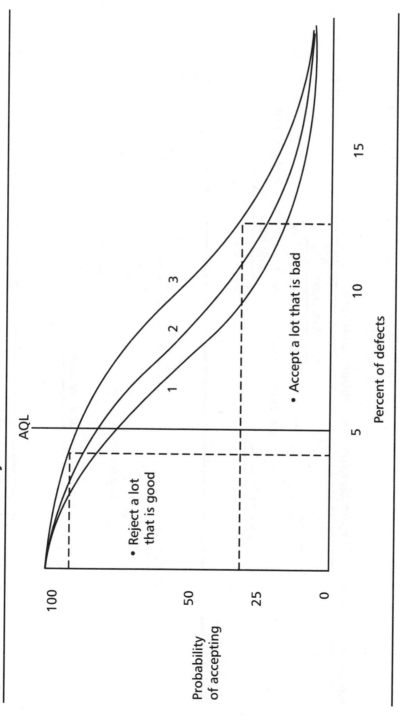

Figure 4-4. Cause and effect diagram, or fishbone diagram.

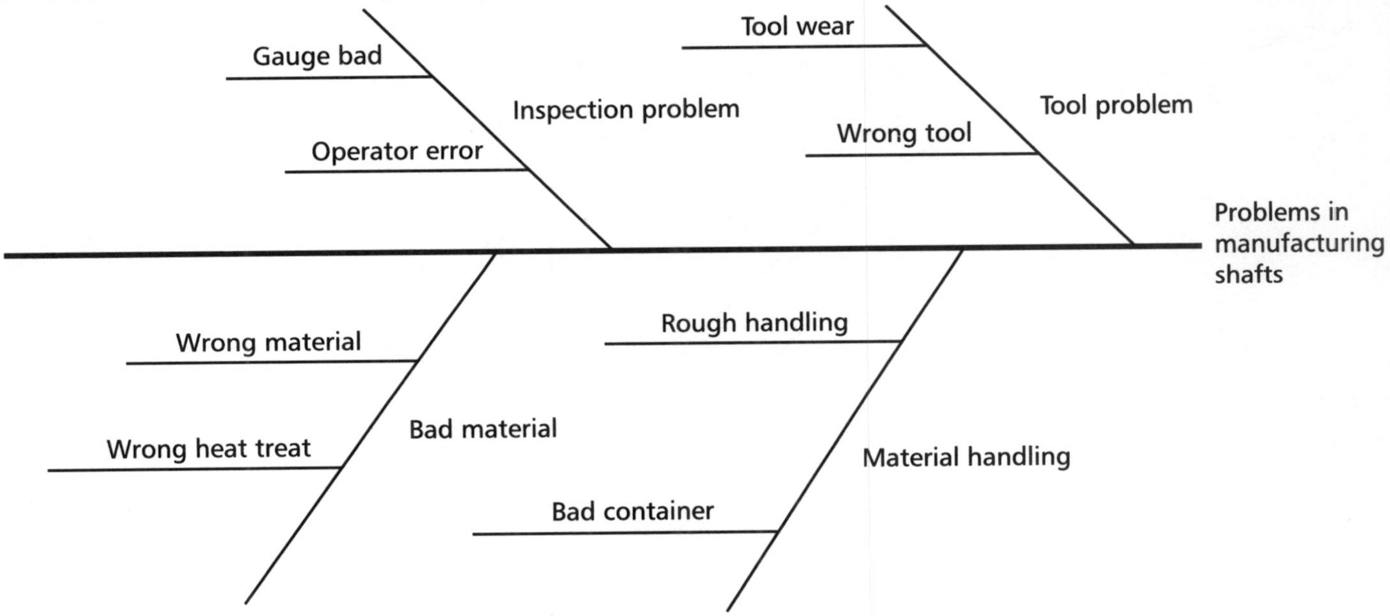

occur in the real world. In terms of quality, it can be said that 80 percent of the cost of defects is caused by 20 percent of the problems. In other words, if there were one hundred possible things that could be considered to be defects in a process, 20 percent, or twenty of the problems, will account for 80 percent of the cost.

By identifying these twenty items it is possible to expend the energy of the organization where it will do the most good. In quality control, as well as in many areas of project management, it is important that the always limited effort available in the organization be concentrated on the problems where the most benefits will result.

The Pareto chart is a simple way of determining the places where this effort might be concentrated. The problems in a process are arranged in the order of importance and are generally arranged by ranking according to the most important factors, such as cost, time delay, or some other parameter (Table 4–1; Figure 4-5).

It can be plainly seen that problem "a" is the most serious problem and will have the greatest effect on the process if it is solved. If problem "a" is solved, we can redraw the Pareto chart to show the improvement (Table 4–2; Figure 4-6).

Control Charts

Control charts are used to determine whether the observed variations in a process are due to normal process variations or whether they are due to the process getting out of control. Control charts allow the observations to be interpreted in such a way as to allow corrections to the process prior to the process producing bad output.

In order to accomplish this goal, the known variations must be determined first. This is done by measuring the dimensions in question on a group of known parts. A lot

Table 4-1. **Ranking of problems.**

Defect	Frequency of Occurrence	Cumulative	Percent of Total Defects by Defect
a	100	100	34.014
b	90	190	30.612
c	30	220	10.204
d	22	242	7.483
e	17	259	5.782
f	14	273	4.762
g	11	284	3.741
h	5	289	1.701
i	3	292	1.020
j	2	294	0.680
Total	294		

Figure 4-5. Pareto chart.

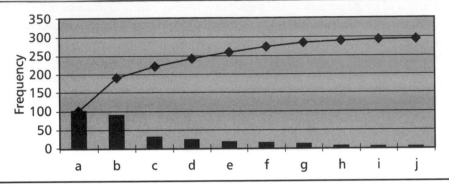

Table 4-2.   Ranking of problems (after solving "a").

Defect	Frequency of Occurrence	Cumulative	Percent of Total Defects by Defect
b	90	90	46.392
c	30	120	15.464
d	22	142	11.340
e	17	159	8.763
f	14	173	7.216
g	11	184	5.670
h	5	189	2.577
i	3	192	1.546
j	2	194	1.031
Total	194		

Figure 4-6. Pareto chart (after solving "a").

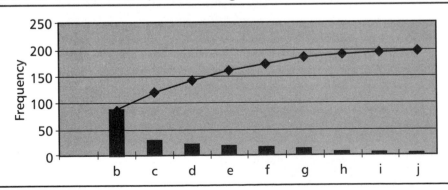

is selected that is known to be acceptable. The dimension is measured on each of the parts, and the mean and standard deviation of the dimension is determined.

By determining the mean and standard deviation of the group of parts we can define the probability distribution of this dimension. In the area of quality we are normally interested in maintaining process control to plus or minus 3 standard deviations. This means that if we consider the dimension of the part in question and the process is under control, then 99.7 percent of the parts coming out of the process should fall in the dimensional range of plus or minus 3 standard deviations from the mean value dimension. If a part is measured and found to be outside this range of values, we have cause for concern. This is a concern even though the part dimensions could still be well within the engineering design tolerance of the part's dimensions.

The control chart is constructed by marking the middle line as the mean value. The upper and lower control limits are determined by adding and subtracting three times the standard deviation of the measurement of the part (Figure 4-7).

If parts are later measured and found to be greater or less than the upper and lower control limits specified, then the process is considered to be out of control and to have an assignable cause. This assignable cause should be investigated to determine what the problem is and appropriate corrective action should be taken. Normally, the upper and lower control limits are less than the engineering dimensional part tolerance for this dimension.

Frequently, a guideline to the use of the control chart is the "rule of seven." If there

Figure 4-7. Control chart.

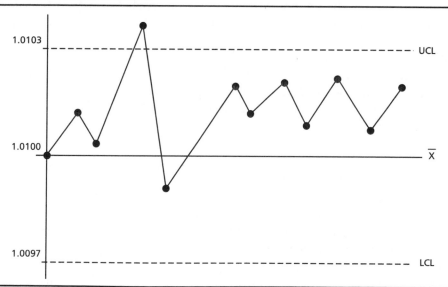

are seven or more points in succession that are either above or below the mean value there is cause for concern about the process. This is because the probability of there being seven measurements in a row that are all on the same side of the mean value is very small, and therefore, it can be concluded that the process is no longer functioning properly.

For example, suppose a part is designed to have a dimension of 1.000 inches, with a tolerance of plus or minus .005 inches. A group of parts are made after the process has been developed and stabilized and been in operation for several hundred parts. These parts are individually measured for this dimension. The mean and standard deviation for the group of parts is determined.

As seen in Figure 4-7, the mean value is found to be 1.0100 inches and the standard deviation is found to be .0001 inches. The upper control limit can be set at 1.0103 inches, and the lower control limit can be set at 1.0097.

Notice that the mean value of the process is not necessarily the nominal dimension on the engineering specification. This is because the process engineer in this situation has determined to run the process deliberately on the high side of the dimension. By taking this approach, if the process goes out of control and bad parts are made, there is a greater chance that the bad parts can be reworked by re-machining them. This is a better alternative than scrapping parts that are too small.

Run Charts

Run charts are simple diagrams that are used to plot an attribute of a product. These are similar to control charts except that upper and lower control limits are not used. Periodically an observation is made of a characteristic attribute. The observation is recorded. Over time, trends may be seen and a history of the observed characteristic is made. Run charts are frequently done prior to the calculation of the control limits of a control chart.

Checklists

Checklists are a sample tool that is used to keep from overlooking items of importance. A checklist is really just an instruction sheet for an inspector to use. The items in the checklist should be significant items. If a checklist is seen as a superfluous document, it will not be used.

Kaizen

Kaizen is one of the many quality techniques that come to us from the work of the Japanese. The Japanese word for continuous improvement is *kaizen*. Using this method, the managers as well as the workers and everyone else are continuously on the lookout for opportunities to improve quality. Thus the quality of a process improves in small increments on a continuous basis.

In this kaizen way of doing things, even the processes that are operating without problems are continuously under scrutiny. A process is observed to be making acceptable parts, but is seen to be slow, or there is an opportunity for even greater quality than is required.

Benchmarking

Benchmarking is the process of comparing the performance of a current process to that of another similar process to determine the differences between them. If a machine can manufacture two hundred parts an hour and a new machine is compared to the old machine, the benchmark for the existing process on the old machine is two hundred parts per hour.

Summary

Quality management is one of the most important aspects of project management. It is the "stuff" that holds a project together. We must have excellent quality in the projects that we produce. Quality management is the process that ensures that we produce each of the deliverables of the project. The three areas of quality management that we are concerned with are quality planning, quality assurance, and quality control.

The cost of quality is actually the profit of quality. The cost of preventing quality problems is less than the cure of having to correct the problem once it has occurred. The savings that are realized in a good quality management plan more than offset the cost of its implementation.

Quality control is the implementation of various control techniques. Various inspection techniques are implemented to prevent defects in processes as well as to prevent the customer from receiving parts that are defective. The acceptable quality level, or AQL, is the allowed number of defective parts that can be delivered without the entire shipment or lot being considered to be bad. This is because trying to produce 100 percent perfect parts becomes very expensive as the 100 percent mark is neared. Buyer's risk is the risk that a lot of parts that is unacceptable will be accepted by sampling inspection. Seller's risk is the possibility that a lot of parts that is truly acceptable will be rejected.

Sampling inspection is a statistical method of inspecting large numbers of parts. It is based on the probability that if there is a certain percentage of defects in a large lot, the probability of finding them can be determined statistically.

Quality is one of the areas in which a remarkable amount of money can be saved. This is because we not only save the direct and observable cost of defective goods and services to our customer, but we save in lost goodwill and future problems that defects bring about.

In the area of project management we must be vigilant and hold to good quality standards at all times, because failure to adhere to good quality practices could end with the ruination of the organization.

CHAPTER 5

Human Resources Management

Human resources management is required to make the most efficient use of the project human resources. This includes all of the people involved in the project—the stakeholders, sponsors, customers, other departments, the project team, subcontractors, and all others.

Organizational planning involves the organizing of the human resources. These are the roles, responsibilities, and relationships of the people who are on the project team. As in all things in project management, human resources management takes place throughout the project. If at any time the project organization needs to be revised, the human resources plan will assist in carrying this out.

On large projects there may be a core team, sometimes called the executive or leadership team, which is responsible for the planning, controlling, and closing of the project. On smaller projects a more participative team is used, with all of the members of the project team participating to get these things done.

With all of this in mind the jobs that must be done relevant to the project from the standpoint of human resources are to create a human resources plan, acquire and develop a project team, and manage that team properly.

Normally on projects, human resources administration is not the responsibility of the project team. There is usually some functional department such as a human resources department that has the responsibility for contracts, employee benefits, and the like. Project managers and project teams should be aware of the human resources functions because the trend in companies using project management is to increase the responsibility of project managers and their teams. The analogy is that projects should be managed like small businesses where the proprietor of the business has many different responsibilities.

Project Manager Roles and Responsibilities

It is a long-standing joke in the project management community that if anyone ever asks you who is responsible for anything in the project, the answer will always be the project manager. Truly it is easier to specify what the project manager does not do than to discuss what he or she actually does and is responsible for.

The nature and scope of the project should dictate the individual roles and responsibilities of the project team. When all of the team assignments and responsibilities have been decided, all of the functions and responsibilities of the project will have been assigned. The responsibility-accountability matrix is useful for determining and tracking the relationship between a given responsibility and who is responsible for it.

Responsibility-Accountability Matrix

As can be seen in Figure 5-1, the responsibility-accountability matrix is a short notational form that allows us to easily see the relationship between the individuals on a project

Figure 5-1. Responsibility-accountability matrix.

	Joe	Mary	Frank	Louie
Requirements definition	S	R	A	P
Functional design	S		A	P
Detail design	S		R	A
Development		R	S	A
Testing			S	P

Key:
P—Participates
A—Accountable
R—Reviews
I—Input required
S—Sign off

team and their responsibilities. Various levels of the responsibility-accountability matrix may be developed for various parts and levels of the project. These are quite simple. The persons involved are listed in the first column on the left and the responsibilities are listed in a row across the top. For each person-responsibility combination there is an intersecting space. The intersection shows the person and their involvement in the responsibility. A third dimension can be shown with a legend listing the different ways that a person can be involved and using symbols at the intersection to show the involvement.

Project Schedule

The project manager, in order to determine when activities are supposed to take place in the project, uses the project schedule (Figure 5-2). It constitutes the schedule for the work that has to be done. Of course, people are involved with the work that has to be done. The project manager in a matrix organization draws the people from the functional organization.

Staffing Plan

Referring to Figure 5-3, the functional manager must have a staffing plan that allows him or her to know where the people in the functional organization are committed. If these commitments are not organized, the utilization of the human resources will be poor. A staffing plan for the functional manager is similar to the project schedule, except that instead of showing the schedule for each task in the project, it shows the schedule for each resource in the functional manager's responsibility.

It is important that the project manager and the functional manager have a clear understanding as to who is being moved to the project to perform work for the project and when they are scheduled to do it. The staffing plan communicates this information very well, and the employees and both managers as well as other project managers seeking resources can easily see what is going on.

Training Plan

Sometimes the project work requires skills that are not available. In these situations it may be necessary for a project to accept a resource who lacks the proper training for the work. A training plan is necessary to support the training for this type of individual.

Figure 5-2. Project schedule.

Task 1	☐	Richard Cordes
Task 2	☐	Jeanette Williams
Task 3	☐	Nancy Brown

Figure 5-3. Staffing plans.

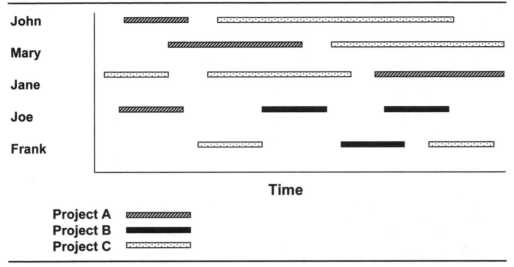

Organization Chart

Hierarchical organization charts are the traditional "Org. Charts" that we are all used to. They show the reporting hierarchy from the bottom of the project organization to the project manager. It is important that these charts be circulated widely so that any misunderstandings about who reports to whom can be avoided. The *Organizational Breakdown Structure* (OBS) is the hierarchical organization chart of the existing departments and their responsibilities, while the *Resource Breakdown Structure* (RBS) is the arrangement of the project by the types of resources employed by the project.

For example, if we had a project to build a ship to transport people to Mars, in the OBS we might have departments responsible for the structure, propulsion, electronics, navigation, and many more. Each of these units may be located in different places or even different cities, and all of them may employ one or more skills that are used in other departments. In the case of the RBS, the resources are organized according to similar skills organized into categories.

Strong Matrix, Weak Matrix, and Balanced Matrix Organizations

Strong Matrix

In a strong matrix organization the project manager has greater authority or power than the functional manager. In this situation, project managers generally get the people they want. In fact the project managers in this type of organization get more than they should. A manager who is assertive will usually get the personnel he or she wants. The functional manager is not able to overcome the project manager's authority and is not free to assign people where their talent is best utilized.

If this type of organization becomes stronger, most if not all of the personnel will be working on projects, and project managers will be able to draw more highly qualified people than are really needed for their projects. The surplus personnel are traded between the project managers themselves, bypassing the functional managers altogether. In this type of organization the project manager has strong authority.

Weak Matrix

In the weak matrix organization, the project manager does not have as much power as the functional manager. This usually occurs in organizations that are moving into matrix management for the first time. The situation occurs something like this: The company's chief executive officer (CEO) decides that matrix management is the thing for the company to do. Almost overnight an attempt is made to change the organization from a functional organization to a matrix management.

When this happens, there is a reaction from the functional managers. After all, these are the major human assets in the company. They would not be in a position of authority if they were not good managers.

The functional managers see the problem in the new organization. In the past, they had responsibility for the administration as well as the directing of work in their part of the organization. Under matrix management they no longer direct some of the work that their people are doing. The fact that project managers will direct that work is a threat to the functional managers. The salary that the company is going to pay the project managers is going to come from someplace. Most likely it is going to come from cuts in functional managers' salary. The functional managers react by convincing the upper management of the company to allow the project managers only to recommend work to be done, and to let the functional managers continue to actually direct the work.

This form of matrix management can be used if there is a transition going on. In the beginning of the transition to matrix management, the project managers are new and inexperienced. As they gain experience, they should be given more authority over the people who report to them. At the same time, the functional managers can be transitioned out of the organization and promoted into higher and more responsible jobs. As the functional managers move on, more appropriate administrative managers can replace them, and direction of the work can be managed by the project manager.

Balanced Matrix

In the balanced matrix organization, the power levels of the functional manager and the project manager are in balance. By that I mean that the functional manager cannot force the project manager, and the project manager cannot force the functional manager. The functional manager makes the decisions about where the people in his or her department will be assigned, and the project manager works with the functional manager to recruit the proper person for the project assignment.

A balancing rule can be applied. By setting a specific interval of time as a requirement for moving a person to the project team, balance can be achieved. For example, a person who is required to work full time on a project for two months is transferred to the project, while persons who are required to work less than two months remain in their functional department, and under the supervision of the functional manager. Persons working longer than two months would be physically moved to the project space and would return to the functional area when the work is completed. The project manager authorizes any work to be done in the functional area by generating a work order or some other device.

By adjusting the balance point, more or less work can be made to happen in the functional areas. If more work is being handled on the project, the project manager has more people reporting to him or her, increasing the project manager's power level. At one extreme we have a strong matrix, where the length of time required to move a person to the project team is very short. At the other extreme we have a weak matrix, where the length of time required to move a person to the project team is very long.

Making Matrix Management Work

Matrix management is not without its problems. The organization is quite complex in comparison to the functional or pure project types of organization. Since the resources are shared, people working in this type of organization also share their bosses. This increases problems in communications, and many more management skills are required to make it all work.

These problems are offset by the flexibility that is achieved. The matrix organization is able to respond quickly and correctly to the needs of the customer in a proper fashion. The project team has greater focus on the customer's needs. Good project direction and participative management lead to high motivation and a sense of achievement and recognition on the project team.

Moving from a functional organization to a matrix organization may take two to three years in some organizations. This is necessary because it takes time to move the functional managers out of their positions and into other productive areas. If movement from functional organizations to matrix organizations is too fast, the result can be chaos and the loss of important personnel. The objective must be to create the impression that people are going to be promoted to other positions and not that their positions are going to be degraded. The functional managers in the existing organization are the major assets of the company and must not be lost.

Personnel and Personal Evaluations

Many project managers tend to have trouble getting enough people to work on their projects in the beginning. Frequently this problem can be helped by looking at key people who are still assigned to other projects but are close to finishing. Many of these project managers want to keep their key persons "just in case" something goes wrong. However, these people are often underutilized and their project managers may welcome the opportunity to have some of their time charged to another project.

Once a project is in the execution phase some of the work of the project will be done in the functional departments. This means that the project manager must have good negotiating skills. The project manager must also be able to negotiate with the functional manager to arrange assignment of people to the project.

Project managers may also need skills in the procurement of personnel from outside the company. Because of the nature of projects there may be unusual skills or unusual quantities of skills required by the project that are simply not available in the company.

Today many project teams are virtual teams, with team members located in different offices, buildings, or even countries. This has been made possible by today's excellent communications through the Internet, cell phones, videoconferencing, and e-mail. We thus can have more skilled individuals working on our project teams than we could in the past. For example, it makes it possible for parents who work at home, mobility-impaired people, and people living in other countries to be an integral part of any project team.

Co-location of project teams becomes more difficult today with the increasing use of virtual teams. What we mean by co-location is physically moving the members of the project team to the same location. This improves casual communication between team members and increases their awareness of what is happening in the project. People working in virtual teams or just in different offices in the same building have a more difficult time becoming a true part of the project team. A good project manager must deal with this fact when forced to work with a virtual project team. Special team building activities must be employed to create a sense of teamwork on a virtual team.

On all project teams a formal set of ground rules should be used, which make all of the team members' expectations clear and avoid misunderstanding during their time spent on the project. These ground rules can cover items like flex time, voluntary and mandatory overtime, training and conferences, travel, formal recognition, and rewards.

It is critically important that functional managers and project managers work together to evaluate employees. This is a problem, because the project team members may be assigned to the project for only a short time and may be assigned to several different projects with several different project managers during the course of the evaluation period. Project managers are oriented toward the goals of the project and frequently think of employee evaluations as administrative work that is the responsibility of the functional manager.

One simple method for accomplishing this and solving the problem is to have the project managers or subproject managers meet individually with people on their project team and review progress being made toward their project assignments. Something as simple as a lined tablet can be used for this. The project manager meets with an individual and makes notes on the tablet. When the meeting is over, a copy of the notes is given to the individual and a copy is filed away by the project manager.

When the person leaves the project, the notes are reviewed by both the individual and the project manager, a summary is written by the project manager with comments by the individual, and the whole package is copied and sent to the functional manager. In this way, when the time of appraisal is due, the functional manager has the notes from the project managers and can make a proper evaluation of the employees.

Motivation

Importance of Motivation

Until modern times there has been little interest in motivation of people in a work environment. From the beginning of the industrial revolution until the end of World War II there was some compelling reason for people to work and work hard.

Industrial Revolution

In the beginning of the industrial revolution people moved to the cities to find work that would give them a better standard of living than the farm work that was available to them. Thus there were many people available for all jobs. If someone did not want to work the hours required under the conditions given, someone else was happy to take the job immediately.

After the rise of unions, the lot of workers improved. In the beginning of the twentieth century, the First World War brought industrial expansion and more jobs, but the patriotic motivation brought even more workers to the workplace.

Scientific Management

The concept of scientific management was implemented by Henry Ford and Fredrick Taylor. In this concept the problem of motivation was essentially ignored. A person was considered to be like a machine. If a person was defective and could not perform the work required, the person was simply replaced with another person who would do the work. The idea behind the assembly line is to have short repetitive jobs for people to do. This results in a rapid slide down the learning curve. If a person has to be replaced, another can quickly learn the job and become productive.

Learning Curve Theory. The concept of the learning curve is quite simple. If people do a job repeatedly, each time they double the number of times they repeat the job, the time to do the work is reduced by a constant percentage.

Figure 5-4 shows a 70 percent improvement learning curve. This means that when the number of times the job is done is doubled, the cost is reduced to 70 percent. If the first time the job is done the cost is $1,000, the second time the cost will be $700. The fourth time the job is done the cost will be $490, and so on. It should be noted that this is similar to the law of diminishing returns in that, for every doubling of repetitions, the amount of reduction is less and less.

Depression Era

In the 1930s the Depression once again caused more people to look for jobs than there were jobs for them. Again, people who did not like the work conditions simply were replaced. When people are trying to satisfy their basic needs, they will work under harsh conditions.

World War II

World War II brought about the patriotic reaction to work. The war engendered prosperity for those who were not in the armed services. The war effort involved total mobilization of industry to defeat the Axis countries. This in itself created a sense of motivation sufficient for people to work their best.

Figure 5-4. Learning curve.

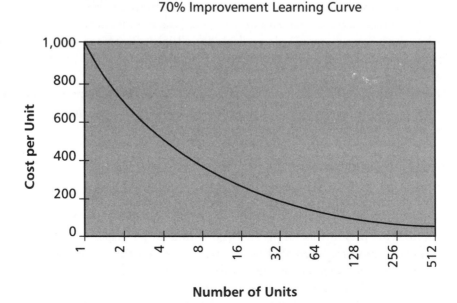

Post–World War II

Postwar prosperity created a new challenge in terms of motivating workers. For the first time in history the basic needs of U.S. citizens were essentially satisfied. There were enough jobs so that people were generally not afraid of starving or having enough money to buy clothing and supply other basic needs.

The problem was that in this prosperity it was difficult to get people to perform the way that they had during the war. This resulted in high levels of absenteeism, poor performance, and a general lack of motivation to do good work.

Companies recognized this problem and began to spend money to try to find solutions to the problem. For this reason much research was done on the problem of motivation, and a great body of knowledge was accumulated.

Research in the area of motivation is money well spent. Motivated employees come to work every day and produce high quality work. Employees who are not motivated have high absenteeism, produce lower quality work, and actually work a smaller percentage of the time. Millions of dollars could be saved by reducing absenteeism by only 10 percent.

Motivational Ideas

Because we have a limited amount of space available we will look at only a few of the most popular and widely accepted ideas on motivation.

Procedures vs. Motivation

We begin with the theory of scientific management, the idea that efficiency and better use of human resources result if clear and specific procedures are used. The idea behind this is that when people know exactly what they are supposed to do and exactly when they are supposed to do it, they will be satisfied with their jobs, be more motivated, and become more efficient. Studies conducted in this area indicated that the creation of procedures improved performance where nothing else was done to improve the performance of employees. The studies also showed that doing things that were motivational to employees improved performance and efficiency still more.

Typical of these studies is the graph shown in Figure 5-5, which simplifies a number of these studies. A large number of companies were studied. Each company was assessed for the amount of effort that was made to do things that were considered to be motivational. At the same time an assessment was made of the actual performance of the company. Performance was measured by looking at measurable criteria such as employee turnover, dissatisfaction, quality of output, and so on.

In companies that did little to proceduralize their work and did little to motivate their employees, the expected performance was low. In companies where an effort was made to improve procedures but little was done to improve the motivation of the employees, the performance of the company was considerably higher.

In companies where an effort was made to improve motivation but little was done

Figure 5-5. Policy/procedure and motivational effects on productivity.

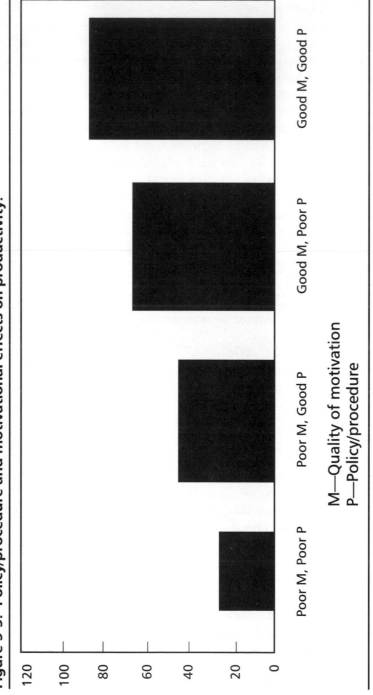

M—Quality of motivation
P—Policy/procedure

to improve the procedures, the performance of the company was considerably higher as well. Not only that, but the performance of these companies was considerably higher than that of the companies that had expended considerable effort creating procedures.

The highest performance was in companies that did both. A certain amount of proceduralization in combination with the creation of a motivational environment created the highest performing organizations.

Expectancy Theory

Expectancy theory focuses on people's ideas about their jobs and their surroundings. It focuses on the idea that people will do a certain thing in order to receive some sort of positive outcome. In other words, people will do good work because they see some sort of reward happening as a direct result. Of course, the difficulty with this is that if people have an expectancy that some outcome will result when they behave in a certain way and then it does not happen, there are problems.

Expectancy theory is a simple concept. It says that if you can create an expectancy in a person, the expectancy may indeed become fact. If a person is told that he or she is a poor performer and is no good at doing a job, the person will eventually become no good at doing the job and become a bad performer. If on the other hand a person is told that he or she is a high performer and does good work, the person may indeed become a good worker and a high performer.

Typical of the studies that were done at this time were studies that were conducted in elementary schools. In these studies the researchers administered an intelligence-measuring test at each school. Without looking at the results of the intelligence tests they randomly selected a small group of students in each class. The teachers and the parents were told that these students exhibited a high capability to learn and perform well in school.

After a period of time the researchers returned to the schools and administered another intelligence-measuring test. The results of this second test indicated that the students who had been randomly selected to be in the advanced capability group had improved their grades considerably. The only reason for this improvement was the expressed attitude of the teachers, parents, and peers toward the advanced students.

In practice, in project management, this concept can be applied by treating people with encouragement, giving them a sense of recognition and achievement, and giving praise publicly and criticism privately.

Maslow's Hierarchy of Needs Theory

The concept of a hierarchy of needs was developed by Abraham Maslow in 1943 (Figure 5-6). Like other concepts, this one is relatively simple. The basic human needs are arranged in a hierarchy. The lower needs must be satisfied before the higher needs can be addressed.

Figure 5-6. Maslow's hierarchy.

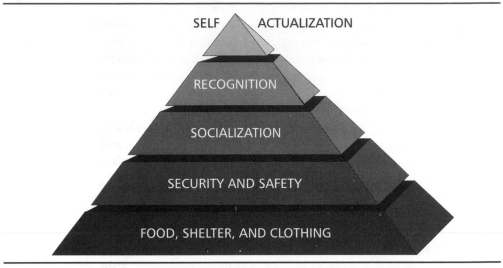

In Maslow's hierarchy, the lowest level—the needs for food, shelter, and clothing—must be relatively satisfied before effort will be made to satisfy the higher needs of safety and security. Someone who is lacking sufficient amounts of food, shelter, and clothing will be highly motivated to obtain them. Once a satisfactory level is obtained for these things, there is a reduced motivation to satisfy them. As one level of needs in the hierarchy is satisfied, the next level becomes the motivating factor, and so on.

According to this concept, people are always in some sort of a "needs" state. This needs state goes to higher, loftier needs as the lower needs are met, but it can also be driven down to the more basic needs if they are reduced.

Several survival biographies and histories of groups have been written over the years about people's reactions to hardship and dire situations. Typically in these stories the group starts out as an agreeable and mutually cooperative group with some goal in mind. As the hardships increase, the motivation moves from satisfying self-esteem to satisfying the need for socialization to the more basic needs. As the lower levels of needs become unsatisfied the individual's motivation becomes more basic and more self-serving. In World War II prison camps, these basic needs became so motivating that people performed acts that they would never have performed under normal circumstances.

The dynamic order of needs from lower to higher is to first satisfy the need for food, shelter, and clothing. These are the basic physiological needs of the individual. Once this has been accomplished or at least relatively well satisfied, the need for safety and security becomes the motivating factor. In satisfying this need the individual's immediate need for the basics has been satisfied, and the individual seeks out the protection of these satisfying factors. A person satisfies his or her need for housing and then wants to ensure that the housing is secure far into the future.

The need for socialization is next. Once the security of basic needs has been satisfied, the person is motivated by the need to have social contact or love. In terms of the workplace, a motivating atmosphere would be one where the individual is made to feel welcome and liked by his or her coworkers. Once a person feels accepted and has a satisfactory amount of love and acceptance, he or she can be motivated by the need for self-esteem.

The top of the hierarchy of needs is self-actualization. This need is satisfied by having the feeling that what you are doing is good for its own sake, and it is not necessary to have the recognition of a peer or even a manager. The person's own self-interest is enough to motivate.

In the 1970s many companies tried to implement this method of motivation. It was felt that the basic needs of food, shelter, clothing, security, and safety were already satisfied and that employee motivation could be achieved by increasing workers' ability to socialize. Companies attempted to make their employees "one big happy family." Generally, this was attempted by building golf courses and country clubs and encouraging company sponsored after-hours activities. In general, these programs failed. People's need for socialization was already satisfied, and giving them more of these things did not motivate them further. One side effect of this kind of program was that when these things were later withdrawn there was a great deal of dissatisfaction, and employees became de-motivated.

Hertzberg's Motivation/Hygiene Theory

When it became apparent that there were some problems with Maslow's explanation of motivation, the research continued. In fact, the research was continued by Maslow and his team. One of the team members was Fredrick Hertzberg, who developed the motivation/hygiene theory.

The research behind this theory was based on the need to explain some research where groups of executives and other professionals were interviewed to determine the things that made them feel good or not good about their work. The concept is that if there are things that make you feel good about working, then these things should also be the things that motivate you.

The factors that are linked with people having a good time when they are working are called "motivators" or "satisfiers." These were identified as a sense of achievement and a sense of recognition for things done, the work itself, responsibility, advancement, growth, and so on.

The factors that were linked with people having a bad time at work were called "dissatisfiers" or "hygiene factors." These factors included things like company policies, relationships with supervisors, salary, relationships with peers, personal factors, status, security, and others. These items were considered to be environmental in nature, and their loss seemed to be associated with bad feelings. Bad feelings were de-motivating. People did not like to do their job when it caused them to feel bad.

To summarize Hertzberg's conclusions, when hygiene factors are maintained, dissatisfaction is avoided. When the hygiene factors are not maintained, dissatisfaction occurs and motivation cannot happen. An unhappy person will not respond to things that make a happy person more motivated. Not only that, but if the same thing is given to people after they have reached their point of no dissatisfaction they would not improve performance. The cost for these types of programs, however, would increase.

"Motivators" were the factors that allowed people to become motivated. By becoming motivated they developed a will to get things done. This was much stronger than the feelings they had about their work when they were merely dissatisfied. Motivators must be given to improve productivity once the point of no dissatisfaction is reached. The motivating factors are recognition and a feeling of satisfaction and an increase in a person's self esteem.

The organization must carefully maintain the hygiene factors by having a good personnel policy and good leadership practices. To motivate people a feeling of achievement and recognition for work done must be created. People must feel responsibility for their work and feel empowered to do it. This is of course what the principles behind the human factors in project management are all about.

Supervisory Style and Delegation

All of these theories seem to indicate that the most motivational methods that can be used will center on high maintenance of the hygiene factors that Hertzberg uses in his explanation. Companies must have good and fair pay policies, good supervision and leadership, and all of the other environmental factors that make an employee workplace an environment conducive to doing good work. Without these things the employees will probably not work to their fullest potential.

Work can be designed so that it improves a person's sense of achievement and recognition. People need to be responsible for the work that they do and have the tools and means at their disposal to complete the work. Employees should feel that they participate in the process of work assignment.

Job and Work Design

Many large organizations in the past simply expected employees to perform the job for which they were paid. The employees' happiness was of little concern. The concept was that people were there to do work for the company, and they could be happy on their own time. The attitude seemed to be, "Here is a meaningless repetitive job. In return for doing it we will give you money and other rewards. You have to spend eight hours a day here doing this work that you do not like so that you can ultimately have time to yourself and money to spend."

Under this system employees became very unhappy and resented the company. This was evident in an aggressive attitude toward the organization or apathy or lack of interest in the company at all. The results of this attitude were evident in conflict between company representatives and employees. Managers came to think that the employees did not care about the company and its success or failure, and the employees did not think that the company cared about their well-being.

For these reasons it is necessary for job design to take place. The purpose of job design is to change these attitudes toward work. Job design is particularly important to the project manager, because a project environment is often uncertain and insecure for the project team, and the proper design of the job of the project team is therefore important to the success of the project team and the project.

Job Enlargement. Job enlargement is done by simply making the job larger. Going back to the ideas of Henry Ford and Fredrick Taylor, the idea of the assembly-line job was to have the job as short as possible to minimize training and maximize interchangeability of people on the job. The objective was to be able to keep the assembly line going even though changes in the workers and other problems might occur.

In an assembly line the work is broken down into very small units, and each person does a small amount of the total work required. For example, in a new Saab automobile plant in Sweden, the Saab engineers estimated that a subassembly of the engine could be manufactured in 12.6 minutes using assembly-line techniques. The engineers also determined that a single person, working by himself or herself, could make the same subassembly in 30 minutes. On the assembly line the job of each of the workers was only 1.8 minutes each. By enlarging the job the size of the job went from 1.8 minutes to 30 minutes.

Although the total effort spent to manufacture the subassembly was larger, Saab felt that the total life cycle cost of assembling the engine was lower. This was due to a much higher motivation, lack of boredom, and a feeling of accomplishing something meaningful. The workers felt good about their job and were much more motivated. This resulted in lower levels of waste and rework due to poorly assembled engine subassemblies. The cost of defects in the engine subassemblies was quite high if the defect caused serious damage to other parts or if the engine ultimately failed in the field.

All of the other costs of unmotivated employees also served to offset the additional time of assembly. Disruptions due to worker absenteeism, tardiness, poor attitude, and so on served additionally to offset the total cost of the assembly.

One problem with job enlargement is that in enlarging the job it is possible to take a small meaningless job and make it into a large meaningless job. It would not be particularly motivating for an assembly-line worker who is responsible for tightening four screws if his or her job was enlarged to tightening sixteen screws.

Job Enrichment. Job enlargement was improved by the concept of job enrichment. The crucial difference was that job enrichment programs not only enlarged the job to make it more meaningful to the worker but also changed the nature of the job itself to make it more motivating.

The major difference between an enlarged job and an enriched one is that the enriched job includes a planning and control task as well as the operating task. Previously, the planning and control of work was done by someone else, and the operational part of the work was the only part that was delegated.

An example of job enrichment is the operation of an automotive maintenance facility. Without job enrichment the mechanic is given assignments from the manager. When each assignment is completed the mechanic goes on to the next assignment. The manager does all of the planning and scheduling work. The manager does the entire interface with the customer. With job enrichment, the mechanic is required to talk to the customer and determine what problems need to be addressed in agreement with the customer. The mechanic might actually be required to schedule the work and promise the customer when the work will be completed.

Another important characteristic of job enrichment is that the information flows from the persons furnishing the input information directly to the persons needing the information. This is different from the traditional nonenriched job where most information is first sent to the supervisor and then retransmitted to those in need of the information. In this way a relationship is formed between the person doing the work and the person benefiting from the work being done.

In job enrichment there are four motivational effects that occur:

1. Lack of boredom
2. Feeling that the work is meaningful
3. Feeling of being responsible for the consequences of what work is done and how it is done
4. Feeling of competence in accomplishing the task

In project management, job enrichment is fundamental to the management of the project. Each of the persons on the project team as well as the stakeholders of the project are encouraged to make their own individual plans for the work that they do. In fact, the work that each individual associated with the project does is discovered and self-assigned in the course of the planning and execution of the project. People working on projects should design their own tasks, plan them, estimate the cost and time necessary to do them, and provide feedback to the stakeholder needing the work to be done.

Quality Circles. Quality circles are ad hoc organizations within the company and the project team. They are a volunteer group of people who have mutually agreed to address some sort of problem. They can be composed of anyone in the organization desiring to address the problem, and membership must be voluntary.

Quality circles must be supported by the company organization but not managed by it. Facilities, support, and time to meet and work on issues that the quality circle is addressing must be given to them.

Let us say, for example, that there is a problem with a high number of defects in the paint of an automotive fender. A group of volunteers can form a quality circle to address the problem. The group might consist of assembly workers, inspectors, quality assurance engineers, paint engineers, and so on. The company assigns a facilitator to assist the quality circle in achieving its goal.

The quality circle meets on company time, discusses the problem, and attempts to analyze problems and solutions. The facilitator attempts to make resources available to them and to ensure that they have access to managers who must ultimately approve their solution to the problem.

This is in keeping with the aims of job enrichment in that each person on the quality circle is there voluntarily, is responsible for the planning, execution, and feedback of what he or she does, has an interest in the results, and feels responsible for the process.

Power

Power is the ability of one person to influence the behavior of another. In project management, understanding power and the use of power can have a great effect on the outcome of the project.

Forms of Power

Power is not simply the brute force necessary to bend someone to your will. There are several ways that people can be influenced.

Coercive Power and Reward Power

Coercive power is based on the idea in the mind of the person being influenced that the person having the influence has the ability to inflict punishment or pain. This pain will be unpleasant, and it will be more unpleasant than doing the task.

Reward power is based on the idea in the mind of the person being influenced that the person having the influence has the ability to administer some sort of reward. This reward will be pleasant, and it will be more pleasant than any unpleasantness associated with doing the task.

Coercive and reward power depend on the person being influenced believing that the thing being requested can actually be done, that the reward or punishment can actually be given by the influencer, and that the reward or punishment is sufficient to motivate the person being influenced to do the work.

For example, if parents want to influence the grades of their child, they might try to influence the child by offering to buy him or her a car if the child gets straight A's next year in high school. The child may feel that there is no possible way of achieving this goal. In this case, the influence will not take place. The child may feel that the parents will not be able to deliver the reward if the goal is achieved, and again the influence will not take place. Finally, the child may not care about getting the reward offered, in which case the influence will not take place.

Legitimate Power

Legitimate power is based on the idea in the mind of the person being influenced that the person having the influence has this influence because of the values of the person being influenced. In other words, the influenced person believes that the person influencing has the right to do this through formal authority in the organization.

For example, in medieval societies, the king was obeyed because everyone believed he had that authority from God. Although response to this sort of power may have once been motivated by fear, over time the power is changed into a tradition. The person who is the influencer has power over others even if he or she lacks the power to punish and reward any longer.

When new employees start to work in a firm, the authority and chain of command in the company are clearly explained them. As long as people wish to work for this company they agree to respect the legitimate authority of those in positions above them.

Referent Power

Referent power is based on the idea in the mind of the person being influenced that the person having the influence has this influence based on the person being influenced having a strong desire to identify with the person influencing. A person who leads others by virtue of his or her charisma has this type of power.

This is the kind of power exercised by some charismatic religious leaders. In this type of power people tend to admire certain characteristics of the influencers and follow them blindly in other areas. These kinds of charismatic leaders influence people by the force of their personality. People with this kind of influence can cause individuals under their influence to perform unusual acts. Throughout history there have been many leaders like this. It generally requires a special personality as well as a special set of circumstances to create someone with this kind of power.

Expert Power

Expert power is based on the idea in the mind of the person being influenced that the person having the influence has this influence based on special knowledge or ability. This special knowledge or ability is believed to help the influenced achieve their goals.

In most business situations people are influenced by expert power. This is the belief that someone can influence others because that person knows more about what he or she is doing and what everyone else should be doing. This influence is based on evidence of the person's expertise.

Representative Power

Representative power is based on the idea of one or more persons being chosen by the group from the group and having the power to lead delegated to them voluntarily. Representative power depends on the group's willingness to delegate this power to one or more individuals. People's willingness to give representative power to one of their members may be influenced by all of the other types of power as well.

Leadership

Theory X and Theory Y Managers

Douglas McGregor's theory of X and Y managers says that there are two kinds of managers: type X and type Y.

Type X managers think that all people are basically lazy and that unless they are threatened or in some way forced to do work, they will not do any work. These managers direct work to be done and do not allow very much participation in any decision making, because they feel that the participation by the workers would only lead to less work being done.

Type Y managers believe that people will do a good job for the sake of doing it. They believe in participative management and sharing information with the workers. These managers will also listen to problems that are brought up by their staff.

Theory X managers are good in situations that are either very favorable or very unfavorable, while type Y managers are good in normal types of projects where there are a moderate number of problems. This may explain why many military managers in combat situations use theory X type management. In a combat situation it is necessary to have orders carried out without question or debate. In projects that are in extreme difficulty, this type of manager has an advantage.

Conflict Resolution

Conflict occurs when one party to the conflict thinks that the other party to the conflict has done something to frustrate attainment of a goal or goals. The conflict is said to be resolved when the two parties have had their frustration lowered to an acceptable level.

Project teams and their stakeholders, like any other group, have many interdependent parts that have their own values or interests and goals. Each person in a group seeks to fulfill his or her own goals as well. In project management, one of the major accomplishments necessary for the project manager is the resolution of these differences. Since each member of the group wants to meet his or her own goals, it is sometimes difficult for each person to fully understand the goals of others in the group. The solution lies in the ability of the project manager to keep each member's activities from interfering with and frustrating the other members while allowing all other activities to take place and move the project toward its goal.

Many believe that conflict has a beneficial side. The argument is that if the organization is dynamic and striving toward difficult goals, there is bound to be conflict. If there is no conflict, it follows that the organization is not dynamic and striving. This is not necessarily the case in project management. Disagreements can be settled quickly and amicably without having conflict. The level of frustration in the disagreeing parties is a measure of the conflict. I believe that in a well-run project team it is possible to settle differences without creating frustration.

There are said to be five ways of resolving conflict:

1. Forcing
2. Smoothing
3. Compromise
4. Problem solving
5. Withdrawal

These five conflict-resolving methods have varying results as to the immediate effect and the long-term effect on the conflict resolution. They also have an effect on the temperament of the conflicting parties (Figures 5-7 and 5-8).

Forcing

One way to resolve a conflict is for one party to force the other to agree. This is the kind of conflict resolution that happens when one person has power over another and

Figure 5-7. Conflict resolution styles.

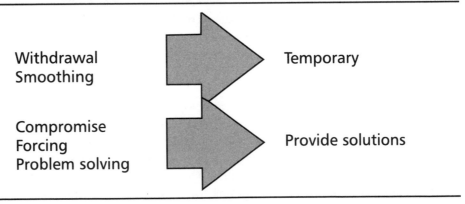

Figure 5-8. Effects of conflict resolution styles.

	Good for Personal Goals	Good for Relationships
Forcing	High	Low
Smoothing	Low	High
Compromising	Medium	Medium
Problem solving	High	High
Withdrawal	Low	Low

exercises it. It amounts to the boss saying, "OK, we have had our discussion, and now I will make the decision." This method of resolving the conflict results in a permanent solution. The solution, although permanent, might not be the best solution that might have been found, but it does save time, and right or wrong, the conflict is resolved. This type of resolution is not good for building teams. People's personal stakes in the decision, especially if the decision is found to be wrong, are frustrated.

Smoothing

Smoothing minimizes the disagreement by making differences seem less important. This kind of resolution occurs when either one of the persons disagreeing or another person in the group attempts to make the differences smaller than they seem. If the tactic is successful, one or both of the conflicting parties will think that the differences are more minor than they had seemed and will accept either a compromise or the group's acceptance of one of the alternatives.

This type of resolution is generally good for the group relations of the team. All of the members of the group are made to feel that the conflict was less important than originally thought. This type of resolution, however, does not lead to permanent solutions. The conflicting parties do not come to an agreement about what was accepted and what was not. At some time later, when the conflicting parties realize that the importance of their differences has been minimized, the conflict is likely to reappear and continue.

Compromise

Compromise is similar to smoothing. Using this type of conflict resolution, each of the parties gives up something to reach a common ground. In this resolution the parties themselves agree to give up on some points but not others. In doing this they reach a common agreement that has relatively few points of disagreement. Compromise is sort of a middle-of-the-road kind of solution. Neither side wins or loses. Without a clear winner, neither of the sides in the conflict is enthusiastic about moving forward with the compromise plan. The effect on team building is neither good nor bad. The destructiveness of the conflict is avoided, but the resolution results in something that neither side supported originally. If compromises are documented, and the parties really make them into firm agreements and stick to them, they become permanent solutions. Many times, as in smoothing the problem, the disagreeing parties will continue to disagree and try to implement the original ideas.

Problem Solving

In problem solving, a group is set up to prove one point or another right or wrong. This method of conflict resolution is based on the idea that all disagreements must have one correct solution. By having additional work on the disagreement, the facts will eventually be uncovered, and it will be clear which of the disagreeing parties is correct. This is actually the best way to resolve conflict. Once indisputable facts are discovered and added to the information available about the conflict, it is difficult for any of the participants to disagree further, and the conflict is resolved. This type of solution produces the best resolution of the conflict for the team. The resolution of the conflict becomes clear, and there is no need for further disagreement.

Withdrawal

Withdrawal may be the worst way to resolve any conflict. In this type of resolution one group leaves the argument and retires. This is the same behavior that occurs when a small child says, "I don't like the way you are playing this game. I am taking my ball and going home." This does not really solve the conflict; it merely postpones it to another day.

This type of resolution has a negative effect on the team. All of the team members feel badly about the end of the discussion and the withdrawal of one person or group.

Managing Meetings

Managers and project managers spend as much as 70 percent of their time in meetings. Nearly all managers complain that they spend more time in meetings than they should and that, for the most part, meetings are a waste of time. If no one likes to go to meetings and everyone feels that they are a waste of time, why do we have so many meetings?

The reason that meetings are held is based on the concept that two heads are better than one, three heads are better than two, and so on. Continuing to add people to a meeting improves the chances that something can be accomplished in the meeting. The problem is that as the number of people attending a meeting increases, the effectiveness of the meeting increases at a diminishing rate. The cost of additional people in a meeting continues to increase in a linear fashion, and very soon the benefit of additional people at a meeting is less than the cost of having them there.

As can be seen in Figure 5-9, as the number of persons who attend a meeting increases, the effectiveness of the meeting continues to increase, but the amount of increase for each additional person is less as more people attend the meeting. The rationale for this is simple. Each additional person comes to the meeting with additional knowledge and experience. There is an ever-increasing probability that the knowledge and new ideas that this additional person brings to the meeting will already be present in someone else. In addition, as the size of the meeting increases, the interest of some of the participants may be less than desired. These less interested people may decide to have their own discussion while the meeting is going on and be effectively lost to the meeting taking place around them for periods of time. With larger meetings, people who simply do not participate may not even be noticed.

Of course, the cost of having these people present increases in a linear fashion. In Figure 5-9 it can also be seen that the cost begins to exceed the benefits of the meeting at around ten people. For most meetings, ten people are optimum. In this size group it is likely that everyone will participate in the meeting, and there will be no side discussions taking place.

There are several reasons to hold a meeting. Meetings can be held for the purpose of giving out information. These types of meetings can violate the ten-person guideline.

Figure 5-9. Meeting size: Effectiveness versus cost.

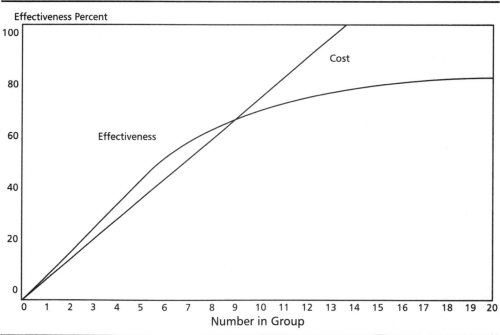

This is the type of meeting where a large group of individuals is told about a new company policy or when some sort of announcement is made. Since there is little participation in this kind of meeting, the group can be quite large. In fact, by using various kinds of media such as closed circuit television, very large groups can be reached.

Most of the meetings that a project manager will have to manage are going to be discussion, idea-generation, and problem-solving types of meetings. To solve the major complaints of those attending these meetings—that they are a waste of time and that they happen too often—the project manager must make the meetings effective.

Managing Meetings Effectively

Before the Meeting

Send out a memo giving notice of the meeting. Notifying people of a meeting by telephone is not the most reliable way to ensure that they will attend. Sending a written message will increase the possibility that they will attend. Most people are busy and are bombarded with meeting notices and telephone calls. Many times meetings are called on short notice at the inconvenience of many of the attendees. This creates a feeling of imposition on the part of attendees and does not make for a good attitude toward the meeting. The participants need to feel that they are a necessary, contributing part of the meeting.

The written notice of the meeting should contain the time and place for the meeting, the subject to be discussed, the tentative agenda, and the list of those invited. In addition, any background information that can be supplied to the participants should be provided.

Attendees should have time to prepare and know who is attending the meeting. They should be specifically informed if they are going to be expected to make any presentation or contribute something special to the meeting.

Beginning the Meeting

Open the meeting by restating the objectives. It should be clear to all of those attending the meeting what the purpose and goal of the meeting is.

Go over the agenda and ask for additions. This is one of the most important aspects of making a meeting effective. One of the problems with meetings occurs when during the meeting one of the participants is inspired to change the subject. Before anyone can stop it, the meeting has headed off in a new direction and is no longer going in the direction of its stated goals. The problem with this is not that the discussion is not useful and that the new discussion is not beneficial. The problem is that the purpose of the meeting is now sidetracked and that some of the people in the meeting are not necessary for the discussion now taking place.

The use of an agenda avoids this problem. When a new and nonrelevant discussion begins, the leader of the meeting can use the agenda to bring things back on track. It is therefore important for the leader of the meeting to ask for additions or corrections to the agenda at the beginning of the meeting. Any additions or corrections made at this time are likely to help achieve the goal of the meeting. Later, when spontaneous discussion ensues, the agenda can be used to guide it back to the purpose of the meeting.

Have someone record all action items assigned and any conclusions reached. The results of the meeting need to be recorded, or they will depend on the individual memories of the participants. In particular, the agreed-upon action items by the participants must be recorded to ensure that they actually take place.

The use of recording devices and video cameras generally has a negative effect on the discussions that take place in meetings. Transcribing tape recordings of meetings is generally time consuming and less effective than good note taking.

Distribute the minutes within one day. Each meeting should be followed up by the distribution of the minutes of the meeting. Like the meeting notes, the information and the results of the meeting must be distributed to the attendees and other interested parties. This written record also ensures that everyone's recollections of the meeting are going to be the same.

Summary

The purpose of human resources management in project management is to make the most effective use of the human resources involved in the project. As always, the project manager is responsible for the human resources management of the project.

Projects work best when the environment around them is organized in a way that is good for project management. The matrix organization is best for project management, because it allows for the flexibility necessary when managing companies on a project basis.

Project teams must be motivated. Much of recent research on the theories of motivation applies directly to the management techniques that are fundamental to project management. These motivating methods favor participative management, responsibility and accountability, and recognition for work done well. The concepts of job enlargement and job enhancement fit well within the project management methodology.

To be an effective project manager, one must have skills in dealing with the normal conflicts that occur from day to day within the project team and between the project team and those external to the project team. Understanding the use of power is necessary for the success of the project.

Project managers spend much of their life in meetings. It is important that meetings be efficient and effective. Meeting agendas allow people to properly prepare for meetings and help participants focus on the subjects that they are supposed to discuss.

CHAPTER 6

Communications Management

The project team must have a communication plan that determines which items of information need to be communicated to all of the stakeholders of the project. It will be determined by who the stakeholders are and to what level they are involved. It will fulfill the stakeholders' need for information when they need it.

The communications management plan contains all of the information regarding the format of the reports, frequency of distribution, and the individual who has the responsibility for generating the reports and distributing them.

Lessons Learned

The lessons-learned document is a document that captures the good and bad things that happened in the project. It should also contain a recommendation for how to avoid or minimize the bad things and enhance the good things. The purpose of the document is to serve other project managers working on future projects. The lessons-learned documents are an excellent starting place for risk identification. Databases can be constructed to classify and store lessons-learned data to simplify the lookup process.

Some companies feel so strongly about the use of this document that their project managers are required to read the lessons learned on relevant projects before they can get approval of the project charter. Project managers are not allowed to close out a project until the lessons-learned document is completed and accepted.

The lessons-learned document is supported by issue logs. An *issue log* is a collection of objections from the stakeholders. Issues are items that do not necessarily become activities in the project but must be answered to keep the stakeholders satisfied. Each issue must be possible to resolve, have a person in charge of it, and have a due date for resolution.

Probably the single most important thing in project management is communications. It is said that if good communications exist in a project, the team will be motivated and the project will succeed in spite of problems that might kill another project. It is therefore essential that project managers have a good understanding of communications.

It is generally agreed among project managers that communications skills are the most important skills that a project manager can have. These skills are considered to be more important than organization skills, team building skills, and leadership skills, and they are certainly considered more important for project managers than technical skills (Figure 6-1). It is often said that if a project manager has good communications skills and no other skills at all, the project team will get the project completed successfully in spite of the project manager.

According to the *Guide to the Project Management Body of Knowledge:*

Communications management in projects is the process required to ensure timely and appropriate generation, collection, dissemination, storage, and ultimately disposition of project information.

Figure 6-1. The importance of communications management (survey of project managers).

Which of the following do you consider important project management skills?

Communication skills	84%
Organization skills	75%
Team building skills	72%
Leadership skills	68%
Technological skills	48%

General Model of Communications

Communicating is the process of delivering a message to another with understanding. Refer to Figure 6-2, the communications model, as we review the terms to make sure we are communicating properly.

Thinking

The sender frames the ideas and creates the message that he or she wants to send.

Encoding

The encoding process consists of formatting the message into some transmittable form. This makes the communication possible. The language, written and spoken words, facial expressions, body language, and other means of transmitting an idea can be used. Some of the time a communication we do not wish to send is sent anyway. We can communicate by physically touching someone. We can communicate by making some sort of a physical gesture such as pointing a finger.

Symbols

All sorts of symbols can be used to communicate. Symbols stand in the place of something we have experienced initially. A picture of a person is a symbol of that person. A

Figure 6-2. Communications model.

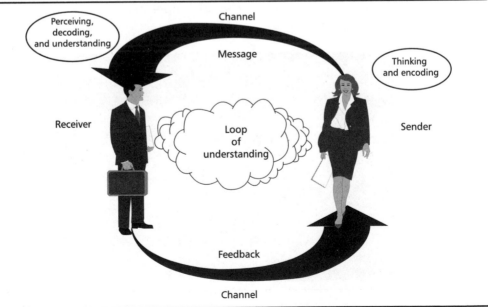

uniform is a symbol for a policeman. Words are symbols for the objects or ideas they represent.

Transmitting

This is the process of moving the message from the sender to the receiver. The medium used might be airwaves, as in the use of the spoken word; electronically, as in e-mail, telephone, and fax; visual signals; or combinations of these.

Perceiving

The receiver must have recognition that the message is coming. If there is no perception of the message, then the message is never received. Ultimately, the message must enter the receiver by means of one of a person's five senses: sight, sound, smell, taste, or touch.

Decoding

The receiver must now take the message and convert it into some form that can be understood.

Understanding

If there is no understanding, there is no message. The message must have some understandable meaning for the receiver.

Barriers to Communications

There can be many barriers to communications. Messages can be blocked or distorted, and as a result, their meaning can be changed considerably.

Distorted Perceptions

Many times the receiver is not in the proper frame of mind to receive the message. This may be due to many factors, such as the environment, the mood of the receiver, or the subject matter being delivered. The status of the person sending the message may have an effect as well. When something is being said by the person working in the next cubicle, the effectiveness of that communication will be different from a message sent by the CEO of the company. So we can say that motivation and needs and even experience affect a person's perception.

The receiver's perception is also affected by the need to connect the new message to already received information that is stored in the receiver's memory. We try to connect new information to old information in order to make it meaningful.

Distrusted Sources

The source of a communication may be wrong about what he or she is communicating. It can be that the source is really wrong or it may be that we are just convinced that the source is wrong. When this condition exists in an extreme way, it makes no difference what is really said. The perception of the message will be similar to what is expected.

Transmission Errors

There are a number of reasons why a message is not properly received, and language is one of the most common problems. Not only are the different words of different languages a problem, but the cultural differences between people who speak different languages can result in errors in communication even if the words and meanings are the same.

Receiving and sending messages can be done only within the framework of common experience and understanding. When the experience and understanding are different, communication is difficult.

When you deal with people from different cultural backgrounds, care must be taken with the choice of words that you use. This is not only necessary when dealing with those who are from a different country than you. There are significant cultural differences among people from different parts of the same country and even from different neighborhoods within the same city.

Improving Communications

The following guidelines will help you improve your communications.

Make the Message Relevant for the Receiver

Good communications come when the receiver is interested and has something at stake in the message. If the message is relevant, then the receiver is more likely to get a more complete meaning. We have all been in situations where someone is telling us about something that is not relevant to us. Our attention wanders off to some other area, and we actually do not hear anything that is said for a period of time.

Reduce the Message to Its Simplest Terms

When you communicate with someone, keep the message as simple as possible. Many times the message is complicated with unnecessary details about the rationale and the justification of a project when the listener is already convinced and just wants to know what to do.

Organize the Message into a Series of Stages

One of the reasons that verbal communication succeeds over written communication is the opportunity to keep things simple. The sender can send a simple part of the message and receive feedback immediately. The sender can send another part of the message and receive feedback on that too. In this way, the message is kept simple, and the receiver is brought to the complete understanding of the full message, one piece at a time. You may have heard this question: "How do you eat an elephant?" The answer is, "One bite at a time." Of course, if it takes too long, the elephant may spoil, and the message may be lost.

Repeat the Key Points

Because listening takes place a very small percentage of the time, it is important to repeat the important points of the message. As we communicate, it is a good idea to go back a few steps and summarize what has gone before. This allows repetition of some of the major points and ensures that the receiver is getting all of the important points in the message.

Verbal and Written Communications

Many people think that there is no better way to communicate than through written messages and that written communications should be used without exception. Today, with the use of e-mail, this feeling is becoming stronger. It is not unusual to see e-mail messages being exchanged between people who sit ten feet from one another. Verbal and written communications each have their place, and it is important that the correct medium be used for each communication.

Verbal communications are faster than written ones; they allow us to keep the message simple and present one thought at a time to the listener. Because verbal communications are two way, we are able to get feedback from the receiver before going on. If the feedback coming from the receiver does not confirm that he or she got the message, the message can be modified and the point made in another way. Questions can be raised by the receiver to help clarify the point.

Written communications can be more detailed than verbal ones and can be used to explain something that is quite complex and requires more explanation than the receiver can absorb in a short verbal exchange. The written communication can be better organized than a verbal communication, and if it is properly organized, the receiver is able to go back and review material already read.

One of the reasons why so many people use e-mail is the timing issue. E-mail can be sent quickly when the sender has the time and motivation to send it. It is read and acted upon when the receiver has the time and motivation to act on it. In many ways this is much better than communicating by telephone. While the telephone gives instant communication, the person being called is usually interrupted while doing something and must change his or her thinking to deal with the person calling on the telephone.

In my classes I usually do an exercise where a group of five or six people is forced to communicate with written communications only. They are given a simple problem to work out that requires input from each of them. They are required to follow strict reporting procedures similar to procedures used in most companies. They are given ten minutes to solve the problem, and fewer than one-tenth of one percent ever solve it. The groups are then allowed to discuss the problem and do anything that they can to communicate. When they are allowed to use free and open communications without restrictions, they all solve the problem in about sixty seconds.

Formal and Informal Communications

Formal Communications

Project managers and members of their project teams are frequently required to make formal presentations to their managers, their customers, and various other stakeholders in the project. In order to accomplish this, it is necessary for them to have good presentation skills.

Today we are fortunate that there is much in the way of computer software for presentations that makes this formerly expensive chore easy and inexpensive to accomplish. One of the most popular software packages is Microsoft PowerPoint. This software package makes formal presentations easy. Digital photography is now widely available, so that photographs can be easily inserted into the presentation to make it more meaningful. Video projection is also widely available, so that the tedious process of making presentation graphics on transparencies is no longer necessary.

Distance conferencing is now widely used. Video and audio connections between conference rooms eliminate the need to have people travel to distant locations to attend meetings. This not only reduces the cost of travel but significantly saves time that can be devoted to more direct project work.

The Internet as well has proven to be a great communication tool for project management. Project data from various parts of a project located in remote parts of the world can be easily shared and combined with other project data through the Internet.

E-mail has already changed the way we communicate. For most of us, the use of e-mail has changed the way we do business. Unlike telephone calls, which are almost always an interruption in what we are doing, the e-mail we receive is looked at when we want to. This allows us to pay close attention to what is being communicated and carefully respond to inquiries. Many decisions made quickly during a telephone call may soon be regretted.

Informal Communications

I have a good friend who is now retired from the U.S. Navy. He was a captain and had a large command of some 1,200 people. We often have discussions about the Navy way of doing things.

One of the problems in any military organization is the structure of the military chain of command. The strict chain of command is required because, when fighting a war, it is critical that legitimate orders be carried out. There is usually no time for discussion, and commanders do not usually have time to explain things to the subordinates who are to carry out the orders. It is important that each subordinate communicates to his or her superior officer and not deviate from that order. It would lead to confusion if an officer would go directly to a subordinate three levels below the officer.

The problem is that the military are not always engaged in war and fighting. Most of the time they are engaged in the business of keeping the forces ready to fight. This part of the military function is more like an everyday business. As we have seen, in a company having free and open communications is a better way to communicate than having a strict chain of command. It is not possible to have an organization work two different ways.

In the military, the problem is solved by having parties. The U.S. Navy has frequent cocktail parties. When I attended such parties, I noticed that very few people were drinking. I also observed that very few people were sitting. This was because the party allowed people to circulate regardless of rank and order in the chain of command. If one person needed to get information from another, he or she could do it this way without going through the formality of the chain of command.

Often in project management there is a need for formal communications. The normal method of communicating between the project team and the stakeholders should be open and free, but there are times when formal communications are necessary. When major milestones in the project are being passed and agreement must be had from all the stakeholders, formal communications are necessary. When authorized project changes are made, it is necessary to have formal communications. As the number of persons involved in a decision is increased, the need for formal communications increases.

Improving Listening

Many times when we listen we do not hear what is being said to us (see Figures 6-3 and 6-4). It is possible to concentrate on what is being said for only a small portion of the time. There are several things to remember: Don't interrupt, put the speaker at ease, appear interested, cut out distractions, and periodically sum up what was said.

Don't Interrupt

One of the most disruptive things that can be done while someone is trying to communicate a message is to interrupt the speaker. This stops the speaker's chain of thought and makes him or her feel that you are not interested in what is being said. The offended feeling on the part of the sender of the message may be enough to make the person angry

Figure 6-3. The manager's time.

- 80% of time is spent in communicating

- Half of communicating time is spent listening

- Most people recall 50% of what they hear immediately after

- After two months 25% is recalled

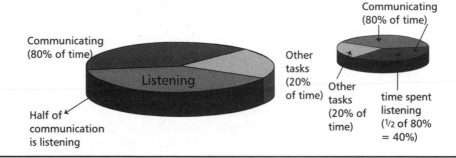

Figure 6-4. Diminishing levels of understanding.

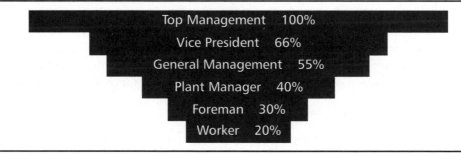

if it is done repeatedly. Eventually, this will reduce the effectiveness of the communication. There are times when this is used as a tactic. If a meeting is going in a direction that you do not like, sometimes by repeatedly interrupting you can get the speaker so upset that the meeting can be postponed, giving you enough time to gather information to make the meeting go along a proper course.

Put the Speaker at Ease

Many times the speaker in a meeting is nervous and uncomfortable in the speaking role. To encourage the speaker you can make comments before and during the meeting to make it known that you are looking forward to what he or she has to say and what an important contribution the speaker will be making to the meeting. During the presentation, nod your head in agreement and smile at some of the speaker's comments. When something is said that you agree with, voice your positive comments, if possible. All of this creates a feeling of confidence and trust in the speaker.

It is important that project managers have good presentation skills. Project managers are frequently called upon to make formal and informal presentations to other managers, clients, stakeholders, and the like. Project managers must be able to convey the information in a way that is comprehensible to their audience.

Appear Interested

Creating the impression that you are very interested in what is being said will do a lot to make the speaker feel at ease with the audience and will also help you retain more of the information that is being sent by the speaker.

Cut Out Distractions

Listening can be improved greatly by improving the environment where the communication is taking place. Noisy distracting places severely inhibit communications, while quiet places with no telephones and a closed door will greatly improve them. Asking all of the attendees to turn off cellular phones and pagers or at least put them on their vibrating mode will help to improve the environment.

Periodically Sum Up What Was Said

Listening can be further improved by periodically summarizing what has been said. By doing this you are essentially repeating what was said, but in a different way. All of the attendees in the meeting will hear again what was said, and their retention will be higher. Summarizing also has the side benefit of making the speaker relax.

Networking

Networking is an important concept in communications management. It is important to understand the relationships between people who are communicating and to realize that the more people communicate the more complex the communications become.

Any network is composed of nodes and links between the nodes. Using the network model can make understanding some aspects of communications much easier. This method of analysis is also useful in measuring the effectiveness of meetings. A meeting can be observed, and the communications between individuals can be recorded as simple lines between them. The more lines of communication there are connecting individuals at the meeting, the more freely communication is taking place. When there are only a few lines, it is an indication of the inhibitions of individuals in the meeting. A good meeting would show lines between each individual in the meeting and every other individual in the meeting.

Circular Networks

A circular network shows communications in a circle (Figure 6-5). Communications in this network require some communications to pass through another communication node before reaching the intended receiver. As the circle becomes larger, there are more intervening nodes between the sender and the receiver.

Chain Networks

The chain network is commonly referred to as the chain of command. To move a message from one end to the other of this network requires that the message pass through all of the intervening nodes. This is the slowest and most error-prone method of communicating, since each time the message is transferred, there is a good chance that some of the information will be lost or changed (see Figure 6-6).

Figure 6-5. Network communications circle.

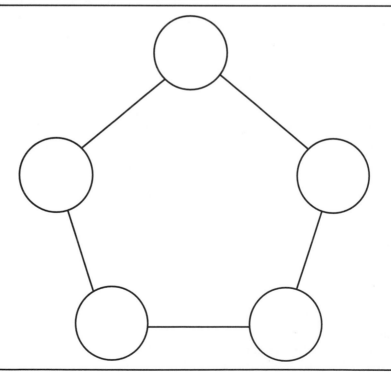

Figure 6-6. Network communications chain.

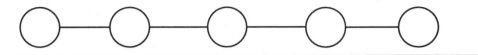

There is a game that is played in communications seminars to illustrate this. A short article from the local newspaper is given to one person to read. That person is then asked to leave the room with another person and accurately retell the story (without looking at the article). The second person tells the story again, in private, to the third person, and this continues until the fifth person is told the story. When this is completed the fifth person is asked to tell the story to the rest of the class. The original article is then read to the class. The two stories will be quite different. The difficulties in communicating using normal chain of command communications are clear.

The Wheel
The wheel network centralizes communications and gives great power to the individual at the center (Figure 6-7). The saying goes that "he who controls the information controls the world." All communications go through the center, and only the center gives information to the other nodes in the network.

Free and Open Communications
The network diagram in Figure 6-8 illustrates the free and open communications model. Each node in the network is able to communicate with every other node in the network.

Figure 6-7. Network communications wheel.

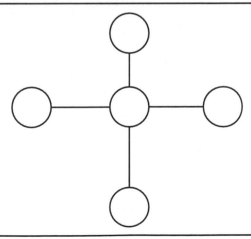

Figure 6-8. Network communications circle: Free and open communications.

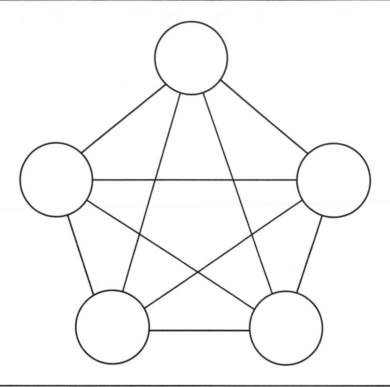

This means that information that any member has can be communicated to any other member of the network.

This network model does not come without problems. This type of communication is difficult to control because of all the possible connections. As the number of participants increases, the number of communication links increases.

The number of communication links can actually be calculated by the formula:

$$\text{Channels} = [\text{N} \times (\text{N} - 1)] / 2$$

For example, if there are five persons on a project team and it is necessary for them to communicate with each other, how many communications channels are there?

$$\text{Channels} = [5 \times (5 - 1)] / 2$$
$$\text{Channels} = 20 / 2$$
$$\text{Channels} = 10$$

Management by Walking Around

Management by walking around is a concept that actually uses a lot of common sense. It is particularly effective for managers who are a little self-conscious about talking to people. Some of these managers are reluctant to come out of their offices and talk to their own people. Such reclusive managers don't communicate well.

It is easier to show how to do management by walking around than to explain it. The manager practicing the technique of management by walking around makes a commitment to do this for a half-hour to an hour each day. This may seem like a lot of time to the manager at first, but the benefits that are derived will save more time than the time spent doing this.

The manager leaves his or her office and starts walking around the project team office space. When a member of the project team is approached, the manager says something like, "How was your golf game this week?" (Of course, the prudent manager would know that the person actually plays golf.) The manager opens up the conversation with a casual statement, and the team member begins to talk about his or her latest escapade on the golf links. Human nature demands that the team member change the conversation in a short time. Because the team member will not want to excessively talk about his golf game to the project manager, he soon will switch to discussing the project. When this happens all of the anxiety that is often present disappears, and free and honest communication takes place.

If the manager had taken a different approach to this conversation, the results might have been different. If the project manager had come to this team member and said, "Hey John, how are things going on your part of the project?" John would have first asked himself things like, "Why is the boss asking me this?" "Something is wrong and I don't even know about it." "The boss wants to give me another assignment and is trying to see how busy I am." "My review is due, what can I say?" All these things go through a person's mind when he or she is put on the spot. This results in anxiety. The team member gives a minimal response to the manager, and poor communication is the result.

Performance Reviews

One of the problems with matrix management is ensuring that all employees and members of the project team have good and fair performance reviews.

In the early days of matrix management, one of the major difficulties was performance reviews. Typically, a person would come to work on a project, work there for a period of time, and then move back to his or her functional department or move to another project. The project manager concentrated on the project and the customer and did not take the time for performance appraisals. When the employee was assigned to the functional department, he or she experienced less stress and less urgency than when working on projects. The employee relaxed more and took vacations and sick days when working in his or her functional area. At the end of the employee's review period, the functional manager had little to base an appraisal on except the times when the employee was working in the functional area. As a result the employee was given a satisfactory appraisal when perhaps his or her project work had been outstanding.

A simple communications device may be used to eliminate this problem. The project manager meets with the person when he or she first joins the project. At this first meeting the project manager starts a plain sheet of paper and makes comments about the suggested assignments for the person. At the end of the meeting the project manager makes a copy of the notes to give to the individual and files the original. In two weeks another meeting is held to review the progress that has been made since the last meeting. Again, notes are made and copied and given to the individual. As time goes on, these notes accumulate and make up a written history of the work the person has done on the project, his or her successes and failures. When the employee leaves the project, the project manager makes another copy of these notes and sends them to the person's functional manager. In this way the functional manager has a good set of notes on the performance of the individual.

Summary

When project management is discussed by project managers it is not very long before the topic of communications comes up. Communications management is the process that allows for the timely and appropriate generation and dissemination of information.

The communications model consists of a sender and a receiver. The sender thinks of what must be communicated, encodes the communication, and transmits it to the receiver. The receiver perceives the message, decodes it, and understands the meaning of the message. If there is insufficient meaning in the message, the receiver can communicate feedback to the sender.

There are many barriers to communications. These serve to inhibit the communication from occurring in an optimal way. The barriers can be overcome by using good communications techniques.

There are many types of communications and many channels through which communications flow. Verbal and nonverbal communications are appropriate at some times and not others. It is important that the proper type of communication be used. A method for communicating that may work well in one situation may not work well in another.

Formal and informal communications are important in project management. Many times the project manager is required to make formal presentations to customers and stakeholders in the project. Good presentation skills are necessary in a good project manager.

The other half of communication is listening. A good project manager must also have good listening skills. These can be improved by following good listening habits.

Network techniques and management by walking around allow for the collection of good information.

One of the problems that occurred in project management when matrix management was first tried was performance reviews being mishandled by project managers. Performance reviews of everyone on the project team are extremely important and necessary. These reviews can be as simple as both the manager and the subordinate periodically adding their comments to a sheet of paper and making copies for one another.

CHAPTER 7

Risk Management

Risk management is one of the most important areas of project management that must be considered. Companies that want to compete with one another have adopted project management as a method of managing their companies. They have had to learn how to define and control project scope, schedule, and cost as baselines, and they have had to learn all of the control elements necessary to make successful projects. But many of these companies have yet to learn to manage the risks involved in managing a project.

A *risk* is an uncertain event that has a positive or negative effect on at least one project objective. All risks have causes. For example the cause of a risk may be that it is necessary to design the wheel of a bicycle in a bicycle design and manufacturing project. The risk may be that the design of the bicycle wheel takes longer than the time that was allowed for it. All risks have uncertainty associated with them and all risks have an impact associated with them. The impacts can affect the project baselines of cost, schedule, and scope. The risk may also affect activities in multiple areas of the project as well as activities outside of the project.

Risks are justified by the benefits that come as a result of taking them. For example, investors or stockholders in companies take the risk that the company will not be profitable and they could lose their investment. On the other hand they could make a profit and share in the success of the venture. Unless the investors feel that the potential benefits justify the investment expenditure they will simply put their money into another venture. The least-risk investment and the one also with the least benefits is investing in United States Treasury Bills. In project risk there are many things that can go wrong in the course of the project. The potential benefits should justify the risks that are taken.

Recall that one of the principles involved in good project management is establishing three baselines. The cost, schedule, and scope baselines are essential to managing a project. These three constraints on a project serve to define the project and give us the goals that are to be obtained. The cost baseline of the project must represent all of the cost that will be incurred in the project. The scope baseline must represent all of the work that has to be done in the project. The schedule baseline must represent all of the time that it is going to take to do the project.

When I discussed scope, I emphasized the importance of discovering and documenting all of the work that has to be done in the project. The scope of the project must also include the work that must be done to handle the work that was not expected to be necessary. When this work is included in the project plan, it affects the scope and schedule baselines as well.

All of this work has some probability of occurring. In other words, work that has a probability of greater than zero but less than 100 percent of occurring is considered to be a risk. Risks can have a positive or negative effect. They can produce benefits for the project, or they can produce loss for the project. The *Guide to the Project Management Body of Knowledge* (*PMBOK*) defines a risk event as "a discrete occurrence that may affect the project for better or worse."

Risks can be divided into known and unknown risks. Known risks are those risks that can be identified. Unknown risks are those that cannot be identified. Even though unknown risks are not identified, we can recognize the effect of these unknown risks and we can plan for them. This planning can be accomplished by looking at expert opinion and observations of similar projects, evaluating the risks that occurred there, and adjusting schedules and budgets accordingly.

When to Do Risk Management

Risk management must be done during the whole life of the project. In the beginning of the conceptual stage of the project, risks are identified almost without effort as the different aspects of the project are discussed. It is important that when these risks are thought of that they be recorded in a risk management file or folder so that they can be dealt with later in the project.

As time goes by and progress is made on the project, the risks need to be reviewed, and the identification process must be repeated for the discovery of new risks. This must be an ongoing, continuous process. Risks that are identified early in the project may change as time goes by. As the project advances, some risks disappear. Other risks that were not thought of earlier will be discovered. As the possibility of each risk approaches, it needs to be reevaluated to ensure that the assessment of the risk made earlier is still valid.

The Risk Process

PMI uses the systems approach to risk management in the *Guide to the PMBOK*. The risk process is divided into six major processes:

1. Risk management planning
2. Risk identification
3. Risk assessment
4. Risk quantification
5. Risk response planning
6. Risk monitoring and control

Risk Management Planning

The planning approach for risk management contains the elements that are necessary to properly prepare and set the ground rules that will allow us to manage the risk of the project. There are several inputs to the risk planning process. The overall project plan is a major input since it defines the stakeholders, size, complexity, and objectives of the project. It also defines the roles and responsibilities of the project team members, decision makers, customers, suppliers, and all of the others who may be involved in the project.

We also need to have an overall company strategy for managing risk. A company that is involved in products that put people's lives in danger will be much more concerned about dealing with these kinds of risk than a company where the risks involve small financial losses.

Templates may be used to assist in making up the risk management plan. This allows much time to be saved by using the already developed content of the plan. Many projects are similar in nature, and you will be able to borrow heavily from already completed or planned project risk management plans.

Risk Breakdown Structure

Much like the work breakdown structure that is the basis for so much of good project management, the Risk Breakdown Structure (RBS) can be considered in much the same way. Starting at the highest level we have the project risks. From there we have a hierarchical structure organized by risk causes. As we move down this structure the description of the risk causes and the risks themselves becomes more and more detailed. For example, a project's risks might first be divided into technical risks, business risks, project management risks, customer risks, and environmental risks. The RBS should continue until all of the detailed risks have been detailed enough that they can be acted on and have one and only one person responsible for them.

Risk Identification

The identification of risks is very important. Each must be described in detail so that it will not be confused with any other risk or project task that must be done. Each risk should be given an identification number. During the course of the project, as more information is gathered about the risk, all of this information can be consolidated about the particular risk.

The first component we need to discuss is the identification of the risk event. In the course of identifying risk events we will call upon the project team, subject matter experts, the stakeholders, and other project managers. Much of the work already done in the project will be utilized in the risk management process. Among these items that will be used are the project charter, the work breakdown structure, project description, project schedule, cost estimates, budgets, resource availability, resource schedules, procurement information, and assumptions that have been made and recorded.

There are many ways to discover and identify risks. I will discuss several of them here:

- Documentation reviews
- Brainstorming
- Delphi technique
- Nominal group technique
- Crawford slip
- Expert interviews
- Root cause identification
- Strengths, Weaknesses, Opportunities, and Threats (SWOT) analysis
- Checklists
- Analogy

Documentation Reviews

Documentation reviews comprise reviewing all of the project materials that have been generated up to the date of this risk review. This includes reviewing lessons learned and risk management plans from previous projects; contract obligations; project baselines for scope, schedule, and budget; resource availabilities; staffing plans; suppliers; and assumptions lists.

Brainstorming

Brainstorming is probably the most popular technique for identifying risks. It is useful in generating any kind of list by mining the ideas of the participants. To use the technique, a meeting is called to make a comprehensive list of risks. It is important that the purpose of the meeting be explained clearly to the participants, and it is helpful if they are prepared when they arrive at the meeting. The meeting should have between ten and fifteen participants. If there are fewer than ten, there is not enough interaction among the participants. If there are more than fifteen people, the meeting tends to be difficult to control and keep focused. The meeting should take less than two hours.

For larger projects it may be necessary to hold several meetings. Each meeting should deal with a separate part of the project and with the risks associated with that project part. This will keep the number of persons involved to a reasonable size, and the meetings will be much more productive.

When the meeting begins, the participants can name risks that they think are important for consideration in the project. No discussion of the items listed is allowed at this time. As participants see ideas listed, they will think of additional ideas. Each new idea will elicit another idea from someone, and many ideas for possible risks will be listed.

Delphi Technique

The Delphi technique is similar to brainstorming, but the participants do not know one another. This technique is useful when the participants are some distance away. The Delphi technique is much more efficient and useful today than it has been in the past because of the use of e-mail as a medium for conducting the exercise. Because the participants in this technique are anonymous, there is little to inhibit the flow of ideas. Where the participants are not anonymous, there is a tendency for one or more persons to dominate the meeting. If one of the participants is a higher-level manager than the others in the meeting, many of the meeting participants will be inhibited or try to show off in front of the upper-level manager. All of this is avoided in the Delphi technique.

The process begins with the facilitator using a questionnaire to solicit risk ideas about the project. The responses by the participants are then categorized and clarified by the facilitator. The categorized, clarified list is then circulated to the participants for comments or additions. The members of the group may modify their position, but they must give reasons for doing so. Consensus and a detailed list of the project risks can be obtained in a few rounds.

The Delphi technique avoids one of the major drawbacks to brainstorming. Because the participants are not known to one another, it avoids peer pressure and the risk of embarrassment from putting forth a silly idea or one that could be ridiculed by others. This does not come without cost. The facilitator must do much more work for the Delphi technique than the facilitator in a brainstorming session. For example, the facilitator frequently has to nag the participants, who may procrastinate in returning their responses.

There is also some risk involved in using this technique. The facilitator is required to analyze and categorize the inputs from the participants, which means that he impresses much of his opinion on the group.

Nominal Group Technique

In the nominal group technique, the idea is to eliminate some of the problems with other techniques, particularly the problems associated with persons' inhibitions and reluctance to participate. In this technique a group size of seven to ten persons is used. The facilitator instructs the participants to privately and silently each list their ideas on a piece of paper. When this is completed, the facilitator takes each piece of paper and lists the ideas on a flip chart or blackboard. At this time no discussion takes place.

Once all of the ideas are listed on the flip chart, the group discusses each idea. During the discussion, clarifications or explanations are made. Each member of the group now ranks the ideas in order of importance, again in secret. The result is an ordered list of the risks in order of their importance. This process not only identifies risks but also does a preliminary evaluation of them.

This process reduces the effect of a high-ranking person in the group but does not eliminate it, like the Delphi technique. The nominal group technique is faster and requires less effort on the part of the facilitator than the Delphi technique.

Crawford Slip

The Crawford slip process has become popular recently. The Crawford slip process does not require as strong a facilitator as the other techniques, and it produces a lot of ideas very quickly. A Crawford slip meeting can take place in less than half an hour.

The usual number of seven to ten participants is used, but larger groups can be accommodated, since there is a fairly small amount of interaction among the persons in the group. The facilitator begins by instructing the group that she will ask ten questions, one at a time. Each participant must answer each question with a different answer. The same answer cannot be used for more than one question. The participants are to write their answer to each question on a separate piece of paper. (Post-it Notes are good for this purpose.) The facilitator tells the participants that they will have one minute to answer each question.

When all the participants are ready, the facilitator begins by asking a question such as, "What is the most important risk to this project?" The participants write down their answers. After one minute, the facilitator repeats the question. This is repeated ten times. The effect is that the participants are forced to think of ten separate risks in the project. Even with duplicates among the members, the number of risks identified is formidable.

Expert Interviews

Experts or people with experience in this type of project or problem can be of great help in avoiding solving the same problems over and over again. Caution must be exercised whenever using expert opinions. If an expert is trusted implicitly and his or her advice is taken without question, the project can head off in the wrong direction under the influence of one so-called expert.

The use of experts, particularly those hired from outside the project organization, can be costly. Care must be taken to ensure that experts are used efficiently and effectively. Before the expert interview is conducted, the input information must be given to the expert and the goals of the interview must be clearly understood. During the interview, the information from the expert must be recorded. If more than one expert is used, the output information from the interviews should be consolidated and circulated to the other experts.

Root Cause Identification

Root cause identification is a process developed by RCA. It helps to identify the what, how, and particularly the why of something going wrong. It seeks to find the underlying causes that can be identified and controlled. The RCA process is aimed at identifying the underlying cause for a problem. Frequently people tend to fix the symptoms of a problem because they are more apparent. By fixing the root cause of a problem we can avoid the same problem in the future.

These root causes are something we can do something about. For example, assume that a risk that parts will be delivered late becomes a risk event that actually happens. As we investigate why this happened we find that there was a severe snowstorm at the vendor's location and that trucks could not move for three days. The root cause of the problem is not the severe weather. It is not ordering the parts early enough to allow for severe weather delays.

Strengths, Weaknesses, Opportunities, and Threats (SWOT) Analysis

SWOT analysis takes into consideration the external and internal environment of an organization. Strengths and weaknesses are usually considered internal environmental factors while opportunities and threats are usually considered external.

As can be seen in Figure 7-1, a matrix can be made showing the possible combinations of the internal and external factors. The S-O strategies are the ones that should be pursued because there is a good fit between the external opportunities and the internal strengths of the company. With W-O strategies, we must overcome our internal weaknesses before we can pursue the opportunity. S-T strategies are strategies where we must use our strengths to overcome the threats to us. W-T strategies are strategies where we must find a defensive position to prevent the threats from taking advantage of our weaknesses.

Checklists

Checklists have gained in popularity in recent years because of the ease of communicating through computers and the ease of sharing information through databases. There are many commercially available databases, and there are many checklists that are generated locally for specific companies and applications.

Figure 7-1. SWOT analysis matrix.

	Strengths	Weaknesses
Opportunities	S-O Strategies	W-O Strategies
Threats	S-T Strategies	W-T Strategies

In their basic form, these checklists are simply predetermined lists of risks that are possible for given projects. In their specific form, they are risks that have occurred in the particular types of projects that a company has worked on in the past. Frequently, certain customers and stakeholders have particular risks associated with them that can forewarn the manager of the new project.

Analogy

The analogous method of identifying risks is quite simple. From the lessons learned and the risk management plan of other projects that were similar, an analogy can be formed. By comparing two or more projects, characteristics that are similar for each project can be seen that will give insight into the risks of the new project.

Diagramming Techniques

Various types of diagramming techniques have been developed that will help in the identification of risks. Cause-and-effect diagrams are used to organize information and show how various items relate to one another. There are several possible risks that contribute to the main risk in question. Each of the contributing risks can be further diagrammed until there is a complete hierarchy of risks. Once diagrammed, the relationships between the risks can easily be seen.

Flowcharts are diagrams that show the sequence of events that take place in a given process. They also show conditional branching. Each point on the flow diagram can be used as a possible point for identifying risks. A comparison of risk identification techniques is shown in Table 7-1.

For other diagramming techniques, see Chapter 4, Quality Management.

Table 7-1. Comparison of risk identification techniques.

Identification Technique	Advantages	Disadvantages
Brainstorming	• Encourages interaction in the group • Fast • Not expensive	• Can be dominated by an individual • Can focus on specific areas only • Requires a strong facilitator • Must control tendency of the group to evaluate
Delphi Technique	• Cannot be dominated by an individual • Can be done remotely by e-mail • Avoids problem of early evaluation • Every person must participate	• Time consuming • Labor intensive for facilitator
Nominal Group Technique	• Reduces the effect of a dominant individual • Allows for interaction of participants • Results in a ranked list of risk ideas	• Time consuming • Labor intensive for facilitator
Crawford Slip	• Fast • Easy to implement • Every person must participate • Large number of ideas generated • Able to do with larger than normal group • Reduces the effect of a dominant individual	• Less interaction between participants
Expert Interviews	• Take advantage of past experience	• Expert may be biased • Time intensive
Checklists	• Focused and organized • Easy to use	• Prejudgment • May not include specific items for this project

| Analogy Techniques | • Use past experience to avoid future experiences
 • Similar projects have many similarities | • Time intensive
 • Easy to obtain data that is not relevant
 • Analogy may be incorrect |
| Diagramming Techniques | • Clear representation of the process involved
 • Easy to generate
 • Many computer tools available for them | • Sometimes misleading
 • Can be time consuming |

Recording of Risks Identified

Once the risks have been identified, they must be recorded. There is nothing worse than identifying a risk and then not thinking about it again until it happens. Since risk management must take place many times during the course of the project, there needs to be a way of organizing and documenting the risks. In the beginning of the project the risks may only be identified. Later in the project, additional information will be continuously added to the risk events that were identified.

This does not need to be a complicated documentation method, but there are certain pieces of information that must be recorded:

1. Name of the risk
2. Description of the risk
3. Date the risk was entered
4. Person responsible for managing the risk
5. Reference to the work breakdown structure
6. Probability that the risk will occur
7. Impact of the risk if it occurs
8. Severity of the risk
9. Mitigation strategies

Risk Assessment

Risk assessment is the stage in our risk management process where the importance of each risk is evaluated. This evaluation will also serve as the guideline for determining the risk strategy. Here we use the list of identified risks that were made as inputs. The list of risks will constantly change as well, since the time of the risk and the progress toward completion of the project will affect the risks that will be on the list of identified risks.

It is critical that the risks be evaluated, since, because of risk tolerance of the stakeholders, some risks will be ignored while others will have rather elaborate monitoring and mitigation plans associated with them. The evaluation or assessment process is necessary to itemize these risks into a ranking that will place them in the order of importance.

In the evaluation process we will be concerned with determining the impact and probability of the risk. From these two factors we can determine the severity of the risk. The severity of the risk will allow its ranking in order of importance.

Qualitative Risk Analysis

Qualitative analysis is a fast, inexpensive way to organize risks according to their importance. Since it is fast and inexpensive it also means that not a lot of detailed information is collected about the risk. This can lead to errors that may rank some risks higher or lower than they deserve to be. As we have said earlier, we must perform risk analysis many times during the course of the project. Risks that are identified long before they can happen need not have a rigorous quantitative analysis since they may never actually happen. Circumstances can often change to make risks that were menacing become trivial or nonexistent.

In analyzing a risk, its probability and impact can be determined in its simplest form by stating its probability as "likely" or "not likely," "bad impact" or "not so bad." We can easily raise the level of discrimination by evaluating the probability and impact of risk as "high," "medium," or "low." This raises the choices of category for a risk from two to three. We could also assess probability by assigning a number from 1 to 10, where 1 is least probable and has least impact, and 10 is very probable and has high impact. As our probability or impact discriminator becomes better, the cost and difficulty of assigning numbers becomes higher. Finally, the most discriminating analysis would be the use of specific probability estimates between zero and one, with accuracy to as many decimal places as can be estimated. Impacts can then be evaluated in terms of dollars.

Many versions of the probability and impact matrix have been done. As can be seen in Figure 7-2, the matrix is formed by assigning a value from 1 to 9 for our assessment of the risk's probability and another value from 1–9 for the risk's impact. By multiplying the values together we get a composite number called severity. The matrix gives a value for severity that can be used to value the importance or severity of the risk. Values of 28 to 81 should be considered high risks. Values from 1 to 9 should be considered low risks, and values from 10 to 27 should be considered medium risks. Expanding the concept to the point of being ridiculous, we could have these matrixes done for each risk and for each type of problem that could develop. Thus we might have separate matrices for cost, schedule, and scope impact, and so on.

Risks can additionally be categorized by their immediacy. Risks that are imminent should have a higher priority than those that are going to happen far in the future. Many of the risks anticipated far in the future may not take place at all.

Risk Tolerance

Risks that have very high probabilities but very low impacts, as well as risks that have very high impacts but very low probabilities, are risks that may not be considered as being

Figure 7-2. Risk probability and impact matrix.

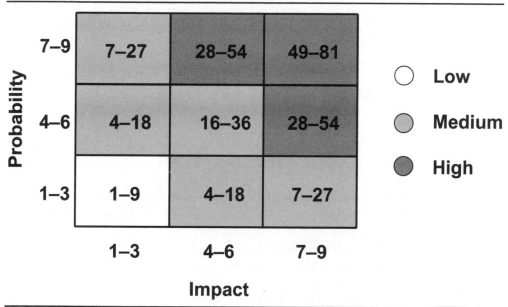

important to the project. It is the combination of probability and impact that causes the risk to be an important consideration to the project.

Consider a risk of very high impact and very low probability, such as the threat to a project caused by a category five hurricane occurring when and where the project work is taking place. This is probably a risk that we would not spend much time and effort worrying about. Although the problems that would occur if the office building were to be blown down or flooded during a hurricane would be great, their likelihood is low enough that we would not worry too much about the risk. Even in New Orleans, where hurricanes are more likely to occur than many other places, they have disrupted business only three times in twenty years, and even then damage was minor.

Let's look at the other extreme of risk: a risk that has a very high probability of occurring but a very low impact. An example of this kind of risk is one person on the project team calling in sick during the project. The probability that this will happen at least one time in the course of the project is close to 100 percent, but the impact is very small. This is a risk that we are not going to spend much time worrying about.

The risks we need to worry about are all the ones that have a reasonably high probability and a reasonably high impact. But what is reasonably high? As in many of the questions that are raised in project management, the answer is: It depends. In this case it depends on risk tolerance.

Risk tolerance is the willingness or the unwillingness of a person or an organization to accept risk. Some individuals and some organizations are risk takers, while others are risk avoiders. One company might be willing to take a large risk of losing a great deal of money on the chance that an even greater amount of money could be made. Another company might not be willing to take the risk of losing the money.

I do this experiment in most of the classes I teach in risk management. I ask all of the students to stand up. I then offer to make a bet with them. I have a single die that I will roll. If the rolled die comes up with a 1 or a 2, I win; if it comes up 3, 4, 5, or 6, then the student wins. The probability of winning is 2 chances in 3, and the probability of losing is 1 chance in 3.

I ask the students, "How many of you would be willing to bet 25 cents on this roll of the dice?" Nearly everyone stays standing. Then I ask, "How many of you would be willing to bet $2 on this roll of the dice?" A few sit down.

Next I ask, "How many of you would be willing to bet $20 on this roll of the dice?" More sit down. The next question is, "How many of you would be willing to bet $200 on this roll of the dice?" Many sit down.

The bet is raised until all sit down. There is usually one in the class who just keeps standing until the bet gets so high that having to pay it off would be impossible.

The people who sit down in the early stages are the risk avoiders. The people who sit down last are the risk takers. Even though the probability of winning is 2 out of 3, as the size of the bet increases people refuse to take the bet. This is because there is still some chance of losing, and the damage to their financial security is too great to be tolerated. It is one thing to bet your lunch money and have to skip lunch if you lose, but it is quite another to bet your house and car and have to do without them if you lose.

Companies work like individuals in this area of risk tolerance. Companies like General Motors have a relatively low tolerance for accepting risk. Their reluctance to accept risk was nearly their undoing in the 1970s when they were forced to compete with Japanese automakers. Other companies are willing to take large risks and even put the entire company at great risk. Amazon.com is an example of a company that is willing to risk a great deal to make a lot of money. At this writing Amazon.com, a billion-dollar (in sales) corporation, has only recently made its first profit in its entire history. Still, investors think that even though the risks are high, there is a good chance to make a lot of money on this company.

As we move into more detail in determining the components of risks to our project, it is important to realize that the techniques discussed can be used to determine all of the components of risk. When I discuss an item like expert interviews or Crawford slip, it is important to realize that these techniques could be used to help determine the probability and the impact of the risk as well as to identify the risk.

Risk Probability

Since all risks have a probability of greater than zero and less than 100 percent, the probability of a risk occurring is essential to the assessment of the risk. Any risk event that has a probability of zero cannot occur and need not be considered as a risk. A risk event that has a probability of 100 percent is not a risk. It has a certainty of occurring and must be planned for in the project plan. Understanding the fundamentals of probability is necessary if we are to understand the role of probability in risk analysis.

Probability is the number that represents the chance that a particular outcome will occur when the conditions allow it. The probability of one possibility occurring is 1 divided by the number of other possible outcomes. In the rolling of die (half a pair of dice), there is 1 chance out of 6 that the result will be a 1. The possibilities are 1, 2, 3, 4, 5, or 6. The probability would be expressed as 1/6 or .167 or even 16.7 percent. All of these terms are commonly used in expressing probability. The outcome of an event is the result of any event taking place. Outcomes cannot be subdivided into smaller outcomes: 1, 2, 3, 4, 5, and 6 represent all of the possible outcomes of rolling our die. The term *event* means the set of all the possible outcomes that could occur.

These events of rolling the die are considered to be mutually exclusive. A mutually exclusive event is one where the occurrence of one of the possibilities eliminates the possibility of the others. In our rolling of the die, all of the possibilities are mutually exclusive, since the rolling of a 5 makes it impossible for a 1, 2, 3, 4, or 6 to occur.

In risk management we frequently have mutually exclusive risks. A risk will occur or it will not occur. If it occurs then it cannot *not* occur. The sum of the probabilities of all the things that can occur in a given set of circumstances will equal 1.0. This is the sum of all the probabilities of all the possible outcomes. In our rolling of the die, all the probabilities that exist are that the die will come up with a 1, 2, 3, 4, 5, or 6. Each of these has a probability of 1/6. The sum of all the probabilities is: 1/6 + 1/6 + 1/6 + 1/6 + 1/6 + 1/6 = 6/6 = 1. In decimals, this is: .167 + .167 + .167 + .167 + .167 + .167 = 1.

In the rolling of a die or in situations where there are only specific outcomes possible, it is assumed that the die is a fair die, that all of the sides weigh the same, and that the corners and anything else affecting the roll of the die are equal. If we had a real die, however, there would be some bias in the die. After rolling the die many times it might be seen that one number comes up more frequently than another. This would be an indication of bias in the die.

The relative frequency definition of probability says that the proportion of past circumstances in which this outcome has occurred determines the probability of a particular outcome. This is the type of evaluation that we use most of the time in business decisions. A business is much better off relying on past experience and observations than assuming that there is no bias in the relevant circumstances. When the relative frequency definition of probability can be used, it is extremely valuable. There are two major difficulties associated with this measure, however.

Let's take the example of a business that operates a theater. The business owner must determine whether it would be better to offer a comedy or a high drama. The risk is that if the owner chooses the wrong type of entertainment, the public will not come to the theater.

Based on past experience, the theater operator determines that when a comedy was offered, money was made 80 percent of the time. When a drama was offered, money was made 60 percent of the time. Based on this past experience, the theater owner should offer nothing but comedy. But this would be a mistake, because the audience changes with each situation. In this situation, the audience would become bored with the constant offering of comedies, and the theater operator would probably lose more money than if dramas were also presented.

The other difficulty in risk management decisions using the relative frequency definition of probability is that there is usually not enough experience in the past to reliably predict the future. For this reason, subjective probability is used. *Subjective probability* is the best estimate that can be made to predict the future outcome based on the conditions that can be known.

As in all mathematical areas there are rules that must be followed if we are going to achieve consistent results. We will need to worry about only a few of these rules.

The Addition Rule

The addition rule in probability explains the probability of one or more of several events occurring. I will start by showing the probability of two events. We can consider the probability of either event A or event B occurring when they are both mutually exclusive events.

Suppose we roll one die again. This time we are interested in two events. Event A is that the die will come up with an odd number. Event B is that the die will come up with an even number. Event A is satisfied if there is a 1, 3, or 5. Event B is satisfied if there is a 2, 4, or 6.

The probability we are interested in is the probability that either event A or event B will occur. This means that if the die comes up with a 1, 2, 3, 4, 5, or 6 we will meet the conditions of the question. The probability of this is 1.0, since there are only six possibilities, and all six are contained in event A or B. Also notice that the probability of event A is .5 (three out of six possibilities) and the probability of event B is .5 as well.

So, for mutually exclusive events we can say that the probability of either of them occurring is the sum of the probabilities of each:

$$P(A \text{ or } B) = P(A) + P(B)$$

With the same explanation we could extend this to more than two mutually exclusive events. In this example, event A would be to roll a 1 or 2. Event B would be a 3 or 4. Event C would be a 5 or 6. The probability of A or B or C would be the sum of the probability of A, B, and C:

$$P(A \text{ or } B \text{ or } C) = P(A) + P(B) + P(C)$$

In fact, we can say that this is true for any number of mutually exclusive events:

$$P(A \text{ or } B \text{ or } \ldots \text{ or } N) = P(A) + P(B) + \ldots + P(N)$$

Well, all this is fine for probabilities that are mutually exclusive, but what about the situations where the events we are interested in are not mutually exclusive? When the events are not mutually exclusive, applying the addition rule as stated will produce a probability that is too high.

Suppose we are interested in two events with our die again. Event A is the rolling of an odd number, that is, 1, 3, or 5. Event B is the rolling of a number less than 4, that is, 1, 2, or 3.

The probability of event A is 3/6. The probability of event B is 3/6. If we apply the mutually exclusive addition rule the result would be: 3/6 + 3/6 = 6/6 = 1. Since rolling 4 or 6 are possibilities, the probability of getting an odd number *or* a number less than 4 cannot be 1.

The problem here is that the two events described are not mutually exclusive. It is possible to have numbers show on the die that satisfy both events at the same time. The numbers 1 and 3 showing on the die are odd and less than 4. When we look at the probability of event A, 1, 3, or 5, and event B, 1, 2, or 3, and apply the addition rule, we get 1, 3, 5, 1, 2, or 3. We can roll only one number in one roll of the die and the numbers that will satisfy either event A or event B are 1, 2, 3, or 5. We should not count the extra 1 and 3. The probability of event A or B is 4/6, or 2/3.

Now the addition rule can include events that are not mutually exclusive:

$$P(A \text{ or } B) = P(A) + P(B) - P(A \text{ and } B)$$

One more example. Suppose we roll a pair of dice, and we want to know the probability of getting at least one 6.

By the addition rule we might say that the probability of getting a 6 on the first roll is 1/6, and the probability of getting a 6 on the second roll is 1/6. The probability of getting a 6 on the first roll or the second roll is 1/6 + 1/6 = 2/6. But this would be incorrect.

In Table 7-2, all of the possible combinations of rolling two dice are shown. If we count the boxes that contain at least one 6 and divide by the number of possible combinations, we should have the probability that we seek.

Doing this we find that there are thirty-six possible outcomes for rolling a pair of dice. In the table, eleven of the combinations would produce at least one 6.

Correctly applying the addition rule, we get the following:

$$P(\text{at least one 6 in two rolls}) = P(\text{6 on the first roll})$$
$$+ \ P(\text{6 on the second roll})$$
$$- \ P(\text{6 on both rolls})$$
$$P(\text{6 or 6}) = 1/6 + 1/6 - 1/36$$
$$P = 11/36$$

The Multiplication Rule

So far we have not explained the term P(A and B) completely. Before we explain this rule of probability, a few definitions are in order: conditional probability and statistical independence.

Conditional probability is the probability of an event given the information that some other event has occurred. Suppose we are interested in the probability of rolling a single die and getting a number less than 4. The probability is 1/2.

Now suppose that I knew that the die had an odd number on it. Does this change the probability of having a number less than 4? There are two numbers that are less than 4 and odd—1 and 3—and there are three numbers that are odd: 1, 3, and 5. If we know that the number facing up on the die is odd, we can say that the probability of it being less than 4 is 2/3, not 1/2. The condition of "being odd" has changed the probability. This is conditional probability. The notation that is used, P(A | B), is read, "The probability of event A given event B."

In our example, event A was a number less than 4, and event B was an odd number. Our statement was the probability of having a number less than 4 given that the number is an odd number.

Statistical independence says that the probability of event A is the same as the probability of event A given the probability of event B. If P(A) = P(A | B), then event A and event B are statistically independent.

The probability of rolling a 6 on the third roll of a die is 1/6. If a 6 had been rolled on the second or even the first and second roll of the die, the probability of getting a 6 on the third roll is still 1/6. These events, rolling a die on the first roll, rolling a die on the second roll, and rolling a die on the third roll are statistically independent.

Table 7-2. Possible combinations of rolling two dice.

1,1	1,2	1,3	1,4	1,5	1,6
2,1	2,2	2,3	2,4	2,5	2,6
3,1	3,2	3,3	3,4	3,5	3,6
4,1	4,2	4,3	4,4	4,5	4,6
5,1	5,2	5,3	5,4	5,5	5,6
6,1	6,2	6,3	6,4	6,5	6,6

Statistically dependent events are events where the probability of A given B is not the same as the probability of A alone. The probability of getting a number less than 4 given that the number is odd is different from the probability of getting a number less than 4. In this case it is 2/3 versus 1/2. Therefore, these events are statistically dependent.

Finally, getting back to the multiplication rule:

$$P(A \text{ and } B) = P(A \mid B)\, P(B)$$

The probability of getting event A and event B is the probability of event A given event B multiplied by the probability of event B.

In the example of the two dice being rolled and finding the probability of getting at least one 6, we had to subtract the probability of getting a 6 and a 6 on a roll of two dice. This value can be calculated by seeing that the P(6 on the second die), 1/6, and the P(6 on the first die given that a 6 was rolled on the second die), 1/6:

$$P(A \text{ and } B) = P(A \mid B)\, P(B)$$
$$P(A \text{ and } B) = 1/6 \times 1/6 = 1/36$$

Notice that event A and event B are also statistically independent. This means that we could have stated the equation this way:

$$P(A \text{ and } B) = P(A)\, P(B)$$

This simplified form of the multiplication rule for statistically independent events is useful. Suppose we want to know the probability of rolling a 6 on a die three times in a row. Since the events are statistically independent, the multiplication rule can be applied:

P(A and B and C) = P(A) P(B) P(C)
P(6 on the first roll and 6 on the second roll and 6 on the third roll)
= 1/6 × 1/6 × 1/6 = 1/216, or .00463

For example, suppose we are interested in the risk of not having a critical part delivered for our project. The vendor that we have chosen has a reliability of delivering parts on time 95 percent of the time. This is an unacceptable risk for the project, and the project manager decides that the order will be split between two different vendors. The project manager hopes that at least one of the vendors will deliver on time.

The probability that vendor A will be late is .05. The probability that vendor B will be late is .05. Events A and B are statistically independent, since the delivery of one vendor on time does not influence the probability of the other vendor delivering on time. The probability of both vendors being late is:

P(A being late *and* B being late) = P(A being late) × P(B being late)
P(A and B) = .05 × .05 = .0025, or 1/4 of 1 percent

To summarize, the assessment of the probability of the risk is important for determining the overall importance of the risk. The rules of probability are important to know so that there is an understanding about what these values mean and that we have some guidance in determining the values to use. Most project risks can be considered mutually exclusive, but not always. Mutually exclusive risks are those where we consider the probability event as "the risk will occur or it will not." If the risk occurs, then it cannot *not* occur. This meets our definition of mutually exclusive.

Risk Impact

The next subject we need to discuss is the next component in risk management, the evaluation of the impact of the risk. Risk impact is the cost of the risk if it occurs. This, in its qualitative measure, is the pain level of the risk. Quantitative measures include the impact of the identified risk in terms of schedule days, effort person-hours, money, and so on.

Risk impacts are those things that affect the cost, schedule, or scope of the project. These impacts can manifest themselves as effects on the level of effort required, labor rates, duration of tasks, technical feasibility, material suitability, material cost, equipment availability, and more.

In determining the impact of a risk it is important to realize that all of the techniques that we have previously discussed, such as brainstorming or the use of probability analysis, can be used to determine the impact of a risk. Likewise, the use of the tools discussed here is not limited to their use in impact analysis. They may yield valuable information about risks that have not been previously identified.

In its simplest terms, *impact* can be described as "real bad" or "not so bad." This separates risks into those that we think have a great impact and those that we think do not. We could improve this by addressing impacts as "high," "medium," or "low." We could further improve this evaluation by giving the risk a numerical value from 1 to 10, or even 1 to 100.

Expected Value

Expected values are a way of combining the probability and the impact of a risk in a meaningful way. The expected value calculation is simply multiplying the probability, in terms of zero to one, times the impact, usually measured in terms of dollars or schedule days. Impact may be measured in any convenient value.

Since this is a more quantitative result than the usual subjective values of probability and impact, it is proper to summarize expected values to total project risk. For example, consider the possibilities of winning money on a lottery ticket. The ticket you buy can win $2, with a probability of 5 percent. It could also win $100 with a probability of 1/2 percent. Of course, there is a 94.5 percent chance of winning nothing. The ticket costs $1.00 to play.

Notice that the three possible outcomes of the event are mutually exclusive. If you were to win $2, it would not be possible to win $100 or nothing (Table 7-3).

With expected values we have a way of evaluating the opportunities and risks involved in the project. The expected value is also a good guideline for the amount of money that might be spent to eliminate the risk.

Let's say that there is a 10 percent chance of a risk occurring that would have a $10,000 impact on the project. The expected value of this risk would be $1,000. If it would be possible to completely avoid this risk by spending $900, it would be considered a good decision to avoid this risk.

Another way of looking at the expected value is to think of the project as being done many hundreds of times (theoretically, that is). For a risk that has a probability of 10 percent, the risk would probably occur in 10 percent of the projects. The average cost of the risk to all the hundreds of projects would be 10 percent of the total risk impact.

It is also interesting to look at the best-case and worst-case situations for the project. This is a simple analytical method that gives us insight into the extreme possibilities that might occur in the project. This is useful when considering the risk tolerance of the individuals or groups involved in the decision-making process.

In the best-case expected value calculation, all of the positive risks are considered to have happened, while none of the negative risks are considered. In the worst-case expected value calculation, all of the negative risks are considered to have occurred, while none of the good risks are considered.

For example, suppose after analyzing risks of a potential project we find the situation shown in Table 7-4. Notice that in the calculation of the worst-case and best-case situations the probability of the risks is not considered. The best case is where everything good that can happen happens and everything bad that can happen does not happen. The worst case is where everything bad that can happen happens and everything good that can happen does not happen.

Table 7-3. The possibilities of winning money on a lottery ticket.

	Probability	Impact	Expected Value
	.05	2	.10
	.005	100	.50
	.945	0	0
Total expected value of revenue			.65
Cost of ticket			−1.00
Expected value of the opportunity			−.35

Table 7-4. Worst-case and best-case situations.

Risk Event	Impact	Probability	Expected Value
Project cost	−2,000,000		−2,000,000
Project revenue	2,200,000		+2,200,000
Fail acceptance test	−100,000	10%	−10,000
Warranty failures	−40,000	15%	−6,000
Additional orders	75,000	30%	+22,500
Penalty for late delivery	−50,000	5%	−2,500
Incentive for early delivery	100,000	30%	+30,000
Expected value of the project (sum of all values)			234,000
Best case (all good risks occur, no bad risks occur)			375,000
Worst case (all bad risks occur, no good risks occur)			10,000

Decision Trees

In a more complex situation it is difficult to calculate the expected value of the project. For these more complex situations a technique called *decision tree analysis* is often used. In this case a large number of individual outcomes are possible.

For example, let's say that you have a large uncut diamond of 6 carats. The diamond cutter says that if the diamond is cut into small stones, the aggregate value of the stones will be $250,000. If the diamond is cut into one large stone, the value will be $100,000. The problem associated with cutting the diamond into smaller stones is that there is a 20 percent chance that the diamond will shatter when cut. If the diamond shatters when it is cut, the aggregate value will be $10,000.

In making the decision to cut or not cut the diamond, expected values could be used. There is a 20 percent chance that the diamond will be worth $10,000, and there is an 80 percent chance that it will be worth $250,000. The expected value of these two mutually exclusive possibilities is:

$$.8 \times \$250,000 + .2 \times \$10,000 = \$202,000$$

If the diamond is not cut, the expected value is $100,000. The obvious choice is to have the diamond cut into smaller diamonds. The decision tree diagram for this situation is shown in Figure 7-3. In the decision tree diagram, boxes are used to represent decisions that can be made, and circles are used to indicate probabilistic events that may occur.

Figure 7-3. Decision tree.

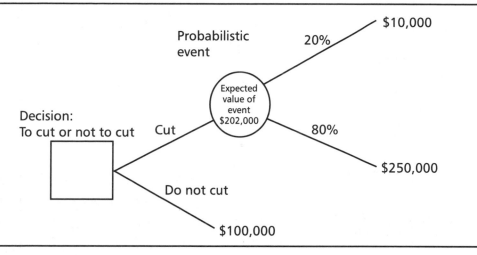

Suppose we now complicate the process. For a $5,000 fee, the diamond can be sent to a firm that can study the structure of the diamond with an electron microscope and microsound echo scanning to improve the chances of cutting the diamond successfully. According to the firm proposing the study, if they predict that the diamond will not shatter, then 99 percent of the time, when the diamond is cut, it will not shatter. If the prediction is that the diamond will shatter, then the diamond will shatter 95 percent of the time. Let's say that the diamond itself has a 20 percent chance of shattering, as before.

The decisions to be made are: Should you pay for the prediction, and should you have the diamond cut?

The decision that must be made is whether to pay for the inspection. Regardless of whether the inspection is performed, a decision must still be made as to whether to have the diamond cut or not. If the decision is made not to go ahead with the inspection, then the choices are the same, with the same expected values that we had in the simpler example. Once the inspection is completed, it will predict 20 percent of the time that the stone will shatter, and it will predict that 80 percent of the time the stone will not. This is not smoke and mirrors; of all the diamonds cut in recent times, 20 percent of this type of diamond have shattered. The question is whether this particular diamond will shatter. That is the point of the inspection.

In the upper part of Figure 7-4, the decision has been made to purchase the inspection. Twenty percent of the time the inspection will predict shattering, and 80 percent of the time the inspection will predict not shattering. Of course, if the inspection predicts shattering, there is a 5 percent chance that the diamond will not shatter when cut anyway. If the inspection predicts that the diamond will not shatter, there is a 1 percent chance that it is wrong and the diamond will shatter anyway.

Figure 7-4. Cutting the diamond.

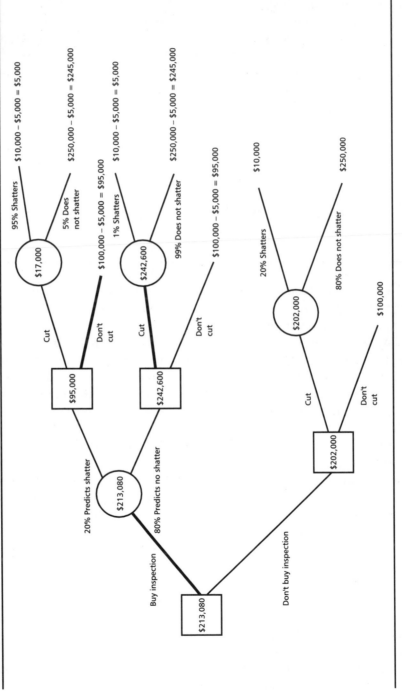

So, what decision should be made?

In the choice to not cut the stone after the lab predicts that it would shatter, the expected value of the decision is $95,000. This is because deciding to cut the diamond under these conditions yields an expected value of $14,600: the $10,000 value of the shattered stone minus the $5,000 fee to the inspection company, or $250,000 less the $5,000 fee. Ninety-five percent of $5,000 plus 5 percent of $245,000 equals $17,000.

The decision not to cut the stone yields $95,000, the $100,000 value of the uncut stone minus the $5,000 fee for the inspection. The decision is made to not have the stone cut after the inspection predicted shattering of the stone.

If the inspecting company predicts that the stone will not shatter, you still must make the decision whether or not to cut the stone. If the decision is made to not cut the stone, the yield is $95,000, the $100,000 value of the uncut stone minus the $5,000 fee for the inspection.

If the decision is made to cut the stone, the expected value is $242,600. If the stone is not cut, the value is $95,000. If the stone is cut, there is a 1 percent chance that it will shatter, yielding $5,000. There is a 99 percent chance that the stone will not shatter, yielding $245,000. The expected value of cutting the stone is:

$$(.99 \times \$245,000) + (.01 \times \$5,000) = 242,600$$

The decision to cut the stone yields $242,600.

Moving to the next branching in Figure 7-4, there is a 20 percent chance that the inspection will predict shattering and an 80 percent chance that it will predict not shattering.

The expected value is:

$$(20\% \times \$95,000) + (80\% \times \$242,600) = \$213,080$$

The last decision is whether to hire the inspection or not. Since the expected value of not having the inspection yielded a value of $202,000, and the expected value of the decision to have the inspection done is $213,080, the inspecting company should be hired.

Risk Quantification

As part of the quantification process in risk management, we need to find a way to organize the risks so that they can be dealt with in a logical way. There are two things we need to consider. The first is that the risks need to be put into groups that can then be managed by individuals who are more familiar with the nature of these risks. The second is that the risks need to be put into some priority order. This is because no organization will ever have the funds or manpower to deal with all the risks. At some point the level of impact and probability will be such that even the most conservative of risk takers will take that risk and accept it.

If we use probabilities between 0 and 1 to estimate the likelihood of our risks, and we use a quantitative number to assess impact, then we could multiply the two values and get the expected value for the risk. If the estimates were done consistently, then we would have a measure to rank them with the highest expected value at the top of the list and the rest below it in descending order. This is the same as the expected value analysis we did previously.

The most qualitative and simple method of evaluating risks can be used in a similar way. The most basic evaluation for risk could be to say the risk is "likely" and "bad," using only the distinctions of "likely" and "unlikely" for probability and "bad" and "very bad" for impact.

A step toward quantitative measure might be to evaluate the risks as, "high," "medium," and "low." Going further, the risks could be evaluated on a scale of 1 to 10 or 1 to 100. Any other system or a combination of any of these is also appropriate. There is nothing wrong in saying that a risk has a high probability of occurring and has an impact of $40,000.

The ultimate goal of this risk prioritization scheme is to get the risks into some hierarchical order. Then the resources of the project can be concentrated on the risks at the top of the list, and effort is spent first on the ones that are the most important. Depending on the risk tolerance of the organization and the stakeholders, acceptable risks may be high or low on the list.

Comparative Ranking

Comparative ranking is one tool that can be used to prioritize risks of the same level of severity. The layout of the diagram in Figure 7-5 compares each risk to every other risk. In the first comparison, the diagonal box at the top of the diagram, risk A and risk B are compared to one another. When the comparison is made, only those two risks are compared. If a group is considering the risk, consensus can be reached for each comparison, or the individual votes of each member of the group can be recorded.

After all of the comparisons are made, the total votes for each of the risks are counted, and the risks are ranked according to the highest vote count. It is important to limit the discussion to the two risks under consideration and not allow discussion of the other risks at that time.

Sensitivity Analysis

Sensitivity analysis can be performed on many of the aspects of the project, from engineering to economics. The basic idea of sensitivity analysis is to look at the parameters that affect the situation that we would like to study. By holding all of the parameters constant and allowing one parameter to have different values we can determine the overall

Figure 7-5. Comparative ranking of risks.

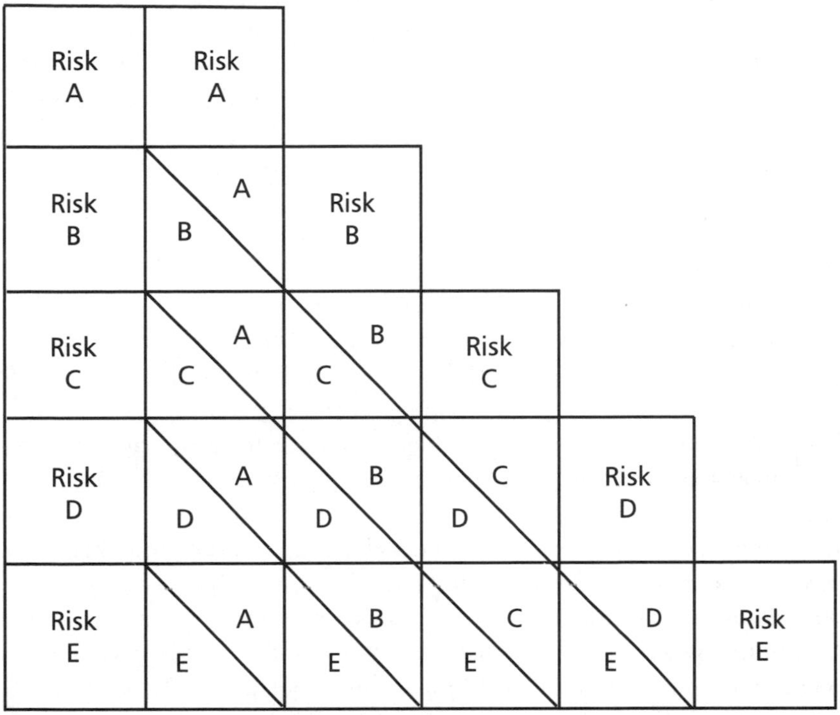

effect on the situation. For example, if we were concerned about the profit to be made from a project we could determine the factors affecting profit. These might be parameters like delivery delays, changes in interest rates, cost overruns, lack of experienced personnel, and so on.

Grouping the Risks

Risks will frequently need to be grouped. This will be more important on large projects than on small ones. The general idea is that if it takes more than ten people to meet and deal with a group of risks, the meeting is too large and will be inefficient. As projects become larger it is necessary to have a series of risk management meetings, whereas in a small project, one meeting might do. To facilitate this, you can use techniques similar to the techniques that were used in the development of the work breakdown structure. In fact, the WBS itself can be used to organize meetings for risk management.

Risks should be assigned to the person who is most closely associated with where the risk will have its largest impact or to the person who has the most familiarity with the technology of the risk. A risk that takes place during the completion of a particular task and directly affects only that task should be a concern to the person responsible for that task. Of course, no task in a project is truly independent of all the others, so for more severe risks a person in the organization above the person responsible for the task may be responsible for the risk.

Oftentimes, in projects where risk is of great concern, the project manager creates the position of risk manager. This person is responsible for tracking all risks and maintaining the risk management plan. As projects become larger or tolerance for risk is low, this approach becomes more necessary.

Affinity Diagramming

Affinity diagramming is a simple tool that can be used to separate risks into groups that can then be managed separately by different groups of people on the project team. All you need for this are pads of sticky-back notes, a room with wall space, and cooperative people.

Members of the project team are brought together for a meeting. You begin the process by writing all of the risks on small pieces of paper. Post-it Notes work well for this purpose.

The members of the meeting then take their pieces of paper and post them on the wall. This is done in strict silence. Each person is allowed to move any of the posted notes. The notes may be moved as often as anyone wishes. Eventually, the notes will form into groups. When all the movement has stopped, the process is complete. At that point, one person in the group or the facilitator must document the results. Sticky-back notes will not stay on the wall for long.

Risk Response Planning

The next task that must be done in our risk management system is risk response planning. At this stage we have discovered all of the risks known to date and have an iterative process for discovering new risks as the project progresses. We have evaluated the risks and assessed their impact and probability of occurrence. We have prioritized the risks in their order of importance. We now must decide what to do about them. This is risk response planning.

Risk response planning is the process of developing the procedures and techniques to enhance opportunities and reduce threats to the project's objectives. In this process it will be necessary to assign individuals who will be responsible for each risk and generate a response that can be used for each risk.

Risk Response Strategies

Risk response strategies are the techniques that will be used to reduce the effect or probability of the identified or even the unidentified risks.

Of course, in the case of opportunities we should want to increase the probability and increase the impact. The opportunity can be exploited by adding resources to encourage and maximize the effect. Opportunities can be shared. In the case where our own organization is not able to maximize an opportunity, a partnership or other arrangement with another organization may be made where both organizations benefit in a greater way than one of them can. By enhancing an opportunity we can maximize the drivers that positively impact the risks. Both impact drivers and probability drivers may be enhanced.

In terms of the risk strategy that should be employed, a qualitative or quantitative evaluation of the severity of the risk will be a guideline as to how much time, money, and effort should be spent on the strategy to limit the risk.

Avoidance

Risk avoidance means just what it says. The strategy is to avoid the risk completely. The project plan or the nature of the project is actually changed to make it impossible for the risk to occur.

Some risks, such as the risk of not having a clearly defined set of user requirements, can be avoided by expending the effort to more clearly define the requirements. This may increase the time and effort previously allowed for this activity, but it will have the result of eliminating the risk.

For example, suppose our project is to design a bicycle. Let's say that during the design phase someone identified a risk of corrosion in the frame of the bicycle. If this corrosion were severe enough, it could cause a failure in the bicycle frame. This failure could cause serious injury to the person riding the bicycle at the time of failure.

The strategy exercised by the project team on this project is to redesign the components that are corrosion problems and use a corrosion resistant material such as stainless steel. This avoids the problem of corrosion in the bicycle frame identified as risky.

The avoidance strategy cannot completely eliminate the risk. In this example, even though the bicycle is redesigned in stainless steel, if the bicycle were left outdoors by the ocean for nineteen years, it might still corrode enough to fail, but the probability becomes so small that the risk is, for all practical purposes, eliminated.

Transfer

Transferring a risk also eliminates the risk from impacting the project. When we transfer a risk, we move the impact of the risk to some other party. When risks are transferred to another party, there is usually some sort of payment involved to induce the third party to take on the risk.

Insurance is a method for transferring risk. In terms of risk management, what we are doing is hiring some third party to take over the impact of the risk. In return for this we pay a premium. For example, in 1995, PMI held its annual meeting in the city of New Orleans. Six months prior to this meeting, the PMI Board of Directors held their quarterly board meeting in New Orleans. The chapter hosted the board for a chapter meeting, and for the program they invited a panel of disaster and emergency management people to discuss hurricane effects on the city.

The discussion at the meeting concerned itself with the possible results of a hurricane hitting New Orleans. The PMI board became somewhat nervous about their meeting, since it would be held in prime hurricane season. PMI recognized that the revenue from their annual meeting was a significant part of their operating budget, and they could not afford to take this loss.

The result of this nervousness was that PMI purchased event insurance for the first time, paying a premium to an insurance company to take the risk. The insurance company agreed to pay PMI in the event of some disaster occurring that would force PMI to cancel their meeting. This was indeed a real risk. Just three years later, a hurricane caused the last-minute cancellation of a similar meeting by the Petroleum Engineers Association, after food and other supplies had already been ordered.

Contracting

Another way of transferring risk is to contract the risk to an outside vendor. If this is done with a firm fixed-price contract, the risk is effectively transferred to the vendor. Generally, in firm fixed-price contracts the vendor will always raise the price of the service to compensate for the effect of the risk. Warrantees, performance bonds, and guarantees are additional methods for transferring risk.

Acceptance

The acceptance of a risk means that the project team has decided not to change the project in any way to compensate for the risk. The risk will be dealt with if and when it occurs. One way to think of acceptance is to visualize the list of risks that was made. The risks were ranked according to the impact they would have on the project. If we imagine a line going through the list at some point, the items above the line are ones that we will do something about in our risk strategy, and the items below the line are the risks that we will accept. The point at which the line is drawn is the point of risk tolerance.

Passive acceptance is when the project team does nothing at all about the risk. If the risk actually occurs, the project team will develop a way to work around the risk or to correct its effects.

Active acceptance is when the project team develops a plan of action to be taken in anticipation of the risk occurring. This action will result in a contingency plan. The contingency plan can be implemented as soon as triggers indicate the possibility of the risk occurring. In addition to the contingency plan, a fallback plan may be made as well. A *fallback plan* is an additional contingency plan to use in the event that the first contingency plan fails.

Mitigation

The strategies that we have discussed have either gotten rid of the risk entirely, transferred it to someone else, or accepted the risk, either passively or actively. *Risk mitigation* is an effort to reduce the probability or impact of the risk to a point where the risk can be accepted. Adding additional tests, hiring duplicate suppliers, adding more expert personnel, designing prototypes, or in other ways changing the conditions under which the risk can occur are ways of mitigating risk.

The important difference in risk mitigation is that it reduces the risk to a level where we can accept it and its consequences. Adding specific work to the project plan employs the mitigation strategy. This work will always be done regardless of whether the risk occurs. The mitigation tasks are specific project tasks that are added to the project plan to reduce the impact or probability of the risk.

It should be clear that an overall risk strategy should be designed to deal with risks by accepting them as they are, avoiding them by eliminating them from being possible, transferring them to another's responsibility, or reducing their impact and/or probability to a level where they can be accepted.

Budgeting for Risk

In keeping with the principle that project baselines are definite commitments for the project, the project budget and schedules should be ones that the project is truly expected to meet. That is, the budget is the budget that is really expected to be spent when the project is complete, and the schedule should allow for sufficient time to do the project. This budget and schedule must include the time for managing and overcoming risks. In Chapter 2, Time Management, we looked at dealing with schedule contingency. Here I discuss planning for budget contingency.

Funds that are to be used for mitigation, avoidance, or transfer are budgeted in with the rest of the committed project work. These are actual tasks that must be done, or they are funds that will be spent regardless of whether the risk occurs. But how do we budget for work that must be done only if the risk occurs?

There are two kinds of risks that must be dealt with, known risks and unknown risks. Known risks are the risks that were identified in the identification process of risk management discussed earlier. Unknown risks are the ones that we know will probably occur on this project, because unknown and unexpected risks have occurred before on projects of this type.

Known risks should be handled by the creation of a *contingency budget*. This money is not assigned to specific project tasks and is set aside and available to fund the work that must be done if and when a risk occurs. This budget should require the approval of the project manager as a means of making certain that the money is truly allocated to solve risk problems. If this money is made available too easily, it will be spent early in the project on problems that might have been solved in the normal course of completing the task.

Unknown risks must be funded as well. In this case the risks are those that could not be identified in the risk identification process. An estimate based on past experience with similar projects can be made. This estimate is used to create a management reserve. The *management reserve* is similar to the contingency budget in that it is made available to fund unknown risks when they occur. In order to prevent the inappropriate use of this budget, a person at a level above the project manager level must approve the use of these funds.

Risk Monitoring and Control

Risk monitoring and control is the process of keeping track of all the identified risks and identifying new risks as their presence becomes known and residual risks that occur when the risk management plans are implemented on individual risks. The effectiveness of the risk management plan is evaluated on an ongoing basis throughout the project.

When a risk is apparently going to take place, the contingency plan is put into place. If there is no contingency plan, then the risk is dealt with on an ad hoc basis using what is termed a "workaround." A *workaround* is an unplanned response to a negative risk event. A *corrective action* is the act of performing the workaround or the contingency plan.

The concern of the project manager and the project team is that risk responses have been brought to bear on the risk as planned and that the risk response has been effective. After they have observed the effectiveness of the risk response, additional risks may develop or additional responses may be necessary.

Risk management is a continuous process that takes place during the entire project from beginning to end. As the project progresses, the risks that have been identified are monitored and reassessed as the time that they can take place approaches. Early warning indicators are monitored to reassess the probability and impact of the risk. As the risk approaches the risk strategies are reviewed for appropriateness, and additional responses are planned.

Risk assessments, reviews, and audits may be performed periodically to review the probability and potential impact of risks that have been identified and are nearer to their possible occurrence. Risks that have already taken place can be reviewed and audited to assess the effectiveness of the risk response.

As each risk occurs and is dealt with or is avoided, these changes must be documented. Good documentation ensures that risks of this type will be dealt with in a more effective way than before, and that the next project manager will benefit from "lessons learned."

Summary

Risk management has become one of the most important aspects of project management. As companies become better at managing projects, the significance of risk management becomes more important. Many companies are not yet adept at determining project cost, schedule, and scope baselines, and they have not yet learned to manage the work that is actually going to have to get done in the project. Until this is done it does not seem worthwhile to consider risk management.

The components of risk identification, probability, and impact must all be considered in order to determine how to deal with a risk. The combination of impact and probability determine the severity of the risk. The severity of a risk determines how it ranks in importance among other risks.

The six steps in risk management—risk management planning, risk identification, risk assessment, risk quantification, risk response planning, and risk monitoring and control—are necessary to manage risk. The steps must be carried out on a continuous basis throughout the project.

Companies and individuals have risk tolerance. They either tend to be gamblers and are willing to take chances to achieve rewards, or they tend to be conservative and less willing to take chances.

Various methods can be used for risk identification. All of the techniques useful for group dynamics are also useful for identifying risks. Risk evaluation must determine the probability of the risk occurring and the impact that it will have if it does. Risks that are either very low in probability or very low in impact need not be considered as a serious threat to the project, even though they may be coupled with high impacts or high probability, respectively.

Expected values for risks are useful in determining the quantitative value of a risk in terms of dollars. The expected value of a risk is the approximate amount of money that could be spent to eliminate the risk.

Once it has been determined that a risk should be dealt with, the proper strategy must be employed. Risks can be avoided by completely eliminating the possibility of the risk through redesign or restructure of the project. Risks can also be transferred by making someone outside the project responsible for the risk. Risks can be mitigated by reducing either their probability or their impact to a level where they become acceptable.

Contingency reserves are monies set aside for dealing with an identified risk when it occurs. The contingency reserve is part of the project budget. Management reserves are monies that are set aside for dealing with unidentified risks when they occur. Management reserves are part of the project budget, but not part of the baseline.

CHAPTER 8

Contract and Procurement Management

M any times it is the project manager who is on the buying end of the project. Most of the time we think of projects as work that we are doing to produce a set of deliverables that will be delivered to some organizations. However, often the project manager is required to hire another project manager to produce goods and services for his or her organization. When this is done, the roles and responsibilities of the project managers change somewhat. It is necessary to have assurance that the hired project manager and his or her team will actually produce what is required.

Contracts provide us with a way of making agreements that can be depended on. After considering the need to protect life, property, and freedom, nearly all of the legal systems of the civilized world are designed to allow business to flow with reasonable ease and allow people to exchange goods and services in a mutually beneficial way. This is called commerce.

Contracts are binding agreements between two or more parties. The terms of a contract are not only binding but enforceable by our legal system and our courts. If this were not the case, our entire economy would soon collapse, and commerce would end. Without the right to property and the enforcement of contracts no one would be a party to any agreement, because the other parties to the agreement might change their minds. Because of the legal nature of contracts there is usually a higher level of approval required. As the value of contracts becomes greater, legal and procurement experts will become part of the project team. Even in the simplest purchases a purchasing agent must sign the purchase order as agent for the organization. Traditionally we refer to the seller and the buyer by several names. A seller may be called contractor, subcontractor, vendor, agency, or supplier. A buyer we may refer to as client, customer, contractor, prime contractor, or acquiring organization.

The contract statement of work is a necessary part of any procurement or contract.

It must be in sufficient detail to allow any of the potential vendors to fully understand what is required of them and if they are capable of meeting all of the requirements. If the purchased items are commodities, the *statement of work* (SOW) is very simple, but if the items being purchased are very specialized, the SOW can be quite lengthy. The SOW should include the items that are required that are not necessarily part of the product delivered. These are items like quality reports, manuals, documentation, and performance and progress reports.

This chapter has two parts: Contract Management and Procurement Management.

Contract Management

The first thing we need is a definition of a contract. Texts on business law define a contract as follows:

> A contract is an agreement between competent parties, for consideration, to accomplish some lawful purpose with the terms clearly set forth.

First of all, the contract is an "agreement." This means that the parties involved must have a meeting of the minds and decide that they will do the things set forth in the contract. By this definition no contract can be forced on someone. If there is any kind of forcing or coercion, there cannot be an enforceable contract. You cannot force someone at gunpoint to sign a contract to buy aluminum storm windows and expect to hold the person to the contract.

The contract must be "between competent parties." This means that the people who make the agreement must be competent to make the agreement. Persons who are impaired in any way that makes them unable to make responsible decisions or people who are not of age cannot make contracts. As a matter of fact, if a minor or another incompetent party enters into a contract, the contract may be enforceable on the competent party and not on the incompetent party.

The contract must be "for consideration." This means that something must be given for something else. If there is no exchange of anything, then there is no contract. There would be no point in going to the trouble to create a contract if there is no exchange. It is important to note that the consideration does not have to be something that is valuable to everyone. The consideration could easily be something that one person values and no one else does. The consideration does not need to be tangible either. An intangible consideration can be involved in any contract.

The contract must "accomplish some lawful purpose." No contract can legally be written that violates the law. You cannot contract with someone to steal a car for you. The contract would be void at its inception.

In discussing contract management for projects we generally are interested in the relationship between a buyer and a supplier.

Make or Buy

The decision to make or buy something must be considered. Many times it is less expensive to purchase something from an outside source than it is to make the item inside the company. Cost is a major consideration for this, but there are many other reasons for deciding whether to purchase or make an item. If a facility has idle capacity, it may make sense to produce a part that is normally made by an outside vendor. The excess capacity is there to be used, and the company is paying for it whether it is used or not. In a make-or-buy decision, it should be necessary to consider only the variable cost in this situation. If there is no extra capacity, then the cost of adding the capacity must be considered as well.

If an item is needed and it is important that strict control be maintained in its production, it may be necessary to make the item instead of purchasing it. Similarly, items that involve trade secrets and innovative products should not be contracted out of the company.

Using the flexibility of the purchasing system to stabilize the workforce is desirable. Many companies have used this strategy to help maintain consistent employment levels in their companies. A company wishing to do this subcontracts some of the work to outside companies. When the demand for its product goes down, the company decreases the amount of work that the outside contractor is doing and maintains the constant level of work in its own facility. It does not take vendors long to figure this out and adjust pricing for the product to compensate them for their own stability problems.

The decision to purchase an item may simply be a matter of a company not having the ability to produce the item. Skills may be unique for this project and may not be needed in the future. Buying equipment to produce items that will be needed only for this project may not be justifiable, and it may be less costly to buy the items in question or to lease the equipment to produce them.

Contract Life Cycle

The contract life cycle must be managed like the project life cycle. The contracting process is very similar to the project management processes of initialization, planning, implementation, and closeout.

In the contracting process, we consider the steps in a little more detail (Figure 8-1). The requirement stage of the contracting process can be considered equivalent to the initialization of the project. The requisition, solicitation, and award stages can be considered equivalent to the planning process. The contract can be considered equivalent to the implementation process. Closeout occurs at the close of the contract.

Figure 8-1. Contracting process life cycle.

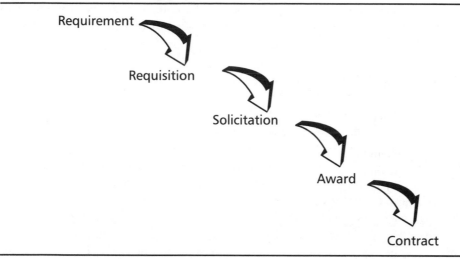

Requirement Process

In the requirement process the needs of the project are identified. As in the requirements definition of the project, the requirements of the contract are identified. These requirements come from a needs assessment, and the needs are further reduced to requirements. Before the decision to purchase a good or service is made, a decision must be made as to whether the item should be purchased or made internally. Requirements are frequently stated in a document called the statement of work.

Cost estimates must be produced to help predict what the correct cost of the item should be. These cost estimates help the person doing the purchasing to determine whether the potential vendor is quoting a fair and agreeable price.

As in the project management requirements definition, the process begins with a determination of needs. These are the items that someone wishes to have delivered. These needs are reduced by mutual agreement to requirements. The requirements are further reduced by excluding the requirements that are not justified.

Requisition Process

The requisition process consists of reviewing the specifications and statement of work and identifying qualified suppliers. It is sometimes called solicitation planning.

During the requisition process, the requirements definition is passed to the purchasing personnel. These may or may not be part of the project team. The specifications and statement of work are reviewed, but now there is input from the purchasing function. This input provides cost information that may further reduce the requirement of items that are now deemed to be impractical.

At this time all of the signatures necessary to procure the item are added to the requisition. Certain signatures are required before the company can be committed to make an expenditure, and other signatures are necessary to be sure that all necessary persons are informed about the purchase being made.

Solicitation Process

The solicitation process involves obtaining bids or proposals. During this process a number of vendors are solicited to participate in the process of becoming the chosen vendor. In the case of commodity purchases it may be necessary to evaluate only the price of the item being supplied. In the case of unique items it may be necessary to evaluate many different aspects of the vendor and the product that is proposed. Frequently procurements are advertised in trade news publications to ensure fairness to all vendors. Oftentimes this is a requirement for any government agency's procurement.

There are two major forms of solicitation, the *request for proposal* (RFP) and the *request for quote* (RFQ). When the RFQ is used, potential vendors must meet all of the requirements of the RFQ and must deliver exactly what has been asked for. When the RFP is used, vendors are at some liberty to meet the functionality described in the RFP. Because of this flexibility each vendor may propose something different and at a different price.

Using the RFQ process makes the vendor decision very simple. Since all vendors are required to supply exactly what was asked for, the only difference between them is the price. The buyer must be very careful in preparing the bid specifications because the vendor will be required to supply what was asked for.

In the RFP process the specifications are more of a functional nature and do not define what is to be delivered as much as they define the functions that the items delivered are supposed to do. While the major part of the work in the RFQ process comes when the bid specifications are written, the RFP process requires most of the work to be done during the evaluation of the proposals submitted.

As an example of how this works, suppose a city government wanted to purchase 500 laptop computers for the city hall staff. They write up the bid specifications for a Pentium 5 processor, with 60 GB of hard drive space, floppy disk drive, and 15-inch screen. The procurement process at city hall is rather lengthy. By the time the laptop computers are delivered, the state-of-the-art laptops have a Pentium 7 processor, 120 GB hard drive, and no floppy drive at all. Not only that, but to meet the specifications the vendor would have to special order the computers, making the overall cost higher than giving the customer something superior to what was asked for. All of this may result in a forced re-bid, and the process could start over and over again.

Vendor conferences, also known as bidder conferences or pre-bid conferences, are used to allow all of the vendors to come to a meeting where they may ask any questions regarding the bid or proposal. A conference of this type allows potential vendors to ask about anything that is unclear about the procurement, and to hear what is being said to the other vendors so there is no risk of one vendor having information that others do not possess.

Qualified Sellers Lists can be developed by the project team or the procurement department. These lists can be constructed based on publicly available information on the Internet; in libraries, Dun and Bradstreet reports, and the Thomas Register; and from various other sources. Potential vendors may also be sent questionnaires to determine their qualifications and interest in doing business in a particular area.

Award Process

During the awarding process, one vendor is selected from the ones solicited. At this time the contract is written, negotiated, and signed by both parties.

The writing and signing of the contract can be simple, as in the purchase of a commodity. In the purchasing of such common items the contract is generally a standard item that is written on the back of a purchase order. Many times these contracts are written in very light ink and in very small type.

In more complex purchases, the contract may have to be negotiated, and specific terms and conditions for this particular contract must be agreed to. The more detailed the contract, the more complex this part of the contracting cycle will be.

Trade-Off Studies

One of the methods of evaluating potential suppliers is the trade-off study. This is a useful process in that it gives us a consistent way of evaluating the potential suppliers and documents each of the reasons why a particular vendor was selected.

Potential vendors may be eliminated through a screening process. By screening we mean that we establish definite requirements of performance, and any vendor that does not at least meet these minimums is automatically disqualified. For example, a vendor might be required to have a project manager assigned who is a certified PMP.

As can be seen in Figure 8-2, a trade-off study is begun by listing all of the potential vendors across the top of the page in columns. The features or the desirable traits of the object being purchased are written down the first column. Another column is added to show the relative importance of each of the features. This is called the weight column. Each of the vendor columns is divided in two: rank and score.

We begin by listing the features. These are all of the important traits that will be part of the evaluation process. Features that might be included include total life cycle cost, price, technical approach, management approach, ability to perform the work, and understanding of what was asked for. For a complex selection this list could go on for several pages. Next, the weight factor is determined, and each one of the features is evaluated for importance. The number here is one of relative importance. A feature that is given a 6 should be twice as important as a feature given a 3. Next, each potential

Figure 8-2. Trade-off study.

Criteria	Weight	Alt. 1		Alt. 2		Alt. 3	
		Score	Wt. x Score	Score	Wt. x Score	Score	Wt. x Score
Total Score							

vendor is ranked according to their ability to supply this feature. If more than one vendor furnishes this feature equally they can receive the same rank, or a scale of 1 to 10 can be used to evaluate how well each vendor supplies the feature. The rank number for each vendor for each feature is then multiplied by the weight factor of each of the features and written in the score column. Summing the score numbers will produce a high score for one of the vendors. This is the preferred vendor.

The trade-off study seems to be quite analytical and quantitative, but in reality it is not. The choosing of the weight factors is very subjective, as is the assignment of ranking numbers for the potential suppliers. Multiplying them together multiplies the errors as well. The method, however, has one great advantage to justify its use. The orderly arrangement of the selection criteria and the evaluation of each supplier is plain to see, and it shows anyone objecting (probably one of the unselected vendors) to the vendor selection exactly what things were considered.

Contract Process
The contract process is the final part of the contracting process. In this process the contract is actually carried out. The vendor and the purchaser must follow the planning process, organize the work staff for the work to be done, and control the contract. The purchaser and the seller must both be responsible for their part of the contract.

Contract Administration
As contracts become more complicated and more valuable the administration of the contract becomes more and more important. In administering a contract we are the client of the project, and we should expect that the supplier's project manager will be able to

furnish us with information regarding the performance of the project team. On large projects, reports from the project manager should include progress reports on scheduling, performance reports on scheduling and cost, quality control reports, risk monitoring and control reports, and change control reports. At times it is desirable that the contract administrator for the buyer visit the facility where the work is taking place and verify that the reports do in fact report what is really going on.

Contract Types

In the world of commerce nearly any kind of agreement can be made that will satisfy the needs of both parties of the contract. Whenever there is a contract, there is always business risk. The business risk is that there can be a positive or negative outcome to the contract, depending on the risks involved and whether they work out favorably or not (see Figure 8-3).

Fixed-Price or Lump-Sum Contract

A fixed-price contract requires that a project be completed for a fixed amount of money. The seller agrees to sell something to the buyer at a price that has been agreed to beforehand. The seller agrees to provide the buyer with something that meets the specifications as agreed, and the buyer agrees to give the seller a fixed amount of money in return. Strictly speaking, in this kind of contract, the seller must do the work specified for the agreed upon amount. In the real world, if problems occur that make it impossible for the seller to perform for the agreed upon price or if the supplier is having severe financial problems, agreements can be modified.

In fixed-price contracting, the seller is taking all of the risk of having things go wrong, but the seller is also setting the price in such a way as to be compensated for

Figure 8-3. Customer and supplier risk.

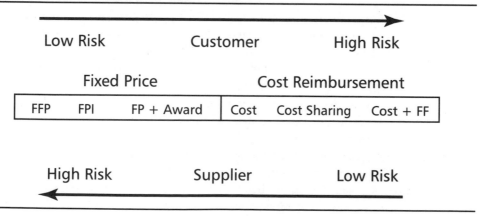

taking the risk. In fact, in this type of contract it may be that the buyer is paying more than would have been necessary if the buyer had been willing to take some of the risk.

In fixed-price contracts there is no need for the buyer to know what the seller is actually spending on the project. Whether the supplier spends more or less should be of no interest to the buyer. The buyer should be interested only in the specifications of the project being met.

There are several variations on the fixed-price contract.

Firm Fixed-Price Contract. In a firm fixed-price contract the seller takes all of the risk. In our discussion on project risk, one of the strategies for handling risk was to deflect or transfer the risk to another organization. The most risk-free way to transfer the risk is to use a firm fixed-price contract. Here the contract terms require that the seller supply the buyer with the agreed-upon goods or services at a firm fixed price. In other words, the supplier must supply the good or service without being able to recover any of the cost of doing the work if cost-increasing risks occur during the fulfillment of the contract.

Frequently, in this type of contract, if the supplier cannot perform for the agreed upon amount, there is some room for negotiating even after the contract has been agreed to and signed. The firm fixed-price contract has the most predictable cost of all of the types of contract.

Fixed-Price Plus Economic-Adjustment Contract. In this type of contract some of the risk is kept by the buyer. All of the risks associated with the contract are borne by the seller except for the condition of changes in the economy. This type of contract can be used when there are periods of very high inflation. The contract price is adjusted according to some formula that depends on an agreed upon economic indicator.

The economic adjustment is important when there are periods of high inflation and the length of the contract is long. During the time of the contract, the value of money may go down considerably and the value of the contract along with it. For example, one company agrees to purchase a project from another company. The time that it will take to complete this project is one year. During the time between the agreement and the delivery of the project, there is high inflation, say 20 percent per year. In our discussion of cost management in Chapter 3, we looked at the effect of present values and saw that money that we receive in the future is worth less than the same money received today. Therefore, it is reasonable that the supplier increase the selling price of the project by 20 percent if the money will be paid at the end of the one-year project.

However, suppose that inflation rates and interest rates are unstable. In this situation the seller does not know how much to increase the price in order to be compensated for the time value of money. Inflation may be 20 percent, or it may be 30 percent. The supplier wants to figure the selling price based on 30 percent, but the buyer argues that the inflation rate could be only 20 percent.

The buyer and supplier agree that they will adjust the selling price up or down according to some economic formula. In this situation it might be reasonable to adjust the selling price at the end of the project according to the average interest rate over the period. In the 1970s many contracts were written with economic adjustments based on the consumer price index. Many other economic indicators can be used for adjusting prices.

Fixed-Price Plus Incentive Contract. In a fixed-price plus incentive contract there is an agreed upon fixed price for the project plus an incentive fee for exceeding the performance of the contract. In this type of contract the buyer wishes to create some incentive for the supplier. The buyer offers to increase the amount to be paid for the completion of the project if the supplier delivers the project early or if the project performance exceeds the agreed upon specifications.

In this situation the risk of meeting the conditions of the project are borne by the supplier, but the buyer assumes some additional risk. The buyer really wants the project to be delivered early or with the enhanced features in the incentive part of the contract but is not able to get the supplier to agree to these terms as part of a fixed-price contract. If the extra enhancements are actually delivered or if the project is completed early, the buyer will pay extra. If the project is completed without the enhancements or is completed in the agreed upon time, the contract terms are met and the incentives are not paid.

For example, the Jones Company wants to buy a new machine. Jones can use the machine as soon as it is delivered to satisfy orders for its product. It contracts with the Ace Machine Company to deliver the new machine. Ace is only willing to promise a delivery of six months because of problems that usually occur in this type of project. If the contract is a fixed-price contract with no incentive fees, the Ace Company will deliver the machine on time. If there is a fixed-price plus incentive contract, the Ace Company may be motivated to deliver early. There may be an incentive of $500 per day for early delivery.

With this type of contract there is usually a penalty for delivering late or for delivering a project that does not meet all of the requirements. The Ace Company may be required to deduct $500 per day for delivering the project late.

Cost-Plus Contract

A major distinction is made between contracts that are fixed price and those that are cost reimbursable. In a *cost-reimbursable contract* the supplier agrees to perform the terms of the contract, but the buyer takes on the risk. The buyer agrees to reimburse the supplier for any work that is done and for any money that is spent. When the contract is completed, the buyer pays a fixed fee to the supplier for the work that was done. This is essentially the profit for doing the project.

Cost-reimbursable contracts are usual when there is a great deal of risk and uncertainty in the project or a significant amount of investment must be made before the final results of the project can be reached.

For example, the U.S. government wants to develop a new tank for the army. The requirements are not clear, and the design of the tank must be modified to accept the latest state-of-the-art designs for its components as it is being developed. The approval and development process may take as long as ten years. There are probably no companies that would agree to a fixed-price contract for this project, so the government awards a cost-plus contract instead.

In a cost-plus type of contract the buyer is actually taking the responsibility for the risk. If problems develop in the project, the buyer will have to pay for the corrective action that is necessary. Some of the time this can actually be economical. In projects with a lot of risk, the supplier usually will estimate the cost of the risks and charge the buyer enough in the price to adequately compensate for taking the risk. In a cost-reimbursable contract the actual costs of the risks that occur are the only ones that are paid for.

One of the problems in a cost-reimbursable contract is the determination of the actual cost. There is always the danger that the seller's report of the actual cost to the buyer may contain costs of some other project. This means that the buyer needs to check to be sure that misallocation of cost is not occurring. In large federal government projects, staffs of auditors check on correct cost reporting to ensure that this is not a problem. Many times the cost of the auditing and tracking system to ensure correct reporting makes these kinds of contracts difficult to apply unless the projects are large.

Cost Plus Fixed-Fee Contract. In a cost plus fixed-fee contract the seller is reimbursed for all of the money that is spent meeting the contract requirements and is also paid a fixed fee. The fixed fee is essentially the profit for managing the project. Without some sort of fee in addition to the actual cost of the contract there would be no profit, and the company would simply be making the money that it spent. No company would knowingly take on this kind of contract.

In a cost plus fixed-fee contract, the supplier has only a small incentive to control cost and complete the project. Regardless of when the contract is completed and as long as the specifications are met, the supplier will get only the profit from the fixed fee.

All of us have had this kind of contract at one time or another. A good example of what can happen is when I hire my teenage child to mow the lawn. Essentially this is a cost plus fixed-fee contract. I am responsible for the equipment and gasoline and maintaining the lawnmower. The labor is supplied by the teenager for a fixed fee. Generally, the results of this contract are that the lawn will get mowed but may not get mowed soon.

Cost Plus Award-Fee Contract. In a cost plus award-fee contract an award system is set up to compensate the supplier for completing parts of the contract. The award fee can be determined by many different criteria including the quality of the workmanship, the correct filling out of reports, and practically any other criteria that are agreed to. As each of these requirements is met the award fee is determined and given to the supplier.

Cost Plus Incentive-Fee Contract. In a cost plus incentive-fee contract an incentive system is set up for the supplier to perform in excess of the agreed upon terms and specifications of the contract. Similar to a fixed-price plus incentive contract, the cost plus incentive-fee contract allows the supplier to exceed the specifications and requirements of the contract. When the project is delivered early or when the design criteria and specifications have been exceeded, the incentive fee is paid.

The cost plus incentive-fee contract is the least predictable of all types of contract. Not only is the variable cost of the work included in the contract but the variable incentive that must be paid to the seller must also be considered.

Time-and-Material Contract

This type of contract is a mixture of fixed-price and cost-reimbursable contracts. In this type of contract the total cost of the contract may vary considerably depending on the total amount of time and material that is expended. There are, however, some fixed costs associated with it. For example, the total amount of engineering labor may not be specified but the cost of the resource per hour may be part of the contract.

Procurement Management

Procurement is the act of acquiring goods and services from outside the organization. The procurement process includes planning for the procurement, solicitation of the sources for the desired product or services, and defining the requirements, source selection, administration, and closeout. In a free market economy, the competitiveness of the product or service that is sought will have a great deal to do with the type of contract that can be written between the two parties. In other words, we must decide whether or not to acquire something, when and how to do it, and how much to acquire.

Commodities

Items that are sought that are widely available and for all intents and purposes identical are considered to be commodities. In the sale of commodities there are many people offering the same product. In all cases the products are identical for the purpose for which they are intended. Familiar examples of commodities are corn, wheat, and soybeans, but electrical components that are made by a number of different firms and are relatively standardized are also commodities.

Since there are many suppliers of the same commodity, competition drives the price to the lowest level. A supplier will not be able to sell a commodity if there is someone else offering the same thing for a lower price.

According to the theory of supply and demand, the price of a product rises as the demand increases. The higher price for the commodity causes other producers to enter the market until the supply increases to meet the additional demand. As demand for a commodity decreases, the price that people are willing to pay for the commodity decreases. Producers of the commodity leave the market, and the supply is reduced to a level that meets the demand. Eventually, in a completely competitive environment, the supply and demand will reach equilibrium.

In contracting for commodity items, the details of the contract and the description of the item being contracted for are relatively standardized. Most of the people in the business of selling commodity items will standardize on the purchase process. With standardization it becomes easier to purchase an item from competing vendors and know that the item will be the same from each vendor.

Unique Products and Services

When we are dealing with unique products and services there will be some risk involved on the part of the buyer and supplier that will modify the truly competitive environment. Unlike commodity buying and selling, the uniqueness of a project will make it impossible to compare the offerings of competitors, and many criteria other than price must be used.

Projects are frequently this type of purchased item. It is necessary to evaluate many different criteria among the offerings that are made. There will be differences in quality, performance, timeliness, and cost for similar projects from different suppliers.

Perfect competition, as in the commodities' type of purchasing, naturally drives the price to the lowest level that allows the producers to make an acceptable profit. In an effort to make a higher profit many companies try to add features to their product that make it unique. Once uniqueness has been established, it is possible to price the unique item higher than it would be in a competitive commodity situation.

Forward Buying

Forward buying is the process of buying items in anticipation of their need. As with all things, it is important to consider the cost and benefits that can result in doing this.

The advantages of forward buying are that there is some protection against running out of an item. In the world of production control this is called a "stock out." Frequently, the vendor will also give a discount for buying larger quantities. The shipping cost will usually be lower to ship a large number of items in one shipment than to make several small shipments. This serves to reduce the cost of the product being made.

On the negative side of forward buying there is the risk that the large number of parts will become obsolete before they are used, as, for example, in the case of a company that purchased a large quantity of buggy whips right before the invention of the Ford automobile. Forward buying requires that the larger inventory of parts be stored in the facility as well. In most businesses floor space is valuable and better used for operating the business than for storing parts.

Blanket Orders

Blanket orders are a form of forward buying. A blanket order allows the buyer to take a quantity discount without actually taking delivery on the large quantity. In a blanket order the buyer agrees to buy all of the material that they need of a certain item from one or more vendors for a specified period of time. The vendor then agrees to sell the items at a discount price based on the expected quantity needed over that period of time.

As the need for the material items occurs, requests to the vendor are filled and tracked against the blanket order. At the end of the time period, the total quantity ordered and delivered to the buyer is checked against the blanket order quantity, and a cash payment is made to the buyer if the quantity has been higher and to the supplier if the quantity is lower.

This arrangement has advantages for both parties. The buyer is assured of a reliable supply of parts because he or she has made a long-term commitment to the vendor. The buyer gets a quantity discount without having to stock a large inventory of parts.

The supplier has the advantage of having a committed customer for the duration of the blanket order. This commitment allows the supplier to plan his or her own operation with the reliability that the customer will continue to purchase these items for a period of time. With the confidence that there will be future business the supplier may be able to invest in equipment and facilities to make these parts for the buyer.

Split Orders

Splitting orders is a process of dividing work between two or more vendors of an item. The purpose of splitting an order is to reduce the risk that the parts may not be delivered on time or may not be of acceptable quality. The advantage of this process is that the probability of one vendor supplying acceptable parts is increased.

Let's say, for example, that we have two vendors that have a 90 percent probability of delivering on time. We could increase the probability of having at least one vendor deliver on time if we give half of the order to each vendor. This is the probability of one vendor or the other delivering. (This is the "addition rule" we discussed in Chapter 7, Risk Management.) The probability of one or the other vendor delivering on time is the probability of one vendor delivering plus the probability of the other vendor delivering given that the first vendor failed to deliver.

The probability of one vendor delivering is 90 percent. The probability of the second vendor delivering given that the first vendor failed to deliver is the probability of both the first vendor not delivering and the second vendor delivering.

Probability of A or B delivering = Probability of A delivering (90%) + Probability of A not delivering (10%) times the probability of B delivering (90%)
P (A or B) = .90 + (.90 × .10) = .99

We can increase the probability from 90 percent to 99 percent by splitting the order between the two vendors.

Splitting the order does not come without a cost. The quantity discount from either of the vendors will be reduced, since only half the quantity is being purchased from each. One of the vendors may not have the same quality as the preferred vendor, and this may add rework to the process.

Summary

Many times a project is not able to produce everything that is needed to complete the project. When this occurs the project manager becomes the client of another project manager, and the roles are somewhat reversed from their normal state.

The project manager now becomes the purchaser. It is important that the project manager understand the purchasing cycle and the basics of contracting. It is quite easy to find ourselves with a significant problem with no legal protection. Contracts provide us with a formal agreement that is binding between the two or more parties involved and is enforceable by our legal system and the courts.

There are many reasons why we may not wish to produce something ourselves. This is known as making a make-or-buy decision. Many factors affect these decisions.

The contract life cycle is similar to the project life cycle in that requirements are developed, requisitions are generated, vendors are contacted and solicited, and finally one is selected and awarded the contract. Once the award is made, the project manager must manage this contractor just as if the contractor were part of the project team.

There are many types of contracts. The various types of contracts can be explained by considering them in light of risk and who accepts the risk. Fixed-price types of contracts have an agreement to pay a fixed price for some specified good or service. Here the risk is on the side of the seller or supplier. If anything happens that increases the cost of producing the good or service, the seller or supplier must bear the additional cost without being able to increase the selling price to the buyer. In cost-plus types of contracts the buyer is willing to reimburse the seller for any costs that have occurred. The risk of increased cost due to unforeseen problems is borne by the buyer.

When purchasing goods and services for projects, there are many different purchasing arrangements that can be made. Forward buying and blanket ordering are methods that are used to make a mutually beneficial arrangement for both the buyer and the seller or supplier.

CHAPTER 9

Professional Responsibility

The Project Management Institute engaged the Columbia Assessment Service (CAS) to study the PMP examination process. This resulted in changes to the PMP examination. In fact, the exam was revised considerably as a result of the work that was done.

CAS began by analyzing the responsibilities of project management professionals (PMPs). Then it specified a plan for the testing of PMPs, wrote and rewrote questions for the exam, and determined the passing score for the test. The *Project Management Professional (PMP) Role Delineation Study* was published in 2000 to address the responsibilities of a PMP and the plan for the test. Since the PMP examination is very important to all of us who are certified as project manager professionals, it is also important that the examination be one that tests what actually happens in project management. The test questions must be fair and accurate and draw information from every aspect of project management.

Those who participated in the studies and interviews that were part of the process were not bound to the topics covered in the *Guide to the Project Management Body of Knowledge*. For this reason the advisers found that it was necessary to add a sixth domain to the examination. So in addition to questions on initiating, planning, executing, controlling, and closing, the exam now contains questions on professional responsibility. These questions will account for 29 questions out of the 200 questions on the exam. This may seem like a lot, but when you consider that there are a lot of questions that are common to all of the domains—such as communications techniques, communicating effectively, coaching, mentoring, personal strengths and weaknesses, instructional methods and tools, stakeholders' interests, competing needs and objectives, conflict resolution techniques, and generating alternatives—it is difficult to relate a specific question on the examination to a particular domain or process area.

In the area of professional responsibility, tasks are defined, along with specific knowledge areas and skills that are required for each task. The examination questions are based on this material. The number of questions for each topic is based on surveys regarding the importance of each task within the project management community.

The following tasks are the basis for the questions that will be on the PMP examination. They are from the *Project Management Professional (PMP) Role Delineation Study*, published by the Project Management Institute.

Task 1

Ensure individual integrity and professionalism by adhering to legal requirements and ethical standards in order to protect the community and all stakeholders.

A project manager must be familiar with the laws that govern the project in the place where the project is being carried out. The project manager is the person in charge. In our classes we refer to the project manager as the one person responsible for everything in the project. If something goes wrong with the project, it is the project manager's responsibility. The project manager has responsibility for everything that happens on the project, much as the captain of a ship is responsible for everything that happens on that ship.

I recently gave testimony in a lawsuit involving a road-milling machine that accidentally broke a gas line while it was removing several inches of old road surface. The issue was to decide which of the several insurance companies would pay for the damages involved resulting from the accident. Since the project manager was responsible for the project, his insurance company should be the one to pay. The road construction company had failed to notify the utility companies, as was their responsibility. Had the utility companies been properly notified that the work was taking place, they might have taken steps to avert the accident.

Even though the project manager had specifically instructed the contractor to notify the utility companies, and even though the contractor said that they had contacted them, the accident remains the project manager's responsibility.

It is important that the project manager have a complete and thorough knowledge of the stakeholders of the project and also of the community that surrounds and mingles with the project. In a real sense the members of the community around the project are stakeholders, and there is a responsibility to protect them from any harmful effects of the project. I am sure that we can all recall the day that the Chernobyl nuclear power plant accident occurred in the Ukraine. Many thousands of lives were lost as a result of this disaster.

Task 2

Contribute to the project management knowledge base by sharing lessons learned, best practices, research, etc. within appropriate communities in order to improve the quality of project management services, build the capabilities of colleagues, and advance the profession.

In this task the project manager is expected to contribute to the improvement of project management knowledge both by increasing the quality and by improving the methods and techniques of project management. In addition to improving the tools of the profession the project manager should contribute time and energy to help improve the capabilities of colleagues.

By being a member of the Project Management Institute and participating in the activities of the chapter, the international organization, and the other international organizations that support project management, you foster the growth and improvement of project management. By attending conferences and meetings and contributing by the presentation of a paper at those conferences you can improve the world of project management. Supporting company training programs and helping to offer training programs through a local chapter of a project management association will go far to reach these ends.

Some project managers offer their time to further the development of research. This does not mean that you must head up a research study, obtain a grant for thousands of dollars, or join the faculty of a university. It does mean, however, that you should fill out questionnaires and surveys when asked, and it does mean that you should respond to students when asked to assist in their research.

Many opportunities present themselves to project managers that foster goodwill and increase the knowledge that others have about project management and what it does. I was once asked to speak before the annual meeting of Meeting Planners International. These are the people who plan conventions and conferences in places all over the world. As it turned out, this group had a great deal of interest in project management. What better places to practice project management than conventions and conferences? They have critical schedules, limited budgets, and high visibility. The convention planner has the opportunity either to upset the plans of thousands of people and lose millions of dollars for an organization or to make thousands of people feel that their time and money were well spent. To accomplish these things we need to have good communication skills and good judgment.

Task 3

Enhance individual competence by increasing and applying professional knowledge to improve services.

This area of professional responsibility involves understanding your personal strengths and weaknesses. For this you will need to have a good knowledge of yourself and make a plan to improve yourself. As project manager you have the responsibility to improve your competencies. To do this you must also have knowledge of methods of personal evaluation. As in modern quality management, it is not the large improvements to our knowledge that are so important, but it is the small increases in our knowledge and capability over the years that will truly improve our value to ourselves and others.

A project manager should do a self-assessment periodically and develop a plan to reach goals for self-improvement and professional competence.

Task 4

Balance stakeholders' interests by recommending approaches that strive for fair resolution in order to satisfy competing needs and objectives.

In the development of any project, one of the most important things that we must do is to accomplish the scope of the project. We have a professional responsibility to make sure that each of the agreed upon stakeholder's needs is met by the completion of the project. We must also take the responsibility of making the stakeholder aware that there may be better and less expensive ways of solving the same problem than how the stakeholder may have suggested doing it. It is an important responsibility of the project manager and the project team to consider all reasonable alternatives as possible solutions to project problems or as possible ways of achieving project goals.

To be able to do this properly we must be aware of the stakeholder's business and interests. In Chapter 7, Risk Management, we discussed stakeholder tolerance, which is the level of risk that the stakeholder is willing to take in the project. It is important that the project manager be able to assess the risk tolerance of the stakeholder so that the proper risk management plan can be worked out.

The stakeholder also must be considered in many other areas of project development as well as in risk management. The project manager and the project team probably know more about the current technology that the project will use. The project team then has a responsibility to keep the stakeholder informed about changes in technology that may affect the project, even if delays and changes in budget are necessary to use the new technology.

In all projects there will be conflicts that arise between participants. In the world of changing needs and expectations, conflicts will need to be resolved. Knowledge of the conflict resolution techniques, discussed in Chapter 5, Human Resources Management, is also the responsibility of the project manager. Negotiating and communications skills serve the project manager well in this area.

Task 5

Interact with team and stakeholders in a professional and cooperative manner by respecting personal, ethnic, and cultural differences in order to ensure a collaborative project management environment.

The project manager needs to ensure that the project team functions without prejudice. Today, many companies and projects are international in nature. Not many companies can afford to run their business without concern for foreign competition and customers. For example, software development contracts are now negotiated in different countries, and the Internet is making us all into one community.

We must be very watchful that we consider the cultural and ethnic differences of our project team and our customers as well. To do this we have to have a thorough knowledge of communications and make a sincere effort to understand the norms of our team and stakeholders. This involves choosing the appropriate communication channels and considering all of the filters and inhibitors that are involved.

It is easy to make mistakes and appear to be uncooperative. A responsible project manager must be able to exercise self-control in situations that involve people with different ethnic and cultural backgrounds. I teach project management around the world, and there have been many times when I have had to forget the practices that I'm used to and adjust my sensibilities and feelings to the surroundings rather than try to make the surroundings conform to my feelings.

Communication with people for whom English is not the first language is always going to present problems, but if you take the time to learn how to say "good morning," "please," and "thank you," you will go far in developing good relations. The technique of speaking louder to someone who does not speak English is not going to improve understanding.

Code of Professional Conduct

It is essential that project management professionals conduct their work in an ethical and legal manner. Without this, team members, customers, colleagues, employees, and stakeholders will have no confidence in a project manager's ability to report on progress or any other aspect of the project. Trust is an element that must be present for any project to succeed.

PMI has instituted the Project Management Code of Professional Conduct in order to encourage self-discipline in the profession. Project managers are required to report violations of the PMI Code of Professional Conduct. This has the effect of maintaining standards of conduct. All certified project management professionals agree to support the Code.

Project management professionals are required by the Code to provide truthful representation of their business in any advertising or public statements regarding cost of services, description of services, and expected results. They have a responsibility to satisfy the scope of the project as agreed upon unless the customer initiates changes. All sensitive information must remain confidential when it is obtained while carrying out professional activities.

Project management professionals must also ensure that there are no conflicts of interest that may interfere with their judgment. This includes not offering or accepting gifts for personal gain unless they are in conformance with the laws and customs of the country in which they take place.

In managing a project, a project manager takes on the responsibility of providing qualified professional service. No project manager should take on a project for which he or she is not qualified. Project managers are required to maintain their level of professional skills for the types of projects that they are managing. Project managers provide leadership to ensure that the maximum amount of productivity is achieved. Quality, cost, and time objectives are to be met as agreed upon.

A project manager must ensure that the workplace is safe, and that all people working in the area that is the project's responsibility are protected from danger. Suitable working conditions must be maintained for the project team and any others in the area of the project's activity.

CHAPTER 10

What Is the PMP Exam Like?

The Project Management Institute (PMI) has constantly improved the PMP examination since it was first given and will continue to improve the exam as time goes on. April 2002 was significant because of the culmination of several factors that have had an influence on the PMP examination. The *Project Management Professional (PMP) Role Delineation Study* was begun in 1999 to help define the roles and responsibilities of project management professionals. From this knowledge, an examination could be designed that would truly test the prospective candidates and prove that the candidates for certification could indeed competently practice the profession of project manager. A good and content-valid examination for project management professionals cannot be developed unless the roles of project managers and how they are practiced are clearly understood.

In order to accomplish this, PMI hired a company experienced in these things, Columbia Assessment Services (CAS). The initial development and evaluation was completed by a panel of thirteen members considered to be subject matter experts in the field of project management. These members represented a variety of fields of practice, industries, geographic locations, and, of course, both genders. This panel determined that there would be six project management domains:

1. Initiating
2. Planning
3. Executing
4. Controlling
5. Closing
6. Professional Responsibility

From each of the domains, a number of tasks were created, and for each of these tasks, the knowledge and skills required were determined. Once this was done project managers were surveyed from various age groups, education levels, industries, regions of the world, levels of experience, and earning levels.

In the survey, the managers were asked to evaluate the importance of the six domains on a scale of 1 to 5. The domains were evaluated according to importance, criticality, and frequency of use. The survey results were then used to determine the number of questions in each of the domain areas that would be in the examination. The results are shown in Table 10-1.

Domain 1: Initiating the Project

Initiating has ten tasks associated with it. The PMP exam will have seventeen questions from domain 1.

Tasks

1. Two questions. "Determine project goals by identifying and working with project stakeholders in order to meet their requirements, specifications, and/or expectations."
2. Two questions. "Determine product or service deliverables by reviewing or generating the scope of work, requirements, and/or specifications to meet the stakeholder expectations."
3. One question. "Determine project management process outputs by applying appropriate practices, tools, and methodologies to ensure required product/service delivery."
4. One question. "Document project constraints through coordination with stakeholders and review of policies and procedures to ensure compliance."
5. Two questions. "Document assumptions by determining information that must

Table 10-1.   Evaluation of domains.

Domain	Percent of Test	Number of Questions
Initiating	8.5%	17
Planning	23.5%	47
Executing	23.5%	47
Controlling	23%	46
Closing	7%	14
Professional responsibility	14.5%	29

be validated or situations to be controlled during the project in order to facilitate the project planning process."

6. One question. "Define the project strategy by evaluating alternative approaches to meet stakeholder requirements, specifications, and/or expectations."

7. Two questions. "Identify performance criteria by referring to product/service specifications and process standards in order to ensure and/or support the quality assurance effort."

8. Two questions. "Determine key resource requirements by referring to deliverables in order to support planning and decision making."

9. Two questions. "Define an appropriate project budget and schedule by determining time and cost estimates in order to support decision making."

10. Two questions. "Provide comprehensive information by producing a formal document to obtain an approval decision from the stakeholders."

Domain 2: Planning the Project

Planning has seven tasks associated with it. The PMP exam will have forty-seven questions from domain 2.

Tasks

1. Eight questions. "Refine project requirements, assumptions, and constraints through communication with stakeholders and/or by reviewing project documents to baseline the scope of work and enable development of the execution plan."

2. Seven questions. "Create the Work Breakdown Structure using the scope of work, other project documents, and decomposition techniques to facilitate detailed project planning and the executing, controlling, and closing process."

3. Six questions. "Develop the resource management plan (Human Resources, Procurement, etc.) by identifying resource requirements and obtaining commitments from internal, external, and procured sources to complete all project activities."

4. Six questions. "Refine project time and cost estimates by applying estimating tools and techniques to all WBS tasks in order to determine project baseline, schedule, and budget."

5. Six questions. "Establish project controls by defining the required correct processes, measures, and controls to manage project change, communications, procurement, risk, quality, and human resources to facilitate project executing and controlling processes, and to ensure compliance with generally accepted industry standards."

6. Seven questions. "Develop a formal and comprehensive project plan by integrating and documenting project deliverables, acceptance criteria, processes, procedures, risks, and tasks to facilitate project executing, controlling, and closing processes."
7. Seven questions. "Obtain project plan approval by reviewing the plan with the client and other required stakeholders to confirm project baselines prior to proceeding with project executing processes."

Domain 3: Executing the Project

Executing has five tasks associated with it. The PMP exam will have forty-seven questions from domain 3.

Tasks

1. Ten questions. "Commit project resources in accordance with the project plan to ensure that all activities are performed."
2. Nine questions. "Implement the project plan by authorizing the execution of project activities and tasks to produce project deliverables."
3. Eleven questions. "Manage project progress by ensuring that activities are executed as planned in order to achieve the project objectives."
4. Nine questions. "Communicate project progress by producing project reports to provide timely and accurate project status and decision support information to stakeholders."
5. Eight questions. "Implement quality assurance procedures by performing project control activities to meet project objectives."

Domain 4: Controlling the Project

Controlling has eight tasks associated with it. The PMP exam will have forty-six questions from domain 4.

Tasks

1. Seven questions. "Measure project performance continually by comparing results to the baseline in order to identify project trends and variances."
2. Four questions. "Refine control limits on performance measures by applying established policy in order to identify needs for corrective action."
3. Seven questions. "Take timely corrective action by addressing the root causes in the problem areas in order to eliminate or minimize negative impact."

4. Five questions. "Evaluate the effectiveness of the corrective actions by measuring the subsequent performance in order to determine the need for further actions."
5. Seven questions. "Ensure compliance with the change management plan by monitoring response to change initiatives in order to manage scope."
6. Four questions. "Reassess project control plans by scheduling periodic reviews in order to ensure their effectiveness and currency."
7. Six questions. "Respond to risk event triggers in accordance with the risk management plan in order to properly manage project outcomes."
8. Six questions. "Monitor project activity by performing periodic inspections to ensure that authorized approaches and processes are followed or to identify the need for corrective action."

Domain 5: Closing the Project

Closing has five tasks associated with it. The PMP exam will have fourteen questions from domain 5.

Tasks

1. Four questions. "Obtain final acceptance of deliverables by obtaining formal approval from appropriate stakeholders to achieve closeout."
2. Two questions. "Document lessons learned by surveying project team members and other relevant stakeholders to use for the benefit of future projects."
3. Three questions. "Facilitate administrative and financial closure in accordance with the project plan in order to comply with organization and stakeholder requirements."
4. Three questions. "Preserve essential project records and required tools by archiving them for future use to adhere to legal and other requirements."
5. Two questions. "Release project resources by following appropriate organizational procedures in order to optimize resource utilization."

Domain 6: Professional Responsibility

Professional responsibility has five tasks associated with it. The PMP exam will have twenty-nine questions from domain 6.

Tasks

1. Eight questions. "Ensure individual integrity and professionalism by adhering to legal requirements and ethical standards in order to protect community and all stakeholders."

2. Three questions. "Contributing to the project management knowledge base by sharing lessons learned, best practices, research, etc. within appropriate communities in order to improve the quality of project management services, build capabilities of colleagues, and advance the profession."
3. Five questions. "Enhance individual competence by increasing and applying knowledge to improve services."
4. Five questions. "Balance stakeholders' interests by recommending approaches that strive for fair resolution in order to satisfy competing needs and objectives."
5. Eight questions. "Interact with team and stakeholders in a professional and cooperative manner by respecting personal, ethnic, and cultural differences in order to ensure a collaborative project management environment."

Types of Questions on the Exam

All of the questions on the PMP exam are multiple choice. There are only four choices for each question, and there are two hundred questions. This means that you will have an average of only 1.2 minutes per question. This is not a lot of time, but it is usually enough, if English is your native language, that is. Otherwise, you may have some problems with the timing of the exam.

The best approach to the exam is to go through it rapidly, answering all of the questions that you are certain about. I can remember doing this on the old PMP exam and realizing that at the end of the process I was not sure of any of the answers. When you are done with those, go back and answer the questions that you skipped. This will take advantage of any information that you can learn as a result of answering the questions you know. If you definitely know the answer to a question, then you also know that the other answers are wrong for that question. This information may allow you to answer a question that you skipped earlier. Be sure to answer every question on the exam. There is no subtraction for wrong answers. Only the right answers are counted.

The trend in the PMP examination is to use questions that are "situational" in nature. This means that the questions will be more like the word problems you had in your high school math classes. Situational questions go something like this: If Joe has four apples and Sally has three oranges, what time will the train from Chicago meet the train from New York? This is thought to test the candidate PMP more thoroughly in the competence of project management and less in the area of rote memorization. This has been accomplished. While the other project management organizations around the world may be critical of PMI for not using the interview methods that so many other organizations favor, PMI has achieved the recognition of the International Organization for Standardization, ISO 9001: 2000 certification for the process of certifying PMPs. This means that the process that PMI uses does what it is supposed to do, and it does act to select project management professionals from those who are not qualified.

PMI uses the Angoff modified technique for constructing the questions. This means that a large number of PMPs are used in the process. First, PMPs are trained to write questions for the exam. These questions are then reviewed by committees of PMPs, after which they are given to an independent professional who reviews the questions again for construction and ambiguity.

Once the questions have been reviewed, they are submitted to another group of PMPs who are asked to rate the questions in terms of whether they think a question tests a person seeking the PMP certification who is "minimally qualified." Each question is evaluated this way.

Although there is a passing grade for the exam, it is not necessarily going to be the same from year to year. PMI rates the difficulty of each question on the exam. A mixture of questions of varying difficulty are then selected so that the difficulty of each version of the exam is about the same. Each question on the exam is given to a group of PMPs who are asked the question, "What is the probability that a minimally acceptable candidate will answer this question correctly?" The probabilities are summarized, and each question receives a difficulty rating. So, if you take the exam with one set of questions and then take it again a year later with a different set of questions, the difficulty rating for the whole exam should be about the same, even though you have a different set of questions. The passing grade for each exam should be about the same as well, but this is not necessarily the case.

The questions fall into three categories. "Recall questions" are similar to what most of the questions on the PMP exam used to be like. These questions give you a definition and then different items, one of which is the item whose definition was stated. The "application questions" ask you to pick out what a project manager should do under the situation described. The "analysis questions" require you to take the information offered and, by looking at the relationships among the various pieces of information, come up with the correct answer.

You can expect that for most of the questions two of the four answers are easily discarded, and the remaining two will often be difficult to separate into the right and wrong answer.

Taking the Exam

The first thing you must do is get a good night's sleep the night before the exam. Don't eat a lot of sugar the morning of the exam. Eat a good breakfast. Try to do things in the way that you do them every day. If you are used to drinking coffee, then do not deprive yourself on the day of the exam.

Get there in plenty of time to take the exam. If you are using public transportation, be sure to allow for waiting time for the bus or train. If you are driving, be sure to allow enough time for traffic delays. You want to be there with enough time to calm yourself and prepare mentally for what will be a tough four hours. A very good friend of mine was totally relaxed about the exam. In fact, she was so relaxed that she forgot to go take it. The proctor phoned her an hour after the exam started and told her that she had not shown up for the exam. She decided to take the exam and rushed over to the exam site. Unfortunately, the proctor could not stay, and so she had to take the exam in two-and-a-half hours instead of four. She passed. But not everyone can do that. Better to be there early, relax, go over your critical notes, and take the exam in a relaxed manner.

There is a fifteen minute tutorial before the exam, and there will be some papers to sign. This activity is not counted as exam time. Take the time to go through the tutorial. It will stop you from making mistakes with the computer that could lose you valuable time in the exam. The four-hour exam time is just the time for answering questions on the exam.

You are allowed one break during the exam. This break can be up to one hour in length, and the timing of the exam will stop for the break. Once you are back at the exam work station, the exam time will continue until the four hours have been completed or you have finished the exam. When you are finished, the proctor will grade your exam, and you will be told whether you have passed or not.

If you are having trouble memorizing formulas and such, my suggestion is to bring the formulas to the exam written on a card. Before the exam, look over the card and leave it outside the examination room. You do not want someone to see you inside the room with something like that. When you get into the exam room, recall the formulas and write them on the approval scrap paper. This is a good idea if you are a person who has trouble memorizing things and who when under pressure gets signs and the order of variables mixed up.

Use of Practice Questions

In the last section of the book I have included nearly three hundred practice questions. Each of these is answered, and the answers are annotated. The questions should give you a good idea of what the exam will be like. I suggest taking several questions from each section and trying to answer them in the same amount of time PMI will give you, that is, 1.2 minutes per question.

Alternatively, you can take several of the questions and answer them after reviewing each of the chapters in the book on the subject of the questions. The questions are organized by the *Guide to the PMBOK* knowledge areas plus another section for the professional responsibility questions. The questions are not mixed as they will be on the actual examination, because I thought it would be more helpful to be able to review at least some of the questions at the end of each chapter. The questions on the actual exam will be randomized; if you have just answered a question from the planning domain about scheduling, the next question may be from any other knowledge area or project management domain.

Many people think that the best way to pass the PMP exam is to practice on the questions from various sources. This has two major problems. One is that the questions that you are likely to get your hands on are questions that someone other than PMI made up. These questions will certainly not have the rigorous inspection that PMI has given the questions on the actual exam. Security around the exam is very tight. None of the questions that are actually on the exam are likely to come into your hands. Prior to the changes in the exam effective April 2002, many of the questions on the exam were one-line type questions. Many of the practice questions you will see are mostly of this type. Practicing them for the exam will not help you when you take the actual exam. You will find that the questions on the actual exam are longer and require you to do quite a bit of analysis and answer the question, "What would a project manager do in this situation?"

The second and most important thing is that practicing on the exam questions will not give you a good knowledge of project management. It will give you only knowledge of the questions you practice with. PMI has gone to extreme lengths to make the exam something that will separate project management professionals from those who are not. This it does very well. It does it well enough that the certification process is itself confirmed by the International Organization for Standardization, ISO 9001: 2000. The exam tests your real knowledge and professionalism. I feel that it actually does a good job of testing your competence as well.

The practice questions are a good way to test your knowledge, but I do not think that they are the only way. A solid understanding of the principles and methods of project management is extremely important to passing the PMP exam. The use of practice questions gives you some idea about the style and form of the questions, which is something you need to know. But using the questions as the principal way of preparing for the exam is a serious mistake and will generally earn you a failing grade.

The Application for PMP Certification

I will not go into all six pages of the application form. Most of the form is straightforward except for the experience section and possibly the education section. For experience you are required to have 4,500 hours of project management experience over the last six years. The same process applies to those who do not have a bachelor's or equivalent degree from a university, only the number of years is increased to eight and the number of hours is increased to 7,500. There is, of course, some confusion for people from countries other than the United States. PMI has included in the application a list of the equivalent degrees that are issued by various countries. If your country is not listed, then you should contact PMI and ask about the validity of the degree that you have earned.

As part of the experience requirements, the number of nonoverlapping months of experience must be 36 months for those with a bachelor's degree and 60 months for those without it. This requirement needs some explanation.

Let's take our applicant with the bachelor's degree. The requirement is for 36 months' experience over the last six years. During this time you must have accumulated 4,500 hours of experience. The easiest way to see whether you qualify is to make a bar chart listing the projects you worked on over the last six years. Show each project bar starting and ending in the month that it started and ended. Of the 72 months in your bar chart at least 36 months should have one or more projects occupying the month. If you go from one end of the time scale to the other, and you can count more than 36 months where there is a project that you worked on, you are qualified. Do not count a month more than once. That is, if you worked on two projects at the same time in a given month, you can count the month only one time.

For example, our candidate works on a project from June to November 2002 and works on another project from August to December 2002. He can count June, July, August, September, October, November, and December for a total of seven months of experience. August, September, October, and November should not be counted two times even though two projects were being worked on at that time.

Be careful that the hours of experience you claim match the start and finish dates of the projects they come from. Do not say you worked on a project for three months and claim 1,000 hours. Even the best of us would have trouble accumulating 1,000 hours of experience in thirteen weeks, so be careful not to do this. It should be perfectly clear to the PMI reviewer that the experience you claim is indeed matched to the projects.

PMI also requires that you separate the experience into the project management process areas. There is really no requirement for this, and you could have all your experience in the project execution area and still qualify. I don't know why PMI requires you to separate your experience hours into the process areas, but as long as it does, you should separate them as instructed. Be careful that the totals also equal the number of hours that you have put on the other pages.

If you fill out the experience sheets of the application carefully, your application should be accepted. By no means should you lie on the application. If you do not have enough experience, then you will have to wait to get your PMP certification.

The last sheet for each project is an explanation of your experience on the project. You should list the deliverables that you were responsible for on the project in some detail. One page should be sufficient for each project. Be sure that the deliverables that you are explaining match the type and hours of experience that you have put on the previous page.

This is the only section of the application that is tedious. You must fill out two sheets minimum for each project you have worked on. For some of you this could be a lot of projects. Take the time and be careful. Put yourself in the mind of the reviewer.

Make the whole application consistent, and be sure that all the hours add up to the same totals. Make sure that your narrative on each project matches and supports the number of hours you are claiming in each domain.

The Education Qualification

There is now a requirement that you receive thirty-five contact hours of project management education. This requirement is relatively simple to achieve. These can be classes that you take at a university, courses taught by training companies or consultants, or courses from a registered education provider or any PMI component (chapter). They can even be courses offered by your own company or distance learning courses. This is a pretty broad classification. The timing of the education has no limits, so you can claim the hours going back in time as far as you wish.

The following is PMI's checklist for the PMP application:

- Name on application matches name on ID (two required)
- Payment or payment information
- Experience verification goes back more than three years
- Experience verification does not go back more than six years
- Experience verification includes more than 4,500 hours involved with project management
- Experience verification includes 36 months total
- Deliverables from each project are summarized
- There are 35 hours of documented project management instruction

Joining PMI

Today the cost of joining PMI and becoming a PMP are very close to the same as becoming a PMP without joining PMI. The benefits of joining PMI are tremendous for the money. Beside being able to network with other PMI members and having the many publications that will be delivered to you, you will be part of an organization of project management practitioners that has grown to nearly 100,000 worldwide.

Here is a list of just a few of the benefits that come to you as a PMI member:

- Discounts on many items
- PMI Knowledge and Wisdom Center
- Project management publications
- *PM Network*®—monthly

- *Project Management Journal*®—quarterly
- *PMI Today*®—monthly
- PMI bookstore
- Networking
- PMI conferences
- Specific interest groups
- PMI chapters
- Career hotline for job searches

Recertification

To be qualified for recertification you must accumulate sixty professional development units (PDUs) over a three-year period. A PDU is equivalent to one hour of contact time in a class on project management offered by a registered education provider. There are also many other ways to acquire PDUs. The different ways of acquiring PDUs will take too much space to review here, but after you have acquired your PMP certification you will have three years or more to accumulate these PDUs. You are able to earn PDUs for attending classes, writing a book or an article on project management, presenting a paper on project management, and many other items outlined in the professional development section of PMI's Web site at www.pmi.org. The timing of the three years starts on January 1 of the January following your certification, so the first time you requalify, you may really have more than three years' time to accumulate enough PDUs.

PRACTICE
QUESTIONS

SCOPE MANAGEMENT

1. Decomposing the major deliverables into smaller, more manageable components to provide better control is called:

   a. Scope planning.
   b. Scope definition.
   c. Scope baselining.
   d. Scope verification.

2. Any numbering system that is used to monitor project costs by category such as labor, supplies, or materials, for example, is called:

   a. Chart of accounts.
   b. Work breakdown structure.
   c. Universal accounting standard.
   d. Standard accounting practices.

3. A person who is involved in or may be affected by the activities or anyone who has something to gain or lose by the activity of the project is called a:

   a. Team member.
   b. Customer.
   c. Stakeholder.
   d. Supporter.

The following should be used for questions 4 through 6.

A project manager is assigned to a project early in the project life cycle. One of the things that must be done is to do a justification for the project. Since very little information is known about the project, the estimates are considered to be rough estimates. The following table is the project manager's estimate of the cash flows that will take place over the next five years.

End of Year	Cash Flow In	Cash Flow Out
1	0	500,000
2	300,000	90,000
3	400,000	100,000
4	100,000	175,000
5	50,000	35,000

4. What is the payback period for this project?

    a. One year
    b. Two years
    c. Three years
    d. Four years

5. What is the net cash flow at the end of five years?

    a. $50,000
    b. −$50,000
    c. $850,000
    d. $100,000

6. If the net present value for each of the cash flows were calculated at a 10% interest rate, the net present value cash flow at the end of five years would be:

    a. Greater than the total cash flow without the net present value applied.
    b. Less than the total cash flow without the net present value applied.
    c. The same as the total cash flow without the net present value applied.
    d. Unable to be calculated with the information supplied.

7. A group of related projects that are managed in a coordinated way that usually include an element of ongoing activity is called a:

    a. Major project.
    b. Project office.
    c. Program.
    d. Group of projects.

8. During the full life cycle of the project, a plot of the project's expected expenditures will usually follow a characteristic "S" shape. This indicates that:

    a. There is a cyclic nature to all projects.
    b. Problems will always occur in the execution phase.
    c. There are high expenditures during closeout.
    d. The bulk of the project budget will be spent in the execution phase.

9. A temporary endeavor undertaken to create a new product or service is called a:

    a. New product development.
    b. Project.

c. Program.
d. Enterprise.

10. A project manager makes a narrative description of the work that must be done for her project. This is called a:

a. Project plan.
b. Control chart.
c. Statement of work.
d. Project objective.

11. An example of scope verification is:

a. Reviewing the performance of an installed software module.
b. Managing changes to the project schedule.
c. Decomposing the WBS to a work package level.
d. Performing a benefit-cost analysis to determine if we should proceed.

12. The process of establishing clear and achievable objectives, measuring their achievement, and adjusting performance in accordance with the results of the measurement is called:

a. Strategic planning.
b. Contingency planning.
c. Detailed planning.
d. Management by objectives.

13. Configuration management is:

a. Used to ensure that the description of the project product is correct and complete.
b. The creation of the work breakdown structure.
c. The set of procedures developed to ensure that project design criteria are met.
d. A mechanism to track budget and schedule variances.

14. A project manager is employed by a construction company and is responsible for the furnishing of the completed building. One of the first things that the project manager for this project should do is to write a:

a. Work breakdown structure.
b. Budget baseline.
c. Project charter.
d. Project plan.

15. A project manager is creating a work breakdown structure for her project. In the breakdown structure the lowest level of the breakdown for the project manager is called the:

    a. Activity.
    b. Task.
    c. Work package.
    d. Cost account.

16. A project manager is reviewing the scope of the project and the scope baseline of the project. This includes which of the following?

    a. The original project schedule, budget, and scope
    b. The original project description and the project charter
    c. The original scope of the project plus or minus any scope changes
    d. The current budget of the project

17. A project manager has just become the manager of a project. The document that recognizes the existence of the project is called:

    a. The statement of work.
    b. The project assignment.
    c. The project charter.
    d. The product description.

18. A project manager is reviewing the work breakdown structure for her project. The WBS for the project represents:

    a. All the tangible items that must be delivered to the client.
    b. All the work that must be completed for the project.
    c. The work that must be performed by the project team.
    d. All the activities of the project.

19. A manager who manages a group of related projects is called a:

    a. Project manager.
    b. Project expediter.
    c. Program coordinator.
    d. Program manager.

20. A new project has begun. The project charter has been written and the project manager has been assigned. The project manager is preparing the work breakdown structure for the project. The WBS is typically used for:

a. Explaining the scope of the project relevant to the client.
b. The basis for organizing and defining the total scope of the project.
c. Showing the resource conflicts that exist in the project.
d. The logical relationship between tasks in the project.

21. During the life of a project, the project will go through several phases—initiating, planning, execution, and closeout. Which phase of the project is likely to have the greatest amount of its funding spent?

a. Initiating
b. Planning
c. Executing
d. Closeout

22. During the course of the project it is important that the stakeholders be informed of the progress of the project. One of the reports that is frequently used is a progress report. Which of the following is true about progress reports?

a. They allow stakeholders to judge the performance of the project according to its plan.
b. They are generally considered to be overkill on very small projects.
c. They require the use of earned value reports.
d. They must be produced by the project manager.

23. The coordinated undertaking of interrelated activities directed toward a specific goal that has a finite period of performance is a:

a. Project charter.
b. Project.
c. Set of project objectives.
d. Program.

24. The document that is proof of upper management's commitment to the project and gives the authority to manage the project to the project manager is called:

a. The project plan.
b. The project goals and objectives.
c. The project charter.
d. The project definition.

25. A project manager works in a company favoring the weakest authority for the project manager. The type of organization that holds the project manager to be the weakest is:

   a. Projectized organization.
   b. Strong matrix organization.
   c. Weak matrix organization.
   d. Balanced matrix organization.

26. A project manager has been asked by the client to meet the promise date of the project. The project manager analyzes the schedule before promising a date to the customer. The project manager uses the program evaluation and review technique to evaluate the project schedule. She decides that based on the results of the PERT calculations she can promise a delivery date of June 30. The expected value of the project completion date is May 30. If the project manager is willing to accept a 5% probability that the project will be delivered later than June 30, what is the standard deviation of the durations of the activities on the critical path? Assume a five-day workweek.

   a. Ten days
   b. Fifteen days
   c. One-half month
   d. One month

27. A project is proposed to a customer. Price and schedule for delivery are agreed upon. The work breakdown structure is agreed to as well. The customer requests that one of the milestones of the project be completed by a certain date. The project schedule is reviewed, and it is found that the expected completion date for this milestone is considerably earlier than the date requested by the customer. The date for this milestone is which of the following?

   a. Consideration
   b. Summary activity
   c. Constraint
   d. Suggestion

28. A project manager is managing a project. The original scope baseline of the project was budgeted at $100,000. Since work on the project started there have been seventeen authorized and approved changes to the project. The changes have a value of $17,000 and the cost of investigating them prior to their approval was $2,500. What is the current budget for the project?

   a. $100,000
   b. $114,500

    c. $117,000
    d. $119,500

29. In a very large project having a budget of $5 million and a project team of over one hundred persons, the project manager constructs a work breakdown structure. The project manager will do the WBS to the detail level of which of the following?

    a. Task
    b. Activity
    c. WBS element
    d. Work package

30. A project manager is managing a project that has reached the end of the planning phase. The work scope has been agreed to and definitive cost estimates have been completed for the project. The total estimated cost of the project is $100,000. It is reasonable to expect that the project will not cost over which of the following values?

    a. $100,000
    b. $110,000
    c. $125,000
    d. $175,000

31. The change management plan should be included in which of the following?

    a. Scope management plan
    b. Communications management plan
    c. Configuration management plan
    d. Quality management plan

32. A project team has made up the work breakdown structure for a project. Senior management for the company and all of the stakeholders including the client have approved the WBS. The client later requests that a change be made in the project, which will cost a considerable amount of money. The client says that the company's salesman promised this feature prior to sign-off on the WBS. Who should pay for the change?

    a. The client should pay.
    b. The company managing the project should pay.
    c. Both the company and the client should pay part of the cost.
    d. The change should not be implemented.

33. A project manager is managing a software development project for a hospital. There is a new computer available that will speed up the development process considerably.

The new computer costs $50,000 including shipping, installation, and start-up. The computer will cause a gross savings of $100,000. What is the net present value of the savings if they occur one year after the expenditure for the computer? Assume a 10% interest rate.

a. $90,000
b. $40,909
c. $45,555
d. $91,110

34. A project manager is managing a project during the planning phase. She chooses to use a precedence network diagram as a graphic planning tool to assist in making the project schedule. The most important reason for using the network diagram as a graphic planning tool is that it makes it easier to see which aspect of the project plan better than the other tools available?

a. The probability that the tasks will be completed on time
b. The logical relationships between activities in the schedule
c. The start and finish dates of the activities
d. The float between activities

The following information and questions 1 through 10 refer to Figure 1.

A schedule was developed for a project to install windows in an apartment building. The project is a rush job, and the contractor has agreed to schedule the work on a single shift basis but will work seven days per week until the job is done. The project is to begin on May 1.

Figure 1. Scheduling practice exercise.

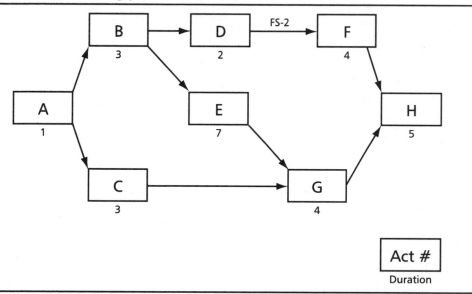

1. What day in May will activity D have for its early finish date?

   a. May 13
   b. May 6
   c. May 7
   d. May 5

2. What is the free float for activity F?

   a. 6
   b. 7

c. 0
d. 8

3. What is the free float for activity D?

a. 6
b. 7
c. 8
d. 0

4. What is the critical path of the project?

a. A B E G H
b. A B D F H
c. A C G H
d. A B E D F H

5. What is the late start for activity F?

a. May 10
b. May 11
c. May 12
d. May 14

6. How long is the project in days?

a. Nineteen
b. Twenty
c. Twenty-one
d. Eighteen

7. What is the early start for activity F?

a. May 7
b. May 6
c. May 5
d. May 4

8. If there is a delay in activity F of six days, what is the effect on the project completion date?

a. Increases one day
b. No change to project completion date

    c. Increases two days

    d. Increases three days

9. What is the early finish date of activity A?

    a. May 1

    b. May 2

    c. May 3

    d. May 4

10. The above diagram is called:

    a. Activity on arrow network diagram.

    b. Network diagram.

    c. Precedence diagram.

    d. Gantt chart.

11. If a project manager were to make Thanksgiving dinner, two of the activities that might be of concern would be roasting the turkey and baking the sweet potatoes. In order to ensure that these two items will be finished cooking and will come out of the oven at the same time, what type of relationship should he or she use in the schedule between these two activities?

    a. Finish-finish

    b. Start-start

    c. Finish-start

    d. Start-finish

Questions 12 through 15 refer to the diagram in Figure 2 and the table that follows.

Activity	Optimistic	Pessimistic	Most Likely
A	1	1	1
B	2	3	3
C	10	13	12
D	5	5	5
E	3	6	4
F	1	1	1
G	5	8	6
H	9	13	10
I	5	5	5

Figure 2. PERT diagram.

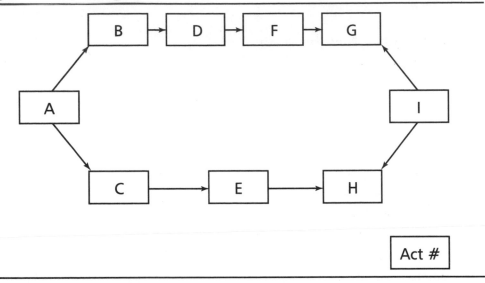

Act #

In a project to install concrete sewer lines there is a lot of uncertainty as to how long the durations should be for the tasks involved. The project manager has determined that the team will use the PERT technique to evaluate the project's completion date. The diagram shows nine activities and the table shows the optimistic, pessimistic, and most likely estimates that the team has already made.

12. What is the expected value of the number of days to complete the project?

    a. 47.3
    b. 22.0
    c. 32.3
    d. 48

13. It is desirable to make an estimate that has a greater than 95% chance of being correct. Which of the following ranges of time for the completion of the project best describes this probability of being correct?

    a. 33.31 to 31.36
    b. 34.28 to 30.39
    c. 14.39 to 33.48
    d. 35.25 to 29.42

14. What is the expected value of the duration for activity B?

a. 5.6
b. 2.8
c. 3.0
d. 2.6

15. What is the standard deviation for the duration of activity B?

a. 1.000
b. .133
c. .166
d. 1.413

16. The project manager decided to improve the predicted completion date for the project by doing in parallel several of the activities that were scheduled to be done in sequence. This is called:

a. Crashing.
b. Increasing priorities.
c. Hurry up defense.
d. Fast tracking.

17. Crashing the schedule means:

a. Making the project shorter by any economic means.
b. Running the project team on overtime.
c. Doing activities that were in sequence in parallel.
d. Getting out of town before the project is in trouble.

18. The original schedule (for a project, a work package, or an activity), plus or minus approved changes, is called:

a. The working schedule.
b. The target schedule.
c. The performance schedule.
d. The baseline schedule.

19. Schedules are used in many ways. In a project to build a bridge the project manager wants to use a tool that will show the scheduled activities in such a way that it is easy to see when each activity starts and finishes and which activities are taking place at the same time. Which tool should be used?

a. PERT chart
b. Gantt chart

    c. Precedence diagram

    d. GERT chart

20. Which of the following is true?

    a. The critical path is the path through the network that has the highest total duration.

    b. The critical path is the path with the least amount of free float.

    c. The critical path is the list of activities that have zero float.

    d. The critical path is the list of activities that have critical risks associated with them.

21. Resource leveling will generally:

    a. Reduce the time needed to do the project.

    b. Increase the total time necessary to do all the tasks.

    c. Reduce the overutilization of resources.

    d. Reduce resources to the lowest skill that is possible.

22. A task was scheduled to use two persons, full time, and take two weeks to complete. Instead, the project manager was only able to assign one person to this task. At the end of two weeks, the person assigned to the task was 75% complete. What is the cost performance index?

    a. .75

    b. 1.5

    c. 1.33

    d. .5

23. Five tasks are scheduled to be completed in sequence. Each task has a finish-start relationship with the next task. Each has one day of total float. As of today, task one and two have been completed on schedule. How many days of float remain in the schedule for these tasks?

    a. Two

    b. One

    c. Zero

    d. Four

24. Which of the following is considered to be a simulation technique?

    a. PERT analysis

    b. GERT analysis

c. Monte Carlo analysis
d. Critical path method

25. The main difference between the two types (ADM, arrow diagramming method, and PDM, precedence diagramming method) of the critical path method (CPM) of scheduling is:

   a. Placement of the activity on the logic diagram line.
   b. Arrow diagramming method (ADM) is a deterministic method, whereas the precedence diagramming method (PDM) is a probabilistic method.
   c. Precedence diagramming method (PDM) is a deterministic method, whereas the arrow diagramming method (ADM) is a probabilistic method.
   d. Precedence diagramming method (PDM) is a more accurate method.

26. The project schedule is *not* used to determine:

   a. The start and finish dates of the activities.
   b. Occasional changes to the activity listing.
   c. The total float of the activities.
   d. The project's budget.

27. The overall duration of the project schedule is not influenced by:

   a. Using mandatory dependencies as constraints.
   b. Using discretionary dependencies as constraints.
   c. The availability of the resources that are assigned to perform the work.
   d. Using the arrow diagramming method instead of the precedence diagramming method (PDM) of scheduling.

28. The program evaluation and review technique (PERT) method of scheduling differs from the critical path method (CPM) because the PERT method:

   a. Uses weighted averages of activity durations to calculate project duration.
   b. Uses "dummy" activities to represent logic ties.
   c. Uses "free float" instead of "total float" in the schedule calculations.
   d. Uses bar charts instead of logic diagrams to portray the schedule.

29. A project manager is managing a project and is considering the reschedule of an activity because one of the project engineers must work on this activity and another activity at the same time. Each of the activities is scheduled to have a duration of two weeks. One of the activities is on the critical path and the other activity has eighteen days of free float. The project manager should:

a. Reschedule the activity that has no float.
b. Reschedule the activity with float.
c. Ask the engineer to work overtime.
d. Reschedule both activities to take advantage of the float on each.

30. A project manager looks at her schedule and sees that there has been a delay in completing a task. It seems practical to move a person from another task who is an expert on the work that is behind. There is a choice of using two different persons who are working on two different tasks. One person is working on a task that has five days of free float and the other is working on a task that has eight days of total float and no free float. Which person should be used to help out?

    a. The person working on the task with free float of five days.
    b. The person working on the task with total float of eight days.
    c. Either person can be used.
    d. A person should be brought in from outside the project.

31. In the first attempt at resource leveling the project schedule, what would you expect to occur?

    a. The number of required resources will increase during certain time periods of the project.
    b. The number of required resources will decrease during certain time periods of the project.
    c. The overall project duration will increase.
    d. The overall project duration will decrease.

32. According to the *Guide to the PMBOK,* work packages can be divided into:

    a. Smaller work packages.
    b. Tasks.
    c. Activities.
    d. Subprojects.

33. A project is nearly 33% complete according to the earned value reporting method. An identified risk has occurred, and the project manager has chosen to draw funds from the contingency fund and add the activities necessary to deal with the problems associated with the risk. What should he do next?

    a. The schedule should not be changed. Original plans should have allowed for this delay.

b. The budget money set aside for the risk should be released, but there is not a need for a schedule change.

c. The schedule and budget baselines should be changed, to show the new work.

d. The budget baseline should be changed, but the work should be done within the schedule as it is.

34. The key inputs to activity definition are:

    a. Work breakdown structure, the project schedule, and the network diagram.
    b. Project schedule, progress reports, and change requests.
    c. The project network diagram, constraints, and durations.
    d. The work breakdown structure, the scope statement, and historical information that supports the applicable activity.

35. A project manager is approached by the major stakeholder in the project and is asked to reduce the time for the scheduled completion of the project. The project manager reviews the project plans and the progress that has been made on the project. He or she decides that the best approach to solving this problem is to fast track the project until the new project completion date can be achieved. Which of the following will be done by the project manager?

    a. Reduce the project schedule by any means that are possible
    b. Reduce the project schedule by applying any practical means necessary
    c. Reschedule activities that would be done in sequence to activities that can be done in parallel
    d. Inform the stakeholder that this will change the project schedule and will require additional funds to comply with the request

36. A project manager would like to manage his project in such a way that he will be able to identify specific tasks that should be watched and managed more closely than others. The project manager should use which method?

    a. The PERT method
    b. The critical path method
    c. The GERT method
    d. The PCDM method

37. A project manager would like to manage his project in such a way that he will be able to predict more accurately the duration of the project even though the estimates for the duration of the activities have a lot of variability. The project manager should use which method to more accurately predict the project completion date?

    a. CPM
    b. GERT
    c. PERT
    d. Activity sampling

38. The project manager for a project is going to use the PERT method of scheduling for the project that she is working on. Using the PERT calculation the variance for the project is found to be 25 days and the duration of the project is found to be 169 days. What is the range of values for the project duration such that there will be at least a 95% probability that the actual project completion will fall between the high and low value of the range of values?

    a. 164–173 days
    b. 144–194 days
    c. 119–219 days
    d. 159–179 days

39. In distinguishing PERT from CPM one could say that:

    a. PERT is probabilistic and CPM is deterministic.
    b. CPM is probabilistic and PERT is deterministic.
    c. Either one is deterministic or probabilistic depending on how they are used.
    d. Neither one is deterministic or probabilistic.

40. According to the *Guide to the PMBOK* the lowest level of the work breakdown structure is:

    a. The task.
    b. The activity.
    c. The work package.
    d. The element.

COST MANAGEMENT

1. A project manager wants to make a trip to California by car. The project manager knows how many miles it will be to drive to California, the current price of gasoline, and how many miles the car will go on a gallon of gasoline. From this information he or she can calculate the estimated cost of the gasoline for the trip. This is a form of what kind of estimating technique?

    a. Definitive
    b. Analogous
    c. Parametric
    d. Quantitative

2. A project manager wants to make a trip to California by car. The project manager knows someone who has made this trip before. This person has a similar car to the one that the project manager has, and the person has kept good records on the money spent for fuel on the trip. The distance that the project manager will travel is 10% farther than the other person's trip. By multiplying the cost of fuel reported by the other person by 1.1, the project manager is performing what kind of estimate?

    a. Definitive
    b. Analogous
    c. Parametric
    d. Quantitative

3. To distinguish top-down estimates from bottom-up estimates, it would be correct to say that the bottom-up estimate would be:

    a. Less accurate.
    b. About equal in accuracy to the top-down estimate.
    c. More accurate.
    d. No different to perform than the top-down estimate.

4. A project manager and the project team identify several specific risks in a project. The expected value of these risks is estimated at $10,000. The impact on the project brought about by these risks is estimated at $40,000. What value should be entered into the management reserve for these risks?

a. $10,000
b. $40,000
c. $0
d. $25,000

5. A project manager and the project team identify several specific risks in a project. The expected value of these risks is estimated at $10,000. The impact on the project brought about by these risks is estimated at $40,000. What value should be entered into the contingency reserve for these risks?

a. $10,000
b. $40,000
c. $0
d. $25,000

6. What characteristic best describes the cost baseline?

a. Total budget for the project
b. Time-phased budget for the project
c. Total budget for the project including the contingency budget
d. Total budget for the project including the contingency budget and the management reserve

7. A project is formed to produce a product that will be used for transporting people. Costs that are associated with the project that occur after the delivery of the product to the customer are considered to be what kind of cost?

a. Prorated costs
b. Expenses
c. Life cycle cost
d. Expected value

8. A project team receives an approved change request from the customer. The team has previously estimated that the cost to implement this change is $10,000. The customer has agreed to pay this amount for the additional work. The customer realizes that there is a 50 percent chance that this change will not work and will later be removed. What change, if any, should be made in the budget?

a. The project budget should not be increased.
b. The project budget should be increased by $15,000.
c. The project budget should be increased by $10,000.
d. The project budget should be increased by $5,000.

9. The act of doing anything that will help to bring future project performance into line with the project plan is called:

   a. Budget update.
   b. Revised cost estimate.
   c. Corrective action.
   d. Contingency planning.

10. Which of the following choices would be an acceptable cause for "rebaselining" a $10 million project?

    a. The monthly consumer price index on some of the commodities used on the project has been identified as having gone up by 1.6%, an increase of 46% over the 1.1% that had been budgeted.
    b. The client has authorized a $10,000 addition to the scope of the project.
    c. The contractor's company has instituted a quality program on which it has pledged to spend $1 million during the next year.
    d. The productivity in the drafting department has been shown to be lower than anticipated, which has resulted in 1,000 additional hours, a 78% increase over what was budgeted.

11. In terms of earned value reporting, a project is considered complete when:

    a. The BAC is equal to the PV.
    b. The EV is equal to the AC.
    c. The PV is equal to the AC.
    d. The BAC is equal to the EV.

12. The time-phased cost of the project that reflects the expenditures rather than the consumption of a resource that will be used to measure and monitor cost performance on a project is the:

    a. Spending plan.
    b. Cost baseline.
    c. WBS.
    d. Schedule.

13. A large piece of equipment is needed for the project. It will be retained and used after the project is completed. The equipment has a value of $500,000, and it has a scrap value of $50,000 at the end of its useful life of ten years. If the sum of the years' digits method of depreciation is used, what is the depreciation that is taken at the end of the third year?

   a. $81,818
   b. $90,900
   c. $65,250
   d. $72,500

14. Using the formula: Present value $= S/(1+i)^n$ where i is the interest rate in percentage, n is the number of periods, and S is the starting amount, the following table is produced:

Periods	10%	12%	14%
1	0.909	0.893	0.877
2	0.826	0.797	0.769
3	0.751	0.712	0.675
4	0.683	0.636	0.592
5	0.621	0.597	0.519

Based on the table, what is the value of an annual income flow of $1,300 each year over the next three years at 12%?
   a. $3122.60
   b. $3900.00
   c. $3497.00
   d. 36%

15. Life cycle costing:

   a. Is a method of including all of the cost associated with the project over its entire life.
   b. Is a federal government accounting method.
   c. Is a method of predicting the life of a project.
   d. Is a method of evaluating projects when they are complete.

The following table and description refer to questions 16 through 22.

A project manager is using the earned value reporting method to manage his project. The following table shows the data collected to date. The plan is for the project to be complete after eight weeks. The earned value report shows data collected for the first four weeks of the project. The figures shown in the table are cumulative.

Week	PV	AC	EV
1	1,000	1,000	1,000
2	3,000	2,000	2,500

3	5,000	5,000	6,000
4	7,000	9,000	7,000
5	13,000		
6	17,000		
7	19,000		
8	20,000		

16. What is the cost performance index for week 4?

    a. 1.000
    b. 0.777
    c. 1.286
    d. 1.250

17. What is the schedule performance index for week 3?

    a. 1.200
    b. 0.833
    c. 1.000
    d. 1.500

18. What is the BAC for the project during week 4?

    a. 7,000
    b. 9,000
    c. 5,000
    d. 20,000

19. During week 5 it is found that some of the work that was reported complete in week 2 was considered unacceptable. It will require $500 to fix the problem and make this work acceptable. The work is scheduled to be done in week 6. No other work is reported to be complete during week 5. What is the EV for week 5?

    a. 7,000
    b. 6,500
    c. 9,000
    d. 5,000

20. What is the cost variance for week 4?

    a. 0
    b. −2,000

    c. 2,000

    d. 7,000

21. What is the schedule variance in week 2?

    a. 500

    b. 1,000

    c. -500

    d. $-1,000$

22. What is the EAC at week 4?

    a. 20,000

    b. 15,555

    c. 25,740

    d. 17,717

23. The calculation of the EAC assumes that:

    a. The schedule performance index will remain the same for the remaining part of the project.

    b. The cost performance index will remain the same for the remaining part of the project.

    c. The BAC will be different by the end of the project.

    d. The EAC will continuously increase for the remaining portion of the project.

24. What factors need to be known in order to be able to calculate the ETC?

    a. Budget at completion, actual cost, and planned value

    b. Budget at completion, earned value, and actual cost

    c. Estimate at completion and planned value

    d. Estimate at completion and actual cost

25. A construction company is being measured by the earned value reporting method. During the project one of the tasks, installing ten elm trees, was completed. The planned value for this task was $4,000, and it was completed two weeks ago. Unfortunately for the contractor, maple trees should have been planted. The customer insists that maple trees be planted and that the elm trees be removed. As of this time the elm trees are still in the ground, but the contractor has agreed to do the work of replacing them. What action should be taken on the earned value report?

    a. Reduce PV by $4,000

    b. Reduce AC by $4,000

c. Reduce EV by $4,000
d. Make no changes since the vendor has agreed to fix the problem

26. Learning curve theory emphasizes that in producing many goods:

   a. Cost decreases as production rates increase.
   b. Average unit cost decreases as more units are produced.
   c. Materials become cheaper when they are purchased in bulk.
   d. Laborers become more productive because of technological advances.

27. A project manager is considering applying learning curve theory to his project. The project involves designing a number of software modules that are very similar. According to the cost figures that have been collected the first unit required 100 person-hours to design and test. The second unit required 90 person-hours to design and test. How many person-hours will the eighth module take to design and test?

   a. 90
   b. 100
   c. 73
   d. 172

28. A project manager decides that for this point in the project life cycle she will use an analogous estimate. One of the things that the project manager will *not* have to worry about in preparing this estimate is:

   a. Activity listings.
   b. Scaling the estimate.
   c. Quantifying the estimate.
   d. Historical support for the figures used.

29. A project manager is preparing the budget for the project. There are several inputs to the budgeting process that the project manager will use. One of the things that the project manager will not use is the:

   a. Cost estimates.
   b. Project schedule.
   c. Cost baseline.
   d. Work breakdown structure.

Use the following information for questions 30 and 31.

A project team has a programmer on the team. The programmer will work on the project for twenty-six weeks as a full-time team member. Her utilization is 72%, productivity is 80%, basic wages are $50 per hour, fringe benefits are 30%, and overhead costs are 50% of wages plus fringe benefits. Use a forty-hour work week.

30. What is the cost of this employee for the project?

     a. $136,760
     b. $126,750
     c. $176,041
     d. $101,400

31. One of the tasks that the person in the above project is assigned requires 100 hours of effort. What is the cost of the task?

     a. $12,187
     b. $16,927
     c. $9,750
     d. $13,541

32. The contingency budget will:

     a. Reduce the probability of scope changes.
     b. Reduce the probability of cost overruns.
     c. Increase the probability of a cost overrun.
     d. Increase the probability of scope changes.

The following table should be used for questions 33, 34, and 35.

A project manager is assigned to a project early in the project life cycle. One of the things that must be done is to do a justification for the project. Since very little information is known about the project, the estimate is considered to be a rough estimate. The following table is the manager's estimate of the cash flows that will take place over the next five years.

End of Year	Cash Flow In	Cash Flow Out
1	0	500,000
2	300,000	90,000
3	400,000	100,000
4	100,000	175,000
5	50,000	35,000

33. What is the payback period for this project?

    a. One year
    b. Two years
    c. Three years
    d. Four years

34. What is the net cash flow at the end of five years?

    a. $50,000
    b. − $50,000
    c. $850,000
    d. $100,000

35. If the net present value for each of the cash flows were calculated at a 10% interest rate, the net present value cash flow at the end of five years would be:

    a. Greater than the total cash flow without the net present value applied.
    b. Less than the total cash flow without the net present value applied.
    c. The same as the total cash flow without the net present value applied.
    d. Unable to be calculated with the information supplied.

36. During the full life cycle of the project, a plot of the project's expected expenditures will usually follow a characteristic "S" shape. This indicates that:

    a. There is a cyclic nature to all projects.
    b. Problems will always occur in the execution phase.
    c. There are high expenditures during closeout.
    d. The bulk of the project budget will be spent in the execution phase.

37. A project manager is using the earned value reporting system to manage his project. At this point in time the EV is $24,000, the BAC is $97,000, the PV is $29,000, and the AC is $45,000. What is the percent complete?

    a. 30%
    b. 25%
    c. 46%
    d. 53%

38. The project manager of a project must buy a large piece of equipment costing $1,543,256. He meets with the accounting department representative to the project team and reviews the different depreciation methods that can be used to depreciate

the equipment over the useful life of the equipment. Which of the following is an accelerated depreciation method?

a. Multiplication of the years' digits
b. Straight line
c. Sum of the years' digits
d. Average deflation

The following situation refers to questions 39, 40, and 41.

In a manufacturing facility that makes electronic widgets, the main widget making machine is getting old and a project is formed to consider the replacement of this machine. The average cost of the operations performed on this machine for making a widget is $5.00 per unit. A new machine can be purchased for $50,000 that will perform these operations much more quickly and with less scrap and rework for an average cost of $3.00 per unit. An alternative machine is even faster than the first machine considered and will perform the same operations for $2.00 per unit. However, this machine will cost $75,000. The company manufactures 1,000 widgets each month.

39. What is the breakeven point for the $75,000 machine compared to the existing machine?

a. 100,000 units
b. Three years
c. Five years
d. 25,000 units

40. What is the breakeven point for the $50,000 machine compared to the existing machine?

a. 100,000 units
b. Three years
c. Five years
d. 25,000 units

41. If the production of widgets is expected to continue for at least three years, what is the preferred action?

a. Do not replace the machine.
b. Replace the existing machine with a new machine costing $50,000.
c. Replace the existing machine with a new machine costing $75,000.
d. Buy both machines.

QUALITY MANAGEMENT

1. The processes required to ensure that the project will satisfy the needs for which it was undertaken include all activities of the overall management function that determines the quality policy, objectives, and responsibilities and implements them by means such as quality planning, quality control, quality assurance, and quality improvement, within the quality system. This is called:

    a. Quality assurance.
    b. Quality control.
    c. Quality planning.
    d. Quality management.

2. Decisions as to the types of projects that should be accomplished and strategic plans as to the quality of the projects that are required should be the decision of which of the following?

    a. Project manager
    b. Procurement manager
    c. Upper management
    d. Stakeholders

3. According to Deming and Juran most of the quality problems that exist are due to a defect or failure in processes that are controlled by:

    a. The project manager.
    b. The procurement manager.
    c. Upper management.
    d. Stakeholders.

4. A project manager is managing a large project and must consider the application of a quality management plan. One of the critical factors in such a plan is the cost of implementing the plan. The project manager should:

    a. Invoice the client for all quality improvements.
    b. Implement the highest quality possible regardless of cost.
    c. Implement quality improvements as long as the benefits outweigh the costs.
    d. Rely on upper management to determine the quality budget.

5. A project manager has discovered a problem and is trying to determine the cause. The process whereby he identifies the variables that have the most influence on the project by holding all the variables constant and changing one at a time is called:

   a. Product correlation.
   b. Design of an experiment.
   c. System integration.
   d. Output processing.

6. A control chart is being used to control a manufacturing process. As part of the control a sample of five parts is taken from the manufacturing process each hour of operation. Each of the five parts is measured and the dimension is recorded on the work sheet. The difference between the highest and lowest measured dimension of the five parts is plotted on the control chart. This is called which of the following values?

   a. R
   b. R bar
   c. X
   d. X bar

7. The totality of characteristics of an entity that bear on its ability to satisfy stated or implied needs is the definition for:

   a. Modern quality management.
   b. Quality assurance.
   c. Quality.
   d. Quality control.

8. A large project is being worked on by a large company. The client is interested in knowing how the company will be able to meet the quality needs of the project. In order to satisfy this request of the client the project manager arranges a meeting between the client and the:

   a. General manager.
   b. Quality control manager.
   c. Quality assurance manager.
   d. Chief designer.

9. One of the fundamental tenets of quality management is that quality:

   a. Must exceed customer expectations.
   b. Is planned in and not inspected in.

    c. Will increase cost.

    d. Costs must all be passed onto the customer.

10. A category or rank given to products that have the same functional use but different technical characteristics is called the product's:

    a. Quality.

    b. Functional characteristics.

    c. Grade.

    d. Technical characteristics.

11. The quality manager of a company wishes to analyze the data that is coming to him in the form of a list of defects that have occurred in the shipping department. The report comes with defects listed chronologically as they occurred, the cost of the repair necessary to correct each defect, the person involved, and a description of the defect. The manager would like to determine which of the defects should be corrected first according to the frequency of the defect occurring. He should use which of the following quality tools?

    a. Cause and effect diagram

    b. Sampling inspection

    c. Pareto diagram

    d. Quality critical path

12. A project manager from the quality control area is trying to categorize the number of mistakes that are made in the area that paints the right front fender of the Mercedes 560 SL. She lists all the possible defects on a sheet of paper and asks the inspector to make a mark each time one of the listed defects is found. This is an example of using which of the following quality tools?

    a. Scatter diagram

    b. Statistical measurements

    c. Check sheet

    d. Random sampling

13. The project management team should be aware that modern quality management complements modern project management. For example, both disciplines recognize the importance of:

a. Completion in the shortest possible time frame.
b. Making a maximum profit.
c. Having lower cost than a competitor.
d. Customer satisfaction.

14. In a manufacturing process that is being controlled by control charts there are variables occurring that will affect the process output. Variations in the process that are considered to be normal process variables are called:

a. Common causes.
b. Uncommon causes.
c. Special causes.
d. Random causes.

15. Work results, quality checklists, operational definitions, and the management plan are:

a. Inputs to quality control.
b. Outputs from quality control.
c. Inputs to quality assurance.
d. Outputs from quality assurance.

16. A control chart is being used to control a manufacturing process. As part of the control a sample of five parts is taken from the manufacturing process each hour of operation. Each of the five parts is measured, and the dimension is recorded on the work sheet. The average of the five parts is plotted on the control chart. This is called which of the following values?

a. X
b. X bar
c. Sample average
d. Control average

17. A project manager for the quality department is trying to solve a problem with a machine that makes die cast aluminum parts that are used in automobiles. These parts are frequently made with defects. The project manager has decided to hold a meeting to discuss the process of making the parts. He creates a diagram that has branches that show the possible causes of the problems. Each of the branches breaks the cause down into more and more detail. This diagram is called a:

a. Pareto diagram.
b. Fishtank diagram.

   c. Cause and effect diagram.
   d. Scatter diagram.

18. As the manager of the production department where electrical circuits are being made you observe the inspection station where the completed printed circuit assemblies are being inspected. In this operation the inspector takes the printed circuit assembly and puts it into a fixture. The fixture is part of a testing machine that has three digital readouts. The inspector records the readings on the three digital readouts on his inspection report. This is an example of:

   a. Attribute inspection.
   b. Variable inspection.
   c. Sampling inspection.
   d. Process control.

19. One of the important advantages of using control charts in managing a production operation is that the control chart tells you when to take corrective action on the process being controlled. Another important result of using control charts is:

   a. The control chart identifies the special causes.
   b. The control chart tells you when you should not take corrective action.
   c. The control chart shows how much the defects are costing.
   d. The control chart shows who is responsible for the defects.

20. According to the ideas behind modern quality management, quality improvements should be made:

   a. In large steps through detailed study of problems and then implemented as comprehensive solutions when they are funded.
   b. In small incremental steps.
   c. By assignment of permanent quality improvement teams.
   d. By hiring ISO certification consultants to point out quality deficient areas.

21. The Japanese developed a method of modern quality management that relies on continuing small improvements involving everyone from the top management to the lowest level worker in the organization. This is called:

   a. Kamban.
   b. Kaizen.
   c. PDCA.
   d. Deming cycle.

22. The primary benefits of meeting quality requirements are:

    a. Cost and delays are reduced, production improves, cost to customer goes up, and profits go up.
    b. Cost and delays are reduced, production improves, market share increases, and profits go up.
    c. Cost and delays are reduced, capital expenditures go down, market share increases, and profits go up.
    d. Cost and delays are reduced, production improves, market share increases, and profits are maintained.

23. When the quality management discipline is implemented, the benefits to costs ratio should at least be:

    a. Unable to be evaluated.
    b. Less than one.
    c. Of little importance.
    d. Greater than one.

24. The quality management plan provides input to _____ and addresses quality control, quality assurance, and quality improvement.

    a. The overall project plan
    b. The WBS
    c. The project scope
    d. External stakeholders

25. Project quality assurance:

    a. Includes policing the conformance of the project team to specs.
    b. Provides the project team and stakeholders with standards, by which the project performance is measured.
    c. Is a managerial process that defines the organization, design, resources, and objectives of quality management.
    d. Provides confidence that the project will satisfy relevant quality standards.

26. The ISO 9001: 2000 standard is used to:

    a. Formalize the tools of quality management.
    b. Set international standards for quality conformance in organizations.
    c. Set USA national standards for quality conformance in organizations.
    d. Develop standards of excellence for manufacturing facilities.

27. What does "cost of acceptance" mean?

    a. The cost of establishing and maintaining the quality function
    b. The life cycle cost of the project
    c. The cost of inspection and reinspection, quality assurance, quality management, and quality planning
    d. The cost of meeting project objectives

28. A control chart controls a manufacturing process. Measurements are taken while the process is operating one time each hour. At each hour five sample parts are measured, and the results are recorded and plotted on a control chart. During the last five hours the following data was observed for X bar and R. The upper control limit for X bar values is 142 and the lower control limit is 102. The value on the control chart for X bar is 122 and the value for R bar is 3. What can be said about this process?

	9 A.M.	10 A.M.	11 A.M.	12 P.M.	1 P.M.
X bar	125	126	127	128	129
R	2	1	4	2	3

    a. The process is not in control and should be adjusted.
    b. The process is in control and should not be adjusted.
    c. The value of R is too high at 11 A.M.
    d. The value for X bar is outside the control limits.

29. The diagram that ranks defects in the order of frequency of occurrence and shows the number of defects and the cumulative percentage from the greatest number of defects to the least number of defects is called a:

    a. Bar chart.
    b. Critical path.
    c. Pie chart.
    d. Pareto diagram.

30. Employees of a company were measured on the amount of scrap that they produced over a period of time. The number of hours of training that they had was also measured. When these results were plotted on a scatter diagram, they were found to be negatively correlated. This means that:

    a. Scrap increased as training hours increased.
    b. Scrap decreased as training hours increased.

c. Scrap increased as training hours decreased.
d. Scrap decreased as training hours decreased.

It was decided to set up a process to control the output of a machine that was manufacturing buttons. The following measurements of the diameter of the button were made. Each hour a sample of four buttons was taken. The measurement shown in the table is the measured ten-thousandths of an inch in excess of 1.000 inches. The engineering tolerance on this part is $1.000 \pm .005$. The following table of data values was collected:

Hour	Item 1	Item 2	Item 3	Item 4
1	10	20	17	31
2	22	43	− 12	40
3	16	29	36	33
4	05	44	− 24	33
5	10	− 44	33	42
6	08	33	− 44	− 23
7	25	27	50	− 12
8	33	41	22	10
9	48	− 33	31	04
10	− 25	28	12	22

Based on the information in the table above answer questions 31, 32, and 33.

31. What is the value of X bar for hour number 7?

   a. .00900 inches
   b. 22.5 inches
   c. 90 inches
   d. .00225 inches

32. What is the value for R on hour 10?

   a. .0037 inches
   b. .0053 inches
   c. 37 inches
   d. 53 inches

33. What is the value for R bar?

   a. .00551 inches
   b. 55.1 inches

c. .010 inches

d. 10 inches

34. In acceptance sampling the ideal operating characteristic curve would:

a. Reject all lots that were above the AQL.

b. Accept all lots that were above the AQL.

c. Have buyer's risk below the AQL.

d. Have seller's risk below the AQL.

35. A company uses sampling inspection to inspect parts that are sent to its customers. If a lot of parts is rejected from sampling inspection, it is inspected 100% and the rejected parts are sent back to the manufacturing department for rework or scrap. What happens to the overall outgoing quality level as the number of defective parts increases?

a. The overall outgoing quality level decreases at first and then increases.

b. The overall outgoing quality level increases at first and then decreases.

c. The overall outgoing quality level decreases.

d. The overall outgoing quality level increases.

36. ISO standards are reviewed and reissued every:

a. Ten years.

b. One year.

c. Two years.

d. Five years.

37. In the Shewhart and Deming cycle, the letters $P\ D\ C\ A$ stand for:

a. Purchase, deliver, cost, and acquisition.

b. Prevent defects caused by anyone.

c. Plan, do, check, and act.

d. Please don't cause accidents.

38. The Deming cycle is usually represented by:

a. PDCA.

b. ABCD.

c. QFAP.

d. CDPA.

39. Attribute inspection is performed on a lot of motor shafts. The lot of parts is rejected. The parts are supposed to have a diameter of 2 inches and have an engineering tolerance of ±.015. What is the average dimension of the parts?

    a. Greater than 2.015 or less than 1.985
    b. Greater than 0.000
    c. Parts should not be rejected.
    d. The inspector should be fired for not writing a better report.

HUMAN RESOURCES MANAGEMENT

1. What are the major advantages of the functional type of organization?

   a. Single point of contact for the customer
   b. Stable organizational structure
   c. Project orientation
   d. Multifunctional teams are easy to form

2. The project manager's leadership style should be matched to the corresponding developmental level of the project team and should move through successive steps in the following order:

   a. Disciplinary, autocratic, participative.
   b. Projectized, matrix, functional.
   c. Team building, team development, responsibility assignment.
   d. Directing, coaching, supporting, delegating.

3. A company has signed a contract for new work that is different from work that it has done before. The company's strategic plan calls for much of this kind of work in the future. It is important that it be able to bring the correct shared resources together to work on different parts of the contract. The type of organization that this suggests is a:

   a. Functional organization.
   b. Contractor organization.
   c. Matrix organization.
   d. Pure project organization.

4. The manager of a large corporation wants to sign a contract to build a nuclear power plant in Botswana several thousand miles away from the home office. The project will take several years to build and test. What type of organization will be best for managing this project?

   a. Functional organization
   b. Contractor organization
   c. Matrix organization
   d. Pure project organization

5. In matrix management organizations, if the organization maintains many of the characteristics of the functional organization and the project managers are considered more like project coordinators or expediters, it is called a:

   a. Strong matrix.
   b. Project team.
   c. Weak matrix.
   d. Project office.

6. A project manager is selecting team members for her project team. She collects the résumés and past performance reviews for the potential team members and discusses each with their functional manager. Which of the following is not a characteristic that the project manager should use in selecting the team members?

   a. Previous experience
   b. Personal characteristics
   c. Personal interest
   d. Salary

7. A project manager is responsible for all that goes on in the project. One of the most important duties that the project manager can perform is the function of:

   a. Risk management.
   b. Quality management.
   c. Cost management.
   d. Integration.

8. The organization that is a formalized structure directed toward the support of the project community within the organization is called:

   a. Matrix organization.
   b. Project office.
   c. Project team.
   d. Project management office.

9. On a project team one of the team members has a problem collecting on a medical insurance claim. The team member comes to the project manager and explains the problem. The problem is the responsibility of the:

   a. Project team.
   b. Project manager.
   c. Executive manager.
   d. Human Resources Department.

10. The organization that is a formalized structure where the project teams and the project managers reside is called:

    a. Matrix organization.
    b. Project office.
    c. Project team.
    d. Project management office.

11. A conflict arises about the method to solve a difficult design problem. The project manager is seeking a method of resolving the conflict. In order to achieve the most long lasting resolution to project conflicts, which of the following approaches should be used?

    a. Problem solving
    b. Compromise
    c. Withdrawal
    d. Smoothing

12. In a large organization a project expediter is being used to manage a project for an important client. The position of project expediter would be found in what kind of an organization?

    a. Strong matrix
    b. Weak matrix
    c. Functional
    d. Projectized

13. The project manager of a project is concerned with managing cost and improving morale and is also concerned about notifying other project managers when individuals from his project team will be available to work on other projects. This is best addressed in the project's:

    a. Communications plan.
    b. Work breakdown structure.
    c. Staffing plan.
    d. Project schedule.

14. The beginning and the end of the project is defined by:

    a. The project plan.
    b. The project charter.
    c. The team charter.
    d. The project life cycle.

15. Herzberg divided motivation factors into two classes: satisfiers and dissatisfiers. Examples of satisfiers are:

    a. Vacation time, assignment of a personal staff assistant.
    b. Work satisfaction, fringe benefits.
    c. Plush office space, performance-based salary raise.
    d. Sense of personal achievement, work satisfaction.

16. The skill of listening involves more than just hearing the sounds. One of the characteristics of a good listener is that he or she:

    a. Finishes the speaker's sentences.
    b. Takes good notes.
    c. Repeats some of the things said.
    d. Agrees with the speaker.

17. Primary outputs from team development are:

    a. Input to performance appraisals.
    b. High project team morale.
    c. Reduced project cost.
    d. Greater customer satisfaction.

18. An automotive oil change station was receiving complaints that service took too long. A coffee machine and television were installed in the waiting room and the complaints went down. This is an example of:

    a. Smith-Carlisle method.
    b. Creative problem solving.
    c. Analytical problem solving.
    d. Decision analysis.

19. A project manager is concerned about team building on her project. One of the mandatory things that she must have in order to have good team building is:

    a. Commitment from top level management.
    b. Co-location of team members.
    c. Establishment of clear negotiated goals.
    d. Open discussion of poor individual performance.

20. The project manager of a new project wants to get things started in a positive way with the project team. The project manager wants the team members to get to know

one another, to introduce the project team and the project manager to one another, to discuss the objectives and goals of the project, and to identify some of the potential problem areas. This meeting is called a:

a. Project team meeting.
b. Project kick-off meeting.
c. Goal setting meeting.
d. Introduction meeting.

21. A project manager is managing a project where there will be a number of persons working together. She wants to enhance the ability of the team to work together and perform as a team. One of the things that she can do to maximize the ability of the team to do this is:

a. Cohabitation.
b. Co-location.
c. Staffing plan.
d. Work breakdown structure.

22. A project manager is in need of a solution to a problem. He decides that the best thing will be to arrange a meeting to solve the problem rather than solve the problem himself or by having one of the project team members solve it individually. Generally, this will result in:

a. The group taking more time than one individual.
b. The solution to the problem being less accurate.
c. The group taking less time than an individual.
d. It depends on the specific problem.

23. A project manager will manage a large complicated project that is located in a remote part of Africa. The project will last for five years and will have the product of producing a nuclear reactor that will generate 900 megawatts of power at start-up. The best kind of organization for managing this project is:

a. Strong matrix management.
b. Weak matrix management.
c. Projectized organization.
d. Functional organization.

24. Project human resources management is divided into which of the following?

a. Organization planning, staff acquisition, and team development
b. Leadership, team building, and negotiation

    c. Recruitment, labor relations, and personnel administration
    d. Team building, communication, and labor relations

25. A project manager wants to do as much as she can to help in developing her project team. A key barrier to project team development is which of the following?

    a. Strong matrix management structure
    b. Major problems that delay the project completion date or budget targets
    c. Team members who are accountable to both functional and project managers
    d. Formal training plans that cannot be implemented

26. A large, complicated software development project is being contemplated by a large company. The project will be done as part of a company strategic plan. The project will be multifunctional and will require many of the project team members to work on multiple other projects during the life of this project. The best kind of organization to support this project is which of the following?

    a. Projectized
    b. Functional
    c. Strong matrix
    d. Weak matrix

27. According to McGregor's concept of theory X and theory Y, which of the following statements is true?

    a. Theory Y managers view their subordinates as lazy, irresponsible, and resistant to change.
    b. Theory Y managers view their subordinates as creative, imaginative, and agreeable to change.
    c. Theory X managers tend to delegate authority.
    d. McGregor did not conceive of theory X and theory Y.

28. A project manager wants to have some of the people trained on his project team. The project team is working in a balanced matrix organization. Generally, the approval for this training should come from which of the following managers?

    a. Project manager
    b. Executive manager
    c. Functional manager
    d. Human resources manager

29. Which of the following is true of management by objectives (MBO)?

    a. The supervisor establishes performance objectives.
    b. The supervisor sets the general objectives and the subordinate reviews and agrees to them.
    c. Objectives do not need to be quantifiable.
    d. The supervisor and the employee jointly establish performance objectives.

30. In the matrix management organization, which of the following is true?

    a. The project manager is responsible for employee skills improvement.
    b. The functional manager is responsible for employee skills improvement.
    c. The project manager is responsible for the employee's annual appraisal.
    d. The employee is responsible for his or her own skills improvement.

31. A project manager wants to better control the procedure for sanctioning work that is done on the project. He initiates a system for doing this. It requires written authorization to begin work on a specific activity or a work package. What is this system called?

    a. Project charter
    b. Team charter
    c. Work authorization
    d. Change management

32. The project management process groups are:

    a. Initiating, planning, expediting, and control.
    b. Plan, organize, develop, and control.
    c. Plan, do, observe, commit.
    d. Initiating, planning, executing, controlling, and closeout.

33. A functional manager needs to communicate the needs of her personnel requirements and the utilization of each person as well as the assignments that they have in the future. To best accomplish this, what type of document should be used?

    a. Gantt chart
    b. Network diagram
    c. Staffing plan
    d. Responsibility matrix

34. There is great difficulty in communicating in a matrix organization. One of the ways that the project manager can make communicating with people on his project team easier is by publishing a:

    a. Gantt chart.
    b. Project charter.
    c. Project team directory.
    d. Staffing plan.

35. The person most responsible for seeing that the proper people are assigned to the projects where they can be used most effectively in a matrix organization is the:

    a. Program manager.
    b. Project manager.
    c. General manager.
    d. Functional manager.

36. In order for a formal reward system to work it must have which of the following characteristics?

    a. The relationship between reward and performance must be explicit.
    b. The reward should be distributed to as many people as possible.
    c. The reward must be of significant monetary value.
    d. The reward must have approval of all team members.

37. One of the major reasons for the pressure to use a matrix management style of organization is:

    a. Pressure for formal communications.
    b. Pressure for shared resources.
    c. Pressure for more accountability.
    d. Pressure to reduce duplication of effort.

38. The disadvantages of using the functional form of organization are:

    a. Poor communications between different parts of the organization.
    b. Potential conflict between the authority of the project manager and the functional manager.
    c. Difficulty of customers recognizing who represents them.
    d. Allocation of resources is complex.

39. A large project is approximately 50% complete. The project manager wants to establish some sort of reward system for the project team members. The project manager hopes that the reward system will help the team morale. Which of the following characteristics for reward systems should the project manager pay the closest attention to?

a. The reward must be a significant monetary value.
b. The reward should be distributed to as many team members as possible.
c. The relationship between the reward and performance must be explicit.
d. The budget for the reward must come from outside the project funds.

40. In a matrix organization there are always people moving between projects. This makes communications difficult if not impossible since people will work on a project for a few weeks and then move to another project or work in their functional department for a time between projects. One of the best tools for assuring that people can be located when they are needed is which of the following?

a. Gantt chart
b. Staffing plan
c. Project team organization chart
d. Work breakdown structure

COMMUNICATIONS MANAGEMENT

1. Which of the following media can a communicator use to present information?

   a. Visual
   b. Audio and visual
   c. Tactile
   d. Visual, audio, and tactile

2. The three principal interests in maintaining good document control are:

   a. Timely communication, collection of performance appraisal data, and assuring proper disposal of sensitive documents.
   b. Timely communication, maintaining proper approvals, and communication cost control.
   c. Effective communication, ability to reconstruct why decisions were made, and historical value.
   d. Security, change management, and procedural documentation.

3. A project manager wants to handle communications well in his project. In order to do this he has chosen to write a communications plan. Of the items listed below, which one is not part of the communications plan?

   a. Collection and filing structure
   b. Distribution plan
   c. Method for accessing information
   d. Project organizational structure

4. Which of the following are filters that the receiver uses to filter messages?

   a. Language and knowledge
   b. Distance
   c. Culture and distance
   d. Language, distance, culture, and knowledge

5. A project manager has many different ways of communicating. Which of the following is a good communication tool for the project manager to use?

a. Sending a videotape of the project progress to the client
b. Inputting a task into the project manager's personal computer
c. Writing notes on a handheld computer
d. Putting the project budget into a spreadsheet

6. The use of brainstorming as a communications technique encourages which of the following?

a. Team building and convergent thinking
b. Divergent thinking
c. Analytical results
d. Use of the scientific method

7. Which of the following techniques allows for the participants to be anonymous?

a. Brainstorming
b. Nominal group
c. Delphi technique
d. Crawford slip

8. Which of the following is not a standard type of communication?

a. Written
b. Verbal
c. Nonverbal
d. Clairvoyant

9. During a project meeting a disagreement between two members of the project team began. The disagreement was over a technical detail of the project. The project manager was in attendance in the meeting. It is important that the conflicting opinions of the two team members be resolved as quickly as possible. It is even more important that the difference of opinion be resolved correctly. What should the project manager do?

a. The project manager should make the decision right away to save time and not let the two disagreeing parties stay in disagreement very long.
b. End the meeting and give everyone a few days to cool off.
c. Assign someone to find out more factual information about the problem.
d. The project manager should suggest a compromise between the two disagreeing team members.

10. In the communications model, communications between the sender and the receiver often are affected by communications barriers. These include all of the following except:

    a. Cultural differences.
    b. Differences in motivation.
    c. Educational differences.
    d. Lack of a communications device.

11. A project manager has one member of the project team working on a critical problem. The person working on the problem verbally communicates to the manager that this correction to the problem will probably cost $1,000. Which form of communication should the project manager use to respond to the team member?

    a. Written
    b. Oral
    c. Form letter
    d. Formal

12. Who is responsible for communications for the project team?

    a. The human resources representative
    b. The representative from the management information systems department
    c. The project manager
    d. The communications department

13. Statements such as "It's never been done before" or "It will cost a fortune" are examples of:

    a. Feedback.
    b. Communication blockers.
    c. Conflict generators.
    d. Forcing.
    e. Facilitation.

14. The project manager has a very complex communication to prepare for the program manager. In order to ensure that the communication will be understood as completely as possible, what method of communication should be used?

    a. Oral
    b. Written
    c. Nonverbal
    d. Oral, written, and nonverbal

15. There are many ways to organize projects. The persons involved with these projects have several titles that describe their management responsibilities. Which of the

following titles describes a person who has a primary responsibility for communications?

a. Project manager
b. Project manager in a strong matrix environment
c. Project manager in a weak matrix environment
d. Project expediter

16. A project manager is responsible for performance reporting. Which of the following is *not* one of the tools and techniques that the project manager can use for performance reporting?

a. Variance analysis
b. Earned value reports
c. Performance reviews
d. Past project review

17. The technologies or methods that are used to transfer information back and forth between project stakeholders can vary significantly. Which of the following is a communications technology factor for projects?

a. Expected project staffing
b. Schedule for the project
c. Work breakdown structure
d. Project scope definition

18. Formal acceptance by the client or the sponsor of the project indicates that they have accepted the products of the project. This document should be signed off during what part of the project?

a. Administrative closure
b. As the last task in the project plan
c. After the project is closed out
d. When requested by the program manager

19. In the model for communications there is a sender and a receiver. The sender is responsible for which of the following?

a. Scheduling the communications to take place
b. Confirming that the message was understood
c. Sending feedback to the receiver
d. Understanding the best channel to use

20. A project manager finds that she is having trouble concentrating on what is being said in meetings. One of the things that she might try to improve her listening ability might be:

    a. Interrupt the speaker to give her own opinion.
    b. Make telephone calls when the subject is not interesting.
    c. Show the speaker that she is interested by showing attention and support.
    d. Concentrate exclusively on the facts the speaker is using.

21. Communication barriers are a more frequent source of conflict in matrix and projectized environments than in functional organizations for all the following reasons *except*:

    a. Communication is the prime focus of an expediter type of project manager.
    b. Team members are often physically separated in a matrix or project environment.
    c. There are increased number of levels of authority in a matrix or project environment.
    d. Team members are often separated in the timing of their contributions to a matrix or project environment.

22. A project manager must be able to effectively manage the communications necessary for the project and the project team. In order to communicate within the project team the project manager should:

    a. Control all communications between project team members.
    b. Control all communications outside of the project team.
    c. Promote communications between project team members and ensure that feedback occurs.
    d. Require all project team members to write formal progress reports each week.

23. A project manager has six people on a team. It is important that each of them communicates information to each of the others. How many lines of communication are there in this group of people?

    a. Fifteen
    b. Twenty-one
    c. Seven
    d. Six

24. The project manager of a project must hold several meetings. The meetings should be efficient and not waste people's time when they are held. One of the things that the project manager can do when he or she is leading a meeting is to:

a. Get out of the way and let the team make all the decisions.
b. Make all of the decisions of importance.
c. Frequently summarize what has taken place.
d. Introduce all new ideas.

25. The study of the way words are used and the meaning that they convey is called:

a. Wordsmanship.
b. Semantics.
c. Language.
d. Communications.

26. A project manager is considering how her time is being spent in the project. One of the things that concerns her is how much time she will be spending communicating. The percent of time that is generally spent communicating by project managers is:

a. 10 percent.
b. 20 percent.
c. 50 percent.
d. 90 percent.

27. The process of collecting and disseminating information in order to provide the stakeholders with information about the project and how the projects resources are being used to reach the project objectives is called:

a. Activity reporting.
b. Performance reporting.
c. Project reports.
d. Status reports.

28. The major processes of project communications management are:

a. Communication, requirements, information distribution, performance reporting, and administrative procedures.
b. Communications planning, information distribution, performance reporting, and administrative closure.
c. Communications planning, response planning, progress reporting, and information distribution.
d. Communications planning, information distribution, schedule reporting, and stakeholder analysis.

29. The three main types of communication are:

    a. Written, oral, and graphic.
    b. Written, oral, and visual.
    c. Verbal, written, and electronic.
    d. Verbal, formal documentation, and informal documentation.

30. A project manager hears a rumor through the project team that the client for the project is supposed to visit the project team office and present the project manager with a purchase order for a large change in the project. The change will authorize a new budget for $50,000. This is an example of what type of communications?

    a. Formal
    b. Informal
    c. Verbal
    d. Nonwritten

31. A project manager uses manual filing systems, electronic text databases, and project management software to manage his project. These are examples of:

    a. Communications technology.
    b. Information retrieval systems.
    c. Project records.
    d. Information distribution systems.

RISK MANAGEMENT

1. A project manager discovers that there is a part of the project that contains some risk. His strategy with this risk is to subcontract the work to an outside supplier by using a firm fixed-price contract. Which of the following must the project manager do?

   a. The project manager should make certain that the project team does not reveal the risk to the supplier until the contract is signed.
   b. The project manager should make every effort to make sure that the supplier is made aware of the risk after the contract is signed.
   c. The project manager should make sure that the supplier understands the risk before the contract is signed.
   d. The project manager should assign a member of the project team to monitor the activity of the supplier to make sure that the supplier deals with the risk properly if it occurs.

2. A project manager is faced with making a decision about a risk that the team has identified. The risk involves the design of a bicycle. It has been found that the neck of the bicycle, where the steering bearing is located and the two supporting bars of the frame come together, will corrode in a high salt environment. If this takes place the neck may fail and injure the rider. The project team decides that the design of the bicycle should be modified by using corrosion resistant materials in the design of the neck. This will eliminate the risk from consideration. This technique is called:

   a. Risk avoidance.
   b. Risk acceptance.
   c. Risk rejection.
   d. Risk deflection.

3. A problem occurs in the design of a grocery cart. In this case it is determined that the wheels will wear out much quicker in areas of heavy snow and ice because the salt will corrode the wheel bearings. Using sealed bearing wheels will significantly increase cost, and it is determined that the carts themselves will be rusty and damaged at about the same time the wheel bearings begin to fail. By injecting the wheel bearings with a high temperature grease the life of the wheel bearings is increased

considerably. The project recommends using the high temperature grease. This is called:

a. Risk acceptance.
b. Risk avoidance.
c. Risk mitigation.
d. Risk deflection.

4. The contingency budget will:

a. Reduce the probability of scope changes.
b. Reduce the probability of cost overruns.
c. Increase the probability of a cost overrun.
d. Increase the probability of scope changes.

5. A risk has four possible outcomes. Given the following information, what is the expected value of this risk?

Probability	Result of Risk
0.4	− 10,000
0.3	− 7,500
0.2	− 5,000
0.1	+ 2,500

a. − $20,000
b. − $14,500
c. $7,000
d. − $7,000

6. The project has done its risk analysis. In the process of risk identification the project team has determined that there are risks that will probably happen that have not been identified or evaluated except by noting that other projects of this type have historically had a certain amount of risk discussed in the lessons learned of the project. This project team should set aside money to handle these risks in which financial category?

a. Risk management fund
b. Contingency budget
c. Management reserve
d. Emergency fund

7. A project manager observes that in one part of the project several activities are being completed late. All of these activities have several days of free float associated with them. These are early warnings of the risk that the project will be late in completion. They are called:

a. Risk triggers.
b. Warning messages.
c. Risk forecasts.
d. Schedule risks.

8. The effect of risk on schedule dates for the project creates an array of dates that are possible for project completion. In a typical project the most likely date for the project will have which of the following relationships with the expected value for the project completion date?

a. The most likely date will be earlier than the expected value date.
b. The most likely date will be later than the expected value date.
c. Both dates will have the same likelihood.
d. The most likely date and the expected value date will occur at the same time.

9. A project manager is reviewing the risks of her project. One of the risks she is reviewing has an impact of $25,000 and an associated probability of 10%. The risk is associated with an activity that is the predecessor to seven other activities in the schedule. All eight activities are on the critical path. The seven other activities have a budget of $75,000. What is the expected value of this risk?

a. $10,000
b. $100,000
c. $25,000
d. $2,500

10. In probability theory, what is the probability that if you roll two dice (cubes with consecutive numbers 1 to 6 on each of the six faces) you will have at least one 6?

a. 1/3
b. 11/36
c. 1/36
d. 1/6

11. A project manager is looking at the risk associated with the project schedule. Realizing that if the risks occur the project will be delivered to the stakeholders late, the project manager decides to consider the risk and promise delivery later than the most

likely project completion date. He then takes the time between the promise date and the most likely completion date and distributes it among the activities of the project schedule. This creates float in the schedule. This process is called:

a. Schedule delay.
b. Critical chain scheduling.
c. Buffering.
d. Contingency scheduling.

12. A project manager wants to give some guidelines to the project team as to how risk events should be described. Which of the following items would *not* be appropriate in describing a risk event?

a. Probability that the risk will occur
b. The cost of the risk should it occur
c. Expected timing of the risk when it is expected to occur
d. The client's outsourcing method

13. A project manager and her project team are analyzing risk in their project. One of the things that they might do to help identify potential risks or opportunities would be to review:

a. The project budget.
b. The goals and objectives of the project.
c. Lessons learned from other similar projects.
d. The monetary value of changes for similar projects.

14. A project manager holds the first risk meeting of the project team. The client is present at the meeting. At the meeting several risks are identified and assigned to members of the project team for evaluation and quantification. The result of the meeting is:

a. Expected value of the risk events.
b. Strategies for the risk events.
c. A list of potential risk events.
d. General statements about risks for the project.

15. In the Monte Carlo technique, what is the criticality index?

a. The number of days the project will be late divided by the project duration
b. The percent of time a given activity will be on the critical path
c. The percent of time an activity will be late

d. The sum of the duration of the critical path activities divided by the project expected value for duration

16. The management reserve for the project contains:

    a. Money to offset missing cost objectives.
    b. Money to offset missing schedule objectives.
    c. Money to offset missing cost or schedule objectives.
    d. Money to handle the effects of known risks in the project.

17. A project manager uses the breakeven point to justify his project. He presents this as a justification for buying a new machine. What risk does the project manager run by using this technique to justify buying a new machine for his company?

    a. Breakeven point will favor buying a cheap, low-quality machine.
    b. Breakeven point will favor buying a machine that is too expensive for the work required.
    c. The company may not have the funds to buy the machine in spite of the justification.
    d. The machine may not be available because the justification method takes a long time to calculate.

18. Goldratt's critical chain theory says that in order to reduce risk in schedules we should:

    a. Start activities in the feeder chains as early as possible.
    b. Start activities in the feeder chains as late as possible.
    c. Start activities in the critical chains as early as possible.
    d. Add buffer to the critical chains.

19. In managing the risk of the project schedule we are managing the risk that the project will not be delivered or completed on time. If we assume that the project's possible completion dates are normally distributed and we promise the client the most likely of the project's possible completion dates, what is the probability that the project will be delivered late?

    a. 5%
    b. 10%
    c. 50%
    d. 77%

20. A risk event in a project is something that can have an effect on the project:

    a. For the better only, a positive effect.
    b. For the worse, a negative effect.
    c. Both better or worse, a positive or negative effect.
    d. Neither better nor worse, neither a positive nor a negative effect.

21. The project team has put together a project plan for a project, and the plan has been approved by the stakeholders. The customer asks the project manager if the project can be delivered seven weeks sooner. The customer offers sufficient monetary incentive for the project manager. The project manager decides to fast track the project. This decision will:

    a. Increase risk.
    b. Decrease risk.
    c. Not affect risk.
    d. Risk change cannot be determined.

22. A project team evaluates risk in the project. As an outcome there are some positive and negative risks that are identified and evaluated. To evaluate the worst case for the project the project team should evaluate and summarize:

    a. All of the risks affecting the project.
    b. Only the negative risks.
    c. The negative risks minus the positive risks.
    d. The positive risks minus the negative risks.

23. The Project Management Institute decided to hold its annual meeting in New Orleans, Louisiana. This conference represents a substantial amount of PMI's operating budget for the year. PMI identified a risk of hurricanes during the month of September, when the conference was to be held. PMI decided to purchase convention insurance to offset the loss of convention revenue if a hurricane caused cancellation of the conference. This is a risk management strategy called:

    a. Avoidance.
    b. Deflection.
    c. Acceptance.
    d. Mitigation.

24. During the project life cycle, in which part of the life cycle will risk be the lowest?

    a. Initiation
    b. Planning

c. Execution

d. Closeout

25. The Monte Carlo technique can be used to:

a. Determine the amount of contingency budget needed for the project.

b. Determine the amount of the management reserve.

c. Determine the criticality index for an activity in the schedule.

d. Determine the risk index for a risk in the project.

26. Three activities are done in sequence. Each activity takes five days to do. There is a 90% probability that each activity will be completed on time and a 10% probability that each activity will be finished late. What is the probability that the last of the three activities will be finished on time?

a. .90

b. .73

c. .27

d. .81

27. The project manager has critical parts that are needed for the project. If the first order of parts is delivered late, the project will be late delivering a critical deliverable to the customer. The seller that has been selected to make these parts for the project has been used in the past and historically has failed to deliver on time 10% of the time. Another vendor can be found that has the same delivery record. The project manager decides to divide the order between the two vendors in hopes that at least one of them will deliver on time. What is the probability that at least one of the vendors will deliver on time?

a. .81

b. 1.8

c. .99

d. 1.0

28. The creative process used to optimize the life cycle costs, save time, increase profits, improve quality, expand market share, solve problems, or use resources more effectively is called:

a. Systems engineering.

b. Value engineering.

c. Project management.

d. Cost management.

29. A project manager is managing a project where a risk occurs. There is no plan to respond to this risk. The response to a negative risk event that has no plan is called:

    a. Repair order.
    b. Workaround.
    c. Risk mitigation.
    d. Risk deflection.

30. A project's schedule completion dates are distributed in an even probability distribution. The earliest that the project can be completed is June 1. The latest the project can be completed is June 29. What is the most likely date for project completion?

    a. June 1
    b. June 29
    c. June 15
    d. There is no most likely date in an even distribution.

31. When using PERT analysis on a project schedule, probabilistic or expected durations are used for activity durations. If there is a concern that the critical path may shift due to durations changing within the expected range, what technique can be used?

    a. CPM
    b. Monte Carlo
    c. Decision trees
    d. Finite element analysis

32. A project manager is dealing with risk analysis on a software development project. There is a risk that the module that creates the most important report that the system will create will not work properly and will require 200 person-hours to correct. The project manager decides to do nothing about this risk. Which of the following risk strategies is the project manager employing?

    a. Acceptance
    b. Avoidance
    c. Mitigation
    d. Deflection

33. The project manager of a large project meets several times with the client for the project. During the meeting the project manager judges that the client has a very low risk tolerance. This means that the client will probably:

    a. Be willing to take large risks to make large profits.
    b. Be unwilling to take large risks to make large profits.

    c. Understand when risks happen on the project.

    d. Not understand when risks happen on the project.

34. Monte Carlo analysis can best be described as:

    a. A deterministic scheduling method.

    b. A probabilistic scheduling simulation method.

    c. A probabilistic cost management technique.

    d. A risk identification technique.

35. A project manager decides to create a model to represent the project risks. The model translates the uncertainties specified at a detailed level into their potential impact and probabilities. This technique is called a:

    a. Risk model.

    b. Simulation.

    c. Computer risk program.

    d. Decision tree.

36. A project manager managing any project should perform risk analysis with his or her project team:

    a. Just before any major meeting with the client.

    b. On a regular basis throughout the project.

    c. Only when justified by the awareness of new risks becoming a possibility.

    d. When preparing the project plan.

37. A project manager working on a large project finds that there are several risks that have a severity that is higher than the acceptable risk tolerance. They cannot be avoided or deflected. The project manager will need to use which of the following approaches?

    a. Change the risk tolerance of the client

    b. Buy insurance for the risk

    c. Ignore the risk

    d. Mitigate the risk

38. The project manager of a project evaluates the risks of the project by assessing the probability of the risk by categorizing the risks as likely or not likely and assesses their impact as high impact, medium impact, or low impact. This would be which type of risk assessment?

a. Quantitative
b. Qualitative
c. General
d. Characteristic

39. A project manager must make a decision about a risk in his project. He examines the extent to which the uncertainty of each of the elements of the project affects the objective being examined when all other uncertain elements are held at their baseline values. This technique is called which of the following?

a. Decision tree analysis
b. Expected value analysis
c. Sensitivity analysis
d. Simulation

40. A project manager is doing risk analysis with the project team members. They are concerned about evaluating the risks in such a way that the risks will be ranked according to their severity in relation to the project. What method should be used to rank the risks in the order of importance?

a. Determine the expected value
b. Determine the cost of the impact
c. Determine the probability
d. Use subjective analysis

CONTRACTS AND PROCUREMENT

1. A project manager must make a narrative description of the project. This narrative description covers the items that will be supplied under the contract with the client. It is called:

   a. The project plan.
   b. The statement of work.
   c. The exception report.
   d. The progress report.

2. A project manager discovers that there is a part of the project that contains some risk. His or her strategy with this risk is to subcontract the work to an outside supplier by using a firm fixed-price contract. Which of the following is true?

   a. The supplier will include an allowance for the risk in the contracted price.
   b. The supplier will lose money on the contract.
   c. The project manager will have to compensate the supplier if the risk occurs.
   d. The project manager will assist the supplier with the project team if the risk occurs.

3. A project manager discovers that there is a part of the project that contains some risk. His or her strategy with this risk is to subcontract the work to an outside supplier by using a firm fixed-price contract. The project manager should:

   a. Make certain that the project team does not reveal the risk to the supplier until the contract is signed.
   b. Make every effort to make sure that the supplier is made aware of the risk after the contract is signed.
   c. Make sure that the supplier understands the risk before the contract is signed.
   d. Assign a member of the project team to monitor the activity of the supplier to make sure that the supplier deals with the risk properly if it occurs.

4. The project manager is considering contracting some of the work of the project to a service bureau. The service bureau has been used in the past by this project manager. The manager has several choices of contracts that can be used to subcontract this work. Which of the following is *not* a type of contract that the project manager might choose?

a. Firm fixed price
b. Make or buy
c. Cost plus incentive fee
d. Unit price

5. A project manager is employed by a construction company and is responsible for the furnishing of the completed building. One of the first things that the project manager for this project should do is to write a:

a. Work breakdown structure.
b. Budget baseline.
c. Project charter.
d. Project plan.

6. A contractor is working on a fixed price contract that calls for a single, lump sum payment upon satisfactory completion of the contract. About halfway through the contract, the contractor's project manager informs the contract administrator that financial problems are making it difficult for the contractor to pay employees and subcontractors. The contractor asks for a partial payment for work accomplished. Which of the following actions by the buyer is most likely to cause problems for the project?

a. Starting to make partial payments to the contractor
b. Making no payments to the contractor
c. Paying for work accomplished to date
d. Negotiating a change to the contract

7. Under a blanket order arrangement, which of the following is correct?

a. The cost of carrying the inventory is borne by the buyer.
b. The seller delivers all of the material ordered at one time.
c. Payments for all of the material are made at one time.
d. At the end of the blanket order, prices are adjusted for the actual amount of material delivered.

8. Forward buying will:

a. Decrease storage costs.
b. Decrease capital investment.
c. Decrease transportation costs.
d. Decrease inventory.

9. Which of the following would not be a part of the procurement management process?

   a. Purchasing
   b. Contract negotiations
   c. Inspection
   d. Marketing

10. The equivalent of cost-reimbursable contracts is frequently termed:

    a. Back-charge contracts.
    b. Fixed-price contracts.
    c. Progress payment contracts.
    d. Cost-plus contracts.

11. The project team has delivered a deliverable to the customer. The deliverable contains defects that are easily correctable. There is a good relationship with the customer and the customer agrees to make the repairs and correct the defects on the item and invoice the supplier for the work that was done. This is considered to be a:

    a. Bid cost reduction.
    b. Payment authorization.
    c. Back charge.
    d. Release payment.

12. A project manager decides to go out for bids on some of the project work that must be done as part of a contract to do a project for another customer. The bids are received and evaluated, and the seller with the lowest bid is selected. The cost of the contract to the project can further be reduced by what action?

    a. Illegal methods
    b. Procurement leverage
    c. Selecting another seller
    d. Contract negotiation

13. A buyer extends a formal invitation that contains a scope of work that seeks a response that will describe the methodology and results that will be provided to the buyer. This is called:

    a. Invitation to bid.
    b. Request for information.
    c. Request for proposal.
    d. Request for bid.

14. A project manager wants to subcontract part of the project. This part of the project is quite complicated, and there are many ways that the work can be done. What method of solicitation should be used by the project team?

    a. Request for bid
    b. Request for quotation
    c. Request for proposal
    d. Request for information

15. The project team is considering whether to purchase a service or do it themselves. One of the items that should not be considered in their analysis is:

    a. The seller's price.
    b. The cost and availability of floor space at the team's facility.
    c. The seller's technical staff.
    d. A competitor's method of outsourcing.

16. A request for bid (RFB) differs from a request for proposal (RFP) in that:

    a. The request for proposal is used when source selection will be price driven.
    b. There is no difference.
    c. The request for bid is used when source selection will be price driven.
    d. The request for proposal disregards price considerations.
    e. The request for bid is concerned with price exclusively.

17. A project has subcontracted part of the work of the project to an outside vendor. The work involves writing modules of software for the project. The first delivery of the subcontracted software has been made, and it is found that the software will not perform the functions that were specified in the contract. The vendor says that the software cannot do what was specified in the contract and refuses to do the work. What should the project team do?

    a. Cancel the contract and find another vendor.
    b. Hold additional meetings with the vendor to determine the problem and the solution to the problem.
    c. Seek legal advice form the company's attorney.
    d. Offer the vendor an additional incentive to finish the contract.

18. A project manager is about to request bids on a large part of the work that must be done on the project. This work amounts to over $1 million. The best reason that the bid should be advertised is:

a. It is a legal requirement to do so.
b. Advertising will notify more companies that you are interested in contracting the work.
c. It will avoid criticism from other potential vendors.
d. It avoids having pressure from the public.

19. A project manager must have some work done by an outside contractor. This work has a great deal of risk associated with it, and it has become very difficult to find a contractor willing to take on the job. Which of the following types of contract would offer the greatest incentive to the contractor?

a. Cost plus percentage of cost as an award fee
b. Cost plus fixed fee
c. Cost plus incentive fee
d. Firm fixed price

20. A project manager purchases 3,500 widgets for his project. The widgets are delivered on time, but there are many defects in the paint that is on the surface of the widgets. The project manager returns the parts to the vendor for repair and rework. The vendor complains that the paint job quality was not specified in the contract and it is not his responsibility to repair the parts. It is likely that the parts will be repaired by the vendor because of:

a. Expressed warranty.
b. Implied warranty.
c. Past business practices.
d. Threat of legal action by the project team.

21. A project is coming to a close, and the project manager is listing the things that must be done to close out the project. One of the things that must be done by the person responsible for contract administration is:

a. Issue letters of recommendation for the project team.
b. Issue a formal written notice of project completion to the contractors.
c. Put a legal notice in the newspapers indicating that all invoices must be submitted.
d. Request final inspection reports for all vendor-supplied materials.

22. A project is engaged in making electronic devices. It is necessary for the company to purchase materials to make the printed circuit boards. All of the parts are common parts that are available from several vendors. The most likely contract that should be issued for these parts is:

    a. Unit price contract.
    b. Firm fixed-price contract.
    c. Cost-reimbursable contract.
    d. Award fee contract.

23. A project is being managed by a project manager. A large portion of the work of the project is being subcontracted to an outside vendor. During the project it is found that a significant change in the design of the project is necessary. The project manager should:

    a. Issue a change notice to the contractor immediately.
    b. Issue a purchase order to investigate the change.
    c. Notify the contractor of the design change possibility.
    d. Rebid the contract.

24. An automotive design project is under way. The project is to design the new body style for the upcoming season. Body styles are considered to be one of the more important items for competing in the next season. The completion date for the project is moved up to three months earlier than planned. Because of this change in the project completion date, there is the possibility of having some of the work done by a design bureau in town. The project manager must make a decision as to whether or not to subcontract this work out to the design bureau. What is the most important consideration in making this decision?

    a. Cost of work to the design bureau
    b. Security of the design bureau
    c. Communications between the project team and the design bureau
    d. Ability of the design bureau to deliver on time

25. At the request of the project team for a large project, the company's purchasing department advertises that they intend to let a contract for construction work associated with the project. This is called:

    a. Procurement planning.
    b. Solicitation.
    c. Advertising.
    d. The procurement process.

26. An agreement between competent parties, for valid consideration, to accomplish some lawful purpose with terms clearly set forth is called a:

    a. Procurement.
    b. Solicitation.
    c. Contract.
    d. Letter of intent.

27. A project manager is managing a project to design a software system for a client. She decides to subcontract the work to a programming subcontractor. The subcontractor fails to deliver the work on time, and the project manager invokes a penalty clause that was written into the contract. It is found that the person signing the contract was under twenty-one years of age (the legal age where the contract was signed). What can be done?

    a. The company can invoke the penalty clause, and it must be honored.
    b. The work must be completed by the subcontractor, and the penalty clauses must be deducted from the amount paid to the subcontractor.
    c. The company should renegotiate the contract.
    d. The contract is void for lack of competent parties, and no additional work should be done.

28. A company wants to buy steel machine screws for a project it is working on. The screws are an example of what type of purchase?

    a. On the shelf
    b. Commodity purchase
    c. Normal procurement
    d. Blanket order

29. The procurement manager of a company decides to solicit bids on a contract. On the basis of the bid the company must clearly specify exactly what it intends to purchase. The selection of the vendor will be on the basis of:

    a. Price and features of the proposal.
    b. Price alone.
    c. Overall desirability of the products offered.
    d. Comprehensive evaluation of the vendor and the proposal.

30. A trucking company expects to purchase 525 truck tires over the next year for its fleet. The company places a blanket order for the tires to a local tire vendor. At the end of a year the company has purchased only 500 of the tires. What should be done to close the contract?

a. The trucking company should pay for the 25 tires and the tire vendor should deliver them.
b. The total price of the blanket order should be adjusted.
c. The contract should be closed because the year is up and no adjustments are necessary.
d. A new blanket order should be negotiated.

PROFESSIONAL RESPONSIBILITY

1. You are a project manager working on a project to market a new product. The deliverables of the project have been established, and the project work has begun. A contract to deliver the deliverables has been signed. The customer who has signed the contract has telephoned you to request additional work to be done on the project. This work will affect the budget but not the schedule of the project. This project has a high priority with your company. What should you do next?

   a. Do what the customer asks you to do and add the additional requirements to the original contract.
   b. Refuse the request and send a memo to your management explaining the situation.
   c. Respond to the customer's request by explaining the change procedure and asking that he or she submit a request for change.
   d. Arrange to meet with the project team to discuss this change.

2. You are the project manager for a high visibility project. The margin on this project is low, and it is extremely important that the cost estimates for the work on the project be accurate. While reviewing the cost estimates for this project you notice that one of the cost estimates for an element in the WBS is 10% higher than two previous projects for very similar work. What should you do?

   a. Accept the estimate because you trust all of the people on your project team, and they are responsible for estimates.
   b. Reduce the estimate and add the additional budget to the management reserve.
   c. Ask the person responsible for the estimate to explain the difference and bring supporting information to you.
   d. Reduce the estimate and add the additional budget to the contingency reserve.

3. You are managing a project in a foreign country. In this country there is a normal practice for businesspeople to exchange gifts when very large contracts, such as the one you are working on, are signed. The gift is of a greater value than your company's policy for gift exchange will allow. You have given a gift of similar value to the customer's representative already. What should you do?

   a. Take the gift.
   b. Contact your company's management and seek assistance.

c. Refuse the gift graciously, explaining your company's policy.

d. Ask the customer's representative to give the gift to your manager.

4. You are the manager of a research group that is developing a new chemical material. You hire a person from a competing company who has a great deal of expertise in this area. The person contributes greatly to the progress of your project. During conversations with the person you determine that many of this person's ideas were developed by the competing company. What do you do?

a. Tell the person that he or she should not mention that the ideas came from another company.

b. Sign a nondisclosure agreement with this person before he or she leaves your company.

c. Accept the new ideas.

d. Investigate the employee for security reasons.

5. You are managing a project that is in process. A large and unexpected problem occurs that will cause a delay in the schedule in excess of the contingency schedule for the project. What should you do?

a. Look at other tasks in the schedule and see which ones should be reduced to allow time for this problem to be worked.

b. Reduce testing on the completed tasks.

c. Require mandatory overtime for the project team.

d. Speak to the stakeholders about getting additional time and budget for the project.

6. You are the project manager for a large project. Some members of the project team have come to you and asked that they be permitted to work on a flexible schedule. Some of the other team members feel that it is important that all team members be on site at all times unless they are absent for business reasons. What should you do?

a. Turn down the request for flexible time schedules.

b. Accept the request for flexible time schedules.

c. Arrange a meeting of the project team members and allow them to decide.

d. Discuss this problem with your manager and act on the results of the meeting.

7. You are the project manager for a project that has high visibility. Your manager wants you to prepare a presentation for him to present at a conference. Most of the material in the presentation will be facts that are the results of your project. Your manager intends to present the material under his own name. Your name will not appear. What should you do?

    a. Refuse to work on the presentation unless you are listed as a coauthor.
    b. Do the work as you were told by your manager.
    c. Present your own presentation.
    d. Meet with your manager's manager and discuss the problem.

8. You are managing a project and the customer's engineers visit your facility on an inspection and general getting acquainted tour. During the tour they make the comment that the parts that are being designed should be in stainless steel instead of plain steel with enamel. What should you do?

    a. Authorize the change in design to your engineers.
    b. Continue with the present design.
    c. Speak to the visiting engineers and discuss having an informal meeting between your engineers and the visiting engineers.
    d. Ask the visiting engineers to submit a change proposal to the change system.

9. Which of the following is an example of a conflict of interest?

    a. You are the fourth cousin of a vendor supplying parts to a project in your company.
    b. You are the owner of a company that is supplying parts to a project that you are managing.
    c. You receive a gift from a supplier of parts for your project.
    d. A supplier tells you sensitive information, in confidence, that allows you to select another supplier for your project.

10. You are the project manager for a large project that is completed on time and on budget. The customer and all of the stakeholders are pleased with the results. As a direct result of the successful completion of the project, your manager approves a bonus of $25,000 to you. There are fifteen members of the project team. One of the people on the project team has been a very low contributor to the project; the other fourteen have all been above standard. What should you do with the money?

    a. Keep the money yourself; you deserve it, and the manager gave it to you.
    b. Divide the money equally among all the team members.
    c. Ask the team members how they would divide the money.
    d. Divide the money equally among the team members except for the substandard team member.

11. One of the members of your project team comes to you and says that he heard that one of the suppliers to the project had given a substantial gift to one of the project

team members in hopes that the team member would favor his company with a purchase order. The company was favored with a purchase order for the parts. What should you do?

a. Talk to the person and get him or her to give back the gift.
b. Investigate the matter completely.
c. Cancel the purchase order with the supplier.
d. Meet with your manager and discuss the problem.

PRACTICE QUESTIONS
ANSWER KEY

SCOPE MANAGEMENT

1. Answer: b

   Scope definition is defined by PMI as "decomposing the major deliverables into smaller, more manageable components to provide better control."

2. Answer: a

   The chart of accounts is the system used to monitor project costs as defined by PMI.

3. Answer: c

   A stakeholder is an individual or organization that is involved in or may be affected by project activities.

4. Answer: c

   The actual payback period is between two years and three years. It is the point where the net or cumulative cash flows equal zero. This occurs between year 2 and 3 and is 2 and 29/30 of a year from the first cash flow. Cumulative cash flow in years are: 1, −500,000; 2, −290,000; 3, +10,000.

5. Answer: b

   The net cash flow is the total of all the cash flows in and out of the company caused by the project. In this example 850,000 in and 900,000 out for a negative 50,000.

6. Answer: b

   Calculating the net present value of the cash flows for the project involves adjusting the future cash flows to allow for diminishing value due to the time that we must wait to get them. Money received today is more valuable to us than money that is received in the future.

7. Answer: c

   From the *Guide to the PMBOK* 2000: "Program. A group of related projects managed in a coordinated way. Programs usually include an element of ongoing activity."

8. Answer: d

   Most of the project money will be spent during the execution phase. At the beginning of execution the rate of expenditures rises as people and materials are brought into the project.

Later the expenditures peak and slow down. By the end of the execution phase expenditures are approaching a minimum.

9. Answer: b

From the *Guide to the PMBOK* 2000: "Project. A temporary endeavor undertaken to create a new product or service."

10. Answer: c

A statement of work is the description of what the project is about and what will be delivered. The project plan is complete and contains the detailed work that the project will do, complete with task descriptions and schedule, cost, and scope baselines containing a real schedule and budget. An exception report describes items that are not as planned and a Pareto analysis is a quality management tool used to prioritize defects according to those most frequently occurring.

11. Answer: a

Verifying scope is the process of verifying that the project made or delivered is what was asked for.

12. Answer: d

In management by objectives, the employee and supervisor meet to discuss the objectives of the employee over the next review period. At the end of the review period the performance of the employee is reviewed relative to the objectives, and adjustments are made. This is generally considered a good approach for project managers to use when managing the project team. In many cases the review period is as little as two weeks.

13. Answer: c

Configuration management is the process of making sure that the product meets the design criteria in terms of form, fit, and function.

14. Answer: c

The project charter is one of the first things that must be done in any project. The project charter according to the *Guide to the PMBOK* 2000 is: "A document issued by senior management that provides the project manager with the authority to apply organizational resources to project activities."

15. Answer: c

In the work breakdown structure the lowest level of breakdown is the work package. This does not mean that work cannot be divided any further. Work packages are usually broken down into tasks, and tasks can be further broken down into activities. The point here is that the project manager is concerned about things down to the work package level. In a relatively large project the project manager would have subproject managers or work package managers who would further breakdown the work in their own work breakdown structures.

16. Answer: c

The current project baseline for scope includes the original scope of the project plus or minus any scope changes that have taken place since the baseline for scope was established.

17. Answer: c

A project charter is a document that formally recognizes the existence of a project. It should include, either directly or by reference to other documents, the business need that the project was undertaken to address and the product description.

18. Answer: b

The work breakdown structure represents all the work that must be done in order to complete the project. Doing all the work will deliver all the tangible results to the client. In most projects there will also be deliverables that will be delivered to other stakeholders. Work that is done by contractors and those not on the project team is included in the WBS. The lowest level of the WBS is the work package (according to PMI). Work packages can be broken down into tasks, and tasks can be broken down into activities.

19. Answer: d

A program manager is a manager who manages a group of related projects in a coordinated way.

20. Answer: b

A work breakdown structure is a deliverable-oriented grouping of project elements that organizes and defines the total scope of the project: Work not in the WBS is outside the scope of the project. Although the WBS can and is used for many other project-related things, the best answer is b, since it is the most comprehensive answer.

21. Answer: c

The execution phase of projects will nearly always cost the bulk of the project budget. This is because there are more people working on the project, and they are spending more money than at other times.

22. Answer: a

Progress reports should be used even on the smallest of projects. They allow all of the stakeholders to judge the performance and progress of the project according to the project plan.

It is not necessary to use the earned value reporting system. The overhead of using a formal reporting system may not be justified on very small projects. Reporting may frequently be delegated to someone on the project team or even a member of the project management support office.

23. Answer: b

This is the definition of a project.

24. Answer: c

The project charter is the first document to be created in the project. It gives the project manager the authority to manage the project. It will frequently contain a business case and a set of goals and objectives for the project as well.

25. Answer: c

Balance is the strength or weakness of the project manager to have authority over the people who actually do the work in the project. In the projectized organization the project manager has complete authority over the people on the project team. In the strong matrix organization the project manager has more influence over the people on the project team than the functional manager. In the weak matrix organization the functional manager has more authority to direct the project team members than the project manager. In a balanced matrix organization the project manager and the functional manager are at about the same authority level.

26. Answer: c

In order for the project to have a 5% probability of being late, there is a 95% probability that the project will be delivered on time or earlier. In terms of the PERT calculation this means that 2 standard deviations should be added to the expected value date of May 30. Since there is a one month difference between the 95% promise date of June 30 and the expected value of May 30, the standard deviation must be one-half month. This is a better answer than fifteen days because on the basis of a five-day workweek this is close to three weeks.

27. Answer: c

The request for and agreement to a specific date for completion of a particular milestone in the project is called a constraint. Constraints for project tasks and activities that do not put them on the critical path are not necessarily a problem as long as delays in the schedule do not ultimately place them on the critical path. Some process constraints may be predefined as constraints. For example, management may specify a target completion date rather than allowing it to be determined by the planning process. Constraints are factors that will limit the project management team's options. For example, a predefined budget is a constraint that is highly likely to limit the team's options regarding scope, staffing, and schedule.

28. Answer: d

The current budget of the project contains all of the authorized funding for the project including additions to the project since the setting of the original baselines. This includes any and all authorized work done on the project, including the investigation of work that may be done to investigate the feasibility of changes.

29. Answer: d

The project manager will normally break the WBS down to the work package level. Work packages can be broken down further into tasks and activities.

30. Answer: b

It is generally accepted that for most projects, once a project's definitive estimate has been completed, the actual project cost will be not more than 5% below the definitive estimate and not more than 10% above it.

31. Answer: a

The change management plan is generally a document or procedure that is normally found in the scope management plan.

32. Answer: a

The client should pay, because the signing of the WBS constituted an agreement between the company managing the project and the client. Work that is not specified in the WBS is not part of the project scope. In reality this is sometimes not the case. Companies will frequently do work that is outside of the project scope as defined by the WBS in order to ensure the goodwill of the client.

33. Answer: b

The calculation for net present value is based on the compound interest formula.

$$FV = PV (1 + r)^n$$

Where FV is future value and PV is present value.
      Solving this for the present value gives:

$$PV = FV / (1 + r)^n$$
$$NPV = -50,000 + (100,000 / 1.1) = 40,909$$

Note that all the negative cash flows occur at the beginning of the year when the machine is purchased and that the positive cash flows all occur at the end of one year.

34. Answer: b

The precedence network diagramming tool is used because it best shows the logical relationships between the activities in the schedule. The Gantt chart shows the project schedule graphically indicating the start and finish for each activity. The milestone chart shows the start or completion for specific groups of activities on a summarized chart.

TIME MANAGEMENT

Answers to the following questions can be found in Chapter 2, "Time Management," unless otherwise noted.

1. Answer: b

   Note that activities in a calendar schedule start on the beginning of the time period that they start on and end at the end of the time period that they finish on. A two-day activity starts on May 5 and ends on May 6, ES and EF.

2. Answer: b

   The free float or slack is the amount of time that an activity can be delayed before it affects the schedule of any other activity. Activity F has free float but activity D does not. Both have seven days of float, total float, or plain old float. When calculating schedules and float with leads and lags, it is best to look at the next activity with no lead or lag and, after determining the dates, change them by the amount of the lead or lag.

3. Answer: d

   The free float or slack is the amount of time that an activity can be delayed before it affects the schedule of any other activity. Activity F has free float but activity D does not. Both have seven days of float, total float, or plain old float.

4. Answer: a

   Critical path is the list of activities that have zero total float. It is dangerous to find the path that has the longest sum of the durations. Path A B D F H has a duration of eight days but has a sum of the durations of ten days.

5. Answer: c

   The late start for activity F is May 12. It has a late start that is calculated to be two days before the late finish of activity D. With leads and lags it is best to calculate the LS of the dependent activity, then the LF of the independent activity, and then adjust the LF of the independent activity to consider the FS lead.

6. Answer: b

   The first work of the project is done on May 1, and the last work of the project is finished on May 20.

7.   Answer: c

There is a lead of two days associated with the finish-start relationship between activities D and F. If the relationship were a normal FS relationship, the ES of activity F would be May 7. A two-day lead means it will start two days earlier, or May 5.

8.   Answer: b

Since activity F has seven days of float it can be delayed for as much as seven days before it has any effect on the project completion.

9.   Answer: a

The early finish date of activity A is the same as its start date and the start of the project. Activities start on the beginning of the time period that work begins and end on the end of the time period that work finishes. This activity takes one day beginning in the morning of May 1 and finishing in the afternoon of May 1.

10.   Answer: c

The figure is called a precedence diagram. It is recognizable because boxes are used to indicate the activities. The arrows in a precedence diagram indicate the logical relationship between the activities. The information about the activity is inside or around the box. An activity on arrow diagram will use circles to indicate events and the activity information will be put on the arrows. The Gantt chart has no logic shown normally (now available on some project management software). The length of the Gantt bar is proportional to a time scale showing the duration of the activity. Although this diagram is also a network diagram, there are many other network diagrams in the world. Precedence diagram is a much better answer.

11.   Answer: a

The finish-finish relationship in a precedence diagram says that the independent activity must finish before the dependent activity is permitted to finish. In the schedule, if the turkey took five hours to roast and the sweet potatoes took one hour, the turkey would be scheduled to start at 1:00 P.M. and the sweet potatoes would be scheduled to start at 5:00 P.M. Both would finish at 6:00 P.M.

The following table refers to questions 12 through 15.

	o	p	ml	EV	SD	CP EV	CP SD	CP VAR
A	1	1	1	1	0	1	0	0
B	2	3	3	2.833333	0.166667			
C	10	13	12	11.83333	0.5	11.83333	0.5	0.25
D	5	5	5	5	0			
E	3	6	4	4.166667	0.5	4.166667	0.5	0.25
F	1	1	1	1	0			
G	5	8	6	6.166667	0.5			
H	9	13	10	10.33333	0.666667	10.33333	0.666667	0.444444
I	5	5	5	5	0	5	0	0

		Total	32.33333	Total	0.944444
Total	47.33333			Sqrt of Total	0.971825
		Prob 66% sd 1		33.30516	31.36151
		Prob 95% sd 2		34.27698	30.38968
		Prob 99% sd 3		35.24881	29.41786

12. Answer: c

The expected value of the project is the expected value of each of the tasks that are on the critical path, A C E H I. The approximate expected value is the sum of each of these task's optimistic, pessimistic, and four times the most likely estimate divided by 6. When calculating the length of time that the project takes, it is important that you remember to include only the critical path activities. Other activities in the schedule are done in parallel with the critical path activities.

13. Answer: b

The 95% probability of the estimate is the expected value ± 2 standard deviations of the total standard deviation of the critical path items. To total the standard deviation, first square the value for each critical path item's standard deviation, add them up, and take the square root of the total.

14. Answer: b

The expected value for activity B is the sum of the optimistic, pessimistic, and four times the most likely value, all divided by 6.

15. Answer: c

The standard deviation for activity B is the difference between the optimistic estimate and the pessimistic estimate divided by 6.

16. Answer: d

Fast tracking a schedule is finding activities that can be done in parallel that were originally scheduled to be done in sequence.

17. Answer: a

Crashing a schedule is improving the project completion date by any means that is economical and feasible. In crashing a schedule an effort is made to find the largest schedule reduction for the least additional cost.

18. Answer: d

The baseline schedule as well as the baseline budget and the baseline scope are the original project plans plus or minus any approved changes. There are many other terms used to describe schedules, but the definition given is the definition of the baseline schedule and therefore the best answer.

19. Answer: b

Bar charts, also called Gantt charts, show activity start and end dates as well as expected durations, but do not usually show dependencies. They are relatively easy to read and are frequently used in management presentations. In a Gantt chart there is a horizontal time scale. Activities are represented as bars above the time scale in such a way that the length of the bar is proportional to the elapsed time of the activity. The start of the activity is on the left side of the bar and is above the date that it starts. The right-hand side of the bar is located over the finish of the activity.

20. Answer: c

The critical path activities are those activities that have zero float. There are exceptions. When activities are forced to be done on specific dates (date constraints), it is possible to create negative float. When the project is resource constrained the critical path may change due to resource constraints.

21. Answer: c

Resource leveling is a tool in most project management software and can also be done manually. In resource leveling an attempt is made to reduce overutilization of resources to their normal utilization.

22. Answer: b

At the end of two weeks this task is 75% complete. The PV was to be 4 person-weeks, two people working full time for two weeks. The EV is therefore 3 person-weeks, .75 × 4. The AC is 2 person-weeks. The cost performance index is the EV / AC. CPI = 3 person-weeks / 2 person-weeks = 1.5.

23. Answer: b

Although total float is assigned to each of the tasks in the sequence, the total float can be used by any of them and it can be used only one time by any of them. If the tasks are A B C D E and each has one day of float, if A is delayed by one day, the total float at B C D E reduces to zero.

24. Answer: c

Monte Carlo analysis is a simulation technique that assigns durations to tasks in a schedule and then calculates the schedule information. It repeats this assignment and calculation many times and then reports statistical results, including the percent of time a task is on the critical path.

25. Answer: a

Precedence diagramming method (PDM). This is a method of constructing a project network diagram using nodes to represent the activities and connecting them with arrows that show the dependencies. This technique is also called activity-on-node (AON) and is the method used by nearly all project management software packages.

Arrow diagramming method (ADM). This is a method of constructing a project network diagram using arrows to represent the activities and connecting them at nodes to show the dependencies. This technique is also called activity-on-arrow (AOA) and, although less prevalent than PDM, is still the technique of choice in some application areas.

26. Answer: d

The project schedule includes at least planned start and expected finish dates for each detail activity. A schedule update is any modification to the schedule information that is used to manage the project. Float is the amount of time that an activity may be delayed from its start without delaying the project finish date. Although the project's budget is the time phased expenditure of the project funds, it is not the project schedule and therefore the best answer.

27. Answer: d

Mandatory dependencies are those which are inherent in the nature of the work being done. Discretionary dependencies are those which are defined by the project management team. They should be used with care (and fully documented) since they may limit later scheduling options.

Resource requirements. The resources assigned to them will significantly influence the duration of most activities and the project itself.

Resource capabilities. The duration of most activities will be significantly influenced by the capabilities of the humans and material resources assigned to them.

28. Answer: a

Critical path method (CPM) calculates a single, deterministic early and late start and finish date for each activity based on specified, sequential network logic and a single duration estimate. Program evaluation and review technique (PERT) uses sequential network logic and a weighted average duration estimate to calculate project duration. Although there are surface differences, PERT differs from CPM primarily in that it uses the distribution's mean (expected value) instead of the most likely estimate originally used in CPM and associates the standard deviation of the estimate to allow the range of values and a probability of occurrence to be calculated for the project.

29. Answer: b

The activity that has eighteen days of free float can be rescheduled without having to reschedule any other activity in the project. If this activity is rescheduled to start two weeks later, the resource will not be overutilized, and the project will remain on schedule.

30. Answer: a

The person who is working on the task that has free float of five days can be used on the task that is in trouble for five days without affecting the other task schedules in the project. The person working on the task that has total float of eight days can be used on the task that is in trouble, but since there is zero free float for this task, there will have to be a rescheduling of other tasks to allow this.

31. Answer: c

The logical analysis of the schedule often produces a preliminary schedule that requires more resources during certain time periods than are available, or requires changes in resource levels that are not manageable. Heuristics such as "allocate scarce resources to critical path activities first" can be applied to develop a schedule that reflects such constraints. Resource leveling, because of the limited availability of the resources, often results in a project duration that is longer than the preliminary schedule.

32. Answer: b

The *Guide to the PMBOK* defines the lowest level of the work breakdown structure as the work package. It goes on to say that the work package is a unit of work that can be assigned to a person or organization. It also says that the work package can be broken down into tasks, and that tasks can be broken down into activities.

33. Answer: c

When a risk is identified, budget and schedule time are identified and put into the contingency reserve. If the risk actually occurs the money is used from the contingency reserve and added to the operating budget of the project. The total project budget contains the operating project budget or baseline, contingency reserve, and the management reserve. The project budget baseline is increased by the amount of the risk although the total project budget stays the same. The schedule baseline is changed to reflect the new activities that have to be done.

34. Answer: d

The *Guide to the PMBOK* gives the following as inputs to the activity definition:
• Work breakdown structure
• Scope statement
• Historical information
• Constraints
• Assumptions

35. Answer: c

Fast tracking a project means that project tasks and activities are rescheduled from being done in sequence to being done in parallel. Crashing a project means doing anything practical that can be done to reduce the schedule. Fast tracking involves only doing things in parallel that would have otherwise been done in sequence.

36. Answer: b

The CPM or critical path method is used to determine the activities that have zero float or close to zero float. These activities should be managed more carefully than other activities in the schedule since other activities not on the critical path will have free float and total float that allows their schedules to be more flexible.

37. Answer: c

PERT stands for program evaluation and review technique. In PERT each of the activities has the optimistic, pessimistic, and most likely duration estimated. A weighted average is then taken to estimate the expected value of the activity. The weighted average is calculated by adding the optimistic, pessimistic, and four times the most likely duration and dividing by 6. The standard deviation of the activity can also be calculated by subtracting the optimistic duration from the pessimistic duration and dividing by 6.

38. Answer: d

In the PERT calculation the standard deviation is calculated by squaring the standard deviation for each of the activities on the critical path of the project, adding them together, and then taking the square root. This is the standard deviation of the project. Plus or minus two standard deviations from the expected value of the project duration will have a range of values such that the project has a 95% probability of actually finishing within the dates calculated.

39. Answer: a

PERT is a probabilistic method used to determine the estimated project completion based on the statistical estimating of the project durations. CPM is a deterministic method using specific values for activity and task durations.

40. Answer: c

The *Guide to the PMBOK* defines the lowest level of the work breakdown structure as the work package. It goes on to say that the work package is a unit of work that can be assigned to a person or organization. The work package can be broken down into tasks, and tasks can be broken down into activities.

COST MANAGEMENT

1. Answer: c

   Both the cost and accuracy of parametric models vary widely. They are most likely to be reliable when the historical information used to develop the model was accurate, the parameters used in the model are readily quantifiable, and the model is scalable (i.e., it works as well for a very large project as for a very small one).

2. Answer: b

   An analogous estimate is one that is arrived at by taking a project or part of a project that is already completed and adjusting the cost on the basis of size.

3. Answer: c

   A bottom-up estimate is a detailed estimate taking into consideration a number of small estimates and summarizing them to a total for the project or subproject being estimated. A top-down estimate is usually a less accurate method that estimates the cost of the entire project by means of parametric, analogous, or some other estimating method.

4. Answer: c

   The management reserve is money that is set aside for dealing with unknown risks. These unknown risks cannot be specifically identified. The risks mentioned in the question are identified and therefore no money should be put into the management reserve for them.

5. Answer: a

   The contingency reserve is money that is set aside for dealing with known risks. These known risks can be specifically identified. The risks mentioned in the question are identified and therefore money should be put into the contingency reserve for them. It would not make sense to budget for the impact of every risk, since all risks have a probability associated with them that means that there is some chance that the impact will not occur; therefore, the expected value should be used.

6. Answer: b

   The cost baseline is the time-phased budget for the project. It is usually shown as the PV curve on the earned value report and is usually shown as a cumulative value of the project budget over time. It will usually have a characteristic "S" shape to it. The contingency reserve and the management reserve are added to the project budget and baseline when and if they are needed to resolve risks that have actually taken place.

7. Answer: c

Life cycle costs are those associated with the project during the entire life of the project. These costs affect the way we think of the project since a poorly done project may finish below its intended budget but result in long-term warranty and repair costs that are greater than the money saved.

8. Answer: c

The project budget should be increased by $10,000 because the only work actually approved at this time is the change notice for the work to be done. If the work done must be undone at a later time and additional work is required to do it, another change notice must be approved and funding added to the project budget.

9. Answer: c

Anything that is done to help bring the project closer to its project plan is called corrective action. Updating the budget and revising the cost estimate are possible corrective actions. Contingency planning is not used to adjust project performance; it is used to budget money for known risks that may occur.

10. Answer: b

The only reason for changing the project's budget is a change in the project budget baseline. This can be brought about by the customer authorizing an addition to the scope of the project.

11. Answer: d

The project is completed when all of the work is done. The EV represents the work that is completed. The BAC represents the total of the work that is planned to be done. When the EV equals the BAC, all of the work must be done.

12. Answer: a

The project's spending plan is the plan for the flow of money to pay for the project.

13. Answer: c

The sum of the years' digits calculation for depreciation is done by summing the digits of each of the years of the useful life, $1+2+3+4+5+6+7+8+9+10 = 55$. The digits are reversed and divided by the total to get the percent of the value to be taken that year. In the third year it would be $8/55=.145$. The value is the equipment minus the scrap value, or $450,000. So we have $.145 \times \$450,000 = \$65,250$.

14. Answer: a

The calculation for the present value is done by consecutively taking the appropriate factor from the table and multiplying it by the money flowing for the year. In this example $1,300 × .893 + $1,300 × .797 + $1,300 × .712, since there is a $1,300 payment each year.

15. Answer: a

Life cycle costing is a way of including the cost of the project even after delivery to the customer. Many projects have warranty repairs, support, and other costs that add to the cost of the project.

16. Answer: b

The cost performance index is calculated by dividing the EV by AC. CPI = .7 /.9 = .777.

17. Answer: a

The schedule performance index is obtained by dividing the earned value by the planned value. SPI = EV / PV; SPI = 6,000 / 5,000 = 1.200.

18. Answer: d

The BAC or the budget at completion is the sum of the expenditures that are currently planned for the project. It is the sum of the EV for each task in the project and will not change from week to week unless the budget for any task is changed.

19. Answer: b

When it is found that work that had been previously credited with its earned value and then later it is found that the value of the completed work was not completely delivered, the earned value should be reversed from the total earned value. In this case, since the amount of undelivered work was identified, only that amount was reversed. If the value missing was not identified but the work was shown to be incomplete, the entire earned value of the work would be reversed. When the work is finally completed, the earned value is credited to the earned value column again.

20. Answer: b

The cost variance is the earned value minus the actual cost. CV = EV − AC; CV = 7,000 − 9,000 = −2,000.

21. Answer: c

The schedule variance is the earned value minus the planned value. SV = EV − PV; SV = 2,500 − 3,000 = −500.

22. Answer: c

The EAC is calculated by dividing the BAC by the CPI for the week being calculated. It is the estimated cost of the project that is expected at the end of the project based on what we know about cost performance today. EAC = BAC / CPI; EAC = 20,000 / .7777 = 25,740.

23. Answer: b

The assumption in calculating the EAC by dividing the BAC by the CPI is that the CPI will stay the same for the remaining part of the project. The BAC may or may not be different by the end of the project but has nothing to do with the CPI and the EAC calculation. The BAC will change only if the budget is changed, and this happens only if new work is added to or taken from the project baseline. The schedule performance index has nothing to do with the EAC calculation.

24. Answer: b

The estimate to complete is calculated by EAC − EV. It is the difference between the work completed, EV, and the estimate of the project at the end of the project. Since the EAC and the EV are not choices, we need to look further. The EAC is BAC / CPI. The CPI, EV, and the BAC are not offered either. The CPI is EV / AC. Therefore, the three factors needed are the BAC, EV, and AC.

25. Answer: c

The EV should be reduced by the amount of the $4,000 already credited to the earned value report for planting the trees. The AC should not be reduced, and since there is no increase in budget the PV will not be changed. When the vendor installs the new trees, the $4,000 will be added to the EV once again.

26. Answer: b

In learning curve theory, each time a task is done the amount of time and cost involved in doing the task decreases. For each doubling of the number of units produced, the cost of producing the units decreases by a fixed percentage.

27. Answer: c

According to learning curve theory, the cost of a unit of production, the software module, will decrease by a fixed percentage for each doubling of the units produced. Since from unit 1 to unit 2 there was a 10% change in cost, the fixed percentage of reduction in cost was 90%. For unit 4, cost would be 81 person-hours, 90% of 90 person-hours. For unit 8, it would be 90% of 81, or 73 person-hours.

28. Answer: a

Listings of activities are usually not part of an analogous estimate. In analogous estimates large portions of the project are estimated by comparing and scaling similar parts of other projects.

29. Answer: c

The cost baseline is not available when the budget is created, since it is the result of taking the completed budget and allocating it over the time of the project. The project budget can be calculated without being time phased, but the cost baseline must be time phased.

30. Answer: d

The programmer will be paid for twenty-six weeks of work. The productivity and utilization factors affect the amount of time that someone is paid in comparison to the hours of effort required to complete the work. In this case the utilization and productivity are not required to calculate the cost: 26 weeks × 40 hours per week × $50 per hour × 1.3 fringe benefits × 1.5 overhead = $101,400.

31. Answer: b

To calculate the cost of 100 hours of effort we must adjust for the person's utilization and productivity. People of lower productivity take longer to do work and make more mistakes but usually cost less since they are usually younger and less experienced. This can often be economical. The calculation is 100 hours / .72 / .8 × $50 per hour × 1.3 fringe benefit × 1.5 overhead.

32. Answer: b

Including a contingency budget will set aside money for known, identified risks. This will give more control to the project and reduce the problem of known risks using budget that was set aside for the work of the project and causing a cost overrun in the project.

33. Answer: c

The actual payback period is between two years and three years. It is the point where the net or cumulative cash flows equal zero. This occurs between year 2 and 3 and is 2 and 29/30 of a year from the first cash flow. Cumulative cash flow in years are: 1, −500,000; 2, −290,000; 3, +10,000.

34. Answer: b

The net cash flow is the total of all the cash flows in and out of the company caused by the project. In this example there was a flow of $850,000 in and $900,000 out for a negative $50,000.

35. Answer: b

Calculating the net present value of the cash flows for the project involves adjusting the future cash flows to allow for diminishing value due to the time that we must wait to get them. Money received today is more valuable to us than money that will be received in the future.

36. Answer: d

Most of the project money will be spent during the execution phase. At the beginning of execution the rate of expenditures rises as people and materials are brought into the project. Later the expenditures peak and slow down.

37. Answer: b

The percent complete is the work completed, or the earned value divided by the total work to be done. EV / BAC = percent complete; PC = 24 / 97 = 25%.

38. Answer: c

Sum of the years' digits is an accelerated depreciation method. Each year of the useful life of the asset is given a sequential number; the numbers are summed and used as the denominator for a fraction of the asset's book value to be taken each year as depreciation. The numerator of the fraction for each year is the reverse of the years' sequence numbers.

$$1+2+3+4+5+6+7+8+9+10 = 55$$

First year use 10/55; second year use 9/55, and so on.

39. Answer: d

The breakeven point is the point where the sum of the investment and the unit cost times the number of units is the same.

Breakeven between $75,000 investment and keeping the existing machine:
$75,000 + 2x = 5x; x = 25,000$ units

Breakeven between $50,000 investment and keeping the existing machine:
$50,000 + 3x = 5x; x = 25,000$ units

Breakeven between $75,000 investment and the $50,000 machine:
$75,000 + 2x = 50,000 + 3x; x = 25,000$ units

40. Answer: d

41. Answer: c

If production were expected to continue for three years, this would mean the production of another 36,000 units. This is beyond the breakeven point for the most expensive machine, the one representing the $75,000 investment. Beyond the 25,000th unit this is the preferred machine to buy.

QUALITY MANAGEMENT

1. Answer: d

   Project quality management includes the processes required to ensure that the project will satisfy the needs for which it was undertaken. It includes "all activities of the overall management function that determine the quality policy, objectives, and responsibilities and implements them by means such as quality planning, quality control, quality assurance, and quality improvement, within the quality system." (*Guide to the PMBOK.*)

2. Answer: c

   Projects are typically part of an organization larger than the project—corporations, government agencies, health care institutions, international bodies, professional associations, and others.

   Projects are typically authorized as a result of one or more needs. These stimuli may also be called problems, opportunities, or business requirements. The central theme of all these terms is that management generally must make a decision about how to respond.

   Projects are authorized by upper management, which is responsible for setting strategic company goals.

3. Answer: c

   According to Juran and Deming, 85% to 95% of the quality problems that occur in organizations are from processes controlled by upper management.

4. Answer: c

   Quality programs save money. Each improvement in quality will yield benefits to the project that are in excess of the cost of the implementation and operation.

5. Answer: b

   Experiments are used to determine the impact of the different variables. The design of the experiment is a controlled study of the problem. Holding all variables constant and varying one of them is sensitivity analysis. The results will show which variable has the most impact on the process.

6. Answer: a

   The averaging of the five parts that are sampled is called the X bar value. In control charts the two values that are normally plotted on the control chart are the X bar value and the R value, the difference between the highest and lowest value of the dimension in the sampled parts.

7. Answer: c

This is the *Guide to the PMBOK* definition for quality. Stated and implied needs are the inputs to developing the requirements of the product or output from the project.

8. Answer: c

Quality assurance is all the planned and systematic activities implemented within the quality system to provide confidence that the project will satisfy the relevant quality standards.

9. Answer: b

Quality must be planned into the product, not inspected in. The design and building of the product should be such that the quality will be designed or built in rather than expecting the inspection of the product to catch the mistakes and defects and rework them into a quality product.

10. Answer: c

Products that are able to perform and function acceptably but are different technically are graded into different categories. For example, wood is graded according to the number of knots that are present in the wood. The wood performs the function of being structurally sound in all grades, but the desirability of knot free wood leads us to higher grades of wood.

11. Answer: c

A Pareto diagram is a histogram, ordered by frequency of occurrence, that shows how many results were generated by type or category of identified cause. By using this tool the manager can identify the defects that occurred most often.

12. Answer: c

This is a check sheet. Check sheets are simple devices that can be used almost anywhere. On them you make a mark in the appropriate category. After many marks are made, they can be added up to give the number of each defect passing the point.

13. Answer: d.

Quality management and project management are very concerned about customer satisfaction.

14. Answer: a

Common causes are those that are the normal variables produced in the process output when the process is operating normally. Special causes are the causes of variability in the process when the process is not operating normally.

15. Answer: a.

    Work results, quality checklists, operational definitions, and the management plan are the
    items listed in the *Guide to the PMBOK* as the inputs to the quality control function.

16. Answer: b

    The averaging of the five parts that are sampled is called the X bar value. In control charts
    the two values that are normally plotted on the control chart are the X bar value and the R
    value, the difference between the highest and lowest value of the dimension in the sampled
    parts.

17. Answer: c

    The diagram the manager is using is a cause and effect diagram, also known as a fishbone
    diagram. These diagrams are often called Ishikawa diagrams as well.

18. Answer: b

    This is an example of variable inspection. If the testing machine had had a light that showed
    green when the parts were acceptable, then it would have been attribute inspection. We don't
    know whether sampling or 100% inspection is taking place.
        A variable is an actual measurement of some characteristic of a part. An attribute is a
    yes or no determination of whether the part is good or bad.

19. Answer: b

    One of the most important things in using control charts is that they not only show when
    the process is out of control but also show when the process is in control and only normal
    variations are taking place. This means that we have a guide that tells us when we should not
    be taking corrective action as well as a guide to tell us when we should take corrective action.

20. Answer: b

    In modern quality management the idea of making small incremental improvements is used
    rather than making up large projects to make giant changes in the operation.

21. Answer: b

    Kaizen means improvement in Japanese. It actually applies to all aspects of life. In terms of
    quality management it means continuing improvement involving everyone, including manag-
    ers and workers alike, from the top to the bottom of the organization.

22. Answer: b

    Cost and delays are reduced, production improves, market share increases, and profits go up.
    Cost to the customer should not go up when quality management is implemented properly.

Capital expenditures should not necessarily go down or up as a result of quality management. Profits should increase.

23. Answer: d

The benefits should always be greater than the cost of implementing quality management. The benefit-cost ratio should always be greater than one.

24. Answer: a

The quality plan is part of the overall project plan and is an important input to the project plan.

25. Answer: d

Quality assurance is all the planned and systematic activities implemented within the quality system to provide confidence that the project will satisfy the relevant quality standards.

26. Answer: b

The International Standards Organization attempts to ensure consistency in organizations that can be relied upon by their customers. To qualify, an organization must meet six requirements regarding the control of documents, control of records, internal audits, control of nonconformance, corrective action, and preventive action.

27. Answer: c

The acceptance costs of quality are the things that must be done to ensure that the quality of the product or service is acceptable. This includes the cost associated with inspection and reinspection, the cost of the quality plan, quality assurance, and quality management.

28. Answer: a

The process is not in control. Although the values of X bar are all within the upper and lower control limits of the process, there is a trend showing five values in a row all increasing. There are several observations on the control chart that can indicate that the process is out of control even though the values measured are within the upper and lower control limits.

29. Answer: d

The Pareto diagram shows a histogram where the defect classes are arranged in the order of the highest to lowest frequency of occurrence of the defect. It also shows the cumulative percent of defects from the highest to lowest number of defects.

30. Answer: b

In a scatter diagram a plot is made with two variables. If there is a correlation between the variables and the two variables increase at the same time, it is called positive correlation. If one variable increases while the other variable decreases, it is called negative correlation.

31. Answer: d

The value of X bar for hour number 7 is the sum of the four observed values for hour 7 divided by 4.

25	27	50	− 12

This is 90 / 4 or 22.5. Since this is the number of ten-thousandths of an inch, the correct answer is .00225.

32. Answer: b

The value of R is the difference between the highest value recorded and the lowest value recorded for the hour.

− 25	28	12	22

This value is 28 − (−25) or 53. Since this number is in ten-thousandths of an inch the correct answer is .0053.

33. Answer: a

To calculate the value for R bar, we take the value for R for each hour and find the mean or average value.

Value for R for each hour is:

Hour	1	2	3	4	5	6	7	8	9	10
R	21	52	20	68	86	77	62	31	81	53

The sum of the values is 551, which is 55.1 when divided by 10. Since this number is in ten-thousandths of an inch, the correct answer is .00551.

34. Answer: a

In sampling inspection the ideal operating characteristic curve would correctly pass or reject all lots that were below or above the AQL point. Any lot that truly had more than the allowed AQL would be rejected, and any lot that had less than or equal to the AQL would be accepted.

35. Answer: a

When sampling inspection is used, it will discover lots that are above the AQL. These lots are then returned for 100% inspection. When the 100% inspection is done, the defective parts are removed, and the acceptable ones are sent to the customer. As the number of defective parts increases, more lots will have to be inspected 100%. Initially, the quality delivered to the customer will fall, but because of the added work of the 100% inspection, the quality will then improve.

36. Answer: d

Five years.

37. Answer: c

In the Shewhart and Deming cycle, an idea is first identified and planned for implementation. Then an experiment is performed to see if the idea will work. The results are checked, and then evaluated. If the evaluation is positive, the idea is fully implemented, and the next idea is planned.

38. Answer: a

The Demming cycle refers to the process of making continuous improvements: Plan, Do, Check, Act. In the Demming cycle we plan an improvement, and then we attempt the new process with the change on an experimental level. We check the results and then act to make the permanent improvement.

39. Answer: b

Because the parts are attribute inspected, we do not have data other than the parts failed to pass a Go–No Go gauge. We know only that an unacceptable number of parts were either above or below the allowed dimension. It is possible that the average for the rejected parts is 2.000 inches. The only thing we know for sure is that the part diameters are greater than 0.000, or they would not exist.

HUMAN RESOURCES MANAGEMENT

1. Answer: b

   The major advantage of the functional organization over those listed is that the organization is quite stable. Project organizations are created and disbanded as the need for them arises. Functional organizations are also able to have high levels of expertise in specific skill areas. These organizations also resist change.

2. Answer: d

   Managing is primarily concerned with "consistently producing key results expected by stakeholders," while leading involves:
   - Establishing direction—developing both a vision of the future and strategies for producing the changes needed to achieve that vision.
   - Aligning people—communicating the vision by words and deeds to all those whose cooperation may be needed to achieve the vision.
   - Motivating and inspiring—helping people energize themselves to overcome political, bureaucratic, and resource barriers to change.

3. Answer: c

   The matrix organization allows for multifunctional teams to be formed as the need arises with different projects being contracted for by the company.

4. Answer: d

   The pure project organization is best used in cases where the project is very large and some distance from the home office. The project manager has a high level of authority.

5. Answer: c

   A weak matrix organization is one where the project managers have less authority over their projects than in the strong matrix or balanced matrix organizations. In many organizations these managers are not called project managers but project expediters or coordinators.

6. Answer: d

   When the project management team is able to influence or direct staff assignments, it must consider the characteristics of the potentially available staff. Considerations include, but are not limited to:

- Previous experience—have the individuals or groups done similar or related work before? Have they done it well?
- Personal interests—are the individuals or groups interested in working on this project?
- Personal characteristics—are the individuals or groups likely to work well together as a team?
- Availability—will the most desirable individuals or groups be available in the necessary time frames?

7. Answer: d

Since the project manager is responsible for a temporary multifunctional team of people who are brought together for the purpose of one project it is most important that the project manager perform the function of integration.

8. Answer: b

The project office is an organization for supporting many project teams. This organization may support the project teams with common services that each of the teams needs, such as training, software, tools, and methodologies.

9. Answer: d

Human resource administrative activities are seldom a direct responsibility of the project management team. Many organizations have a variety of policies, guidelines, and procedures that can help the project management team with various aspects of organizational planning. For example, an organization that views managers as "coaches" is likely to have documentation on how the role of "coach" is to be performed.

10. Answer: d

The project management office is the place where the project teams and the project managers reside. It should not be confused with the project office, which is a support organization for the project teams and the project managers. The manager of the project management office has the project managers report to him or her.

11. Answer: a

Of the four conflict resolution techniques listed, problem solving is the most long lasting. In problem solving more additional facts are gathered until it becomes clear that there is one solution to the problem that is the best solution. The others listed do not provide permanent solutions, as the persons in conflict will later disagree again.

12. Answer: b

Weak matrices maintain many of the characteristics of a functional organization, and the project manager role is more that of a coordinator or expediter than that of a manager. In similar fashion, strong matrices have many of the characteristics of the projectized organization—full-time project managers with considerable authority and full-time project administrative staff.

13. Answer: c

    Particular attention should be paid to how project team members (individuals or groups) will be released when they are no longer needed on the project. Appropriate reassignment procedures may:
    • Reduce costs by reducing or eliminating the tendency to "make work" to fill the time between this assignment and the next.
    • Improve morale by reducing or eliminating uncertainty about future employment opportunities.

14. Answer: d

    The project life cycle defines the beginning and the end of the project. Depending on the project life cycle definition, the beginning and ending parts of the project may or may not be included in this project. For example, transition at the end of the project to some ongoing effort may be part of the project or the ongoing effort.

15. Answer: d

    Projects must often have their own reward and recognition systems since the systems of the performing organization may be not appropriate. For example, the willingness to work overtime in order to meet an aggressive schedule objective should be rewarded or recognized; needing to work overtime as the result of poor planning should not be.

16. Answer: c

    Good listening is an important skill for any manager. One of the ways that you can become a skilled listener is by repeating some of the things that are said. Summarizing gives yourself and others a repeat of important points and makes the speaker feel more relaxed and in a friendly atmosphere.

17. Answer: a

    The outputs from team development are performance improvements and input to performance appraisals.

18. Answer: b

    Creative problem solving is when an innovative approach to the problem is used. The problem was solved not by improving service but by making the area where the customers wait more friendly and enjoyable.

19. Answer: a

    The project management team must identify the stakeholders, determine what their needs and expectations are, and then manage and influence those expectations to ensure a successful project. Key stakeholders on every project include:
    - Performing organization—the enterprise whose employees are most directly involved in doing the work of the project.
    - Sponsor—the individual or group within the performing organization who provides the financial resources, in cash or in kind, for the project.
    - The structure of the performing organization often constrains the availability of resources or terms under which they become available to the project. Therefore, commitment of top levels of management is important to every aspect of the project.

20. Answer: b

    The project team kick-off meeting is the first meeting of the project team. It should aim to do all of the items mentioned.

21. Answer: b

    Co-location involves placing all, or almost all, of the most active project team members in the same physical location to enhance their ability to perform as a team. Co-location is widely used on larger projects and can also be effective for smaller projects (e.g., with a "war room" where the team congregates or leaves in-process work items).

22. Answer: a

    Groups of people will generally take longer to solve a problem, but the quality of the solution will be superior to the individual solutions that are reached.

23. Answer: c

    The projectized organization has a very strong project manager because there is little chance for the home company organization to be able to correctly judge and make decisions for the project. The project manager has nearly autonomous authority.

24. Answer: a

    From the *Guide to the PMBOK*, project human resource management includes the processes required to make the most effective use of the people involved with the project. The following are major processes:
    - Organizational planning—identifying, documenting, and assigning project roles, responsibilities, and reporting relationships.
    - Staff acquisition—getting the human resources needed assigned to and working on the project.
    - Team development—developing individual and group skills to enhance project performance.

25. Answer: c

Team development on a project is often complicated when individual team members are accountable to both a functional manager and to the project manager. Effective management of this dual reporting relationship is often a critical success factor for the project and is generally the responsibility of the project manager.

26. Answer: c

In a projectized organization, team members are often co-located. Most of the organization's resources are involved in project work exclusively for this project, and project managers have a great deal of independence and authority. In functional organizations the project manager may not exist and therefore little attention is paid to individual projects. In the weak matrix organization the project manager is given little authority to get things done and is primarily concerned with communication problems with managers who direct the work of people for the project.

In a strong matrix organization the project manager manages the people and usually co-locates them at the project's location. This would be the best organization for the situation.

27. Answer: b

According to McGregor, managers are of two types, theory X and theory Y. Theory X managers believe their subordinates to be lazy and irresponsible and will not work unless forced to by fear. Theory Y managers think that their people are creative and imaginative and want to do good things if only they are given the means to do them.

28. Answer: c

The functional manager in a balanced matrix organization should be the person responsible for the training of the people within his or her organization. It is appropriate for this manager to have this responsibility since this manager knows the skills of the people in the functional department and knows what training is appropriate for them.

29. Answer: d

In management by objectives the supervisor and the employee jointly set the objectives for the employee over the next time period. The objectives do not necessarily have to be quantifiable, and the supervisor should not set the objectives for the employee.

30. Answer: b

In matrix organizations the functional manager is responsible for skills improvement and training since the functional manager is the best person to evaluate skills and development improvement for the employee. The project manager is more expert in the project work and not necessarily the skills of each person on the multifunctional team.

31. Answer: c

The system that controls the starting of activity on a project is the work authorization system. It should be used when it is economical. On large complicated projects the cost of having a formal work authorization system may be justified by adding more control. On small projects this may not be worthwhile.

32. Answer: d

These are the process groups that make up the project management processes.

33. Answer: c

The staffing plan is like the Gantt chart in looks. It has a bar for each person on a time scale, showing the length of time and the dates that each person will be working on which specific projects.

34. Answer: c

A project team directory is like a telephone book of the project team. It shows where people can be found. This is helpful in matrix organizations because teams are being formed and disbanded often, and when they disband, people frequently change their physical locations.

35. Answer: d

One of the major responsibilities of the functional manager in a matrix organization is to see that the right people are in the right place at the right time. Project managers tend to ask for the best person for their projects when a lesser skilled person might do the work just as well.

36. Answer: a

In reward systems it is important that there be a clear connection between the reward and the reason that it is being given. Rewards that are distributed to as many people as possible lose their motivational effect. To have motivational value, rewards need not be valuable in terms of monetary worth. Rewards that are approved by all team members generally end up being popularity contests.

37. Answer: b

When projects are many and resources are few the resources must be shared between projects in a sensible way. The matrix management method of organizing allows the sharing of resources and concentrated focus on different projects.

38. Answer: c

The disadvantage of using a functional form of organization is that there is considerable difficulty for customers to recognize who in the company represents them. This is because as the project progresses through the organization of a functionally organized company, the person responsible for the project changes.

Usually communications in a functional organization are good. This is because the organization is relatively stable and communications are well established.

There is no project manager in a functional organization, so there is little problem of conflict between project managers and functional managers. If there are project managers, they will have little influence in a functional organization.

39. Answer: c

It is important in reward systems that there be a strong connection between something being done that is considered outstanding performance and the reward. Reward systems must be explicitly fair to all participants.

40. Answer: c

A project team organization chart is essential to communicating to others and within the project team where different individuals are working. Of course, this should be kept up to date.

COMMUNICATIONS MANAGEMENT

1. Answer: d

   A communicator can use all three media to communicate.

2. Answer: c

   The project manager has three main reasons for or interests in having good document control: effective communications, making sure that all necessary information is distributed and received by all those who need it; ability to reconstruct why certain decisions were made and the conditions under which they were made; historical value, so that lessons learned can be used in the future on other projects.

3. Answer: d

   From the *Guide to the PMBOK* 2000:
   > "A communications management plan is a document which provides:
   > - A collection and filing structure which details what methods will be used to gather and store various types of information. Procedures should also cover collecting and disseminating updates and corrections to previously distributed material.
   > - A distribution structure which details to whom information (status reports, data, schedule, technical documentation, etc.) will be used to distribute various types of information. This structure must be compatible with the responsibilities and reporting relationships described by the project organization chart.
   > - A description of the information to be distributed, including format, content, level of detail, and conventions/definitions to be used.
   > - Production schedules showing when each type of communication will be produced.
   > - Methods for accessing information between scheduled communications.
   > - A method for updating and refining the communications management plan as the project progresses and develops."

4. Answer: d

5. Answer: a

   The act of communicating involves an exchange of information between two parties. The definition of communications is: An exchange of information between two parties with understanding.

6. Answer: a

   Brainstorming encourages team building if handled properly. Participants feel that they are part of the decision making process and have a sense of participation. In the evaluation part of brainstorming, the participants' thinking converges to a common agreement.

7. Answer: c

   The Delphi technique allows participants to be located in different parts of the world. It lends itself to using e-mail. In the process, the participants submit their ideas anonymously. The facilitator receives the ideas, categorizes them, and returns the list to the participants.

8. Answer: d

   Clairvoyance would be nice to have in many projects, but it is not practical for general use.

9. Answer: c

   The situation described is a conflict. As applied to human behavior it is a disagreement between individuals, which can vary from a mild disagreement to a win/lose, emotion-packed confrontation. There are two basic, but opposing, views of conflict, the traditional and the modern. The traditional view sees conflict as being primarily negative. In this view, trouble-makers cause conflict and it should be avoided. The manager who views conflict in this way avoids admitting that it exists, keeps it under cover, and tries to suppress it. The contemporary view sees conflict in a more positive light. According to this view, conflict is inevitable. It is a natural result of change and is frequently beneficial to the manager if properly managed. In particular, an atmosphere of tension, and hence conflict, is essential in any organization committed to developing or working with new ideas, for innovation is simply the process of bringing together differing ideas and perspectives into a new and different synthesis.

   In resolving conflict there are several methods: forcing, withdrawal, smoothing, compromise, and problem solving. Of these, problem solving is the best, because the new facts allow the two disagreeing parties to resolve their differences with factual information and not opinion.

10. Answer: d

    Communication involves at least two people who may have very different backgrounds, experience, and education. Many times these individuals come from different cultures, speak different languages, and certainly have different drives.

11. Answer: b

    Unless there is reason not to do so, the communication method used to respond to a communication should be the same form as the original communication.

12. Answer: c

The project manager is responsible for the functions of the project team. As such the project manager is responsible for the communications that the team must make. The project manager has a wide range of responsibilities and is responsible for the guidance, motivation, output, planning, and control of the project team.

13. Answer: b

Too many innovative ideas are smothered by negative thinking before they are given any chance to prove their worth. It is much easier to think of dozens of reasons why something will not work than to figure out how to make it work. People who are prone to this type of thinking, particularly if they overdo the "devil's advocate" role, will act as communication blockers and seriously impede the process of team building. These people announce their presence by their typical negative responses when something new is suggested.

14. Answer: d

The most effective way to communicate is to use several methods of communicating. Each method will make some of the message understood, and if all listed were used the level of understanding would be the highest.

15. Answer: d

The project expediter has no directing responsibility for the work that is done on the project. This is left to the functional managers in this environment. Project managers have many responsibilities, one of which is communications. In comparing the roles of the project manager and the project expediter, the expediter's primary role is communications.

16. Answer: d

Past project reviews are not one of the tools and techniques that could be used for performance reporting. Variance analysis, earned value reports, and performance reviews are listed in the *Guide to the PMBOK* as tools and techniques for performance reporting.

17. Answer: a

The expected project staffing is important to the communications technology since it will be necessary for the project staff to be able to use the communications tools effectively.

18. Answer: a

The administrative closure of the project consists of documenting the results of the project to formalize the acceptance of the products of the project. Administrative closure should not be delayed until the project is complete. Each major phase of the project should be closed to ensure that important information will not be lost. Outputs from administrative closure are the project archives, the project closure, and the lessons learned document.

19. Answer: b

The sender of a communication must make sure that the communication is understood and that it is clear and unambiguous and complete so that the receiver can receive it correctly.

20. Answer: c

You can improve your listening ability by doing these things:
- Show the speaker that you are interested.
- Demonstrate active, supportive attention.
- Don't constantly interrupt the speaker.
- Listen for the concepts and the ideas being presented by the speaker.
- Don't concentrate exclusively on the facts the speaker is using to support his or her arguments.
- Make sure that there is sufficient feedback on both sides to ensure that the points being made are clearly understood.

21. Answer: a

22. Answer: c

Project managers must be good communicators. While this does not mean that they must be orators or spellbinders, it does mean three things:
- They must recognize the importance of the interpersonal communication network with the project team, and encourage, not inhibit, informal communication between team members.
- They must recognize the importance of human relations to the success of communication flow and team building. Effective communication will not be achieved if there is not harmony and trust.
- They must recognize that communication is a two-way street. The project manager does not just give orders; the project team must understand, participate, and agree before teamwork is achieved. Feedback in both directions is necessary for team building and is vital for a continuing team effort.

23. Answer: b

There are seven people in the group, including the project manager. The networking formula for the number of lines of communications or connections between seven people is $n \times (n-1)/2$. In this case, $[7 \times (7-1)] / 2 = 21$.

24. Answer: c

One of the best techniques for helping to keep a meeting moving in the right direction is to frequently summarize what has already happened in the meeting. The project manager should not make all the decisions; the team should participate in decision making. Although the project manager can introduce new ideas, he or she should not dominate the meeting with his or her own ideas.

25. Answer: b

    Semantics is the study of words and their meanings. Words like *charge* can have many meanings. For example, *charge* my credit card, get an electric *charge*, the *Charge* of the Light Brigade, *charge* San Juan hill, he was *charged* with murder.

26. Answer: d

    Most project managers spend approximately 90 percent of their working hours engaged in some form of communication. Examples include but are certainly not limited to conferences, meetings, writing memos, reading reports, and talking with team members' top management, customers, clients, subcontractors, suppliers, and so on.

27. Answer: b

    From the *Guide to the PMBOK:* "Performance reporting involves collecting and disseminating information in order to provide stakeholders with information about how resources are being used to achieve project objectives. This process includes status reporting and progress reporting and forecasting."

28. Answer: b

    Communications planning—determining the information and communications needs of the stakeholders; who needs what information, when they will need it, and how it will be given to them.

    Information distribution—making needed information available to project stakeholders in a timely manner.

    Performance reporting—collecting and disseminating performance information. This includes status reporting, progress measurement, and forecasting.

    Administrative closure—generating, gathering, and disseminating information to formalize phase or project completion.

29. Answer: c

    The technologies or methods used to transfer information back and forth among project elements can vary significantly: from brief conversations to extended meetings, from simple written documents to immediately accessible online schedules and databases.

    Information can be shared by team members through a variety of methods, including manual filing systems, electronic text databases, project management software, and systems that allow access to technical documentation such as engineering drawings.

    Project information may be distributed using a variety of methods including project meetings, hard copy document distribution, shared access to networked electronic databases, fax, electronic mail, voice mail, and video conferencing.

30. Answer: b

    This is an example of informal communications. Informal communications are unplanned written or verbal communications. Frequently these communications can bring valuable information to the project manager, but they can also be a source of erroneous information, and care should be taken when using them.

31. Answer: b

   Project data is put into a variety of retrieval systems. These are not necessarily distribution systems but are storage and retrieval systems.

RISK MANAGEMENT

1. Answer: c

   In a fixed-price contract the supplier is obligated to deliver the contracted-for item at a fixed price. The supplier is aware of the risk and will put an allowance for the risk in the contracted price. This often means that the project team will pay the supplier for the cost of the risk regardless of whether the risk occurs.

2. Answer: a

   Risk avoidance is eliminating the risk from consideration by doing something that will eliminate it as a possibility. Risk acceptance is allowing the risk to happen and dealing with it if it occurs. Risk deflection or transfer is transferring the risk to someone other than the project team, such as an insurance company or outside supplier.

3. Answer: c

   Risk mitigation is the process of reducing a risk to acceptable levels. In risk mitigation the risk has either a reduced impact or probability or both. This reduces the risk severity to levels below the risk tolerance.

4. Answer: b

   Including a contingency budget will set aside money for known, identified risks. This will give more control to the project and reduce the problem of known risks using budget that was set aside for the work of the project and causing a cost overrun in the project.

5. Answer: d

   The expected value of a risk is the probability of the risk times the impact of the risk summed up for all possibilities.

$.4 \times -10,000$	$-4,000$
$.3 \times -7,500$	$-2,250$
$.2 \times -5,000$	$-1,000$
$.1 \times +2,500$	$+250$
	$-7,000$

6. Answer: c

   Management reserve is funds set aside to manage unidentified risks. PMI refers to these as the "unknown unknowns." When the management reserve is used, it is moved from the management reserve to the cost or schedule baseline.

7. Answer: a

   Risk triggers, sometimes called risk symptoms, are indications that a risk is about to occur. In this example there is a risk that the project will be delayed. There is a warning that this will occur because several activities are now overdue for completion. They do not affect the project schedule yet, but if this trend continues the project will be late.

8. Answer: a

   Because of risk in most projects the probability distribution is usually skewed. This is because there are more things that will adversely affect schedules than there are that will improve them. If the probability distribution of the scheduled completion of the project is indeed skewed, then the most likely date for project completion will be earlier than the mean value or the expected value.

9. Answer: d

   The expected value is found by multiplying the probability of the risk by the cost of the impact of the risk should it occur. EV = 25,000 × 10%

10. Answer: b

    This is a matter of applying the probability rule of addition. This rule says that the probability of either one of two events is equal to the probability of one event plus the probability of the second event minus the probability of both of the events occurring.

    P(6 or 6) = P(6) + P(6) − P(6 and 6)
    P(6 and 6) = P(6) × P(6)
    P(6 and 6) = 1/6 × 1/6 = 1/36
    P(6 or 6) = 1/6 + 1/6 − 1/36 = 11/36

11. Answer: c

    A buffered schedule is one where float is deliberately created in the schedule. Buffers are deliberately created between tasks on the critical path, and the activities are rescheduled to more closely approximate the schedule to the new promise date.

12. Answer: d

    The client's outsourcing method has nothing to do with risk management; all the other choices are items that should be included in the risk description.

13. Answer: c

The lessons learned document from other similar projects can be a great help in determining the new risks associated with this project. Many times risks repeat themselves from one project to another. This makes the lessons learned document very important for all projects.

14. Answer: c

The result of the first risk meeting of a project team is to identify as many risks as possible in the time allowed.

15. Answer: b

The Monte Carlo technique is a refinement of PERT. In the PERT process the range of values and the probability that they can occur is calculated for the project completion date or parts of the project. The Monte Carlo technique allows for shifts that may occur in the critical path during possible values of the durations of the activities of the project. It is a simulation technique that produces a value called the criticality index, which is the percent of simulations that a particular activity is on the critical path. That is, criticality index is the percent of the number of simulations that an activity is on the critical path.

16. Answer: c

The management reserve is time and money used to offset the effect of unknown risks affecting cost and schedule. These risks can only be approximated since none of them are specifically identified. PMI refers to these risks as the known-unknown risks and the identified risks as the known-known risks.

17. Answer: a

The breakeven-point justification technique predicts a point in time where the benefits offset the costs involved. It is a simple justification technique that takes into consideration a lot of assumptions. Since it predicts the point in time where the benefits exceed the cost, given the choice of an expensive and a cheap machine, the cheap machine will usually have high short-term benefits, and the expensive machine will have higher long-term benefits.

18. Answer: d

In critical chain theory the feeder chains are activities that are not on the critical path. These tasks are scheduled to be done as late as possible and then buffered so that they start earlier than the late schedule dates. Buffer is also added to the critical path of the schedule to improve the probability that the project will finish on time. Feeder chain activities as well as critical chain activities are not started as early as possible or as late as possible. They are started as late as possible minus their buffer.

19. Answer: c

    In the normal probability distribution or any symmetric probability distribution, the most likely value of the distribution is the peak of the distribution curve. This is the value that has the highest probability of occurring. In a symmetric probability distribution this will be the center of the curve as well. There is a 50% probability that the project will finish past the most likely date and a 50% chance that the project will finish earlier than that date.

20. Answer: c

    Risks are events that affect a project for better or worse. Positive risks increase the positive cash flow or benefits to the project, and negative risks increase the negative cash flow or effects of the project.

21. Answer: a

    Fast tracking is changing the project plan to schedule activities that were planned to be done in sequence so that they can be done completely or partially in parallel. This will increase risk, because more work will be done if a problem is discovered.

22. Answer: b

    In determining the worst-case situation, all of the negative risks are included and none of the positive risks are included in the total. This makes the assumption of the worst case as being that all of the bad things happen and none of the good things happen.

23. Answer: b

    Insurance transfers (deflects) the problem of the risk to someone else who takes the responsibility for the loss caused by the risk. In this case an insurance company agreed to compensate PMI if this loss occurred.

24. Answer: d

    During project closeout much of the project work has been completed and many of the risks have passed the time in which they can occur. The total risk of the project is therefore lowest during closeout.

25. Answer: c

    The Monte Carlo technique is a refinement of PERT. In the PERT process the range of values and the probability that they can occur are calculated for the project completion date or parts of the project. The Monte Carlo technique allows for shifts that may occur in the critical path during possible values of the durations of the activities of the project. It is a simulation technique that produces a value called the criticality index, which is the percent of simulations that a particular activity is on the critical path.

26. Answer: b

If any of the activities are late, the entire project of the three activities will be late. To state this as three mutually exclusive events we consider the probability of all three of the events occurring on time. This is .9 for each, and the probability of all three occurring is $.9 \times .9 \times .9 = .73$.

27. Answer: c

The probability is that at least one of the sellers will deliver the parts on time. This is the same as saying either vendor A or B must deliver. This is the addition rule in probability. The probability that the first seller will deliver is .9. The probability that the second seller will deliver is also .9, but the second seller delivering on time is only of consequence if the first seller fails to deliver on time, or .1. The calculation is then $.9 + (.1 \times .9) = .99$.

28. Answer: b

This is the definition of value engineering used in the *Guide to the PMBOK* Glossary.

29. Answer: b

A workaround is the work that is not planned ahead of time to take care of a threat that occurs.

30. Answer: d

In an even distribution any date in the distribution will have the same probability as any other date in the distribution.

31. Answer: b

The Monte Carlo technique is a simulation technique that assigns a value to the duration for each activity in the schedule. This assignment can be by user-selected probability distributions. Depending on the values of the duration for each activity the critical path may change from simulation run to simulation run.

32. Answer: a

Risk acceptance is doing nothing about the risk until it happens. This is done with risks that are below the risk tolerance level.

33. Answer: b

Risk tolerance is the measure of the client's likelihood to take risks. A client with a low risk tolerance will not be willing to take very many or large risks even though they may produce considerable opportunities to make large profits.

34. Answer: b

    The Monte Carlo technique is a computer simulation method that selects durations for schedule events according to a probability distribution on a random basis. For each set of selected durations the simulation is run and the schedule and critical path are calculated. The result is a probability distribution showing the probability of project completion dates that are possible. The criticality index shows the percent of simulations that any activity is on the critical path.

35. Answer: b

    Simulations such as the Monte Carlo simulation are frequently used in risk management. It is far less expensive to model the real world than to actually do things in the real world.

36. Answer: b

    Risk analysis should be done frequently throughout the project.

37. Answer: d

    The risk option of mitigation means that the impact or the probability is reduced to a level below the risk tolerance level. This means that the risk is now acceptable.

38. Answer: b

    Qualitative assessment of risks is often appropriate. When there is little impact from a risk or when little is known about the risk parameters it may only be practical to evaluate risks in a qualitative way.

39. Answer: c

    This is the definition of sensitivity analysis in the *Guide to the PMBOK*.

40. Answer: a

    The expected value of the risk is the probability of the risk multiplied by its cost. This is one method of ranking risks. Risks can also be ranked qualitatively by assigning them qualitative values like "very risky" and "not too risky" and ranking them in groups.

CONTRACTS AND PROCUREMENT

1. Answer: b

   A statement of work is the description of what the project is about and what will be delivered. The project plan is complete and contains the detailed work that the project will do, complete with task descriptions and schedule, cost, and scope baselines containing a real schedule and budget. An exception report describes items that are not as planned.

2. Answer: a

   In a fixed-price contract the supplier is obligated to deliver the contracted-for item at a fixed price. The supplier is aware of the risk and will put an allowance for the risk in the contracted price. This often means that the project team will pay the supplier for the cost of the risk regardless of whether the risk occurs.

3. Answer: c

   The project manager should make every effort to make sure that the supplier is aware of the risk before the contract is signed. The project manager is obligated ethically to reveal the information to the supplier before the contract is signed.

4. Answer: b

   The make or buy decision is not a contract or purchase order type. Make or buy refers to the decision process that is used to decide whether work should be done in our own facility or contracted out to a supplier.

5. Answer: c

   The project charter is one of the first things that must be done in any project. The project charter according to the *Guide to the PMBOK* 2000 is: "A document issued by senior management that provides the project manager with the authority to apply organizational resources to project activities."

6. Answer: d

   Although it is not to the letter of the contract, the buyer is going to have much more trouble if the seller cannot make the payroll and cannot complete the contract because their employees will not work without pay. The best thing would be to change the contract in some way that is mutually beneficial.

7. Answer: d

In a blanket order, a long-term order is placed with the seller. The price is based on the goods or services that will be sold over the period of the blanket order. The seller has a long-term order from the buyer and can invest in the means of production. The buyer has a stable price for the period of the blanket order. If the buyer does not buy all the goods or services that were promised, the price per unit is adjusted at the end of the contract. Since the inventory is delivered as needed, the inventory carrying cost is of no consequence to the buyer.

8. Answer: c

Forward buying is the type of purchasing where the amount of goods required for a long period of time is purchased and delivered at one time. There is a quantity discount for this type of purchase, but it has no effect on capital investment unless it would be to build a place to store the goods. It will decrease transportation cost, increase inventory, prevent the risk of future price increases, and increase the cost associated with obsolescence.

9. Answer: d

The marketing function is not part of the procurement process.

10. Answer: d

Cost-reimbursable contracts are frequently called cost-plus contracts.

11. Answer: c

Work is frequently done after delivery if it is to both the seller's and the buyer's mutual benefit. The cost of doing the work is charged back to the seller, thus back charged.

12. Answer: d

Contract negotiations take place after the vendor has been selected. This is true even in a bid situation. The seller and the buyer negotiate over the specific terms and conditions of the contract and can even adjust the pricing. Care must be taken here lest the unsuccessful bidders protest the adjustments and force a rebid of the contract.

13. Answer: c

A request for proposal is a device used to solicit seller proposals. In an RFP the seller makes proposals as to how the needs of the buyer can be satisfied. The buyer may accept the proposal from the seller even if it is more costly than the lowest proposal.

14. Answer: c

The request for proposal process is the most effective means of obtaining the best seller. It puts the burden of offering the best solution to the problem on the seller, but it creates a problem for the buyer in that the proposals will require careful evaluation by the buyer's team.

15. Answer: d

Our seller's competitor's method of outsourcing is not relevant to the make or buy decision.

16. Answer: c

The terms *bid* and *quotation* are generally used when the source selection decision will be price driven (as when buying commercial items), while the term *proposal* is generally used when nonfinancial considerations such as technical skills or approach are paramount (as when buying professional services).

17. Answer: b

It is better to try to save a contract that is nearly completed than to start all over with another vendor. There are problems in this work, and it seems likely that the work is not clearly defined.

18. Answer: b

Existing lists of potential sellers can often be expanded by placing advertisements in general circulation publications such as newspapers or in specialty publications such as professional journals. Some government jurisdictions require public advertising of certain types of procurement items; most government jurisdictions require public advertising of subcontracts on a government contract.

19. Answer: a

Of the contracts listed, the cost plus percentage of cost as an award fee is the greatest risk for the buyer and the least risk for the contractor performing the work. Not only do costs go up if there are problems but the fee increases with additional cost as well. Generally speaking, buyers prefer the fixed-price contract, which places more risk on the seller, and sellers prefer cost contracts, which place more risk on the buyer.

20. Answer: b

The concept of warranty is based upon one party's assurance to the other that the goods will meet certain standards of quality, including condition, reliability, description, function, or performance. This assurance may be expressed or implied. Recognizing the principal function of a warranty is to establish a level of quality (and title—not discussed herein); it thus gives a source of remedy for loss due to a defect in the quality of the goods. The contract may and should establish a level of quality, and if it does, it is an expressed warranty recognized under Section 2-313 (1) (a) of the Uniform Commercial Code.

21. Answer: b

The person or organization responsible for contract administration should provide the seller with formal written notice that the contract has been completed. Requirements for formal acceptance and closure are usually defined in the contract.

22. Answer: b

Fixed-price or lump sum contracts—this category of contract involves a fixed total price for a well-defined product. To the extent that the product is not well-defined, both the buyer and seller are at risk—the buyer may not receive the desired product or the seller may need to incur additional costs in order to provide it. Fixed-price contracts may also include incentives for meeting or exceeding selected project objectives such as schedule targets.

23. Answer: b

The first thing that should be done is to issue a purchase order to the contractor and find out how much the change is going to cost. It is important in managing changes that work on changes does not take place until the cost of doing the change is clearly understood.

24. Answer: b

Security is a consideration in making a make-or-buy decision. In this situation it might be very important to know how well the service bureau will be able to protect your designs from the competition. Make or buy is a general management technique that can be used to determine whether a particular product can be produced cost-effectively by the performing organization. Both sides of the analysis include indirect as well as direct costs. For example, the "buy" side of the analysis should include both the actual out-of-pocket cost to purchase the product as well as the indirect costs of managing the purchasing process.

A make-or-buy analysis must also reflect the perspective of the performing organization as well as the immediate needs of the project. For example, purchasing a capital item (anything from a construction crane to a personal computer) rather than renting it is seldom cost effective. However, if the performing organization has an ongoing need for the item, the portion of the purchase cost allocated to the project may be less than the cost of the rental.

25. Answer: b

In the procurement process, the solicitation process is the process whereby potential vendors are notified of an impending contract procurement.

26. Answer: c

This is the formal and legal definition of a contract.

27. Answer: d

The contract definition includes the requirement for a contract to be agreed to by competent parties. The person signing the contract was below the legal age for doing so; therefore, the contract is void.

28. Answer: b

    Commodities are those items that are common and readily available from several suppliers. They are interchangeable and can be bought on the basis of price alone, since there is little difference between vendors of these products.

29. Answer: b

    When a procurement is put out for bid the resulting decision to buy from a vendor is based on price alone. If a request for proposal was issued instead, then it would be up to the overall evaluation of the proposal to determine the vendor selected.

30. Answer: b

    Blanket orders are promises to do business for a period of time. In this case the trucking company has negotiated a blanket order with the tire vendor. The discount price per tire is based on the quantities specified and forecast. If they do not happen, the discount on all the tires sold is adjusted at the end of the contract.

PROFESSIONAL RESPONSIBILITY

1. Answer: c

   There should be a change procedure in the project to handle changes that might be initiated by customers. The change procedure should include the cost for managing the change and the cost of developing the estimate for the effects of the change.

2. Answer: c

   Estimating is just that, an estimating process. Perhaps it would have been better for the project manager to have given all the information to the person responsible for the estimate. At this point the best thing to do is to use all of the information available to create the most accurate estimate that is practical.

3. Answer: b

   In this kind of situation it is important that the customs and culture in the foreign country be respected. By consulting with your company's management, the gift can usually be accepted and disposed of in the proper way.

4. Answer: c

   Unless the employee has signed a nondisclosure agreement with his or her previous company, there is no obligation for him or her not to share knowledge that was gained while working for the competitor.

5. Answer: a

   The first thing that should be done is to look for tasks in the project where there is an ability to reschedule to free resources for this problem. If the problem is severe and additional budget and time is needed, it may be necessary to speak to the stakeholders, but the project impacts and plan for the correction should come first.

6. Answer: c

   It is usually in the best interest of the project if the project team decides matters of personal time themselves unless there are significant reasons for the project team to be on site at certain hours or because they are necessary to interact with other people on the team.

7. Answer: a

Intellectual property belongs to the author of the property. If you create a presentation based on your own work, you have a right to receive credit for it. This is not to say that it is necessary to give credit to every person who contributes anything to a presentation or we would have a list of credits like a Hollywood movie. One of the options not offered here is to speak to the manager first.

8. Answer: c

This type of problem occurs frequently. Many times there is a misunderstanding on the part of the customer's engineers, and it can be resolved simply by having an informal meeting and discussing the problem. Later, if the disagreement persists, the customer should submit a request for a change, and a formal investigation can be completed.

9. Answer: b

It would be a conflict of interest to own a company that was supplying parts to a project that you are managing. Receiving a gift of a small amount or one that is within the limits of your company's gift policy is not a conflict of interest. Using sensitive information voluntarily given to you is not a conflict of interest.

10. Answer: c

Probably the best thing to do in this situation would be to divide the money by letting the team decide how to divide it. This is participative management.

11. Answer: b

Unsupported allegations that are brought to you by a third party may often be rumors and mistaken facts. It is best to investigate the allegations first, and complete the investigation before making any changes.

APPENDIX: PROBABILITY DISTRIBUTIONS

In the discussion so far, I have tried to sound less like a statistician and more like a project management practitioner. The material I have covered here is mainly practical. But there are a few more things we should discuss if we are going to use any of the many statistical packages that are available for project management. Many of these software packages require making decisions on the type of distributions to use, so it is important to know the differences.

A probability distribution is a list of all the possibilities that could occur and a probability associated with each of them.

The Even Distribution

The even distribution is perhaps the easiest to understand. In the even distribution, there is an even chance that any of the possibilities will occur. A good example is the rolling of a die. If the die is not loaded, there is an equal chance that any of the possible numbers could come face up. The possibilities are 1, 2, 3, 4, 5, or 6. As you can see from the plot in Figure A-1, there is an equal chance of rolling a 1, 2, 3, 4, 5, or 6.

Binomial Distribution

As we move into more complex distributions, the calculation of the probabilities becomes more complex. The binomial distribution describes the probabilities of all of the possible outcomes of a series of experiments, where each experiment is identical in every way and has only two possible outcomes.

This particular distribution is of value in project management because there are many situations in risk management where there are two possible outcomes, success and failure.

In order to use the binomial distribution, three conditions must be met:

1. Each event must have only two possible outcomes.
2. Each event must be statistically independent of the others. Statistical independence means that the occurrence of one event does not have an effect on the probability of any other event.

Figure A-1. Even distribution plot.

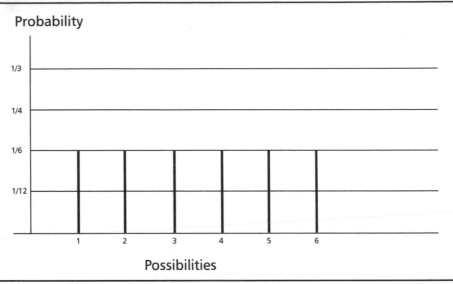

3. The probability of the outcome of any event must be the same from event to event.

In the binomial distribution it is possible to calculate the value of the probability directly. As the distributions become more and more complex, the formulas for making this calculation are too complex to be done without the use of a computer.

$$P(x) = [n! / (n-x)! \, x!] \, \Pi^x (1-\Pi)^{n-x}$$

Where: x is the number of occurrences of a particular outcome; $P(x)$ is the probability that x will occur; n is the number of events that will be measured; Π is the probability of the outcome occurring in one event; and $!$ stands for factorial. Factorial means multiplying the number by successively smaller integers until 1 is reached: 5! is $5 \times 4 \times 3 \times 2 \times 1 = 120$.

For example, suppose a coin is flipped three times. The probability of getting a head on any flip is .5. What are the probabilities of getting two heads in the three tries?

The probability of two heads is:

$$P(2) = [3! / (3-1)! \, 3!] \, .5^2 (1-.5)^1$$
$$P(2) = (6/2) \times 0.25 \times 0.5 = 0.375$$

Poisson Distribution

The Poisson distribution is used to describe the probabilities of independent events spaced over time or some other parameter. This distribution is useful in projects involving queues on lines and the number of occurrences of an event over a time period.

Three rules to the Poisson distribution are:

1. Each occurrence must be statistically independent of the others.
2. There must be an expected number of events over a period of time.
3. The probability of more than one occurrence happening at the same time is very small.

The Normal Distribution

From the illustration in Figure A-2, it can be seen that the normal distribution curve is bell shaped, with a high point in the middle and an ever-decreasing slope toward horizontal at the ends.

One of the important things about the normal distribution is that the formula for calculating it depends on only two factors, the mean value and the standard deviation. The mean value locates the middle of the curve, or the peak. The standard deviation shows whether the curve is clustered tightly around the midpoint or whether it is loosely clustered (Figure A-3).

It has been found that most physical occurrences will fit a normal curve or something close to it. This is true of many of the things that we would like to approximate in project management. The probability distribution of cost and schedule estimates fits this

Figure A-2. Normal distribution curve.

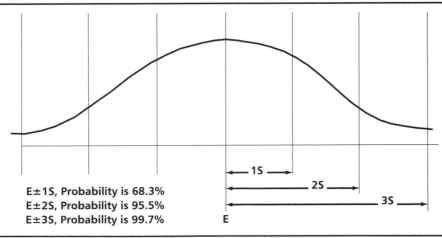

E±1S, Probability is 68.3%
E±2S, Probability is 95.5%
E±3S, Probability is 99.7%

E

1S
2S
3S

Figure A-3. Standard deviation: A measurement of the dispersion of the data.

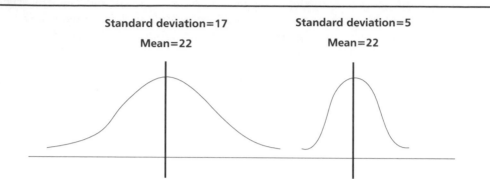

Standard deviation=17   Standard deviation=5

Mean=22   Mean=22

kind of distribution. In the area of scheduling, the PERT method is employed to more closely predict the completion time for a project. In cost estimating, the normal distribution is used to predict the range of values that has a given probability of occurring if that project is actually done.

In PERT and cost estimating, we want a 95 percent probability of being correct in our estimate. As in all probability distribution curves, the area under the curve between the two points we are interested in compared to the total area under the entire curve is the probability that the actual event will be between the two values. This means that we can use the normal distribution to determine the probability that the true value of our project will be between two estimated values.

For convenience, multiples of the standard deviation are used to mark off these ranges in values. The mean value of a project cost, for example, plus or minus one ($\pm$ 1) standard deviation is 68.3%, ± 2 standard deviations is 95.5%, and ± 3 standard deviations is 99.7%. These are values that are used for convenience. Any range of values within the limits of the distribution could be similarly calculated.

In the area of statistical quality control, the term "plus or minus 3 standard deviations" and the term "3 sigma" are frequently heard. Sigma is the Greek letter usually used to represent standard deviation. In statistical quality control, it is usual to want the accuracy of the inspection process to have a 99.7% probability of being correct. That is a 99.7% chance that the lot of parts that is inspected and deemed to be acceptable is really acceptable and a 99.7% chance that a lot of parts that is said to be unacceptable is really unacceptable. More is said about statistical quality control in Chapter 4.

All normal curves have the same percentage of total area between the same multiples of the standard deviation. Suppose point "a" is 1/2 standard deviation above the mean value. Suppose another point called "b" is 2 standard deviations above the mean. The area or probability of the actual value being between these two values is 28.57%.

Now suppose the mean value is 100, and the standard deviation is 10. Point "a" would be 105, and point "b" would be 120. The probability of the actual cost being between 105 and 120 is 28.57%.

If the standard deviation is 5 and the mean is 50, point "a" would be 52.5 and point "b" would be 60. The probability of the actual cost being between 55 and 60 is 28.57%.

Most statistical computer programs make these calculations directly. In fact most inexpensive calculators that have only the most basic statistical functions perform these calculations.

In the appendix of most statistics books you will find Z tables. These tables are used to find the probability or the area under the normal distribution curve for any point on the horizontal axes and the mean value. To use the tables, standardize the values desired by dividing them by the standard deviation.

In the previous example, the standard deviation was 10, the mean value was 100, and the desired probability was between "a" at 105 and "b" at 120. To use the table we must standardize the values:

$$Z = (x - \text{mean value}) / \text{standard deviation}$$
$$Z \text{ for the "a" value} = 5 / 10 = .5$$
$$Z \text{ for the "b" value} = 20 / 10 = 2.0$$

From this we can find the probability in the Z table for .5 and the value for 2.0. Both of these values are on the same side of the mean, so we must subtract the smaller one from the larger one to show the area we are concerned with (see Figure A-4):

Figure A-4. Probability using Z values.

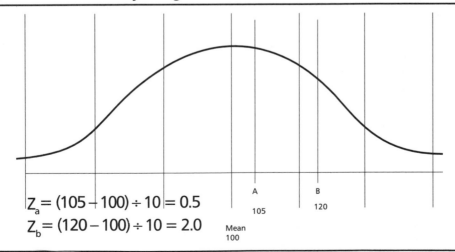

$$Z_a = (105 - 100) \div 10 = 0.5$$
$$Z_b = (120 - 100) \div 10 = 2.0$$

A 105
B 120
Mean 100

$$P(Z_a) = .6915$$
$$P(Z_b) = .4772$$
$$P(Z_a - Z_b) = 28.57\%$$

Beta Distribution

The beta distribution is used frequently in project management since it closely resembles the phenomena in cost and scheduling. The beta probability distribution is bell shaped like the normal distribution, but it is not symmetrical (Figure A-5). The rationale behind this is that the cost or time to complete a task or project can be only a limited amount under or below expectations but could be an unlimited amount over or above our expectations. If a task were scheduled to be completed in ten days, the task could not be completed in less than zero days, but there is a possibility that the task could take ten or twenty or even thirty days. Similarly, if a task were budgeted at $5,000, it could take many times $5,000 to complete, but it is not likely to take more than $5,000 less than the budget.

Figure A-5. Beta distribution.

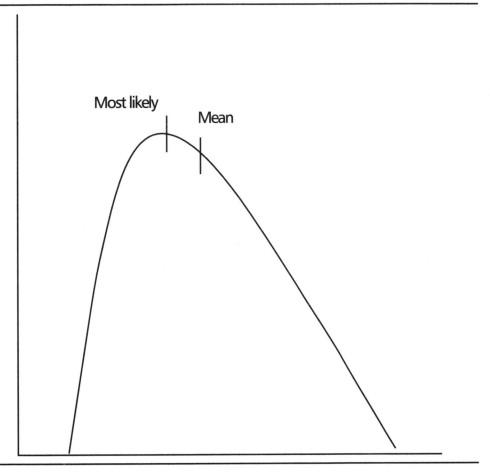

BIBLIOGRAPHY

Bach, George Leland. *Economics: An Introduction to Analysis and Policy.* 6th ed. Englewood Cliffs, NJ: Prentice-Hall, 1968.

Cleland, David I., Karen M. Bursic, Richard Puerzer, and A. Yaroslav Vlasak, Eds. *Project Management Casebook.* Newtown Square, PA: Project Management Institute, 1998.

Eckes, George. *The Six Sigma Revolution: How General Electric and Others Turned Process into Profits.* New York: Wiley, 2001.

Ferraro, Gary P. *The Cultural Dimension of International Business.* Upper Saddle River, NJ: Prentice-Hall, 1998.

Frame, J. Davidson. *Managing Projects in Organizations.* Rev. ed. San Francisco, CA: Jossey-Bass, 1995.

Goldratt, Eliyahu M. *It's Not Luck.* Great Barrington, MA: The North River Press, 1994.

Grant, Eugene L., and Richard S. Leavenworth. *Statistical Quality Control.* 5th ed. New York: McGraw-Hill, 1980.

Hamburg, Morris, *Statistical Analysis for Decision Making.* 3rd ed. New York: Harcourt Brace Jovanovich, 1983.

Hampton, David R., Charles E. Summer, and Ross A. Webber. *Organizational Behavior and the Practice of Management.* 4th ed. Glenview, IL: Scott, Foresman, 1982.

Hellriegel, Don, and John W. Slocum, Jr. *Management.* 3rd ed. Reading, MA: Addison Wesley, 1982.

Hendrick, Thomas E., and Franklin G. Moore. *Production/Operations Management.* 9th ed. Homewood, IL: Richard D. Irwin, 1985.

Imai, Masaaki. *Kaizen: The Key to Japan's Competitive Success.* New York: McGraw-Hill, 1986.

Ishikawa, Kaoru. *Guide to Quality Control.* Tokyo: JUSE Press, Ltd., 1980.

Kerzner, Harold. *Project Management: A Systems Approach to Planning, Scheduling, and Controlling.* 2nd ed. New York: Van Nostrand Reinhold, 1984.

Lewis, James P. *Project Planning, Scheduling, and Control.* Chicago, IL: Probus, 1991.

Lial, Margaret L., and Charles D. Miller. *Mathematics with Applications in the Management, Natural, and Social Sciences.* 2nd ed. Glenview, IL: Scott, Foresman, 1979.

Meredith, Jack R., and Samuel J. Mantel, Jr. *Project Management: A Managerial Approach.* 3rd ed. New York: Wiley, 1995.

Morrison, Terri; Wayne A. Conaway, and George A. Borden. *Kiss, Bow, or Shake Hands.* Holbrook, MA: Adams Media Corp., 1994.

Newbold, Paul. *Principles of Management Science.* Englewood Cliffs, NJ: Prentice-Hall, 1986.

Project Management Institute. *Project Management Professional (PMP) Role Delineation Study.* Newtown Square, PA: Project Management Institute, 2000.

Project Management Institute. *A Guide to the Project Management Body of Knowledge,* 3rd ed. Newtown Square, Pa.: Project Management Institute, 2004.

Project Management Institute Standards Committee. *A Guide to the Project Management Body of Knowledge.* Upper Darby, PA: Project Management Institute, 2000.

Sashkin, Marshall, and Molly G. Sashkin. *The New Teamwork.* New York: AMA Membership Publications Division, 1994.

Scholtes, Peter R., et al. *The Team Handbook.* Madison, WI: Joiner Associates, 1995.

Tenner, Arthur R., and Irving J. DeToro. *Total Quality Management.* Reading, MA: Addison-Wesley, 1992.

Timms, Howard L. *The Production Function in Business.* Homewood, IL: Richard D. Irwin, 1966.

Wetherill, G. Barrie. *Sampling Inspection and Quality Control.* 2nd ed. London: Chapman and Hall Ltd., 1977.

Williams, Terry M., Ed. *Proceedings of the NATO Advanced Research Workshop on Managing and Modelling Complex Projects.* Dordrecht, The Netherlands, and Kiev, Ukraine: Kluwer Academic Pub., 1996.

AC, *see* actual cost
accelerated depreciation, 99–101
acceptable quality level (AQL), 109
acceptance (of risk), 188
acceptance criteria, 27, 33
accounting equation, fundamental, 95
active acceptance, 188
activity definition process, 47–48
activity duration estimating, 47, 57–58
activity level, 31
activity on arrow diagramming (AOA),
     49–50
activity on node network diagram, 50
activity sequencing process, 47–53
   AOA diagramming used in, 49–50
   Gantt/milestone charts used in, 50, 51
   logical relationships in, 52–57
   PDM used in, 51–53
actual cost (AC), 86–91
actual cost of work performed (ACWP), 86
addition rule (risk probability), 174–176
affinity diagramming, 186
agendas, meeting, 142–143
"agreement," 193
Amazon.com, 172
American National Standards Institute
     (ANSI), 1–2
analogous estimates, 80
analogy method, 167, 169
analysis questions, 219
Angoff modified technique, 219
ANSI, *see* American National Standards Insti-
     tute
AOA diagramming, *see* activity on arrow dia-
     gramming
Apollo Project, 5, 9, 30
application questions, 219

AQL (acceptable quality level), 109
Armstrong, Neil, 9
assembly-line work, 133
assets
   in fundamental accounting equation, 95
   process, 21
assumptions, 22
attribute sampling, 108
average rate of return on investment, 36–38
avoidance, risk, 187
award process, 197

BAC (budget at completion), 90
balanced matrix organization, 12, 122–123
balance sheet, 95, 97
barriers to communication, 147–148
baseline, 3
   cost, 82
   and risk management, 161
   scope, 26–28
BCWP (budgeted cost of work performed),
     86
BCWS (budgeted cost of work scheduled), 86
benchmarking, 117
benefit cost ratio, 93
beta distribution, 70, 363
bidding, 24–26
bids, 20
bill of material (BOM), 33
binomial distribution, 357, 358
blanket orders, 205
BOM (bill of material), 33
bottom-up estimates, 78–80
brainstorming, 163–164, 168
breakeven charts, 35–36
budget at completion (BAC), 90
budgeted cost of work performed (BCWP),
     86

budgeted cost of work scheduled (BCWS), 86
budgeting
    cost, 82, 84
    for risk, 189–190
buffering the schedule, 63–67
business needs statement, 20
buyer's risk, 109–111

calendars, 59, 66
capital, cost of, 98
CAS, *see* Columbia Assessment Service
cash flow, 37, 38, 42–46
cash flow analysis, 35–46
    average rate of return used in, 36–38
    breakeven chart used in, 35–36
    internal rate of return used in, 40, 42–46
    present value of money used in, 37, 39–41
cause and effect diagrams, 110, 112
certification, 221–223
chain networks, 154, 155
chain of command, 151, 154, 155
change management, 16, 21, 33–34
changes, cost of, 27
charter, *see* project charter
checklists, 116, 166–168
Chernobyl nuclear accident, 208
circular networks, 154
clients, 5
closing process group, 16
closing the project, 16, 217
Code of Professional Conduct, 211–212
coercive power, 135–136
co-location, 124
Columbia Assessment Service (CAS), 207,
    213
commodities, 203–204
communications
    barriers to, 147–148
    formal/informal, 150–151
    improving, 148–149
    and listening, 151–153
    and management by walking around, 157
    model of, 146–147

and networking, 153–158
and performance reviews, 157–158
verbal vs. written, 149–150
communications management, 144–159
    definition of, 145
    importance of, 145
    lessons-learned documents for, 144–145
    practice questions about, 274–280,
        337–342
community, 208
comparative ranking, 184, 185
"competent parties," 193
compound interest formula, 39
compromise conflict resolution, 139–140
conceptual estimates, 79
conditional probability, 176
confidentiality, 212
conflict resolution, 137–140
conflicts of interest, 212
"consideration," 193
constraints, 22
contact, points of, 7
contingency budget, 82, 84, 189–190
continuous improvement, 116
contract administration, 198–199
contract life cycle, 194–198
    award process of, 197
    contract process of, 198
    requirement process in, 195
    requisition process in, 195–196
    solicitation process of, 196–197
    trade-off studies in, 197–198
contract management, 193–203
    and contract administration, 198–199
    and life cycle of contract, 194–195
    and make-or-buy decision, 194
    practice questions about, 291–298,
        349–353
contract process, 198
contracts
    cost-plus, 201–203
    with customer, 19
    definition of, 193

fixed-price, 199–201
   reasons for using, 192
   as risk response plan, 188
   terms used in, 193
   time-and-material, 203
   types of, 199
contractual WBS (CWBS), 33
control charts, 113, 115–116
control estimates, 79
control estimating, 81–83
controlling the project, 216–217
corrective action, 190
cost(s)
   of changes, 27
   and make-or-buy decision, 194
   price vs., 23–26
   during project phases, 14–15
   of quality, 105–107
   and requirement process, 195
cost baseline, 82
cost budgeting, 82, 84
cost control, 84–101
   cumulative reporting used in, 85–86
   data collection problems in, 87, 88
   and depreciation, 98–101
   earned value reporting used in, 84–94
   examples of, 88–91
   financial measures for, 93, 95–97
   reporting work complete for, 88
cost estimating, 79–83
   analogous, 80
   bottom-up, 79–80
   control, 81–83
   parametric, 80–81
   top-down, 79
cost management, 77–102
   budgeting for, 82, 84
   controls for, 84–101
   estimating for, 79–83
   importance of, 77–78
   and life cycle of project, 78
   practice questions about, 245–254,
      318–323
   WBS used in, 78–79

cost performance index (CPI), 91–92
cost-plus award-fee contracts, 202
cost-plus contracts, 201–203
cost-plus fixed-fee contracts, 202
cost-plus incentive-fee contracts, 203
cost-reimbursable contracts, see cost-plus con-
      tracts
cost variance (CV), 90
CPI, see cost performance index
CPM, see critical path method
crashing a schedule, 62
Crawford slip, 23, 165, 168
"creeping elegance," 32
Critical Chain (Eliyahu Goldratt), 75
critical chain theory, 74–76
criticality index, 74
critical path method (CPM), 61–62, 68, 69
cultural differences, 211
cumulative reporting, 85–86
customer, 18–19
CV (cost variance), 90
CWBS (contractual WBS), 33

data collection, 87, 88
decision trees, 180–183
decoding, 147
defects, costs of, 106–109
definitive estimates, 79
delegation, 132
deliverables, 14, 27, 222
Delphi technique, 164, 168
Deming, Edward, 107
Deming's fourteen points, 107
dependencies, 49
depreciation, 98–101
   accelerated, 99–101
   straight-line, 99
Depression Era, 126
design, job and work, 132–135
diagramming
   for quality control, 110, 112–117
   of relationships, 56–57
   of risk identification, 167, 169

difficulty rating, 219
discretionary dependencies, 49
dissatisfiers, 131–132
distance conferencing, 150
distorted perceptions, 147
distractions, eliminating, 153
distrusted sources, 147–148
documentation reviews, 163
domains (of project management), 213–218
double declining balances, 101
duplicate activities, 65
duration of activity, 57–58

EAC, *see* estimate at completion
earned value (EV), 86–91
earned value reporting, 84–94
    calculations for, 90–94
    as cumulative reporting, 85–86
    data collection problems in, 87, 88
    examples of, 88–91
    parameters for, 86–87
ease, putting speaker at, 152–153
economic adjustment, 200–201
economic value added (EVA), 97–98
education requirement, 221–22
efficiency, 127
effort, 57
elementary schools, 129
e-mail, 149, 150
encoding, 146
environment, 4
environmental factors, 21
environmental responsibilities, 211
estimate at completion (EAC), 92–93
estimates, 15–16
estimate to complete (ETC), 93, 94
estimating
    activity duration, 47, 57–58
    cost, 79–83
ETC, *see* estimate to complete
ethical responsibilities, 208
ethnic differences, 211
EV, *see* earned value

EVA, *see* economic value added
even distribution, 357, 358
exam questions, 218–221
executing process group, 16
executing the project, 16, 216
expectancy theory, 129
expected value, 71, 81–83, 178–180
experience requirement, 221–223
expert interviews, 165–166, 168
expert power, 136–137
external dependencies, 49

fallback plan, 188
fast tracking, 49, 62–63
feeder chains, 75–76
FF relationship, *see* finish-finish relationship
50–50 rule, 88
final phase of project, 15
financial measures, 93, 95–97
financial ratios, 96
finish-finish (FF) relationship, 54–55
finish-start (FS) relationship, 52
firm fixed-price contracts, 200
fishbone diagrams, 110, 112
fixed-price contracts, 199–201
fixed-price plus economic-adjustment contracts, 200–201
fixed-price plus incentive contracts, 201
flexibility, 123
float, 61–62, 68, 73, 75
flowcharts, 110
forcing conflict resolution, 138, 139
Ford, Henry, 9, 133
formal communications, 150
formulas, 220
forward buying, 204
free and open communications model, 155, 156
free float, 68, 75
frequency histogram, 74
FS (finish-start) relationship, 52
functional managers, 121–125
functional organizations, 9–11
fundamental accounting equation, 95

Gantt charts, 2, 50, 51
General Motors, 172
Goal, The (Eliyahu Goldratt), 75
goals, 4
"Go" gauge, 108
Goldratt, Eliyahu, 74–76
    on feeder chains, 75, 76
    on price, 23
grade, quality vs., 103–104
grouping of risks, 185–186
Guide to the Project Management Body of Knowledge (PMBOK), 2
    on communications management, 145
    on earned value parameters, 86
    on goal of project, 103
    on quality assurance, 105
    on quality management, 104
    on risk events, 161

hard dependencies, 49
Hertzberg, Fredrick, 131
Hertzberg's motivation/hygiene theory, 131–132
hierarchy of needs theory, 129–131
human resources management, 118–143
    and leadership, 137–140
    in matrix organizations, 121–123
    and meetings, 140–143
    motivation function of, 125–135
    and organization chart, 121
    personnel/personal evaluations functions of, 124–125
    and power, 135–137
    practice questions about, 265–273, 330–336
    and project schedule, 120
    roles/responsibilities of, 119–120
    and staffing plan, 120, 121
    and training plan, 120, 121
hygiene factors, 131–132

incentives, 201, 203
income statement, 95, 96

indexes, 91–92
individual competence, 209–210
industrial revolution, 125
informal communications, 150–151
information flows, 134
initial phase of project, 14
initiating process group, 15–16
initiation of project, 19–22, 214, 215
inspection, 108–111
insurance, 187–188
intelligence tests, 129
interest, showing, 153
interest rates, 42–46
internal deliverables, 14
internal rate of return on investment (IRR), 40, 42–46
International Organization for Standardization (ISO), 1, 218, 221
Internet, 150
IRR, *see* internal rate of return on investment
Ishikawa, Kaoru, 110
ISO, *see* International Organization for Standardization
ISO 9001: 2000, 1, 218, 221
issue log, 144–145
It's Not Luck (Eliyahu Goldratt), 23, 75

job design, 132–135
job enlargement, 133
job enrichment, 134
justifications, project, *see* project justifications

kaizen, 116–117
Kennedy, John F., 9
key points, 149
key stakeholders, 22–23
knowledge areas, 16, 17
knowledge base, 21, 209
known risks, 161, 189–190

labor cost, 87, 88
lags, 56, 64
language, 211

"lawful purpose," 193
leadership, 137–140
leads, 56
learning curve theory, 125–126
legal responsibilities, 208
legitimate power, 136
lessons-learned documents, 144–145
liabilities, 95
life cycle, 14–15
    of contracts, 194–198
    of project, 2–4, 78
life cycle costing, 93
life cycle costs, 4
listening, 151–153
logical precedence diagram, 57
logical relationships, 52–57
    diagramming of, 56–57
    finish-finish, 54–55
    finish-start, 52
    and leads/lags, 56
    start-finish, 55–56
    start-start, 52, 54
lump-sum contacts, *see* fixed-price contracts

make-or-buy decision, 194
management by walking around, 157
management information systems, 21
management reserve, 84, 190
managers
    in functional organizations, 9–11
    in matrix organizations, 11–12
mandatory dependencies, 49
Manhattan Project, 5
Maslow, Abraham, 129–131
material cost, 87
matrix organizations, 11–12
    and performance reviews, 157–158
    project managers in, 121–123
McGregor, Douglas, 137
McGregor's theory of X and Y managers, 137
mean value, 70
meeting management, 140–143
Meeting Planners International, 209

meetings, 141–142
memos, 142
Microsoft PowerPoint, 150
milestone charts, 51
mitigation, 189
monitoring and control, risk, 190
monitoring and control process group, 16
Monte Carlo simulation, 73–74
motivation, 7, 125–135
    in Depression era, 126
    expectancy theory of, 129
    Hertzberg's theory of, 131–132
    importance of, 125–127
    in industrial revolution, 125
    and job/work design, 132–135
    Maslow's hierarchy of need theory of,
        129–131
    in post–World War II, 127
    procedures vs., 127–129
    and scientific management, 125–126
    and supervisory style/delegation, 132
    in World War II, 126
motivation/hygiene theory, 131–132
multiplication rule, 176–178

NASA, 9
needs, hierarchy of, 129–131
net operating profit after taxes (NOPAT), 96,
    97, 100
net present value, 40
net profit, 96
networking, 153–156
"No go" gauge, 108
nominal group technique, 165, 168
NOPAT, *see* net operating profit after taxes
normal distribution, 70, 359–362
note taking, 143

objectives, 4, 142
OBS, *see* organizational breakdown structure
order of magnitude estimate, 28
organizational breakdown structure (OBS),
    33, 121

organizational factors, 21
organizational knowledge base, 21
organizational process assets, 21
organization chart, 121
organizations, 7–12
    functional, 9–11
    matrix, 11–12
    projectized, 7–9
overbidding, 24–26
owner's equity, 95

parametric estimates, 80–81
Pareto, Vilfredo, 110
Pareto charts, 110, 113, 114
passive acceptance, 188
PDM, see precedence diagramming method
PDUs (professional development units), 224
perceiving, 147
performance reviews, 124–125, 157–158
personnel administration, 21, 124–125
PERT analysis, see program evaluation and review technique
physical environment, 4
physiological needs, 130–131
planned value (PV), 86–91
planning
    project, 16, 215–216
    quality management, 104–105
    risk management, 162
    risk-response, 186–190
planning process group, 16
PMBOK, see Guide to the Project Management Body of Knowledge
PMI, see Project Management Institute
PMO, see project management office
PMP exam, 207, 213–224
PMPs, see Project Management Professionals
Poisson distribution, 359
Polaris Missile Program, 68
political environment, 4
portfolio management, 3
post–World War II era, 127
power, 135–137

precedence diagramming method (PDM), 51–53
preliminary estimates, 79
preliminary project justification, 16
present value of money, 37, 39–41
prevention, costs of, 106
price, cost vs., 23–26
probability and impact matrix, 170, 171
probability distributions, 357–363
    beta, 363
    binomial, 357, 358
    even, 357, 358
    normal, 359–362
    Poisson, 359
probability of risk, 172–178
problem-solving conflict resolution, 140
procedures, motivation vs., 127–129
process assets, 21
process groups, 16–17
procurement management, 203–206
    with blanket orders, 205
    of commodities, 203–204
    with forward buying, 204
    practice questions about, 291–298, 349–353
    with split orders, 205–206
    of unique products/services, 204
product, quality of, 104
product scope, 26
professional development units (PDUs), 224
professional responsibility, 207–212, 217–218
    balancing stakeholders' interests (task 4), 210
    and code of conduct, 211–212
    environmental (task 5), 211
    individual competence (task 3), 209–210
    knowledge base (task 2), 209
    legal/ethical (task 1), 208
    practice questions about, 299–302, 354–355
program, project vs., 3
program evaluation and review technique (PERT), 2, 68, 70–73

"progressive elaboration," 3, 4, 16
project(s)
    cost of, 78–79
    definition of, 2
    end of the, 3–4
    environment of, 4
    life cycle of, 14–15
    life of, 2–4
    limited resources of, 5
    program vs., 3
    quality of, 104
    scope of, 3
    teams for, 4–5
project charter, 16, 19–21
project finish events, 57
projectized organizations, 7–9
project justifications, 34–46
    average-rate-of-return method of, 36–38
    breakeven charts used in, 35–36
    internal-rate-of-return method of, 40,
        42–46
    present-value-of-money method of, 37,
        39–41
project management, 1–17
    advantages of, 6–7
    case example of, 5–6
    definition of, 2
    domains of, 213–214
    growth of, 1
    and life cycles, 14–15
    manager's role in, 13
    organizing for, 7–12
    PMO for, 12–13
    processes of, 14–17
    terms used in, 2–5
Project Management Code of Professional
        Conduct, 211–212
Project Management Institute (PMI), 1, 187–
        188, 207, 208, 213, 218
    joining, 223–224
    membership in, 1
    Web site of, 224

project management office (PMO), 12–13
Project Management Professional (PMP) Role
        Delineation Study, 207, 208, 213
Project Management Professionals (PMPs)
    CAS analysis of, 207
    certification of, 221–223
    number of, 1
    recertification of, 224
project managers
    and communication, 152
    in matrix organizations, 121–123
    roles/responsibilities of, 13, 119–120
    skills of, 13
    see also human resources management
project office, 12
project schedule, 120
project scope, 26
project selection methods, 22
project start events, 57
project team
    and customer, 18–19
    as organizational asset, 21
PV, see planned value

qualified sellers lists, 197
qualitative risk analysis, 170, 171
quality, grade vs., 103–104
quality assurance, 104, 105
quality circles, 134–135
quality control, 104, 107–117
    with benchmarking, 117
    with cause and effect diagrams, 110, 112
    with checklists, 116
    with control charts, 113, 115–116
    with flowcharts, 110
    with kaizen, 116–117
    with Pareto charts, 110, 113, 114
    with run charts, 116
    with sampling inspection, 108–111
quality management, 103–117
    assurance function of, 105
    control function of, 107–117

and cost of quality, 105–107
  planning process of, 104–105
  practice questions about, 255–264,
    324–329
quality plan, 104–105
quality planning, 104–105

ranking of problems, 113, 114
RBS, *see* resource breakdown structure
RBS (risk breakdown structure), 33
RCA, 166
recall questions, 219
recertification, 224
referent power, 136
regulation, 2
relevance (of message), 148
repetition (of key points), 149
representative power, 137
request for proposal (RFP), 20, 196
request for quote (RFQ), 196
requirement process, 195
requirements list, 26
requisition process, 195–196
research, 209
resource availability, 66
resource breakdown structure (RBS), 33, 121
resource cost rates, 80
resource histogram, 66–67
resource requirements, 66
resource scheduling, 65–67
responsibility, *see* professional responsibility
responsibility-accountability matrix, 119–120
return on assets (ROA), 96, 97
return on sales (ROS), 96
reverse resource allocation scheduling, 67
reward power, 135–136
RFP, *see* request for proposal
RFQ, *see* request for quote
risk(s)
  buyer's vs. seller's, 109–111
  definition of, 160
  known vs. unknown, 161
  and scope development, 28

risk assessment, 169–183
  decision trees in, 180–183
  and expected value, 178–180
  qualitative risk analysis for, 170, 171
  and risk impact, 178
  and risk probability, 172–178
  and risk tolerance, 170–172
risk avoidance, 187
risk breakdown structure (RBS), 33, 162
risk events, 161, 163–169
risk identification, 163–169
  analogy method of, 167
  brainstorming used for, 163–164
  checklists for, 166, 167
  comparison of techniques for, 168–169
  Crawford slip process of, 165
  Delphi technique for, 164
  diagramming techniques for, 167
  documentation reviews used for, 163
  expert interviews for, 165–166
  nominal group technique for, 165
  recording of, 169
  root-cause, 166
  SWOT analysis for, 166, 167
risk impact, 178
risk management, 160–191
  assessment process of, 169–183
  charter description of, 21
  identification process of, 163–169
  monitoring and control process of, 190
  planning process of, 162
  practice questions about, 281–290,
    343–348
  processes of, 162
  quantification process of, 183–186
  response planning process of, 186–190
  timing of, 161
risk management planning, 162
risk monitoring and control, 190
risk probability, 172–178
  addition rule in, 174–176
  multiplication rule in, 176–178
risk quantification, 183–186

risk response planning, 186–190
  acceptance strategy of, 188
  avoidance strategy of, 187
  and budgeting, 189–190
  contract strategy of, 188
  mitigation strategy of, 189
  strategies for, 186–187
  transfer strategy of, 187–188
risk tolerance, 21, 170–172
risk transfer, 187–188
ROA, *see* return on assets
rolling wave planning, 16, 48
root cause identification, 166
ROS (return on sales), 96
rule of seven, 115–116
run charts, 116

safety, 212
satisfiers, 131
schedule control, 47, 68–76
  CPM used in, 68, 69
  critical chain theory of, 74–76
  Monte Carlo simulation for, 73–74
  PERT used in, 68, 70–73
schedule development, 47, 58–67
  adjustments in, 62–63
  buffering in, 63–67
  conventions used in, 59, 60
  float in, 61–62
  for resources, 65–67
schedule performance index (SPI), 91–92
schedule variance (SV), 90
scientific management, 9, 125–127
scope
  and quality, 103
  and risk management, 161
scope baseline, 26–28
scope definition, 18
scope description, 20
scope management, 18–46
  and baseline, 26–28
  and change management, 33–34
  constraints/assumptions addressed in, 22

  and cost vs. price, 23–26
  and initiation of project, 19–22
  practice questions about, 227–234,
    305–310
  and project justifications, 34–46
  project selection methods section of, 22
  and stakeholders, 22–23
  and verification, 33
  WBS used in, 28–33
scope of project, 3
scope verification, 33
security, 131
self-actualization, 131
seller's risk, 109–111
sensitivity analysis, 184, 185
SF relationship, *see* start-finish relationship
sign-off, 27, 28
simplicity (of message), 148
situational questions, 218
skills, 8
slack, 61
smoothing conflict resolution, 139
social environment, 4
socialization need, 131
solicitation process, 196–197
SOW, *see* statement of work
span of activity, 58
specialists, 8
SPI, *see* schedule performance index
split orders, 205–206
sponsors, 5
SS relationship, *see* start-start relationship
staffing plan, 120, 121
stakeholders, 5, 7
  balancing interests of, 210
  community as, 208
  expectations of, 103–104
  and life cycle of project, 15
  and scope baseline, 27
  and scope management, 22–23
standard deviation, 71
standards, 1, 2
start-finish (SF) relationship, 55–56

start-start (SS) relationship, 52, 54
statement of work (SOW), 20, 192–193
statistical sampling, 109
straight-line depreciation, 99
strengths, weaknesses, opportunities, and threats (SWOT) analysis, 166, 167
strong matrix organization, 12, 121–122
subjective probability, 174
summarizing, 153
sum of the years' digits, 100
sunk cost, 93, 95
supervisory style, 132
supply and demand, 203–204
SV (schedule variance), 90
SWOT analysis, *see* strengths, weaknesses, opportunities, and threats analysis
symbols, 146, 147
systems management approach, 15

task 1, 208
task 2, 209
task 3, 209–210
task 4, 210
task 5, 211
task level, 31
tasks of professional responsibility, 208–210
Taylor, Frederick, 9, 133
teams, 4–5, 18–19
ten-person guideline (for meetings), 141
termination, 9
test criteria, 27–28
theory of X and Y managers, 137
thinking, 146
time-and-material contracts, 203
time management, 47–76
    activity definition process of, 47–48
    activity duration estimating process of, 57–58
    activity sequencing process of, 48–57
    definition of, 47
    practice questions about, 235–244, 311–317

processes of, 47
schedule control process of, 68–76
schedule development process of, 58–67
timing
    of cost information collection, 77
    of risk management, 161
top-down estimates, 79
trade-off studies, 197–198
traditional organizations, 9–11
training plan, 120, 121
transfer of risk, 187–188
transmission errors, 148
transmitting, 147
trust, 211
truthfulness, 212
tutorial, 220
type X managers, 137
type Y managers, 137

underbidding, 24–26
understanding, communication and, 147, 152
uniqueness, 4
unique products/services, 204
unknown risks, 161, 190
U.S. Navy, 68, 150–151
U.S. Treasury bills, 42

vendor conferences, 196–197
vendors, 196–197
verbal communications, 148–150
video projection, 150
virtual teams, 124

WACC (weighted average cost of capital), 98
walking around, management by, 157
WBS, *see* work breakdown structure
weak matrix organization, 12, 122
weighted average cost of capital (WACC), 98
wheel network, 155
withdrawal conflict resolution, 140
"workaround," 62, 190

work breakdown structure (WBS), 28–33
    in activity definition process, 47–48
    in cost management, 78–79
    definition of, 29
    dictionary used in, 32
    organizational, 33
    resource, 33
    risk, 33
    systems approach to, 31–32

work breakdown structure dictionary, 32
work calendar, 66
work complete, 88
work design, 132–135
work package, 29, 31, 48
World War II era, 126
written communications, 142, 149–150

zero float, 61, 73, 75

ABOUT THE AUTHOR

Michael Newell is a certified Project Management Professional (PMP) who has been managing projects for the past thirty-five years. In that time he has managed such diverse projects as those involving many manufacturing systems, electronics assembly, foundry operations, rubber molding, robotics, aerospace manufacturing, and automation of manufacturing process and control. More recently, Mike has been involved in the management of projects for developing and implementing computer systems.

Mike has been teaching project management professionally for the past fifteen years and has taught in many countries throughout the world. He has recently established a branch of his firm, PSM Consulting, in Moscow, Russia, to teach and consult in project management.

He is Vice President of Operations for PSM Consulting. He has authored several courses in project management. Mike's courses are approved by the Project Management Institute for recertification as a Project Management Professional and as part of the PMI Professional Development Program. PSM Consulting is a Charter Member of the Registered Education Providers of the Project Management Institute.